D1272984

FDR
—and the—
News Media

FDR
— and the —
News Media

Betty Houchin Winfield

University of Illinois Press
Urbana and Chicago

Publication of this work was supported in part by a grant from
the Andrew W. Mellon Foundation.

© 1990 by the Board of Trustees of the University of Illinois
Manufactured in the United States of America
C 5 4 3 2 1

This book is printed on acid-free paper.

Library of Congress Cataloging-in-Publication Data

Winfield, Betty Houchin
    FDR and the news media / Betty Houchin Winfield.
        p. cm.
    Includes bibliographical references.
    ISBN 0-252-01672-6
    1. Roosevelt, Franklin D. (Franklin Delano), 1882–1945.
  2. Government and the press—United States—History—20th century.
  3. Government publicity—United States—History—20th century.
  4. Press and politics—United States—History—20th century.
  5. United States—Politics and government—1933–1945. I. Title.
  E807.W58   1990
  973.917—dc20   89-20485
                                                                CIP

To three important people in my life:

Mildred Bock Houchin
Sidonie Karen Winfield
Sharon Rebecca Winfield

Contents

Preface

The Great Depression and World War II marked a turning point in many Americans' lives. The events were overpowering in a personal sense. When my unemployed engineer father left West Virginia to survey the newly purchased Sam Houston National Forest in east Texas for the Civilian Conservation Corps (CCC), he met the woman who was to be my mother. One of their first dates was to the Roosevelt Birthday Ball, a national event to raise money for the campaign against infantile paralysis. Following their marriage, my dad worked on public works projects for the Army Corps of Engineers until he entered the army after Pearl Harbor. My earliest memory was of a strange, tall, smiling man in a uniform and my mother's explanation that this returning soldier was my father.

My Texas grandmother Reba Bock, once Walker County treasurer, often told me how the Democratic party had helped her as a widow raise four children. She would say, "I was born a Democrat and I will die one." To her, Franklin D. Roosevelt was the greatest of all Democrats.

Since my childhood, I have continued to hear and read about Roosevelt's impact and those depression and war years. My peripheral knowledge did not make me curious until the more recent presidential eras. In the 1970s that hereditary seed began to germinate as I began to reflect on the issues of presidential power, political news coverage, and especially presidential news management. When I read that Franklin D. Roosevelt had the reputation of having had one of the best if not the best possible press relations, I wondered how. Thus, I began this study. I have published several preliminary pieces on this topic in *Presidential Studies Quarterly, Journalism Quarterly,* and *Journalism History* (see bibliography).

Many people have added bits and pieces to the larger mosaic of this book. For years my colleagues, friends, and family listened patiently to my ideas and reflections. They will never know how very much I appreciate their patience and interest. While it would be impossible to mention them all, I have very much valued the penetrating questions from University of Washington professors Don R. Pember and the late William E. Ames; the quiet encouragement from University of Missouri Provost Lois B. DeFleur, New York University Professor Emeritus Hillier Krieghbaum, Washington State University Dean John C. Pierce, and professors Edward M. Bennett, Thomas L. Kennedy, and Thomas H. Heuterman; and the assistance of Paul Eisenberg, Claudia Miner, and Sidonie Winfield.

There are also those Roosevelt-era people who have willingly given me new insights into the press-presidential interaction, such as the Washington correspondents, several of whom are now deceased. The Franklin D. Roosevelt Library archival assistance has been invaluable, especially from Frances M. Seeber, Raymond Teichman, Robert H. Parks, Susan Elter, Mark Renovitch, Paul McLaughlin, and William Stewart, now at the National Archives. I also thank Richard Wentworth and Jane Mohraz of the University of Illinois Press for their encouragement and assistance. Lastly, I am deeply obligated to Frank Freidel and most especially to Robert E. Burke, who enthusiastically followed this project from its birth, spent endless hours arguing with me, and offered indispensable advice.

For travel to Hyde Park and research assistance, this study received financial support from a National Endowment for the Humanities Summer Fellowship, an Eleanor Roosevelt Fellowship, the University of Washington Graduate School, the Washington State University Office of Graduate Research and Development, the E. O. Holland Research and Travel Fund, and the Washington State University College of Science and Arts. During the early part of my fellowship at the Gannett Center for Media Studies, I worked on the final editing of this book.

Introduction

Within the past decade, scholars have wondered about two major presidential press conflicts: the executive's manipulation of the American mass media and the overriding power of the national press, an unelected "other government." This study concerns one strong president's efforts to influence newsgathering: the reporters' reactions and what they wrote. One overall question is asked: How did President Franklin Delano Roosevelt attempt to manage the news, especially during such domestic and international crises?

Here is one president's attempt to reconcile the inherent conflict between crisis decision making and a free press. Traditional First Amendment theory places a free press in the role of a separate estate, a watchdog of government for the American public. Yet can the press really play this role during the administrations of a president who has had the reputation of having had among the best press relationships to date? If Roosevelt was as tactically adroit in handling the press as he was said to have been, especially during such major crises as the Great Depression and World War II, did he actually reduce the press to a mere publicity arm of the government?[1]

In general, scholars who have done extensive research on FDR have presented other topics and have skimmed Roosevelt's news management tactics. In fact, few scholarly studies concern Franklin D. Roosevelt's press interactions. Certainly, there are no comparisons of the executive branch's New Deal and World War II publicity efforts as well as the press of the 1930s and 1940s. Richard W. Steele's *Propaganda in an Open Society: The Roosevelt Administration and the Media, 1933–1941* (1985) except for one chapter deals with the challenge of isolationism from 1939 to 1941. Even Graham J. White's *FDR and the Press* (1979) focuses on Roosevelt's philosophy about reporters, editors, and publishers, rather than how Roosevelt actually interacted with them. White all too readily accepts Roosevelt's press conferences at face value. Despite his press secretary's preparations for these conferences and Roosevelt's press conference remarks about such preparations, White writes, "The unique importance of the press conferences is that they enabled Roosevelt to speak for himself, to reveal his mind." In addition, White makes such statements as "Roosevelt won additional credit for not launching 'trial balloons,' " even though the Roosevelt papers demonstrate the president's constant reliance on such a tactic.[2]

Other scholars—including Elmer Cornwell, James E. Pollard, John Tebbel, and Sarah Miles Watts—have referred to FDR's record number of press conferences and his proficient press relations. Such political studies usually cover a number of presidents and only cursorily refer to the Roosevelt manuscripts. Researchers also have not discussed how FDR coped with the democratic principle of disclosure during the crises of a devastating depression and a tragic world war, periods involving a possible need for secrecy and the nation's survival. In fact, William L. Rivers and others have noted that relatively few studies have examined both media and government and that there has been too little research that offers a better understanding of the relationship between the two institutions.[3]

This book attempts to add to political communication research with a case study of President Franklin D. Roosevelt and the press. The work here does not presume to cover every single aspect of Roosevelt's relationship with the press from 1933 to 1945. Rather, the focus is twofold: the nexus between the American press and a president who reached a certain apex of presidential press relations and an interpretive examination of Franklin D. Roosevelt's overall news management attempts. The goal here is to contribute to a better understanding of the interaction between presidents and the press in a democratic society. The analysis and evaluation are presented chronologically, capturing changes over time. Mostly, the study examines Roosevelt's own publicity role and his personal communications with the journalists of the period, based on presidential notes and letters; the diaries and accounts of those who worked closely with FDR; the 1933–1945 press conference transcripts; journalists' responses, news articles, memoirs, and letters to the White House; and the era's newspapers. These documents are used in the context of Roosevelt's tactics to influence newsgathering—what he planned to do, what he did, and how the press reacted.[4]

Notes

1. "Press" in this study refers primarily to the print media, the daily newspapers. The "press" in a personalized sense refers to those reporters who covered the president—the White House correspondents. When "press" includes other media, a distinction is made, such as photography, newsreels, and radio broadcasts. Other refer-

ences in the text which refer to media workers are consistent with the terminology used by the journalists, the president, and the press secretary, such as "newspapermen," "camera men," and "spokesmen." Very few women were in those positions, as noted in chapter 4.

2. Richard W. Steele, *Propaganda in an Open Society: The Roosevelt Administration and the Media, 1933–1941* (Westport, Conn.: Greenwood Press, 1985); Graham J. White, *FDR and the Press* (Chicago: University of Chicago Press, 1979), pp. xi, 8. See also David Brinkley, "An Age Less than Golden: Roosevelt vs. the Wartime Press," *Washington Journalism Review* 10 (June 1988): 39–44, which discusses Roosevelt's problems with newspaper publishers, and David Brinkley, *Washington Goes to War* (New York: Alfred A. Knopf, 1988).

3. Elmer E. Cornwell, Jr., *Presidential Leadership of Public Opinion* (Bloomington: Indiana University Press, 1965); Elmer E. Cornwell, Jr., "Presidential News: The Expanding Public Image," *Journalism Quarterly* 36 (Summer 1959): 275–83; Elmer E. Cornwell, Jr., "The Presidential Press Conference: A Study in Institutionalization," *Midwest Journal of Political Science* 4 (November 1960): 370–89; James E. Pollard, *The Presidents and the Press* (New York: Macmillan, 1947); John Tebbel and Sarah Miles Watts, *The Press and the Presidency* (New York: Oxford University Press, 1985); William L. Rivers, Susan Miller, and Oscar Gandy, "Government and the Media," in *Political Communication, Issues and Strategies for Research,* Steven H. Chaffee, ed. (Beverly Hills, Calif.: Sage Publications, 1975). William L. Rivers has also written *The Adversaries: Politics and the Press* (Boston: Beacon Press, 1970), *The Other Government: Power and the Washington Media* (New York: Universe Books, 1982), and *The Opinionmakers: The Washington Press Corps* (Boston: Beacon Press, 1967). See also Otis L. Graham, Jr., and Meghan Robinson Wander, eds., *Franklin D. Roosevelt, His Life and Times: An Encyclopedic View* (Boston: G. K. Hall, 1985).

For important Roosevelt studies, see James MacGregor Burns, *Roosevelt: The Lion and the Fox* and *Roosevelt: The Soldier of Freedom* (New York: Harcourt, Brace, 1956, 1970); Frank Freidel, *Franklin D. Roosevelt,* 4 vols.: *The Apprenticeship; The Ordeal; The Triumph; Launching the New Deal* (Boston: Little, Brown, 1952–1973); William E. Leuchtenburg, *Franklin D. Roosevelt and the New Deal, 1932–1940* (New York: Harper and Brothers, 1963); Arthur M. Schlesinger, Jr., *The Age of Roosevelt,* 3 vols.: *The Crisis of the Old Order, 1919–1933; The Coming of the New Deal; The Politics of Upheaval* (Boston: Houghton Mifflin, 1957–60); George Wolfskill and John A. Hudson, *All but the People: Franklin D. Roosevelt and His Critics, 1933–1939* (Toronto: Macmillan, 1969).

Major studies of public opinion and the press include Samuel L. Becker, "Presidential Power: The Influence of Broadcasting," *Quarterly Journal of Speech* 47 (February 1961): 10–18; Daniel Boorstin, "Selling the President to the People," *Commentary* 20 (November 1955): 421–27; H. G. Nicholas, "Roosevelt and Public Opinion," *Fortnightly,* May 1943, pp. 303–8; James F. Ragland, "Franklin D. Roosevelt and Public Opinion, 1933–1940" (Ph.D. dissertation, Stanford University, 1954). See also Leo C. Rosten, *The Washington Correspondents* (New York: Harcourt, Brace, 1937); John H. Sharon, "The Psychology of the Fireside Chat" (Senior honors thesis, Princeton University, 1949).

4. This historical interpretation rests heavily on the press conference transcripts found in Franklin D. Roosevelt, *Complete Presidential Press Conferences of Franklin D. Roosevelt,* Vols. 1–25 (New York: Da Capo Press, 1972), although there are several problems concerning both the number and their accuracy. For example, several conferences are missing from the listed 998. The numbers are off by two because the stenographer was on vacation, and conferences 138 and 139 were accidentally skipped. See Vol. 4: 27, between August 24 and 29, 1934.

The publishers note in volume 1 that "except for correction of unmistakable typographical errors and for slight changes in the alphabetizing of the indexes, the text of the transcripts and the indexes are unedited and unaltered" (p. v). However, the transcript references to *Chicago Tribune* publisher Robert McCormick call him *Bert* McCormick, despite the fact that Roosevelt is well known for the statement "You tell Bertie that he is seeing things under the bed." See ibid., Press Conference (henceforth PC) 64, October 27, 1933, Vol. 2: 383; PC 81, December 27, 1933, Vol. 2: 579; "Fourth Estate," *Newsweek,* November 4, 1933, p. 26. *Newsweek* quotes the president as saying, "You tell 'Bertie' he is seeing things under the bed. That power is in no wise different from that of the fire marshall or the building inspector. . . . Lip Service from autocratic steel barons and the Red baiting publishers is no honor to Zenger. The same kind of Tories sent him to jail." This quote is not in the October 27 or November 3 press conferences. Stanley Walker, *City Editor* (New York: Frederick Stokes, 1934), p. 22, refers to the press conference quote, "Tell Bertie McCormick that he's seeing things under the bed." Ragland, "Franklin D. Roosevelt and Public Opinion," p. 368, and Pollard, *The Presidents and the Press,* p. 797, both quote the well-known phrase with the name "Bertie." In PC 620, August 26, 1938, Vol. 12: 53, and PC 620, February 2, 1940, Vol. 15: 117, the president does say "Bertie."

In addition, Roosevelt's reported "horse and buggy" statement in the May 31, 1935, press conference differs from the transcript. As another example, James MacGregor Burns states that "more than once Roosevelt had told a reporter to go into the corner and don a dunce hat" as a type of punishment, but the transcripts indicate that Roosevelt gave a dunce hat only once during the press meetings. See James MacGregor Burns, *Roosevelt: The Lion and the Fox,* p. 409; Roosevelt, *Complete Press Conferences,* PC 377, June 29, 1937, Vol. 9: 466. No other mention is made of Dunce Hat Awards being given in the 1937, 1938, 1939, and 1940 press conferences. Such dunce hats might have been given informally at those press interchanges during the president's trips. For a reference to the club, see Roosevelt, *Complete Press Conferences,* PC 660, July 12, 1940, Vol. 16: 34–35.

In addition, despite the disclosure that Justice Hugo Black had been a member of the Ku Klux Klan, that press conference discussion was not recorded and those transcript deletions are noted. PC 399, September 21, 1937, Vol. 10: 221, refers to Hugo Black. The Nazi Iron Cross to be given *New York Daily News* correspondent John O'Donnell was presented at the December 18, 1942, conference, not earlier as stated by correspondent Walter Davenport. Davenport gave April 1941 as the date and said the incident had to do with the U.S. Navy's convoys to England. See Walter Davenport, "The President and the Press," *Collier's,* January 27, 1945, p. 47.

FDR
and the
News Media

"When I was a journalist." Roosevelt *(front row center)*, as president of the *Harvard Crimson,* with its senior board, 1904. Courtesy of the Franklin D. Roosevelt Library.

1

The Roots of Presidential Press Relations

No government ought to be without censors; and where the press is free, none ever will.
> —Thomas Jefferson to George Washington, September 9, 1792

Power is persuasion.
> —Richard E. Neustadt, *Presidential Power,* 1960

Political scientists and historians have long acknowledged Franklin Delano Roosevelt's ability to seize, expand, test, and communicate presidential powers so successfully. Roosevelt's formidable presidency has continued to be a point of political and economic reference for measuring those presidents who followed him. Scholars nearly always rank Roosevelt among the great presidents for leadership qualities. FDR could resolve most policy problems and give authoritative answers to the crucial crisis questions. He could set the political agenda and persuade Americans of the rightness of most of his proposals.[1]

Franklin Roosevelt has also provided the baseline in the contemporary evolution of the relationship between the presidency and the press. His press relations are so well known that they have continually been referred to for almost sixty years. His difference was immediate. When Roosevelt came into office, even Theodore Joslin, Herbert Hoover's former secretary in charge of the press, said, "Roosevelt has come nearer than any of them to meeting the expectations" of the press corps. Columnist Heywood Broun, who had never before seen anything like Roosevelt's adroitness, accessibility, and intermittent candor, called him "the best newspaperman who has ever been President of the United States." It was not just the president's personal style, but much more. Historian Daniel Boorstin wrote that "perhaps never before had there been so happy a coincidence of personal talent with technological opportunity as under his administration." Press historian John Tebbel wrote that "he understood the press as no president has before or since." In fact, Roosevelt may have publicly personalized the presidency so much through his astute use of the existing mass media that he created unreasonable expectations for those less personable and less talented presidents who followed him.[2]

Franklin D. Roosevelt's presidency also signaled a rise of the president as the number one newsmaker. FDR skillfully demonstrated that presidents who dramatize and personalize issues and policies will receive favorable news coverage. He showed that to communicate well and to control information can be tremendous political power. Most vital to any presidential authority is the ability to maintain public confidence in a governing ability. To get Congress to do their bidding, presidents must use their public persuasive arts. Presidents can garner and keep the attention of the people through the national media. Because presidents have the power of initiative and definition, they can set the terms of the political debate as well as define their political agenda. Thus, presidents, more than any other national political figures, have the greatest opportunity for educating the public with information of their choosing. In fact, FDR's definition of political leadership was "persuading, leading, sacrificing, teaching, always, because the greatest duty of a statesman is to educate."[3]

This study is an examination of Franklin D. Roosevelt's news skills with the mass media from 1933 to 1945 within the context of public information in a democratic society. Roosevelt's news management actions and reactions had theoretic and historical precedent. In one sense, FDR's communication efforts fit the democratic ideal of an informed public: an ideal developed from John Locke's seventeenth-century natural rights principles of a rational man and those of John Milton's "self-righting process" in the unlimited marketplace of ideas, where truth and falsehood grapple, and truth wins. The Roosevelt era also tested Thomas Jefferson's reasoning that for the popular majority to make sound decisions and to facilitate the democratic process, the citizen must not only be educated but also be kept informed. Jefferson had maintained that "where the press is free, and every man able to read, all is safe."[4]

American press-government relations have been based on a strong libertarian foundation of free expression with political purpose. Franklin Roosevelt's presidency has been only one stage in that political communications relationship. Thomas Jefferson also argued that for a press to be free from governmental control, it must serve in a "watchdog" capacity to guard against the government's deviation from its original purposes. During strong anti-federalist press criticisms, Jefferson assured George Washington in 1792, "No government ought to be without censors; and where the press is free, none ever will."[5]

The Roosevelt era tests that principle in several ways. When the federal government became more directly involved in the lives of people, especially during major national upheavals, as it did during the Roosevelt years, the environment became ripe for the correspondents to allow themselves to be compromised. Reporters then and now could become so anxious to get the inside story from the highest level news source that they may be unwilling collaborators in the process by which the chief executive can determine their news content. The press could also become so much a part of the executive branch's public relations efforts during national crises that Thomas Jefferson's watchdog press would be impossible.

Yet, at the same time, some kind of political symbiotic relationship between the president and the press is a democratic necessity. James Madison, author of the First Amendment, wrote after his presidency, "A popular government without popular information or the means of acquiring it, is but a prologue to a farce or a tragedy, or perhaps both." Leaders like Jefferson and Madison, who built America's early political framework and who suffered from savage criticism, knew that a free press should be a keystone to democracy. They insisted that political opinions and criticism be free from federal legal restraint. Today, some two hundred years later, scholars are still grappling with what free expression means in a popular government. Generally, the First Amendment prohibited prior restraints on publication, although it is less clear that the amendment also precluded seditious libel, often used as a means for stifling or punishing political dissent.[6]

In theory, America's presidents, including Franklin D. Roosevelt, have often said they wanted a free press as a check on government. In practice, most of them have found such media independence difficult to tolerate. The conflict was there from the beginning. President George Washington cursed "that rascal Freneau" in cabinet meetings when Philip Freneau's *National Gazette* became such a critical adversary. Washington and other presidents sensed that news management was important to transmit their own viewpoints beyond those critical adversaries and to sway public opinion for passing laws and levying taxes. Nevertheless, at the same time, deeply embedded in American tradition and laws has been the implicit right of the president to decide which executive branch's records may be withheld or disclosed. Such specific information controls began at the country's inception, when the deliberations of the Constitutional Convention were held in secret to limit premature speculation.[7]

Roosevelt had the legacy of a long line of presidential news management tactics, including the information access prerogatives. Previous presidents had sought direct information channels to explain their political viewpoints, depending on the technology of the time. The earliest presidents or their supporters awarded government printing contracts to favored political party newspapers, which became presidential mouthpieces. When the independent popular penny press attracted mass readership, nineteenth-century presidents began favoring several well-known editors by giving them exclusive information and informal interviews. Abraham Lincoln carried on an extensive correspondence with Horace Greeley and James Gordon Bennett and used his excellent sense of timing for releasing dramatic news. Lincoln wrote of the importance of public persuasion: "In this age, and this country, and like communities, public sentiment is everything. *With* it, nothing can fail; *against* it, nothing can succeed."[8]

During FDR's formative adult years in the early twentieth century, the presidency became the preeminent source of national opinion leadership. Roosevelt's distant cousin Theodore Roosevelt created the turning point. The first Roosevelt set a pattern for actively influencing the news with organized press conferences for favored reporters, direct quotes, "off-the-record" stipulations, and trial balloons for testing public opinion. Many correspondents were so taken by Teddy Roosevelt's magnetism that they were coopted. Those turn-of-the-century newspapers emphasizing human interest stories capitalized on this Roosevelt's colorful personality and his flair for the dramatic. He used such favorable publicity to build an extensive positive reputation. FDR was impressed and would later emphasize TR's bully pulpit: "I want to be a *preaching President*—like my cousin [Theodore]."[9]

Between Roosevelts, other presidents coupled their personalities and various news management methods with the latest mass media technologies. Just as FDR was first entering politics, President William Howard Taft gave exclusive information to friendly reporters who would not quote him directly. As assistant secretary of the navy, Franklin Roosevelt must have noticed Woodrow Wilson's lasting news management possibilities. Wilson held the first regular press conferences with the Washington correspondents en masse. Wilson, not understanding the press's speculative nature, used the 1915 sinking of the Lusitania as a much-needed excuse to discontinue what had become for him unpleasant, uncontrolled semiweekly meetings. He preferred to leak information to favorite journalists and rely on other tactics: advance copies of well-written speeches, catchy phrases for headlines, and news access though a secretary, who had a flair for public relations. During World War I, Wilson organized the unprecedented executive branch propaganda and censorship agency, the Committee on Public Information.[10]

While Roosevelt was running for vice-president and then convalescing and reentering politics, three presidents of the 1920s added to the repertoire of news management tactics. Warren G. Harding deliberately staged dramatic newscatching events during his 1920 presidential campaign with celebrity visits by Al Jolsen and the winning Chicago Cubs baseball team to his home town of Marion, Ohio. During that tabloid news era, Harding willingly posed for photographers and even tried the embryonic radio. He revived the semi-weekly press conferences, although he controlled the queries by requiring written questions submitted in advance. His warm personality was in sharp contrast to Calvin Coolidge's reticent style. Coolidge's five years of regular press conferences created an expectation of regular White House news. Without attribution, Coolidge spoke to the American people indirectly through the medium of "the White House spokesman." Since nothing of substance was happening, the print media built with Coolidge's assistance the myth of a strong, silent president, "the Sage from Vermont." The press emphasis shifted from what the president did to who he was, a representation of a leader.[11]

Having developed an image of superman and a reputation for accessibility as secretary of commerce, Herbert Hoover shocked the reporters when he did not solve the country's economic problems and tried to avoid direct contact with journalists. During the depression he would go for months without a press conference, and when he did see journalists it was mainly for disseminating handouts. He continued the Harding/Coolidge technique of requiring that written questions be submitted before the press meetings. Radio addresses became his one-way, direct public contact, although he was a dull, monotonous speaker. When he tended to lie about the extent of the depression and the administration's corrective measures, journalists and others accused him of endangering public confidence in the federal government.[12]

By the time Franklin D. Roosevelt took office in March 1933, the Washington correspondents were grumbling so much that *Brooklyn Daily Eagle* reporter Henry Suydam suggested that perhaps press conferences should be abolished. The journalists wondered how Roosevelt would communicate to the public, if at all. At the time, FDR and his advisers were thinking about garnering public support for emergency actions. They had certain expectations for the press. The president would communicate publicly his policies and goals, tell the truth, and provide access to information. In turn, the press would be accurate, fair, and certainly responsible about the White House news. At the same time, journalists would transmit enough information to educate the public about governmental leadership.[13]

Yet, another set of conditions existed in the presidential relationship with the correspondents. Roosevelt came into office during a major domestic crisis; he had an international crisis by the end of his second term. During crises, the chief executive assumes greater responsibilities for governing, and the media have found their traditional role as the Fourth Estate in jeopardy. Such crisis news management has not been exclusive to Roosevelt or this country. Media scholar Frederick S. Siebert wrote in his classic *Freedom of the Press in England, 1476–1776,* "The area of freedom contracts and enforcement of restraints increases as the stresses on the stability of government and of the structure of society increase." According to Siebert's proposition, free expression would switch from a more open to a more closed form of political communications during times of societal stress. The study here proposes that the *type* of societal stress would make a difference: internal or external crisis would partially determine a president's informational system. More specifically, it hypothesizes that there would be a more open communications system during an internal crisis, whereas there would be a more autocratic, secretive communications system during an external crisis when there is an outside enemy. To test this hypothesis, this study emphasizes the differences in Franklin D. Roosevelt's communications system during those two major different crises: the Great Depression, the internal crisis; and World War II, an external crisis.[14]

Roosevelt had to offer strong leadership, garner public support, and cope with continual crises—times involving the nation's economic survival during a depression and a possible need for secrecy to protect military and diplomatic information during a world war. In each situation, the public expected the president to seize the moment and act. During such major upheavals, there was still the need for public order and public access to information. After his first two years in office, Roosevelt lacked newspaper editorial support when he was reacting to the Great Depression. He worried about his access to the public through the biased daily newspapers. The editorial criticism of him and his administration was vicious at times, even when he had vast public support. Thus, Roosevelt's careful news management policy might have been justified.[15]

The Franklin D. Roosevelt era provides crucial lessons in the viability of Madison's popular government in the larger context of popular information. While there might be a difference between secrecy concerning the internal reactions to an economic upheaval and secrecy concerning the external reactions to military and diplomatic conduct, there is also the problem of secrecy for circumventing possible public opposition. With the latter, there might be a greater danger of misfeasance or malfeasance on the part of administrators whose actions are undetected. Moreover, without public discussion of alternative courses by the opposition party or other public figures, the danger would be that the weakness of programs and policies may not easily emerge before the actions are put into effect. Further, without having their transactions and proceedings constantly under public scrutiny, officials of the executive branch may not be kept "up to the pitch of duty." The Roosevelt years provide one measurement of public scrutiny.

On March 4, 1933, President Franklin Delano Roosevelt began his "pitch of duty" and the American press began their twelve-year odyssey. It was a relationship full of many conflicts—conflicts between a president performing his executive functions as he saw fit and the press wanting information about those actions and, at the same time, supposedly remaining independent of the president's control. The battle had been fought many times. For over two centuries that restless American contradiction had persisted in theories, policies, and statutes. Indeed, it was and still is a clash as old as that found in Article II of the United States Constitution: "The Executive power shall be vested in a President of the United States," and "he shall take care that the laws be faithfully executed;" and the First Amendment: "Congress shall make no law . . . abridging the freedom of speech, or of the press."

Notes

1. David L. Porter, "American Historians Rate Our Presidents," in *The Rating Game in American Politics,* William Paterson and Ann McLaurin, eds. (New York: Irvington Publishers, 1987), pp. 13–25; Thomas Kelly and Douglas Lonnstrom, "Political Science and Historians Poll," based on twenty different qualities or characteristics, in Betty Boyd Caroli, *First Ladies* (New York: Oxford University Press, 1987), pp. 387–88. See also David C. Nice, "The Influence of War and Party System Aging on the Ranking of the President," *Western Political Quarterly* 37 (September 1984): 443–55; William E. Leuchtenburg, *In the Shadow of FDR: From Harry Truman to Ronald Reagan* (Ithaca, N.Y.: Cornell University Press, 1983).

2. Arthur M. Schlesinger, Jr., *The Coming of the New Deal,* Vol. 2 of *The Age of Roosevelt* (Boston: Houghton Mifflin, 1959), p. 563; William L. Rivers, *The Opinionmakers: The Washington Press Corps* (Boston: Beacon Press, 1967), pp. 134–35; Daniel J. Boorstin, *America and the Image of Europe: Reflections on American Thought* (New York: Meridian Books, 1960), pp. 107–8; John Tebbel, *The Media in America* (New York: Mentor Books, 1974), p. 416.

3. Elmer E. Cornwell, Jr., "Presidential News: The Expanding Image," *Journalism Quarterly* 36 (Summer 1959): 275–83; Donald Richberg, *My Hero* (New York: G. P. Putnam's Sons, 1954), p. 279.

4. John Locke, "Two Treatises of Government," in *The Works of John Locke,* Vol. 5 (Aalen, Germany: Scienta Verlag, 1963 reprint), pp. 132–207; John Milton, "Areopagitica," in *Areopagitica and Of Education with Autobiographical Passages from Other Prose Works,* George H. Sabine, ed. (Northbrook, Ill.: AHM Publishing Corporation, 1951), pp. 50–51; Thomas Jefferson to Colonel Charles Yancy, January 6, 1816, *The Writings of Thomas Jefferson,* Vol. 9 (Monticello, Va.: Thomas Jefferson Memorial Association, 1903), p. 384.

5. Thomas Jefferson to George Washington, September 9, 1792, *Writings of Thomas Jefferson,* p. 406.

6. James Madison to W. T. Barry, August 4, 1822, *The Complete Madison,* Saul Padover, ed. (New York: Harper and Brothers, 1953), p. 337; Leonard W. Levy, *Emergence of a Free Press* (New York: Oxford University Press, 1985), pp. 301, 304–8, 316, 318; Harold L. Nelson, "Seditious Libel in Colonial America," *American*

Journal of Legal History 3, no. 2 (1959): 160–72; Jeffery Smith, *Printers and Free Expression: The Ideology of Early American Journalism* (New York: Oxford University Press, 1987).

7. Edwin Emery and Michael Emery, *The Press and America: An Interpretative History of the Mass Media,* 5th ed. (Englewood Cliffs, N.J.: Prentice-Hall, 1984), p. 98; Douglas Cater, *The Fourth Branch of Government* (New York: Vintage Books, 1965), p. 25.

8. Abraham Lincoln, "Public Sentiment Is Everything," Lincoln-Douglas Debates, 1858, Private Notes, in *Abraham Lincoln's Philosophy of Common Sense: An Analytic Biography of a Great Mind,* Part 2, Edward J. Kempf, ed. (New York: New York Academy of Sciences, 1965), p. 576.

9. Leo C. Rosten, *The Washington Correspondents* (New York: Harcourt, Brace 1937), p. 22. See also Robert C. Hilderbrand, *Power and the People: Executive Management of Public Opinion in Foreign Affairs, 1897–1921* (Chapel Hill: University of North Carolina Press, 1981); George Juergens, *News from the White House: The Presidential-Press Relationship in the Progressive Era* (Chicago: University of Chicago Press, 1981), who covered the presidencies of Theodore Roosevelt, William Howard Taft, and Woodrow Wilson. For quote, see Schlesinger, *The Coming of the New Deal,* p. 558.

10. James E. Pollard, *The Presidents and the Press* (New York: Macmillan, 1947), pp. 601–27; James Kerney, *The Political Education of Woodrow Wilson* (New York: Appleton Century, 1926), p. 345; Elmer E. Cornwell, Jr., "Wilson, Creel and the Presidency," *Public Opinion Quarterly* 23 (Winter 1959): 189–202.

11. Robert K. Murray, *The Harding Era: Warren G. Harding and His Administration* (Minneapolis: University of Minnesota Press, 1969), p. 50; "Harding's Question Box in the White House," *New York Times,* November 30, 1921; "Harding First Disputes, Then Accepts the Four-Power Treaty," *New York Times,* December 21, 1921; Murray, *The Harding Era,* p. 114; Donald R. McCoy, *Calvin Coolidge: The Quiet President* (New York: Macmillan, 1967), pp. 166–67, 292; Howard Quint and Robert Ferrell, *The Talkative President: The Off-the-Record Press Conferences of Calvin Coolidge* (Amherst: University of Massachusetts Press, 1964), pp. 1–2.

12. Craig Lloyd, *Aggressive Introvert: A Study of Herbert Hoover and Public Relations Management, 1912–1932* (Columbus: Ohio State University Press, 1972), pp. 156, 161, 168, 175; Joan Hoff Wilson, *Herbert Hoover, Forgotten Progressive* (Boston: Little, Brown, 1975), pp. 130, 138–42.

13. *Conference on the Press under the Auspices of the School of Public and International Affairs,* Princeton University, April 23–25, 1931 (Princeton, N.J.: School of Public Affairs, 1932), p. 6.

14. Frederick S. Siebert, *Freedom of the Press in England, 1476–1776* (Urbana: University of Illinois Press, 1952), p. 10. For testing this proposition, see Donald L. Shaw and Stephen W. Bauer, "Press Freedom and War Constraints: Case Testing Siebert's Proposition II," *Journalism Quarterly* 46 (Summer 1969): 243–54; John D. Stevens, "Press and Community Toleration: Wisconsin in World War I," *Journalism Quarterly* 46 (Summer 1969): 255–59. For other international crises and a newspaper reporting study, see Montague Kern, Patricia W. Levering, and Ralph B. Levering,

The Kennedy Crises: The Press, the Presidency, and Foreign Policy (Chapel Hill: University of North Carolina Press, 1983).

15. David Brinkley, "An Age Less than Golden, Roosevelt vs. the Wartime Press," *Washington Journalism Review* 10 (June 1988): 42–43.

"No pictures of me getting out of the car, boys." Campaign trip to Hollywood, California, September 24, 1932. Courtesy of the Franklin D. Roosevelt Library.

2

The Development of FDR's Media Skills

I'm going where there's no depression,
To the lovely land that's free from care—
I'll leave this world of toil and trouble;
My home's in heaven, I'm going there.
                    —A. P. Carter, "No Depression in Heaven"

Get aboard the freedom car—
Cast your vote for F.D.R.;
Cactus Jack and Franklin D.,
They're the ones for me.
                    —"Cactus Jack and Franklin D.,"1932 campaign song

The United States was in the depths of the Great Depression during the winter of 1932–33. The country's catastrophic illness was more than economic, the collapse was total—unexpected, unprecedented, and devastating. So anxious were the people to get aboard FDR's freedom car that 22 million voted for a change on November 8, 1932. Franklin Delano Roosevelt had also gained the enthusiastic support of reporters and such publishers as Roy Howard, Cissy Patterson, and William Randolph Hearst.[1]

Roosevelt's relationship with the press began long before March 4, 1933. His media's roots were deep, based on his own personal interest in the media and his press interactions during a twenty-two-year political history. These pre-inaugural press experiences laid the groundwork for his early days in the presidency and set the tone for his subsequent media relationship.

Franklin Delano Roosevelt, born into an aristocratic, well-to-do, upstate New York family, had the benefits of an education at Groton, Harvard, and Columbia Law School and travel in Europe. He was not to be intimidated by corporate opulence or wealthy media owners. Much like many turn-of-the-century progressives, including the muckraking reporters, FDR had a sense of responsibility—a noblesse oblige, inherited from his parents, developed by Endicott Peabody at Groton, and influenced by his cousin, President Theodore Roosevelt.[2]

During his presidential years, Roosevelt loved to reminisce about his own newspaper days on the *Harvard Crimson.* By his junior year, he was the editor in chief. His editorials, although filled with a 1903 obsession for football, also advocated the much-needed fire escapes and boardwalks. He had an innate sense of timing and certainly understood the importance of a dramatic scoop. Through luck, connections, or sheer doggedness, he was the first to announce that the president, his cousin Theodore, would lecture in a Harvard course. His biggest scoop was when he beat the *Yale News* by ten minutes with a play-by-play account of the Yale football home win over Harvard.[3]

FDR transferred the understanding that news was the unusual and the startling to politics. In 1910, when Roosevelt ran for state senator from upstate Dutchess County, he aggressively campaigned as an unusual reformer against party bossism. While much of the Republican district press discounted his charges, the press had to notice him. Roosevelt had the advantage of a well-known last name and a nonpartisan strategy of a face-to-face campaign. Most important, he surprised people, as he was to do throughout his political career. The press covered his travels in what was then an unusual automobile—his two-cylinder Maxwell. And, Roosevelt won his first election—only the second Democrat to win in the heavily Republican district since the Civil War.[4]

Franklin D. Roosevelt's initial political experience paralleled the American press's increasing emphasis on social concerns and economic change. Just as State Senator Roosevelt urged political reform, newspapers and magazines from 1910 to 1914 crusaded against governmental graft, industrial evils, bossism, and utility company payoffs. In his early political dealings with the press, Roosevelt conducted a confident, witty, and superior propaganda campaign. He became widely known as the leader of an insurgent revolt against the Tammany choice for U.S. senator. As a result of his daily press statements, friendly newspapers began painting him as the "Galahad of the Insurgency" and the Tammany leaders as the unmitigated villains. Before he had voted on a single bill, FDR had become one of the most widely known state politicians. His fight against bossism and for the direct election of U.S. senators had also won him national press attention.[5]

An Albany correspondent for the *New York Herald,* Louis McHenry Howe, assisted the senator in his 1912 reelection campaign when Roosevelt was stricken by typhoid fever. Howe admired Roosevelt and through his columns had given the revolt some of its best state coverage. To begin what became a twenty-two-year publicity partnership, Howe devised a campaign strategy to send thousands of "personal" letters from Roosevelt to farmers throughout the district, publish large newspaper advertisements, and mail ready-to-print boiler-plate articles emphasizing specific Roosevelt proposals, such as standard-size fruit barrels. The publicity helped, and Roosevelt easily won a second term.[6]

When Franklin Roosevelt went to Washington, D.C., as the assistant secretary of navy in 1913, he continued gaining valuable publicity through his news management skills and Howe's help. Although the cabinet members met with the press daily, Roosevelt held his own regular press conferences and applied other news tactics. He was an advocate of military preparedness and would leak information concerning the inadequate state of national defense. He also created regional media attention by conducting numerous naval yard inspections with the marines at attention, brass bands blaring marches, and well-staged guns booming salutes.[7]

Throughout it all, Howe's main news strategy was to control the new content for the most supportive image of Roosevelt, without setting the pose so much that it could not immediately be dropped. According to biographer Alfred D. Rollins, Jr., Howe said, "If you say a thing is so often enough, it stands a good chance to become a fact." Rollins noted that Howe's major weakness was his immense confidence in his ability to trick the ordinary person: "While he often doubted the press, he assumed that the ordinary voter would believe what he read."[8]

Howe and Roosevelt occasionally misjudged their news management power. Roosevelt's 1914 race for the U.S. Senate lead to a resounding defeat. Howe had used many news tactics, some of which were reckless. For example, Howe wrote scores of notes to Democratic and independent editors who published "good editorials" telling them how valuable he found their newspaper advertising and then requesting their rates. Besides flattering these rural editors, Howe "helped" them with a steady supply of weighted stories to fill their columns. He also would capture free space with a boiler-plate item featuring FDR's picture and an unrelated headline claiming the national administration supported Roosevelt. He then carefully compiled his efforts in a clipping file of editorials and news stories.[9]

When Roosevelt ran for vice-president in 1920, Howe again helped, along with navy publicity agent Marvin McIntyre and Democratic party publicity agent Stephen Early, who had covered the Navy Department for the Associated Press. Each night Roosevelt and Howe would give Associated Press reporter Stanley Prenosil a rough draft of the high points of the next day's speeches. Prenosil could then file "background" stories in advance and accurately quote "off-the-cuff" comments. Overall, Roosevelt kept a positive image even though his ticket lost. Journalist Henry Pringle recounted, "I cannot recall whether Franklin D. Roosevelt said anything worth saying or whether anyone listened. I do remember he had a pleasing personality, that he was 38 years old, and that he had a magnificently strong physique."[10]

Such news management skill became most important when Franklin Roosevelt was stricken by polio at the Canadian island of Campobello in 1921. Howe immediately took charge and fed vague explanations to the Associated Press correspondent. In fact, he managed to keep the severity of Roosevelt's illness out of the newspapers for over two weeks. Newspapers at that time were racier and more sensational and were filled with pictures, emotional appeals, and gossip about public figures. So little was known about polio that even the words "infantile paralysis" could have dire implications. So when Howe did talk to the press, he coupled the information with the statement "He is now improving." From the outset, he helped create an illusion of a mild illness. In fact, no one outside the immediate family was told Roosevelt was seriously ill.[11]

Such a managed image could work. When Roosevelt was flat on his back and needed to be moved to New York City, a private railroad car arrived amid a crowd of well-wishers and reporters. Howe started a rumor that Roosevelt would land on a dock at the far end of town and then signaled the motorboat to bring Roosevelt to the near end so that his stretcher could be passed through the railroad car window secretly. FDR was comfortably settled before the crowd spied him. A *New York World* correspondent wrote, "Mr. Roosevelt was enjoying his cigarette and said he had a good appetite. Although unable to sit up he says he is feeling more comfortable." Thus, Roosevelt returned to the city, assuring everyone, including himself, that he was not suffering from anything more than a passing illness.[12]

Following FDR's arrival at the Presbyterian Hospital, Howe announced that Roosevelt did have poliomyelitis. Yet he quoted the physician, a Roosevelt school chum, "He will not be crippled. No one need have any fear of permanent injury from this attack." When the *New York Times* ran the good news on its September 16 front page, Roosevelt jokingly reinforced such optimism in a letter to publisher Adolph S. Ochs: "While the doctors were unanimous in telling me that the attack was very mild and that I was not going to suffer any permanent effects from it, I had, of course, the usual dark suspicion that they were just saying nice things to make me feel good, but now that I have seen the same statement officially made in the New York Times I feel immensely relieved because I know of course it must be so." Nevertheless, Roosevelt was seriously ill. He never again would be able to walk or even stand without support.[13]

Howe, who had planned to accept a lucrative business position, now was to function as Roosevelt's morale booster, press agent, political guide, and administrative assistant. He immediately handled the business and political correspondence Roosevelt could not even sign. Despite his physical handicap, Roosevelt continued to capture newspaper publicity. Rollins noted that from

1921 through 1927, Roosevelt had been noticed in one way or another on nearly two hundred occasions by the *New York Times* alone.[14]

Through his understanding of what had happened to news style, Roosevelt himself would help. More and more newspapers had begun using columnists to fit in every type of news, and by 1933 there was a variety of specialized columns, including Walter Winchell's gossip column, Walter Lippmann's more serious political column, and Drew Pearson's and Robert S. Allen's "inside story," called the "Washington Merry-Go-Round." Washington correspondents also wrote syndicated articles to give readers the background, motivations, and probable consequences of official acts. Well-known public figures, including Roosevelt, also wrote columns.[15]

For a short while during his long convalescence, Roosevelt wrote a regular news column, "Roosevelt Says," which appeared in the *Macon* (Geo.) *Telegram* in 1925, and "Between Neighbors," which was carried by the *Beacon* (N.Y.) *Standard* in 1928. FDR admitted to his former navy chief Josephus Daniels, an editor and publisher as well as a columnist, that he found it difficult to do such writing and to have an "honest" topic on hand for each deadline. Yet Roosevelt continued to express himself publicly in one form or another. He condemned the Republicans in the quarterly *Foreign Affairs* for their unproductive international disarmament conferences, their backward steps in Latin America, and their abdication of the nation's "moral leadership."[16]

Governor Alfred Smith, the Democratic presidential candidate, pressured FDR into running for governor in 1928, despite his handicapped condition. Although he had only four weeks to campaign, Roosevelt had the expert support of his wife Eleanor, New York's Athletic Commissioner James Farley, Howe, and a former state legislator and young lawyer named Samuel I. Rosenman. The *New York Herald-Tribune* response was typical: "The nomination is unfair to Mr. Roosevelt. It is equally unfair to people of the state, who, under other conditions, would welcome Mr. Roosevelt's candidacy for any office."[17]

Smith and Roosevelt handled such concerns with humor. Among the numerous stories about Roosevelt's health was the rumor that he would have to resign and permit Lieutenant Governor Herbert Lehman to succeed him. Governor Smith retorted that Roosevelt was mentally as competent as ever: "Even though he lacks muscular control in his legs, he didn't need to be an acrobat to be governor." The state's editors, mostly Republican, soon dropped the subject, which easily could have backfired into public sympathy. Knowing that the public was keenly interested in his physical condition, Roosevelt could appear to be perfectly candid about the issue. The *New York Herald-Tribune*'s description of Roosevelt as he entered his headquarters that fall captures both his humor and his apparent frankness.

[He was] Supporting himself on the left side with a crutch and on the right side with a cane, and leaning forward on these supports so that he could draw his feet after him in a sliding gait.

"How's your state of optimism?" he was asked.

"Fine," he said. "I told them in Poughkeepsie this afternoon that most people who are nominated for the governorship have to run, but obviously I am not in the condition to run, and therefore I am counting on my friends all over the state to make it possible for me to walk in."[18]

When Roosevelt focused attention on the state's problems, the audience forgot his legs. His speeches, expressing his enthusiasm, brought him positive headlines. His energetic stumping throughout the state served to convince journalists and audiences alike that he was in magnificent health. Although it sometimes took him as long as five minutes to walk painfully to a platform and once he had to be carried up a fire escape and in through a back window, he appeared unruffled. His spectacular display of physical endurance endowed him with media celebrity status. However, he would have to keep proving his physical ability again and again.[19]

It was not just proving his physical ability that was so important but the image of doing so. Photography in one form or another had become an integral part of American journalism, from the first 1914 rotogravure sections of the *New York Times* through the tabloid newspapers of the 1920s to the newsreels. Politicians, particularly presidents, were important subjects, symbolized by the formation of the White House News Photographers Association in 1921. By 1930 successful tabloids began filling 40 percent of their editorial space with pictures and some eight-column newspapers used as much as 25 percent for illustrations. The upcoming decade was ripe for the launching of the successful weekly pictorials, such as *Life* and *Look* magazines. Before World War II, picture transmission by cable and radio had become possible. Associated Press members could have wire photo service and regional pony service.[20]

Photographers were careful to respect Roosevelt's wishes concerning his pictorial coverage. For example, on the morning of November 6 when Roosevelt arrived at Hyde Park Town Hall to cast his ballot, a group of newspaper and newsreel photographers prepared to take his picture as he left the car. He requested, "No movies of me getting out of the machine, boys." And, indeed, they turned away until he had alighted, adjusted his braces, and posed. According to William Leuchtenburg, "News photographers in the 1920s voluntarily destroyed their own plates when they showed Roosevelt in poses that revealed his handicap." FDR appeared so vigorous that few Americans thought much about his crippled legs.[21]

FDR vaulted into the governorship and immediately began unfolding his program to reporters day by day. He fully understood that daily revealing one or another aspect of his program would attract more attention than presenting a single, complicated parcel. He used the same tactic with the names of his appointments.[22]

Right after his inauguration, Roosevelt told Democratic leaders that "it is a moral duty for us to spread the Democratic gospel." At his urging, the State Democratic Committee raised the necessary $100,000 for a Democratic Publicity Bureau. Under the direction of Louis Howe, the bureau's tactics included providing a schedule of stories for the county weeklies, news notes on the governor's actions, and texts of his speeches and pertinent editorials. The press releases appeared as straight news to encourage direct publication.[23]

Roosevelt's press strategy included feeding Democratic news to the rural press to offset the dominant Republican bias. Howe immediately sent letters to district leaders and even phonograph records with Roosevelt's words welcoming any political suggestions. He mailed copies of Roosevelt's inaugural address to other state and national editors to supplement the Associated Press reports, since the address dealt "largely with problems of equal interest to every state in the union." Howe not only sent news out but also reorganized the personal clipping service to provide a daily state survey of legislative issues and a composite of the nation's editorial opinions of Roosevelt.[24]

At the same time, Roosevelt was accessible to reporters. He tried to meet daily with the working press, although he would not take responsibility for his words and used an "off-the-record" stipulation. Several writers observed his every move from the time he awoke until he went to bed. In fact, biographer Frank Freidel noted that "he was seldom alone even with his family."[25]

Roosevelt also experimented with radio. FDR's rise to national prominence paralleled the growth of radio as an important mass medium. Programming become more than just hearing another human voice read dispatches. With radio capturing spot news, newspaper editors and even feature writers were now news listeners. As publishers began recognizing a natural affiliation with broadcasting, they began acquiring more and more stations. Roosevelt thought he could circumvent a virtual state Republican monopoly of the press outside New York City with broadcasts.[26]

The Democratic party thus contracted for an hour of radio time each month on a statewide hookup, which Roosevelt used to discuss the latest developments in Albany. As a follow-up to these monthly radio addresses, James Farley sent out questionnaires to local Democrats asking them about their reception. When faced with the 1929 legislative impasse, Roosevelt used the microphone to make a public appeal. By April 1929 Roosevelt was using his radio time in the manner of what was later called a "fireside chat," "an intimate, quiet way" of speaking. He projected his personality as a friend of the people with speeches that were logical, simple, and authoritative. The House Speaker and one powerful senator jointly reacted by declaring that they would not sit by quietly while the governor vetoed budget items and "bombards the Legislature through the press and over the air with ridiculous and groundless charges." Already fascinating to many listeners, the radio became New York's classroom. Roosevelt effectively discussed his proposals for prison reform, public power, public utility regulation, tighter banking laws, and old age security, and a responsive public helped him gain passage of his legislative program.[27]

Roosevelt was also able to influence the era's feature writers through his warmth and gaiety and by giving them numerous human interest stories. During the spring of 1929 when many people were interested in stock investments, FDR told reporters about a company he formed with Henry Morgenthau, Jr., to grow squashes. He recounted his letter to Morgenthau concerning the enterprise "Squashco": "Please write me any further directions as to how the common stock should be planted, whether it should be watered, whether the distribution should be wide or closely harrowed, whether it carries any bonus (besides bugs), other stock in the same row, etc." The reporters and the public enjoyed such humor, especially when there was a news lull in Albany.[28]

During his first summer as governor, Roosevelt made a number of politically effective and "official" inspection tours, similar to those in his Navy Department days. He met many people as he cruised along the barge canals and made side trips to state schools, hospitals, and prisons. The carefully orchestrated inspections and Eleanor Roosevelt's "eyes and ears" trips gave reporters an "event" to cover. FDR was seen as an energetic, busy executive who sought facts while others vacationed and who had deep interest in upstate affairs. He sold his program to the public and press so well that the Republican majority in the legislature had to acquiesce.[29]

Roosevelt's 1930 campaign strategy was to emphasize the positive achievements of his administration through novel publicity efforts. Howe, who canvassed radio stations to find those with the largest audiences, and the Democratic Publicity Bureau spent $25,000 on radio time. After surveying those theaters willing to rent for rallies, Howe began a movie campaign. A talking motion picture, still so new in 1930, was made as a campaign documentary. "The Roosevelt Record," covering the governor's inspection tours, was shown at two hundred theaters and distributed for small meetings by five movietone sound trucks.[30]

Yet newspapers continued to point to Roosevelt's health. Even after the legislature adjourned in 1929, newspapers such as the *Elmira Advertiser* observed that "he was an exceedingly tired man when he went South" and that "the office proves a severe tax upon his strength, for he is by no means well." Roosevelt strongly refuted such statements, asking editors not only to correct the misimpression but also to let him know the source of such erroneous news. One terrible rumor circulating around the country was that Roosevelt's incapacity was not polio but syphilis. Roosevelt acted dramatically. Rather than just letting his record as a vigorous, hardworking governor stand, he had an examination by a group of New York physicians representing several insurance companies. Roosevelt announced he had passed his physical tests so successfully that twenty-two companies had granted him insurance policies totalling $560,000 at the normal rates and had offered the option of a million dollars worth. Before assembled newspaper reporters, the Equitable Life Assurance Company medical director publicly told the governor that rarely had it been his privilege to see such a splendid physical specimen, and Roosevelt accepted the policies, naming the Warm Springs Foundation as the beneficiary. The campaign continued, and FDR won by a staggering plurality of 725,000 votes.[31]

Before that 1930 gubernatorial election, Roosevelt had been prominent as a prospective Democratic presidential nominee. Afterwards, newspapers from all over the country called him a front-runner, despite such public denials as "I am giving no consideration or thought or time to anything except the duties of the Governorship."[32]

When the National Democratic Club met in New York City for a Jefferson Day dinner, Franklin D. Roosevelt was one of the two featured speakers. The NBC Blue Network carried his address to all parts of the nation except the Pacific coast. When Senator Burton K. Wheeler of Montana spoke and proclaimed his support for Roosevelt as the "general" to lead the country to victory in 1932, Roosevelt's friends were delighted with a chance to test the political winds.[33]

Immediately after the reelection, Louis Howe launched another letter-writing and publicity effort. The "Friends of Roosevelt," centered in New York City, invited influential leaders to the governor's second inauguration and quietly began garnering national support. Notables such as Colonel Edward M. House, Woodrow Wilson's friend and adviser, carried on extensive correspondence in Roosevelt's behalf.[34]

At the same time, Roosevelt kept after the critical press and chastised such media owners as Henry Luce and his "distasteful" *Time* magazine because of articles connecting Roosevelt to Tammany. *Time* magazine was growing in influence, and newspapers were beginning to copy, in one form or another, *Time*'s weekly synthesis—an outline of events and departmentalized news. Unlike newspaper editors, who publicly declared they tried to be objective, the *Time* editors made no pretense about being impartial. Conservative Henry Luce was a formidable multimedia owner who continued to expand his influence by producing a radio program called "March of Time" as well as a motion picture version of it, and by establishing *Fortune* and *Life* magazines in the 1930s.[35]

As Roosevelt gained more and more national prominence as a possible 1932 presidential candidate, his critics and the press once again questioned his physical condition. The question was, Could he withstand the presidential pressures? The memories of Warren G. Harding's collapse and Woodrow Wilson's breakdown were all too recent. FDR responded with a spectacular media stunt in 1931. Earle Looker, professedly a Republican writer who had been a playmate of Theodore Roosevelt's children, challenged Roosevelt to have the Director of the New York Academy of Medicine select a committee of eminent physicians, including a brain specialist, to examine him. They produced affidavits of his buoyancy, reaffirmed his fitness, and invited Looker to come and see for himself whether Roosevelt was competent to carry out his gubernatorial duties. After three visits, Looker reported in the July 15 *Liberty* magazine: "In so far as I had observed him, I had come to the conclusion that he seemed able to take more punishment than many men ten years younger. Merely his legs were not much good to him." Howe purchased thousands of reprints to send to every county Democratic chair in the country and to any correspondent who doubted Roosevelt's general health.[36]

From 1931 on, magazine articles and books increasingly focused on Franklin D. Roosevelt as a presidential candidate. *Liberty* contracted to buy a 400-word magazine article every two weeks over Roosevelt's signature, ghostwritten by Earle Looker. Howe furnished the materials and enlisted the aid of others for terse, professional pieces on taxes, crime, and relief. By the fall campaign, Roosevelt's *Government Not Politics* appeared, based on the *Liberty* articles. The Albany correspondent for the *New York World,* Ernest K. Lindley, wrote a friendly biography, *Franklin D. Roosevelt.* Looker turned out his own helpful campaign book, *The Man Roosevelt,* and followed that in 1933 with *The American Way: F.D.R. in Action.* Even Roosevelt's mother, with the assistance of Howe's staff, helped by writing *My Boy Franklin.*[37]

After Roosevelt officially announced his candidacy on January 22, 1932, he and his "Friends for Roosevelt" organization expanded their news tactics to include a type of public opinion polling. Newspapermen Cornelius Vanderbilt, Jr., and Marvin McIntyre scouted rumors, gathered political opinion, and cemented relationships with state organizations to create a springtime bandwagon effect. Jesse Straus, a department store owner and one of the most active members of the "Friends for Roosevelt," polled not only delegates and alternates from the 1928 Democratic convention but also bankers, directors of corporations, and small-business owners. These early surveys attracted so much media attention that they led newspapers and magazines to conduct further polls to satisfy the public's interest. One of the most important, a poll conducted by twenty-five Scripps-Howard newspapers, led to the prediction that Roosevelt not only would be nominated but would win in November. By fall Roosevelt began using analyst Emil Edward Hurja to weigh the tabulations of the Hearst papers and the *Literary Digest.* These unique, embryonic polls and the press coverage accorded them did much to create the desired bandwagon effect.[38]

Despite such publicity efforts, all was not perfect. Roosevelt had to battle the intellectuals as well as some newspaper critics. Walter Lippmann expressed misgivings about Roosevelt's straddling the issues: "Franklin D. Roosevelt is not crusader. He is not tribune of the people. He is not enemy of entrenched privilege. He is a pleasant man who, without any important qualifications for the office, would very much like to be President." FDR retorted with an elitest accusation: "In spite of his brilliance it is very clear that he [Lippmann] has never let his mind travel west of the Hudson or north of Harlem!"[39]

When William Randolph Hearst broadcast a speech and ran front-page editorials accusing Roosevelt of being an internationalist, Roosevelt had Colonel E. M. House assure the publisher that he was *not* an internationalist. FDR publicly spoke at the Albany Grange and neutralized the issue by saying that the League was no longer the League conceived by Woodrow Wilson. "I do not favor American participation," said Roosevelt, and he called Hearst himself in an attempt to free himself publicly from the League of Nations' "legacy." Hearst was a major newspaper owner and by the mid-1930s would have the largest media empire, with 13.6 percent of *all* American dailies and 24.2 percent of all Sunday circulations. He also would control the major news syndicate, King Feature, as well as International News Service, Universal Service, International News Photos, thirteen magazines, eight radio stations, and two motion picture companies.[40]

While some delegates were wavering between Roosevelt, John Garner, and Al Smith during the preconvention weeks, Howe pulled out the previous technological successes and charmed and amazed convention delegates by sending each of them an autographed photograph of Roosevelt and a small phonograph record "containing a message especially for you, from the Governor." When the convention delegations arrived in Chicago at the end of June, Howe had in his room a direct wire from Albany with a microphone attached. Roosevelt's booming voice would greet each arriving delegation with "My friends from Nebraska . . . ," or wherever, and then would call the delegates by their first names and ask them personal questions.[41]

Millions of Americans were able to follow step by step each phase of the candidate's nomination, which excited the popular imagination. When the convention reached the fourth ballot without the necessary two-thirds vote, both the print media and radio led with stories about the convention's tenseness and nomination struggle. After winning the nomination, Roosevelt's first act was to make a dramatic break with tradition. He not only would make an unprecedented appearance at the convention but also would fly to Chicago. Both of these decisions were indeed newsworthy, especially his boldness in flying when commercial air transport was still in its infancy. Never before had a nominee delivered an acceptance speech in person, and certainly never before had an airplane been utilized in national politics. As Roosevelt's plane bumped along in the turbulence—slowed down by strong headwinds and gradually falling more and more behind schedule—the press, including radio, gave progress reports and anticipated the landing. With the nation listening, a buildup began for the candidate's acceptance speech. In a clear, confident voice, Roosevelt pointed out that he was breaking traditions and pledged his party to the task of destroying foolish practices. Two words in his final paragraph stuck—"new deal." Although not original, the magic ring that Franklin Roosevelt gave the phrase caught the imagination of newspaper reporters and cartoonists alike.[42]

The Democratic National Committee emphasized positive publicity, with more than 475,000 news releases and campaign expenditures of almost $2.5 million, the largest expense of $340,000 going for radio time. Although the Republicans bought more network time than the Democrats did—seventy as opposed to fifty hours—Herbert Hoover could not approach Roosevelt's broadcast or publicity skills.[43]

At the end of the summer when the showdown over Tammany corruption came, Roosevelt shrewdly summoned Mayor Jimmy Walker to Albany on August 11, the day of Hoover's acceptance speech. Roosevelt's action became the lead story in many newspapers, even Republican ones. His quiet dignity in taking personal charge of the hearings further contributed to the election drama. After Walker resigned, Judge Robert Bingham, publisher of the *Louisville Courier-Journal,* wrote Roosevelt, "I am convinced you made no new enemies, but, on the other hand, you gave a host of people throughout the country an opportunity to know you. It was a grand job, fearlessly, fairly, nobly done."[44]

Despite warnings from numerous campaign advisers to play it safe by staying home and giving a few national radio speeches, Roosevelt campaigned strenuously, gave masterful speeches, and courted the press. Many advisers feared he might collapse. Yet Senator Thomas J. Walsh prevailed with advice that such a trip might dispel the remaining whispers about Roosevelt's lack of physical endurance. After FDR entertained his old schoolmate Colonel Robert R. McCormick of the *Chicago Tribune,* the publisher assigned a trusted young reporter, John Boettiger, to cover the campaign. FDR granted Anna O'Hare McCormick of the *New York Times* an exclusive interview, and he invited to lunch Cissy Patterson, who was leasing Hearst's *Washington Herald.* When he was in California, Roosevelt made sure that he saw Hearst, and Hearst's star columnist Arthur Brisbane visited Hyde Park. Hearst newspapers endorsed FDR, although the *Tribune* did not.[45]

Franklin D. Roosevelt's campaign had tremendous news coverage and press support. FDR's landslide win was only surpassed by Andrew Jackson's. Even Walter Lippmann now saw favorable omens in the governor's win and wrote, "Luckily for him, he has not made or had to make very many specific pledges to the voters which will rise to plague him."[46]

From January 1 until March 4, Roosevelt saw reporters daily and parried their queries in a gay, informal way. When he had something important to tell them, he would write a precise statement. He gave the newspaper reporters the correct impression that he was actively exploring a number of approaches to conquer the depression. However, he did not dribble the names of his cabinet as he had done in 1928; he officially announced only two of his selections before the end of February. Amid all the speculations, he told the Hearst emissary that it would be a "radical" cabinet with no Wall Streeters or international bankers. Although he remained cautious on most issues, he gave reporters sufficient news and enough pleasant banter to retain their enthusiastic support. He continued to court the largest publishers for editorial support by inviting them to Warm Springs. Cissy Patterson came, but Hearst, who was recuperating from an operation, did not. Yet he assured Franklin Roosevelt that he had his backing: "I have been following your course very closely and I think I have a good general idea of your plans; and I can assure you that I am in hearty accord with those plans as I understand them to be."[47]

The journalists who followed the president-elect's travels witnessed the February 15 assassination attempt on Franklin Roosevelt's life. Their accounts of Roosevelt's courageous reaction to this brush with death brought a surge of public confidence in him as none of his other actions had. FDR now became the symbol of courage and hope for the country. The winter of 1932–33 was catastrophic: there was a new series of bank failures, one-fourth of the population was unemployed, and desperate people were stricken by famine despite farm overproduction.[48]

In the midst of these staggering blows, Franklin D. Roosevelt prepared to take the oath of office. The American people needed a dramatic, innovative, and strong leader. America, too, was suffering a handicap, a crippling economic disease that was bringing it to a standstill. As Franklin Delano Roosevelt had met his crippling infantile paralysis head on, so too would the country meet the paralyzed economy. The challenge was great. And, clearly, the press would continue to help.

Notes

1. William E. Leuchtenburg, *Franklin D. Roosevelt and the New Deal, 1932–1940* (New York: Harper and Brothers, 1963), p. 17; Frank Freidel, *Launching the New Deal*, Vol. 4 of *Franklin D. Roosevelt* (Boston: Little, Brown, 1973), p. 63.

2. Frank Freidel, *The Triumph*, Vol. 3 of *Franklin D. Roosevelt* (Boston: Little, Brown, 1956), p. 5; Arthur M. Schlesinger, Jr., *Crisis of the Old Order*, Vol. 1 of *The Age of Roosevelt* (Boston: Houghton Mifflin, 1957), pp. 474–77; James MacGregor Burns, *Roosevelt: The Lion and the Fox* (New York: Harcourt, Brace, 1956), pp. 14–16.

3. Burns, *Roosevelt: The Lion and the Fox*, pp. 17, 20; William D. Hassett, *Off*

the Record with F.D.R., 1942–1945 (New Brunswick, N.J.: Rutgers University Press, 1958), p. 119; Schlesinger, *Crisis of the Old Order,* p. 324.

4. Schlesinger, *Crisis of the Old Order,* p. 331–34; Burns, *Roosevelt: The Lion and the Fox,* pp. 31–34, 36, 40.

5. Burns, *Roosevelt: The Lion and the Fox,* pp. 39–40.

6. Ibid., p. 44.

7. Frank Freidel, *The Apprenticeship,* Vol. 1 of *Franklin D. Roosevelt* (Boston: Little, Brown, 1952), p. 324.

8. Alfred D. Rollins, Jr., *Roosevelt and Howe* (New York: Knopf, 1962), pp. 14–15.

9. Ibid., pp. 102–3; Lela Stiles, *The Man behind Roosevelt* (Cleveland and New York: World Publishing, 1954), p. 62.

10. Stiles, *The Man behind Roosevelt,* p. 69; Burns, *Roosevelt: The Lion and the Fox,* pp. 74–75; Henry F. Pringle, "Franklin D. Roosevelt," *The Nation,* April 27, 1932, p. 488.

11. Silas Bent, *Ballyhoo: The Voice of the Press* (New York: Boni and Liveright, 1927), pp. 21–45; Edwin Emery and Michael Emery, *The Press and America: An Interpretative History of the Mass Media,* 5th ed. (Englewood Cliffs, N.J.: Prentice-Hall, 1984), pp. 387–98; Burns, *Roosevelt: The Lion and the Fox,* pp. 87–88; Frank Freidel, *The Ordeal,* Vol. 2 of *Franklin D. Roosevelt* (Boston: Little, Brown, 1954), p. 101; Stiles, *The Man behind Roosevelt,* p. 77.

12. Freidel, *The Ordeal,* p. 102, cites *New York World,* September 14, 1921, and an interview with Eleanor Roosevelt, May 1, 1948.

13. Rollins, *Roosevelt and Howe,* pp. 180–81; Ernest K. Lindley, *Franklin D. Roosevelt: A Career in Progressive Democracy* (New York: Blue Ribbon Book Co., 1931), pp. 202–3. The *New York Times,* September 16, 1921, discussed FDR's polio on page 1.

14. Rollins, *Roosevelt and Howe,* p. 205. In addition, Howe encouraged Eleanor Roosevelt to expand her political activities and write. She edited the *Women's Democratic News,* and Howe taught her to make up a dummy, proofread, and quickly read the daily newspapers.

15. *Conference on the Press under the Auspices of the School of Public and International Affairs,* Princeton University, April 23–25, 1931 (Princeton, N.J.: School of Public Affairs, 1932), pp. 13, 17.

16. Thomas H. Greer, *What Roosevelt Thought: The Social and Political Ideas of Franklin D. Roosevelt* (East Lansing: Michigan State University Press, 1958), p. 155: Franklin D. Roosevelt, *Foreign Affairs* 6 (July 1928): 573–86.

17. Lindley, *Franklin D. Roosevelt,* p. 21.

18. Freidel, *The Ordeal,* p. 258 for acrobat quote and p. 260 for newspaper quote, which cites *New York Herald-Tribune,* October 9, 1928.

19. Ibid., pp. 260–66, cites the *New York Times,* November 2, 3, and 5, 1928; Burns, *Roosevelt: The Lion and the Fox,* p. 103.

20. Frank Luther Mott, *American Journalism, a History: 1690–1960* (New York: Macmillan, 1962), pp. 461–62.

21. Freidel, *The Ordeal,* p. 26, cites the *New York Post,* November 6, 1928; Leuchtenburg, *Franklin D. Roosevelt and the New Deal,* p. 169, cites *Post,* November 6, 1928, and William McKinley Moore, "F.D.R.'s Image: A Study in Pictorial Sym-

bols" (Ph.D. dissertation, University of Wisconsin, 1946), pp. 427, 477, 634, nn. 135–36.

22. Rollins, *Roosevelt and Howe,* p. 258; Freidel, *The Triumph,* p. 14, *Launching the New Deal,* p. 15, and *The Ordeal,* p. 268.

23. Freidel, *The Triumph,* p. 29; Roy V. Peel and Thomas C. Donnelly, *The 1932 Campaign: An Analysis* (New York: Farrar and Rinehart, 1935), p. 69.

24. Rollins, *Roosevelt and Howe,* pp. 260–61.

25. Ibid., p. 260; Freidel, *The Triumph,* p. 30.

26. Sydney W. Head, *Broadcasting in America* (Boston: Houghton Mifflin, 1972), p. 138; *Conference on the Press,* p. 36.

27. Freidel, *The Triumph,* p. 31; Burns, *Roosevelt: The Lion and the Fox,* p. 118; Freidel, *The Triumph,* p. 61 for first quote and p. 64, which cites the *New York Post,* April 11, 1929, for second quote. For other mention of his radio appeals, see Freidel, *The Triumph,* pp. 54, 61–64, 112, 119, 130.

28. Freidel, *The Triumph,* p. 67.

29. Ibid., pp. 80–81; Rollins, *Roosevelt and Howe,* pp. 260–61, 280; Burns, *Roosevelt: The Lion and the Fox,* p. 118.

30. Freidel, *The Triumph,* pp. 156, 159.

31. Ibid., pp. 68–69, 157–58. See also Rollins, *Roosevelt and Howe,* p. 297.

32. Freidel, *The Triumph,* pp. 165, 169.

33. Ibid., p. 136.

34. Ibid., p. 175.

35. Emery and Emery, *The Press and America,* pp. 450, 458–60; Mott, *American Journalism,* pp. 461–62, 683.

36. Looker article quoted in Freidel, *The Triumph,* p. 211.

37. Rollins, *Roosevelt and Howe,* p. 313; Freidel, *The Triumph,* p. 342.

38. Freidel, *The Triumph,* pp. 202–6, 242, 360; Peel and Donnelly, *The 1932 Campaign,* p. 60.

39. Lippmann is quoted in Schlesinger, *Crisis of the Old Order,* p. 291; Franklin D. Roosevelt to Morris Llewellyn Cooke, January 18, 1932, *F.D.R.: His Personal Letters, 1928–1945,* Vol. 1, Elliott Roosevelt, ed. (New York: Duell, Sloan and Pearce, 1950), p. 254.

40. Schlesinger, *Crisis of the Old Order,* p. 289; Emery and Emery, *The Press and America,* pp. 398–406, 428; William Weinfeld, "The Growth of Daily Newspaper Chains in the United States: 1923, 1926–1935," *Journalism Quarterly* 13 (December 1936): 357, 368–69, 377.

41. Freidel, *The Triumph,* p. 297.

42. Ibid., pp. 308, 316; Peel and Donnelly, *The 1932 Campaign,* p. 95.

43. Democratic National Committee, President's Secretary's File, Franklin D. Roosevelt Library. The budget of the National Committee was $382,000, with the bulk going for radio, $340,000. See also Peel and Donnelly, *The 1932 Campaign,* pp. 115–16.

45. Ibid., pp. 338, 341.

46. Freidel, *Launching the New Deal,* pp. 16–17.

47. Ibid., p. 62.

48. For a most vivid description, see Leuchtenburg, *Franklin D. Roosevelt and the New Deal,* pp. 1–2, 18, 21–23, 38–39.

THE NATIONAL CAPITAL

Press Conference at the White House

Drawing by Gluyas Williams; © 1942, 1970 by The New Yorker Magazine, Inc.

3

The New Deal Press Conferences

Roosevelt and the press were united in holy newslock.
—Walter Davenport, "The Presidency and the Press,"
Collier's, January 27, 1945

As a President with an almost always critical press, he took them in and
made the press conference not theirs but his. What an artist and
performer he was! But it takes an artist to make the press conference a
Presidential work of art, and unfortunately not all Presidents, though
stuck forever with the open press conference, can play on it as he did.
—Jonathan Daniels to Frank Freidel, May 22, 1971

When Franklin Delano Roosevelt recited the oath of office at one
o'clock on Saturday afternoon, March 4, 1933, radio listeners throughout the
world heard him promise, "I am certain that my fellow Americans expect that
on my induction into the Presidency I will address them with a candor and a
decision which the present situation of our nation impels. This is preeminently
the time to speak the truth, the whole truth, frankly and boldly." Such a plan
to communicate frankly and boldly with the people had to be executed in some
manner. While Roosevelt astutely used radio, newsreels, and photojournalism, he most consistently communicated through his regular press meetings. While FDR was an acknowledged master in conducting press conferences, not so well known have been his methods. This chapter examines
those Roosevelt press conference efforts to "speak the truth," just as he had
promised, and at the same time scrutinizes those news management attempts.[1]

If Franklin D. Roosevelt had followed the path of his recent predecessors,
he could have abandoned press conferences. By the end of Herbert Hoover's
presidency, they were moribund. The depression crisis would also be excuse
enough. The correspondents themselves found the conferences most un-
satisfactory. Echoing others at the 1931 Princeton University Conference on
the Press, Henry Suydam, Washington correspondent for the *Brooklyn Daily*

Eagle, complained that the meetings were unproductive for journalists, "an arrangement which is more to the advantage of the President than to the press."[2]

Roosevelt's meetings would indeed be to his advantage, but they would also benefit the correspondents. FDR had specific purposes in mind when he reinstituted the press conferences. Just before his inauguration, Steve Early, his secretary who would be in charge of the press, confided to *Washington Post* correspondent Raymond Clapper that he wanted the coverage of the White House to be prestigious and not a separate estate. In fact, Early said that the president wished "to make the White House assignment an important one and not a watchdog affair, one that would require the very best correspondents to swing."[3]

Such proposals were leaked not only to Clapper but also to the wire services. News articles began appearing about the planned press conference format, meetings which were to be more like FDR's Albany sessions. They did not mention that Roosevelt would avoid "a watchdog affair." Even when the president himself later relayed his purposes, he obviously only stressed his desire for accuracy: "I have endeavored to see an organization under a trained and experienced newspaper man, which would be helpful to the correspondents by furnishing a continuous supply of accurate information and which would at the same time prevent them from 'getting out on a limb' with inaccurate stories which would later have to be repudiated." He immediately wanted that accuracy and started giving that continuous supply of information. On March 5, he met with representatives of the four press associations to explain the banking holiday proclamation.[4]

Four days after his inauguration, Franklin D. Roosevelt began his twelve-year press meeting odyssey. At 10:10 A.M. on March 8, John Russell Young, a former president of the White House Correspondents' Association, introduced each correspondent to the president as they filed into the Oval Office. Roosevelt gave the hundred or so reporters an individual handshake and a few words of greeting. He explained, "I am told that what I am about to do will become impossible, but that I am going to try it."[5]

The president assured the journalists that he thought they could have profitable meetings. He cautioned them that there would be many questions he could not answer, either because they were conditional questions or because he did not know enough. He promised to meet twice weekly, "off the record," much as he had done in Albany and in the Navy Department. He provoked laughter by remarking that he did not want to revive Theodore Roosevelt's "Ananias Club," a make-believe negative organization of those reporters who had erroneously published confidential remarks.[6]

Roosevelt then introduced four rules on the release of press conference information: all news stories based on news announcements from the White House were to be without quotations; direct quotations could be used only when given out in writing by the press secretary Steve Early; background information would be given to reporters on their own authority and responsibility, not to be attributed to the White House; and the off-the-record information was to be confidential, given only to those reporters present.[7]

Despite the introduction of informational boundaries, FDR's first news conference was a tremendous success. After four years of Herbert Hoover's reticence, the correspondents were captivated by Roosevelt's more open attitude. FDR had eliminated the loathsome written-question requirement dating from the Harding era. Even though the president told the reporters little they could attribute to him, the discussion was so frank about the banking crisis that when the meeting ended thirty-five minutes later, the reporters broke into spontaneous applause. They now had enough background information to put the spot news into context. Yet, as an omen, Steve Early warned the departing journalists that he would make an example of anyone who violated the president's confidence.[8]

Besides the rules, other factors influenced the press conference news. The very meeting timetable, even the location, would help. Initially, Roosevelt alternated his Oval Office conferences between 10:30 A.M. and 4 P.M. on Wednesdays and Fridays, later Tuesdays and Fridays, to meet the spot-news requirement for a front-page story for both the morning and afternoon editions. Such scheduling was so important that even when his own timetable changed, FDR still alternated the meetings. When he was on the road, Roosevelt would hold miniconferences for the dozen or so traveling correspondents elsewhere: aboard the Presidential Special Train, on the deck of a ship, at his Hyde Park home, or in front of his Warm Springs cottage. The traveling reporters had a greater chance to ask more questions. Sometimes when FDR was ill with a cold or a sinus infection, he would still value the sessions enough to meet with a small wire service delegation in his bedroom. They in turn would relay information to the other correspondents.[9]

By scheduling meetings on a regular basis, the president had another news management tactic. He could set an important White House news agenda that day. He could respond to events and other political happenings immediately. He could also hinder or aid developing news. In addition, he could learn from the correspondents what they thought was newsworthy. Moreover, like Calvin Coolidge, he could maintain a regular, expected flow of news from the White House. Reporters appreciated such an expected news flow. During the depression years, many smaller newspapers and news services overloaded correspondents with "the hill" responsibilities, regional interests, as well as White House coverage. Roosevelt's regular meetings, open to all hundred or more journalists, kept the correspondents from being "scooped" by their competition. The meeting also saved them time by removing some of the tension of covering Washington.[10]

The conferences were so important that Roosevelt carefully prepared for them. Steve Early refers in his diary to the daily morning meetings in FDR's bedroom to discuss possible news subjects and materials. Early usually brought statements, telegrams, and letters as well as suggestions from others in the administration. For example, in reference to a summary of FDR's 1938 messages and letters submitted to Congress, Early wrote, "You wanted this to refresh your memory and guide you in preparation for the press conference 'round-up' or rewrite story for use tomorrow morning."[11]

Such preparations were not secret. Roosevelt was candid enough about them to tell national journalism educators in 1935, "Sometimes I think that a perfectly tremendous matter of great importance is going to be the subject of the press conference, and I get ready. It is obvious to me that is news, and when the conference comes, nobody asks about it!" The academics roared with laughter.[12]

To make sure that somebody asked about it, Roosevelt and his press secretary would plant questions. On April 24, 1935, Early wrote in his diary that he told Earl Godwin of the *Washington Times-Herald* to "ask the President what part he personally is going to play in the administration on this work relief bill." During that morning's press conference, that question was one of the first asked. Roosevelt then launched into the subject with numerous proposals as well as a theoretical chart to explain the relationship between the new agencies and his projects. The planted question and the president's answer dominated the conference. Afterward, Secretary Early followed the wire service and the newspaper accounts. This particular instance and others occurred, despite Roosevelt's assurances in his *Public Papers and Addresses* that "I have not tried to create a Publicity Bureau for the Administration or to 'plant' stories on its behalf."[13]

Early had those favorite correspondents, such as Godwin and George Durno of the International News Service, take planted questions. In his study of the New Deal correspondents, Leo C. Rosten also reported "that reporters 'in the front row claque' permitted themselves to be used for 'planted questions.' " Early's memos to the president gave instances of such assistance: "The Murphy report can be brought into the press conference by having someone planted with the following question . . ." and "George Durno will at Friday's press conference ask this question. . . ."[14]

Roosevelt might declare, "I just take 'pot luck,' " yet he was accused of requiring correspondents to warn Steve Early of prospective controversial questions. This might have been true in some instances. On one occasion a correspondent declared, "I wish to ask you a question about the State Department release you have on the desk." The president replied, "Steve said you were going to. . . ." FDR was warned, yet such warnings could be indirect. After Raymond "Pete" Brandt of the *St. Louis Post-Dispatch* sent a copy of his paper's editorial, Early wrote that he suspected Brandt would ask for a comment about it at the next press conference.[15]

In the final analysis, FDR was skillful enough to be able to cover whatever information he wished. Pete Brandt even defended the president's conference style in 1939: "The White House has been accused of planting questions, but such overt action is unnecessary. Mr. Roosevelt has shown no hesitancy in initiating announcements and if he has prepared himself to answer questions which reporters do not ask, he has a way of bringing up the subject." After all, the president did have an excellent "news sense," and he certainly kept abreast of events of the day and would even make such press conference statements as "Somebody is sure to ask a question about. . . ."[16]

Overall, the press conferences were exclusive affairs. The president and his secretary controlled access to information by limiting the meetings mostly to those Washington correspondents who had credentials from either the House and Senate press galleries or the White House Correspondents' Association. Although the press secretary would allow occasional visitors, only accredited correspondents could ask questions or make comments.[17]

Another format requirement made them exclusive. The meetings were supposed to be confidential. No cameras or recording devices were allowed in the room. As a protective device, the White House had conferences taken down in shorthand and kept a copy of the meeting transcripts. Steve Early contended that the rule "has been not to permit any of these conferences to be transcribed or be distributed to anyone in government," especially the opposition party. Initially, FDR had explained that he wanted to keep the conferences informal and extemporaneous, open only to newspapermen, so he would not have to worry about his style or be overly concerned about grammar and language. During the second term, Early wrote Richard Neuberger of the *Portland-Oregonian* that stenographic records were available to those journalists present. However, they could be used only to check their notes and could not be published verbatim without permission. Such information release was selective. Roosevelt included 48 edited excerpts out of the 337 first-term meetings in his *Public Papers and Addresses* published in 1938.[18]

In addition, the president sometimes waived his policy on confidentiality, notably after reacting to the famous 1935 Schechter case, the Supreme Court ruling against the National Industrial Recovery Act. Here, he did not waive enough of what he said. During that unprecedented hour-and-a-half press meeting, the president unleashed his fury, reading excerpt after excerpt of supportive letters to make his points about the dire implications of the Court's decision. The correspondents may have needed some kind of "news handle," an overall catchy phrase in which to explain the president's viewpoints. They found it in Roosevelt's statement that "we have been relegated to the horse and buggy definition of interstate commerce." The president said that the correspondents could quote that one phrase directly. Taken out of context, however, that sentence was misunderstood and created an uproar.[19]

Many people wanted a transcript of the conference. Steve Early sent copies to Democratic Publicity Director Charles Michelson "to be used for his own information and for the guidance of Senator Robinson to let other Senators read." He also sent copies "TO ALL MEMBERS OF THE CABINET OR ACTING SECRETARIES IN CHARGE OF THE EXECUTIVE DEPARTMENTS" to help them understand what the president actually had said about the effects of the Court ruling. But he turned down correspondent Ruby Black's request. As far as can be determined, no correspondent received a transcript of this very important press conference. If Roosevelt and his press secretary had released the president's remarks, or at least the context of the "horse and buggy" phrase, there probably would not have been such a public uproar over what was taken figuratively as an attack on conservative judges. Perhaps that is why copies of the various press conference transcripts later went to particular cabinet officials and were temporarily made available to reporters to compare their notes.[20]

Overall, it was Roosevelt's warm personality and his informal style which greatly influenced his press conferences. His numerous news management techniques meshed with his character from the very outset of the meetings. The president usually began by sounding his buzzer to signal that he was ready to receive the press. The secretary then informed White House Usher Pat McKenna, who clapped his hands twice, and the journalists rushed past a group of Secret Service men. As the newsmen entered, Roosevelt began teasing them with the camaraderie of someone who knew not only their first names but also their lifestyles and secrets, and certainly what they wrote. A familiar rapport set the scene, such as this August 11, 1936, press conference:

THE PRESIDENT: Don't you think the boys look well?
A. (answer—John Russell Young): They look a little pale.
THE PRESIDENT: They got all washed out. Had too much clam juice.
A. (Mr. Young): Yes, but the taproom sun didn't burn them any. (Laughter)[21]

The conference transcripts continually demonstrate Roosevelt's informality, humor, and small hospitalities. With the president's encouragement, the reporters kept up a repartee on the correspondents' baseball team, a singing group, and the reporters' clothes-buying spree for a Florida trip. FDR asked if the journalists had a place to stay near Hyde Park and if they were comfortable in a cottage at Warm Springs. In his efforts to be helpful, he once mentioned holding a press release until he found a particular reporter. He also was amenable to answering the questions of correspondents who lingered after the meetings to inquire about their specific regions or specialities.[22]

During the New Deal years, the press conferences became an informal club, a center of capital news, a place to see other correspondents as well as the president. Journalists could gather not only White House information but also news tips that other reporters could not use. All parties gained. The president gave out his story and provided the correspondents with several laughs as well as a couple of top-head dispatches in a time-saving twenty-minute visit. The president's press meetings became the greatest regular show in Washington. Roosevelt knew it too. He once remarked, "Most of the people in the back row are here for curiosity. Isn't that right?"[23]

Roosevelt's personality, his familiarity, his good humor, and his small kindnesses all might be considered a form of psychological bribery to promote "good stories." James Martel said that being called "Bill" by the president left a glow that lingered while the news was being written. Even as he sparred with reporters, FDR's good-humored repartee could also "soothe the beast." Following several questions which tried to pin him down on a possible position for Triple A Administrator George Peek, this quick retort exemplifies how effective FDR could be: "Really, this is not a cross-examination!" Laughter followed, and the mode of questioning changed.[24]

Besides having a fast retort, Roosevelt also used anecdotes to divert or soften a line of questioning. For example, when a reporter tried to find out if anything was being done about the nation's money crisis, the president answered, "I would not tell you if there was but there isn't." He then launched into the financial losses of Appointments Secretary McIntyre when his pocket was picked and he lost his watch. That tactic successfully diverted the line of questions.[25]

Certain formalized signals also gave the press conferences important boundaries. Although a back-and-forth bantering initially began the conferences, there was a more formal signal by January 1934. Bill Donaldson of the House press gallery would shout "all in" from the rear of the room, and the door was then shut until the conference ended. The closed door was symbolically important. At the second press conference the president had asked the correspondents to stay in the room until the meeting was over to be fair to all. The journalists had been "locked in" on an equal basis, not to be "scooped." Occasionally this rule was waived for the afternoon meetings to allow the reporters on early deadline to be excused immediately following the president's statements to get the story in the final edition.[26]

Roosevelt's very manner of starting the conferences helped too. He usually began with "What's the news?" or "I don't have any particular news," or some variation thereof. In fact, after he set up the conference rules at his first press meeting, he jokingly quipped, "Now, as to news, I don't think there is any," amid the correspondents' laughter. FDR said this, even though he had much new information on the banking crisis and possible new legislation. Roosevelt overstated the "no news, except . . ." refrain throughout his years in office. In an August 1940 press conference, he began with "I haven't got any news this morning except the release Steve will give you afterwards." He then said, "There isn't any news. You saw the appointment of the Permanent Joint Board on Defense yesterday." He then said, "There is no news whatsoever on conversations with Great Britain in regard to bases or destroyers. . . ." He then had four transcribed pages of "no news." Despite Roosevelt's use of such qualifying statements, the New Deal conferences averaged thirty-two questions, and reporters would remind the president, "You told us no news on Friday and we filled the paper."[27]

Initially, Roosevelt closed the meetings himself. By September when the fast-moving action of the first months of the New Deal had slowed down somewhat, the most senior wire service member, usually Francis H. Stephenson of the Associated Press, began the traditional closing of "Thank you, Mr. President," or a similar variation. Such a termination could also rescue the president from embarrassing situations.[28]

Roosevelt, in fact, used this tactic to contain information he did not wish to divulge. For example, during the 1933 Cuban leadership revolt, a correspondent asked if the president was considering abrogation of the Platt Amendment, which included a provision for the United States to intervene to preserve order and maintain Cuban independence. In answer to the question, FDR shook his head in the negative and the signal, "Thank you, Mr. President," was given, even though the usual twenty- to thirty-minute conference period had not elapsed. The press carried his head-shaking response. Despite Roosevelt's negative answer, the administration did indeed appear to be considering changes in the Platt Amendment. In December Roosevelt publicly announced "the definite policy of the United States from now on is one opposed to armed intervention." By May 1934 the United States and Cuba signed a treaty to abrogate the amendment.[29]

Roosevelt's most clearly defined news boundaries were his press conference rules, announced at his first meeting. Those stipulations could determine the type of attribution as well as the manner in which material could be released. Many times FDR's style was to start the meetings with an announcement, which set an agenda for a news story. As a master of timing, Roosevelt also knew when released news would make the greatest impact. As an example, at the beginning of the January 31, 1934, afternoon conference, he began with the following statement: "Will you please not go out for five minutes. It will be a very short conference because I would very much like to have you all get this on the wires as soon as possible. The reason for the haste is that the gold market over here stays open until five or half-past and it will probably be advantageous for the American gold market to be open instead of having this operate only on the European gold market tomorrow morning. Therefore, the quicker you get it out the better I will be pleased." The president's announcement to those hundred or so newspaper correspondents would get "better press" than a cold, mimeographed White House "handout." Roosevelt often used the technique for positive news coverage. *New York Times* correspondent Arthur Krock wrote that by personally making the statement, Roosevelt invested the announcement with his own charm and gave it the prestige of coming directly from the president.[30]

For the most part, FDR's direct-quotation rule meant that the correspondents had to have the exact quotable remarks in mimeographed form. Usually encompassing messages to Congress and presidential addresses, the copy also stipulated the release time and date, which gave the president a contractual agreement with reporters over the release time, the accuracy of his words, and his point of view. For example, Roosevelt began his June 4, 1935, conference with "Today's announcement is confined to the following, in other words all the news that is, as one of the newspapers says, fit to print." He went on to explain, "I am going to tell you about two steps, three things really and they are all down in mimeographed form, so you won't have to take notes." The president then began a long discussion of the operation of the National Recovery Administration following the Supreme Court decision against the codes.[31]

Although initially Roosevelt's rules stipulated that direct quotes could be used only when given out in writing, reporters would sometimes ask in the middle of the conference if they could quote a remark, as they did with the "horse and buggy" conference. When the president gave permission for an exact quotation, Steve Early piped up with "Just that one sentence," which the president carefully reiterated.[32]

Roosevelt's off-the-record rule gave the president another effective method for containing information. He defined the rule again and again with such statements as "I want to repeat very simply that 'off the record' means merely 'in confidence.' It is only for information to prevent more than anything else, the wrong kind of stories from being written." With such a rule he could contain the discussion of pending courses of action or changes in policy. He could spike rumors by revealing facts in confidence as well as attempt to prevent reporters from blundering into delicate foreign negotiations. Roosevelt first used that category to cover little pleasantries about himself, personnel appointments, and later foreign relations. His budget meetings were strictly off the record until the White House officially released the budget message.[33]

Although admittedly a convenience to the president, the off-the-record stipulation could assist reporters too. Many correspondents liked receiving quotable copy early enough to give them a chance to read the material carefully and to write the story before an event occurred. In one sense, the rule kept them all at the same "scoop" level. When their competition broke a confidential story, they complained loudly. The rule also provided points of orientation amid Washington rumors and political controversy and served as a possible check on the authenticity of stories. An off-the-record stipulation gave reporters Roosevelt's ideas, motives, possible courses of action, and policy changes while at the same time the regulation relied on the journalists' professional ethics concerning secrecy. At least initially, some reporters were flattered by the president's confidences.[34]

Yet, as Roosevelt began using the off-the-record category more frequently during his first term, many journalists complained that the rule was "silly" or "unnecessary" and that it "sewed up a story" the reporters wanted to write. *New York Times* bureau chief Arthur Krock found the rule so inhibiting that he said it was one of his reasons for staying away from press conferences.[35]

When the reporters openly broke the off-the-record rule, Early would react immediately. He particularly tried to enforce the rule when information concerned the confidential budget conferences and foreign policy. In 1936 he chided Phelps Adams of the *New York Sun* about violating the off-the-record rule: "All previous conferences on the budget . . . have been strictly 'off the record.' . . . A formal complaint has been made by me in regard to the story mentioned above."[36]

Early's enforcement appears to have been successful, although the off-the-record stipulation was confusing when it kept changing as to meaning. After the first two years, the rule meant that reporters were not even to infer that particular information came from the president's press conference. Later they were merely forbidden to quote the information directly. Such regulation worked so well that Roosevelt himself told journalism professors the rule was 80–90 percent effective in keeping material from being published. Certainly, the president could define and interpret the rule, depending on the story or stress on the president.[37]

Such off-the-record stipulation might have been a good news control, but it did not completely stifle information. Visitors at the National Press Club could hear half a dozen stories an afternoon that fell into the off-the-record category. Columnist Drew Pearson wrote Steve Early that much of the information he gathered from others for his "Daily Washington Merry-Go-Round" column had fallen within the rule.[38]

Perhaps such a stipulation was impossible to follow, as well as enforce. Roosevelt should have known the reporters' first allegiance was to the newspapers and editors. Moreover, the president possibly knew his remarks ultimately would find their way into press dispatches in some disguised form. Correspondent James Martel wrote that the off-the-record information might have even been a clever and deceptive "trial balloon" for testing public reaction. If the particular information was inconvenient or the viewpoint wrong, then a denial or a reprimand could be used.[39]

The off-the-record rule also applied to the president's special press meetings, such as his "school" sessions on the Gold and Silver Message to Congress and on his proposed governmental reorganization plan, as well as his special press sessions with the American Association of Teachers of Journalism, farm journal editors, and editors of trade papers. Using the off-the-record rule, Roosevelt restricted the information discussed in these meetings, sometimes, as in 1939, to "prevent the story from breaking on the Hill before the word had been given by the White House."[40]

His special conferences to go over the proposed budget were also off the record until the release date. Roosevelt explained why he had these rather tedious financial meetings: "The average of the newspaper profession know less about dollars and cents—c-e-n-t-s—than almost any other profession—except possibly the clergy." In addition, FDR could display his detailed knowledge of the budget and present a sympathetic interpretation. Although the budget conferences initially were held in the Oval Office as exclusive seminars, limited to one newspaper and press association member each, by 1936 they had to be moved to the Executive Offices for the approximately 125 reporters who were interested.[41]

For the bulk of the press conferences, Franklin Roosevelt released a variety of information under the background stipulation. As many as thirty to forty different background questions could be answered. In 1933 the queries ranged from "Are we going to have a war?" after Roosevelt announced that the Japanese admiral was coming to talk to him, to the resignation of the governor of Puerto Rico, the protests of cotton farmers, a report of sugar quotas, a possible war in Cuba, and his message to Congress. With their queries, reporters hoped to gain some kind of information. The president could give as much or as little detail as he wished and then hold the correspondents responsible for the final printed news product.[42]

The background rule also changed as the president redefined the boundaries to suit his purposes. At first FDR stipulated that background information could not be attributed to the White House. By November 1933 he was telling journalists that they could make a limited attribution to the chief executive. After Roosevelt's proposal to pack the Supreme Court was defeated in 1937, Early suggested that background news could then be attributed to the president if written in the third person. By 1941, as the international crises worsened, the president insisted that information was not to be attributed to him or the White House: "You call it the best information obtainable in Washington or something like that." The reality was that if the president disagreed with the news account or the indirect reference, Steve Early could reprimand the reporters. Thus, journalists could never be sure what kind of White House attribution to use: the third person, or a limited reference, or a paraphrase of a limited attribution. Such a rule remained confusing to reporters, although it remained a useful White House news management device.[43]

During his background sessions, Roosevelt employed the full range of news management techniques for not revealing or releasing information. He openly let reporters know that he would not tell everything he knew. At one press conference, he told the journalists he was exhausted after talking to 105 editors. When asked if he could relate his discussion, he answered, "Not by a jugful. I was franker with them than I ever am with you. That is awful, isn't it."[44]

One of his techniques for stopping discussion was to label certain speculative questions "iffy." Roosevelt warned from his first press conference that he would not answer "if" questions; that designation also came to mean different things during the conferences. During that first year, the president retorted, "A terrible 'if' question," in response to questions about a proposal on expanding the credit, possible farm legislation, and congressional adjournment. Areas in which policy had not been made he labeled as "too much if," and he emphatically answered speculative foreign policy questions with "if." He would also say, "That is an opinion question, an 'if' question," even though he often gave his opinions. The ambiguous nature of an "if" retort was useful to the president. In its inexactitude, the label gave Roosevelt enough latitude both to rule out those queries he did not want to answer and to stop a particular line of questioning.[45]

The president used other evasive techniques in answering questions. In one press conference, his answers included "I haven't the faintest idea. I haven't enough information," "I haven't looked at it," and "haven't thought of it." Sometimes, he would just repeat a question, resort to laughter, not answer the question, or answer "No comment." Another method he used to avoid questions was simply to repeat a previous answer and add, "I think that is all there is to say about it."[46]

Although the press conference transcripts indicate his verbal skill, FDR had a tremendous talent for nonverbal communication. When John Gunther visited a 1934 press conference, he noted that within twenty minutes Roosevelt's features showed "amazement, curiosity, mock alarm, genuine interest, worry, rhetorical playing for suspense, sympathy, decision, playfulness, dignity and surpassing charm. Yet he said almost nothing."[47]

The president's elusive tactics, verbal and nonverbal, were all the more noticeable in the delicate area of foreign relations. His skill can be seen in this December 7, 1934, conference:

Q. Do you share Ambassador Bingham's views that a great opportunity exists at the present time for Anglo-American cooperation?

THE PRESIDENT: Where did you get that?

Q. He expressed that in his speech in London last week.

THE PRESIDENT: I will have to get a copy of it. (Laughter)

Later at his National Emergency Council meeting, Roosevelt used this particular question as a lesson on handling potentially explosive queries. He said
that if he had commented on the Bingham statement and supported the ambassador, it would have implied he advocated a working alliance between the
United States and Great Britain. This would have been a sensational story, an
Anglo-American alliance against Japan. On the other hand, if he had said, "I
have no comment to make on the speech of the American Ambassador," it
would have made headlines intimating the president disagreed with his ambassador's statement. Either way, Roosevelt knew he could be misinterpreted. As
it was, he implied that he had not seen it, when in fact he had.[48]

Roosevelt effectively used various other tactics to stop or divert questions.
His interruptions, labeled "interposing" in the transcripts, would cease or
divert questions. While in some cases he might have been only too eager to
answer, he would also hurry through a pointed question with a kind of irrita-
tion. As the number of Supreme Court decisions against the New Deal programs increased, FDR became increasingly impatient with pointed questions
and would often interrupt. In answer to the question, "Does the lower court
decision stump anything you are doing? Does it make any difference in the
Administration . . . ?" FDR interposed with "I think that particular decision
only affects that one project." Sometimes when asked if he had a comment on
something, he would just say "no." Other times he would ignore a question,
or openly show his contempt for a question he did not want to discuss, or as
mentioned tell a reporter to put on a dunce hat.[49]

Correspondent Raymond Clapper noted that in a February 1935 conference
Roosevelt's face tightened and he remarked sharply to a question about his
attitude on the Wheeler-Rayburn public utilities holding company bill: "I have
never seen it. This is the same old thing. There isn't a story. When I say I
haven't seen a thing you can't write a story that the President discussed the
paternity of this, that or the other thing. I don't comment on pending legislation one way or the other, and no deductions are to be made from the statement one way or the other. I don't comment on pending legislation." Despite
the president's reiteration about pending legislation, he had referred to bills in
progress from his very first press conference. But this particular utilities bill
was controversial: the giant holding companies were fighting the proposed
curbs on operating subsidiaries. The timing was wrong. Roosevelt, although
committed, found February 15 too early to discuss the bill, which was modi-
fied, renamed, and passed six months later.[50]

Roosevelt's method of stopping questions was so successful that correspondents such as Raymond Brandt wrote in 1939 that the president's method became an unwritten rule. Whenever Roosevelt signaled he did not intend to answer a question, correspondents would not press on the topic.[51]

As another news management tactic, Roosevelt would tell the correspondents exactly how to write stories. He had not only a great news sense for timing but also a public relations instinct about what would produce the most favorable impact and interpretation. In suggesting *when* to use a story, he once advised, "Instead of using it right now, jot your notes down and let me give you a hint. . . . Let me dig that up for you. Don't use it today—use it for a Sunday or Monday story. . . . Wait until you know more about it." He also gave the adverbs and adjectives he wanted: "In regard to the Message, I suppose if I were writing your stories for you, I would say it is the most brutally frank Budget Message ever sent in." He would emphasize the exact substance of the story: "If I were writing the story I would say that there will undoubtedly be a recommendation to the Congress for permanent legislation."[52]

FDR had no compunction about stretching the truth to create a desired image. In reference to his housing program, he said, "In other words, if I were writing the story today I think it would be perfectly all right to say this, without putting it on me: It has been made perfectly clear by people coming to Warm Springs to see the President (laughter), meaning the Press (laughter), that the Government recognizes as a matter of policy its obligation to those people in the United States whose standards of living are so low that something has to be done about it. . . ."[53]

President Roosevelt attempted to influence the news in other ways. He referred reporters to the agency public relations officers or to particular articles that articulated his viewpoint. On the topic of exporting gold, he directed the correspondents to Walter Lippmann's column: "If I were going to write a story, I would write it along the lines of the decision that was taken last Saturday. . . . If you want to know the reason why, I think the best exposition of it was by Walter Lippmann yesterday morning."[54]

The reporters became so used to his demands that by 1934 they began asking him for his news interpretations. For example, when asked, "Mr. President, if you were going to write a story today for the morning papers, what would you write?" Roosevelt answered, "I would write that the power people were all down here and were discussing power and legislation, just a preliminary talk."[55]

FDR could complain too, sometimes with humor, sometimes not. At his December 27, 1933, press conference he answered a query on the danger to press freedom with the required National Recovery Administration code of fair practices for all businesses, including newspapers. Roosevelt referred the reporter to "Dave Stern's editorial in the New York *Evening Post* last night; I commend it to John Boettiger and, John, entirely off the record, I wish you would give a dare to Bert (referring to Robert McCormick) to reprint it. (Laughter)." The *Chicago Tribune* correspondent assured the president that he would get the editorial published and that he would even mail Roosevelt a copy. FDR's remark must have been effective even with the opposing *Chicago Tribune* because on December 29 Boettiger said that the Stern *New York Post* editorial was to be in the December 30 *Tribune,* "compliments of Colonel McCormick."[56]

If nothing else worked, Roosevelt openly criticized particular news stories. He initially complained about the reporters' inaccuracy, misleading headlines, and speculative stories, but he later lost his temper, especially over the crucial financial stories. He would lash out at a reporter by name: "The number of people who have come to me, . . . and said—readers of these papers—'Why are people trying to destroy the credit of their own Government?' . . . It is a bit like that front page of the *Sun* that came out two weeks ago Saturday that I wrote Will Dewart (New York Sun) about." Then FDR promised he would someday read the letter.[57]

His exasperation was there, planned or not. Such tirades could be useful. Roosevelt could put on the armor of his office and use a "jawbone" as a sword. His complaints were but another effective method of evading topics. They changed the mode of questioning for the moment. Yet as the president became more vigorously open in his criticism, he also risked losing some of his following among the correspondents.[58]

Roosevelt's angry protests became especially noticeable in 1935. Often using sarcasm, he clamored about "fool stories in fool press," "cuckoo stories in the press," "the opposition of the Hearst Press," the eastern managing editors' inadequate understanding of farming in references to the Agricultural Adjustment Act, and editorial inability to interpret unemployment statistics. FDR maintained that there was a tendency to "color the news stories." By the end of the year, he said he did not believe what he read in the press because of editorial decisions. He explained: "Lack of confidence today is not because of the editorials but because of the colored news stories and the failure on the part of some papers to print the news. Very often, as you know, they kill a story if it is contrary to the policy of the owner of the paper. It is not the man at the desk in most cases. It is not the reporter. It goes back to the owner of the paper."[59]

That year Roosevelt was facing his own domestic crisis; too many aspects of his New Deal program were faltering: the budget grew more unbalanced, the courts were ruling against some of his programs, and public expectations had exceeded his attempts to curb the depression. The American press covered the situation. To the prying White House correspondents, he now became more of an antagonist. He often complained to reporters as representatives of their publishers and editors. Publishers, overwhelmingly Republican, had looked askance at Roosevelt and the National Industrial Recovery Act's ever-increasing requirements, especially section 7a, which guaranteed collective bargaining rights and labor's right to organize. The subsequent Wagner Act, compelling employers to accede to the unionization of their plants, seemed even more drastic. To powerful publishers like Robert McCormick and William Randolph Hearst, government requirements meant that the freedom of the press was at stake.[60]

As his ultimate news management tactic, Franklin D. Roosevelt cut off personal access and the flow of news from the White House. During the 1936 election year, American dailies with the largest circulations openly supported Alfred Landon and made vicious attacks on FDR. For the president, it was a domestic crisis. During that busy campaign year, Roosevelt curtailed his regular press meetings. He reduced the number of press conferences, which had averaged 86 a year, to 70, the fewest until 1943. He also decreased the length, which had averaged 779 transcript pages per year to 520, the fewest until 1945. By 1937 Roosevelt had returned to his regular schedule and press conference length.[61]

Yet, no matter what he did, as long as he would meet with the correspondents, they defended his news impositions. Even the Republican *Buffalo Evening News* correspondent Jim Wright wrote in 1938, "I don't care how many inhibitions or restrictions a President may impose on the handling of his news or how he may attempt to propagandize, I want the press conferences held. If I can get a look inside his head to see how the wheels are going around, and along what line he is thinking, I believe that is an advantage in attempting to interpret him to my readers. If he gets away with propaganda then I am too dumb to be a Washington correspondent."[62]

Although James MacGregor Burns wrote that Roosevelt's press transcripts rarely contained strikingly important ideas or statements, FDR never sent the reporters away empty-handed. Whatever FDR said candidly or not, whatever he did, made news. It was a symbiotic relationship. The correspondents used Roosevelt to help them write a story as much as he was trying to use them. Elmer E. Cornwell, Jr., found in the *New York Times* an average of 1.13 articles, a little more than a story per press conference, and a summary story averaging seventeen inches. Through his news management skill, the president defined certain issues and lessened the impact of undesirable information, not always as frankly as he promised. The correspondents, "united in holy newslock" with the highest level news source, watched with a mixture of delight and professional admiration for Roosevelt's adroitness. Raymond Clapper wrote that it was "like admiration for Babe Ruth, Man of War, a skillful surgeon, for the man who knows how to do his stuff."[63]

Although the owners and publishers might have abused him in editorials, Roosevelt was able to make the press conference his. As an artist, he could sculpt with words, chiseling stories, a little here and a little there, with his humor, personality, labels, gestures, and suggestions. If nothing else worked, he jawboned and put reporters on the defensive. But he had no "Ananias Club," as had the previous President Roosevelt. Unlike his predecessor, FDR never completely stopped the conferences, even during a vicious presidential election and domestic crises. Nor did he go back to written questions, even when journalists and the trade journal *Editor and Publisher* suggested he do so. FDR continued holding press conferences on a fairly regular basis. He rescued the preexisting press meetings from the doldrums and as that sculptor, he skillfully carved the meetings into his institution, his own unsurpassed communications forum. With a continuous flow of news from the president, the White House assignment indeed became an important one, though not necessarily a watchdog affair, just as the president had wanted.

Notes

1. *New York Times*, March 4, 1933. See also Frank Freidel, *Launching the New Deal*, Vol. 4 of *Franklin D. Roosevelt* (Boston: Houghton Mifflin, 1973), p. 202.

2. *Conference on the Press under the Auspices of the School of Public and International Affairs*, Princeton University, April 23–25, 1931 (Princeton, N.J.: School of Public Affairs, 1932), p. 68.

3. Raymond Clapper to Bob Bender, March 1, 1933, Raymond Clapper Personal File, Letters 1933, Box 8, Raymond Clapper Papers (henceforth RCP), Manuscripts Division, Library of Congress (henceforth LofC). Clapper became a columnist for the *Washington Post* by December 27, 1933, and later United Features before joining the United Press.

4. Note article in *New York Times*, March 3, 1933. For a reference to the purpose, see Franklin D. Roosevelt, *The Public Papers and Addresses of Franklin D. Roosevelt*, Vol. 2, Samuel I. Rosenman, ed. (New York: Random House, 1938), p. 39; Franklin D. Roosevelt Diary, March 5, 1933, Franklin D. Roosevelt Library (henceforth FDRL). FDR kept a diary for only two days. The press associations were the Associated Press (AP), International News Service (INS), United Press (UP), and Scripps-Howard Newspaper Alliance.

5. Franklin D. Roosevelt, *Complete Presidential Press Conferences of Franklin D. Roosevelt* (New York: Da Capo Press, 1972), Press Conference 1 (henceforth PC), March 8, 1933, Vol. 1: 1. *New York Times*, March 9, 1933; "Mr. Roosevelt 'Ungags' the Press," *Literary Digest*, March 25, 1933, p. 10.

6. Roosevelt, *Complete Press Conferences,* PC 1, March 8, 1933, Vol. 1: 2. In the Bible, Ananias was a man struck dead for lying. See Acts 5: 1–5.

7. Roosevelt, *Complete Press Conferences,* PC 1, March 8, 1933, Vol. 1: 2–16. Indirect attribution and direct-quotation rules had existed since the Theodore Roosevelt era. Herbert Hoover's background rule was FDR's off-the-record stipulation. Theodore Joslin, *Sunday Star,* March 4, 1934, found in Roosevelt, *Public Papers and Addresses,* Vol. 2, pp. 40–41.

8. Raymond Clapper Diary, March 8, 1933, RCP, LofC; *New York Times,* March 9, 1933.

9. Rarely did the meetings begin exactly on time because of the president's schedule. In 1935 meeting dates changed to Tuesday afternoons and Friday mornings. See Steve Early to Logan C. Harding, March 10, 1936, President's Personal File (henceforth PPF), FDRL.

Early makes diary references in 1935, in particular, May 31 and November 12, 1935, Stephen T. Early Papers (henceforth STEP), FDRL. Franklin D. Roosevelt was not the first president to alternate the weekly format. Warren G. Harding started alternating the biweekly press meetings when he came into office in 1921.

For his press conferences otherwise, see Roosevelt, *Complete Press Conferences,* PC 212, June 12, 1935, Vol. 5: 360–66; PC 287, April 8, 1936, Vol. 8: 207–10; PC 41, 42, 43, August 7, 9, 11, 1933, Vol. 2: 148–80; PC 71, November 22, 1933, Vol. 2: 473–82. See also Steve Early to Alfred Dashiell, August 24, 1934, Official File (henceforth OF) 36, FDRL. Usually only twelve to twenty reporters traveled with FDR on trips. See Roosevelt, "Notes," in *Public Papers and Addresses,* Vol. 2, pp. 39–40. For an example of a meeting with a small delegation, see Roosevelt, *Complete Press Conferences,* PC 63, October 25, 1933, Vol. 2: 365–77.

10. Roosevelt, *Public Papers and Addresses,* Vol. 2, pp. 39–40. See also Charles A. Baird, "Reporter Finds Roosevelt Press Conference Anything but Boring," *Ft. Wayne News Sentinal,* March 8, 1938, Early 1938 Scrapbook, STEP, FDRL. See also Leo C. Rosten, *The Washington Correspondents* (New York: Harcourt, Brace, 1937), p. 60; Ruth Finney Allen, interview at her home, Washington, D.C., June 8, 1976.

11. Note preparations in Alfred D. Stedman to Steve Early, August 23, 1935, OF 36, FDRL; FDR Memo to Steve Early, April 17, 1935, OF 36, FDRL; Early Memo to Murray W. Latimer, July 11, 1936, OF 36, FDRL.

The casualness with which Roosevelt conducted the press conferences was studied. James F. Byrnes remembers after one of his first press conferences that "his hand was trembling and he was wet with perspiration." His personal physician ordered the press conferences cut down during the war because they "took a lot out of him." James F. Byrnes, *All in One Lifetime* (New York: Harper and Brothers, 1958), p. 74; Ross McIntire, *White House Physician* (New York: G. P. Putnam, 1946), pp. 81–82.

For other references, see Early Diary, March 7, 1934, February 15, 1935, April 24, 1935, May 15, 1936, STEP, FDRL; Drew Pearson and Robert S. Allen, "How the President Works," *Harper's,* June 1936, p. 2.

For preparation, see also Commander Leland P. Lovette Memorandum to Steve Early, October 21, 1937, OF 36, FDRL; Samuel I. Rosenman to Early, n.d., filed July 9, 1937, OF 36, FDRL; Roosevelt to Dr. H. A. Morgan, TVA, November 26, 1937, OF 36, FDRL. Follow-up at PC 411, November 23, 1937, Vol. 10: 341–56; STE

Memorandum for the President, June 20, 1938, STEP, FDRL. Follow-up at PC 448, June 21, 1938, Vol. 11: 476–77; Early to Hassett, March 31, 1939, President's Secretary's File (henceforth PSF) 146, FDRL.

In particular, note STE Memorandum for the President, March 3, 1938, STEP, FDRL. Follow-up at PC 439, March 4, 1938, Vol. 11: 208–12.

12. Roosevelt, *Complete Press Conferences,* PC 260-A, December 27, 1935, Vol. 6: 363.

13. Early Diary, April 24, 1935, STEP, FDRL. Roosevelt, *Complete Press Conferences,* PC 198, April 24, 1935, Vol. 5: 225–43. Early 1935–36 Scrapbooks, STEP, FDRL (Early collected not only the United Press wire service copy but also newspaper clippings, mostly from the large East Coast dailies); Roosevelt, *Public Papers and Addresses,* Vol. 2, p. 39.

14. Rosten, *Washington Correspondents,* p. 58; Early Memorandum to the President, August 24, 1938, STEP, FDRL. See also Early Telegraphic Memorandum to Hassett, April 19, 1941, STEP, FDRL. Since the transcripts rarely refer to a questioner by name, it is difficult to determine if the "front row claque" did indeed ask planted questions.

Earl Godwin of the *Washington Times-Herald* sat on the front row during the 1939–40 press conferences and closed many of the 1939 conferences with "Thank you, Mr. President." See press conferences in Volumes 13, 14, 15, 16. During the second term, Godwin defended himself in a press conference against the newspaper accusations that he asked planted questions every time he asked a question. See also Roosevelt, *Complete Press Conferences,* PC 694, November 8, 1940, Vol. 16: 301.

For others, note the FDR Memo to Marvin McIntyre and Steve Early, April 17, 1935, OF 36, FDRL, which concerns problems in the New England cotton mills due to the processing tax, regional wage differences, prices, and import competition. The very first question at the next press conference was on that topic. See Roosevelt, *Complete Press Conferences,* PC 197, April 19, 1935, Vol. 5: 217. Roosevelt asked for a Civilian Conservation Corps report to discuss at the September 25 press meeting. A specific question at the September 24, 1935, conference enabled the president to use that report. See Guy D. McKinny Memo to Steve Early, September 24, 1935, OF 36, FDRL; Roosevelt, *Complete Press Conferences,* PC 241, September 24, 1935, Vol. 6: 198–99.

Elmer E. Cornwell, Jr., refers to planted questions in later administrations in *Presidential Leadership of Public Opinion* (Bloomington: Indiana University Press, 1965), pp. 157–58. See also plant efforts in William Hassett Memorandum to Roosevelt, July 11, 1939, OF 36a, FDRL. See also Memorandum, Press Conference, July 18, 1939, OF 2111, FDRL.

15. Roosevelt, *Complete Press Conferences,* PC 260-A, December 27, 1935, Vol. 6: 363; PC 78, December 15, 1933, Vol. 2: 546; STE Memorandum for the President, February 4, 1939, STEP, FDRL. See also Raymond P. Brandt, "The President's Press Conference," *Survey Graphic,* July 1939, p. 446; George Michael in *Handout* (New York: G. P. Putnam's Sons, 1935), p. 234, went so far as to say that journalists had to inform Early of questions they planned to ask.

16. Brandt, "The President's Press Conference," p. 446; Roosevelt, *Complete Press Conferences,* PC 86, January 10, 1934, Vol. 3: 48.

17. Early to Joseph Ness, November 15, 1933, OF 36, FDRL. See also Walter Davenport, "The President and the Press," *Collier's*, January 27, 1945, p. 11.

18. Early to Richard L. Neuberger, August 22, 1939, OF 36, FDRL; Roosevelt, *Complete Press Conferences*, PC 202, May 8, 1935, Vol. 5: 274–75. See also Lindsay Rogers, "President Roosevelt's Press Conferences," *Political Quarterly* 9 (July–September 1938): 366. Stenographers were Grace Tully, Jack Romagna, Henry Kannee, and the various navy men who worked aboard ships, including Charles K. Claunch, Francis J. Terry, and William M. Rigdon. Henry Kannee took most of the conferences between 1933 and 1938 and only intermittently afterwards. See Grace Tully, *F.D.R., My Boss* (New York: Charles Scribner's Sons, 1949), pp. 89–91.

Early also wrote to Ruby Black about this, June 6, 1935, OF 36, FDRL. In later years transcripts made by *New York Herald-Tribune* reporters, such as Emilie Tavel Livezey in 1944–45, were sold but not published and then made the rounds to various correspondents. See Fauneil J. Rinn, "The Presidential Press Conference" (Ph.D. dissertation, University of Chicago, 1960); Emilie Tavel Livezey, telephone interview, August 18, 1985. See also Robert E. Kennedy of the *Chicago Times,* "Letters," *The Quill,* January 1989, pp. 5–6. Kennedy remembered that the transcripts were made during the war years, 1941–44, and delivered to the National Press Building an hour or so after the conference.

See also Early to Judge Samuel Rosenman, December 1, 1937, STEP, FDRL; Roosevelt's notes after the first press conference in *Public Papers and Addresses,* Vol. 2, p. 40. Other information is in Roosevelt, *Complete Press Conferences,* PC 209, May 31, 1935, Vol. 5: 309–37.

19. Roosevelt, *Complete Press Conferences,* PC 209, May 31, 1935, Vol. 5: 336. Steve Early gives this account in his diary, May 31, 1935, STEP, FDRL.

20. Early Memo to Charles Michelson, May 31, 1935, OF 36, FDRL; Early Memo and Enclosure to all Members of the Cabinet, June 1, 1935, Of 36, FDRL; Early to Ruby Black, June 6, 1935, OF 36, FDRL; *Literary Digest,* June 29, 1935, p. 7.

Brandt, "The President's Press Conference," p. 447, wrote that Roosevelt's remarks needed background not only on the Schechter case but also on constitutional history and law. See also James MacGregor Burns, *Roosevelt: The Lion and the Fox* (New York: Harcourt, Brace, 1956), p. 223. Roosevelt himself refers to the inadequate reporting from this press conference in a letter to Harry L. Stimson, June 10, 1935, *F.D.R.: His Personal Letters, 1928–1945,* Vol. 1, Elliott Roosevelt, ed. (New York: Duell, Sloan and Pearce, 1950), p. 484.

Arthur M. Schlesinger, Jr., interprets the statement literally: "The decision, Roosevelt said, denied the economic interdependence of the nation; it turned back the Constitution, he suddenly said, to 'the horse and buggy days,' when the economy was, in its essence, local and most people were self-supporting within their own communities." See Arthur M. Schlesinger, Jr., *The Politics of Upheaval,* Vol. 3 of *The Age of Roosevelt* (Boston: Houghton Mifflin, 1960), p. 285. For remembered references, see Stephen Early to Charles P. Shaeffer, Public Relations, Treasury Department, June 11, 1943, OF 318-A, also in OF 36, OF 340, OF 101A, FDRL; Early Memorandum for Frances Perkins, April 18, 1944, OF 36, FDRL.

21. Roosevelt, *Public Papers and Addresses,* Vol. 2, p. 42. See also Charles A.

Baird, "Reporter Finds Roosevelt Press Conference Anything but Boring," *Ft. Wayne News-Sentinel,* March 8, 1938, Early 1938 Scrapbook, STEP, FDRL. For quote, see Roosevelt, *Complete Press Conferences,* PC 314, August 11, 1936, Vol. 8: 67.

22. For example, Roosevelt, *Complete Press Conferences,* PC 115, April 25, 1934, Vol. 3: 296; PC 21, May 16, 1933, Vol. 1: 264; PC 109, March 27, 1934, Vol. 3: 262; PC 36, July 26, 1933, Vol. 2: 92; PC 71, November 22, 1933, Vol. 2: 474; PC 149, October 1934, Vol. 4: 113; PC 274, February 11, 1936, Vol. 7: 121. The president told Rudolph de Zappe of the *Washington Times,* "Well, I came across. . . ." Interview with Ruth Finney Allen, Scripps-Howard correspondent, at her Washington, D.C., home, June 8, 1976, who talked about the after-conference questions, as did Robert S. Allen, correspondent for the *Philadelphia Record* and columnist of "Washington Merry-Go-Round" with Drew Pearson, in an interview at the National Press Club in Washington, D.C., June 8, 1976.

23. Frank Freidel makes a similar club analogy in *Launching the New Deal,* Vol. 4 of *Franklin D. Roosevelt* (Boston: Little, Brown, 1973), p. 279; Rosten, *Washington Correspondents,* pp. 50–51, 58. For the quote, see Roosevelt, *Complete Press Conferences,* PC 274, February 11, 1936, Vol. 7: 121.

24. James Martel, "Washington Press Conference," *American Mercury,* February 1938, p. 204; Roosevelt, *Complete Press Conferences,* PC 76, December 8, 1933, Vol. 2: 526. For more on Roosevelt's humor, see M. S. Venkataramani, *The Sunny Side of FDR* (Athens: Ohio University Press, 1973).

25. Roosevelt, *Complete Press Conferences,* PC 74, December 2, 1933, Vol. 2: 506.

26. Ibid., PC 2, March 10, 1933, Vol. 1: 18; PC 86, January 10, 1934, Vol. 3: 48. For other discussion, see Charles Hurd, *When the New Deal Was Young and Gay* (New York: Harper, 1965), p. 232; Martel, "Washington Press Conference," p. 204; Roosevelt, *Public Papers and Addresses,* Vol. 2, p. 41; Steven E. Schoenherr, "Selling the New Deal: Stephen T. Early's Role as Press Secretary to Franklin D. Roosevelt" (Ph.D. dissertation, University of Delaware, 1976), p. 89; Erwin D. Canham, "Democracy's Fifth Wheel," *Literary Digest,* January 5, 1935, p. 6. For a rule waiver, see Early to Louis Ruppel, June 9, 1935, OF 35, FDRL.

27. Roosevelt, *Complete Press Conferences,* PC 1, March 8, 1933, Vol. 1: 1–2; PC 674, August 23, 1940, Vol. 16: 142–48. An examination of press conferences every six months, every three years through FDR's first two terms shows that the number of questions asked in each conference ranged from 24 to 49, with an average of 32 questions for each meeting.

28. Ruth Finney Allen, interview at her Washington, D.C., home, June 8, 1976. For closing the press conferences, see Roosevelt, *Complete Press Conferences,* PC 55, September 22, 1933, Vol. 2: 295. From this date on, a final statement was usually given. Rosten suggested rescues in general in *Washington Correspondents,* p. 58, as did Martel without evidence in "Washington Press Conference," p. 205.

29. For the Cuban revolt quote, see Roosevelt, *Complete Press Conferences,* PC 60, October 13, 1933, Vol. 2: 342; for the December quote, see Thomas A. Bailey, *A Diplomatic History of the American People* (New York: Appleton Century Croft, 1946), p. 737; William E. Leuchtenburg, *Franklin D. Roosevelt and the New Deal, 1932–1940* (New York: Harper and Brothers, 1963), pp. 207–8; Burns, *Roosevelt:*

The Lion and the Fox, p. 253. The Press Intelligence Bulletin included the press accounts with the following headlines: "Thinks U.S. Should Keep Out of Cuban Affairs," October 8, 1933, *Boston Globe;* and "Cuban in Earnest for Political Principles, U.S. Had Better Keep Out," November 2, 1933, *Baltimore Sun.* See Press Intelligence Bulletin 17, OF 36, FDRL.

30. Roosevelt, *Complete Press Conferences,* PC 93, January 31, 1934, Vol. 3: 118. Cornwell found that 102 of the first 250 press conferences began with announcements, statements, or a discussion of a subject the president thought was newsworthy. See Cornwell, *Presidential Leadership of Public Opinion,* p. 157. See also Arthur Krock Speech to the National Republican Club, New York City, January 26, 1935, Arthur Krock Collection, Princeton University.

31. Roosevelt, *Complete Press Conferences,* PC 210, June 4, 1935, Vol. 5: 339.

32. Ibid., PC 235, September 4, 1935, Vol. 6: 130.

33. Ibid., PC 19, May 10, 1933, Vol. 1: 248. For FDR's original definition, see ibid., PC 2, March 10, 1933, Vol. 1: 31; PC 4, March 17, 1933, Vol. 1: 51, 57. See also Early Memo for the Press, January 5, 1936, OF 36, FDRL.

34. Rosten, *Washington Correspondents,* pp. 51, 251–52, 255–70; STE-Dictated Memorandum, October 12, 1937, OF 36, FDRL, which said, "The newspapermen, with one exception, received the information in confidence and did not publish it. The single exception was that of Robert S. Allen who had made the trip to the West Coast with the President for the N.Y. *Post* and other papers. Attached is the report written by Allen and published in the *Post* on October sixth."

35. Roosevelt, *Complete Press Conferences,* PC 161-A, November 20, 1934, Vol. 4: 251; Krock Speech, January 26, 1935.

36. Early to Phelps Adams, January 7, 1936, OF 36, FDRL. For others, see Drew Pearson to Steve Early, January 7, 1936, OF 36, FDRL; Ralph E. Renaud to Stephen A. Early, January 4, 1934, OF 144B, FDRL: "The Washington *Post* also wishes to file a protest against . . . Washington *Herald* . . . and the Washington *Times.* . . ."

37. Roosevelt, *Complete Press Conferences,* PC 19, May 10, 1933, Vol. 1: 248; PC 260-A, December 27, 1935, Vol. 6: 362.

38. Rosten, *Washington Correspondents,* p. 101; Drew Pearson to Steve Early, January 7, 1936, OF 36, FDRL.

39. Martel, "Washington Press Conference," p. 205.

40. Roosevelt, *Complete Press Conferences,* PC 88, January 15, 1934, Vol. 3: 65–78; PC 331, December 22, 1936, Vol. 8: 188–97; PC 260-A, December 27, 1935, Vol. 6: 360–64; PC 193-A, March 22, 1935, Vol. 5: 177–78; PC 275-A, February 14, 1936, Vol. 7: 131–41; PC 556, June 22, 1939, Vol. 13: 430; Early Diary, June 22, 1939, STEP, FDRL.

41. Roosevelt, *Complete Press Conferences,* PC 260-A, December 27, 1935, Vol. 6: 362, where he told the teachers of journalism about the scant economic knowledge. For release dates, see ibid., PC 83, January 3, 1934, Vol. 3: 1; PC 263, January 4, 1936, Vol. 7: 4. Roosevelt was correct in his analysis of reporters. Leo C. Rosten found that 86.6 percent of the 127 Washington correspondents he interviewed agreed that they "often feel the need of knowing more economics for my job." See Rosten, "President Roosevelt and the Washington Correspondents," *Public Opinion Quarterly*

1 (January 1937): 49. Early Memo to the Press, January 5, 1936, OF 36, FDRL. Another off-the-record reference was Lyle Wilson (UP) to Steve Early, January 7, 1935, OF 35, FDRL.

42. Roosevelt, *Complete Press Conferences,* PC 3, March 15, 1933, Vol. 1: 32; PC 50, September 8, 1933, Vol. 2: 274; PC 53, September 20, 1933, Vol. 2: 274; PC 52, September 16, 1933, Vol. 2: 268; PC 42, August 9, 1933, Vol. 2: 149; PC 76, December 8, 1933, Vol. 2: 251.

43. Ibid., PC 65, November 1, 1933, Vol. 2: 393. For particular references to the background rule, see Early to Byron Price (AP), June 3, 1935, OF 36, FDRL; Early to Theodore C. Wallen *(New York Herald-Tribune),* March 23, 1933, OF 36, FDRL; Wallen to Early, March 22, 1933, OF 36, FDRL. Letters concerned Wallen's coverage of the first press conference while he was on background. A. Merriman Smith, *Thank You, Mr. President: A White House Notebook* (New York: Harper and Row, 1946), p. 16. For quote, see Roosevelt, *Complete Press Conferences,* PC 787, November 28, 1941, Vol. 18: 327. For other background rules to third-person attribution, see Roosevelt, *Complete Press Conferences,* PC 384, July 22, 1936, Vol. 8: 74.

44. Roosevelt, *Complete Press Conferences,* PC 298, April 17, 1936, Vol. 7: 218.

45. Ibid., PC 15, April 26, 1933, Vol. 1: 191, for labeling as "iffy." For FDR's first year other warnings about "if" questions, see ibid., PC 1, March 8, 1933, Vol. 1: 2; PC 18, May 5, 1933, Vol. 1: 191; PC 80, December 22, 1933, Vol. 2: 566; PC 45, August 18, 1933, Vol. 2: 200; PC 21, May 16, 1933, Vol. 1: 266; PC 29, June 14, 1933, Vol. 1: 391; PC 67, November 9, 1933, Vol. 2: 432; PC 62, October 20, 1933, Vol. 2: 362.

46. Ibid., PC 331, December 22, 1936, Vol. 8: 185–88; PC 210, June 4, 1935, Vol. 5: 350; PC 264, January 7, 1936, Vol. 7: 55; PC 311, June 2, 1936, Vol. 7: 280–81; Raymond Clapper, "Between You and Me," n.d., Clapper Reference File, Censorship, Box 110, RCP, LofC.

47. John Gunther, *Roosevelt in Retrospect* (New York: Harper and Brothers, 1950), p. 23.

48. Roosevelt, *Complete Press Conferences,* PC 163, December 7, 1934, Vol. 4: 264; exact transcript for December 11, 1934, in *The New Deal Mosaic: Proceedings of the National Emergency Council,* Lester G. Seligman and Elmer E. Cornwell, Jr., eds. (Eugene: University of Oregon Press, 1964), pp. 378–80.

49. In reference to Supreme Court decisions, see Roosevelt, *Complete Press Conferences,* PC 272, February 4, 1936, Vol. 7: 110; PC 296, May 19, 1936, Vol. 7: 261; PC 298, May 26, 1936, Vol. 7: 272. Other tactics of "no" in ibid., PC 198, April 24, 1935, Vol. 5: 243; PC 26, June 2, 1933, Vol. 1: 342. As noted in the introduction, only one dunce hat retort has been found, that in reference to the question of the president running for a third term. See ibid., PC 337, June 29, 1937, Vol. 9: 466.

50. Clapper column, "Between You and Me," *Washington Post* clipping, n.d., and Theodore C. Wallen, *New York Herald-Tribune* clipping, February 15, 1935, Clapper Reference File, Censorship, Box 110, RCP, LofC; Roosevelt, *Complete Press Conferences,* PC 184, February 15, 1935, Vol. 5: 112.

51. Brandt, "The President's Press Conference," p. 449.

52. Roosevelt, *Complete Press Conferences,* PC 160, November 28, 1934, Vol. 4: 245; PC 84, January 3, 1934, Vol. 3: 6; PC 142, September 7, 1934, Vol. 4: 54–55.

53. Ibid., PC 161, November 28, 1934, Vol. 4: 245. For other elaborations, see ibid., PC 13, April 19, 1933, Vol. 1: 159; PC 14, April 21, 1933, Vol. 1: 162–63; PC 14A, April 21, 1933, Vol. 1: 173–79; PC 14B, April 26, 1933, Vol. 1: 180–84; PC 15, April 26, 1933, Vol. 1: 185–95; PC 141, September 4, 1934, Vol. 4: 42–43.

54. Ibid., PC 13, April 19, 1933, Vol. 1: 152.

55. Ibid., PC 160, November 23, 1934, Vol. 4: 232.

56. Ibid., PC 81, December 27, 1933, Vol. 2: 579; PC 82, December 29, 1933, Vol. 2: 592. John Boettiger, *Chicago Tribune* correspondent, later married the president's daughter Anna.

57. Roosevelt, *Complete Press Conferences,* PC 25, May 31, 1933, Vol. 1: 314–15; PC 19, May 10, 1933, Vol. 1: 240–42; quote in PC 141, September 5, 1934, Vol. 4: 48. See also Franklin Roosevelt to Will Dewart, Telegraphs and Letters of August 13, 14, 15, 1934, PPF 780, FDRL.

58. *Jawboning* is slang for challenging, embarrassing, or urging to comply in a face-to-face discussion. In the Bible (Judges 15: 15), Sampson took an ass jawbone and slew a thousand of his enemies. See Rosten, *Washington Correspondents,* pp. 54–57.

59. Roosevelt, *Complete Press Conferences,* PC 198, April 24, 1935, Vol. 5: 226; PC 222, July 19, 1935, Vol. 6: 46; PC 209, May 31, 1935, Vol. 5: 332; PC 243, October 25, 1935, Vol. 6: 217; PC 244, October 30, 1935, Vol. 6: 231; PC 220, July 12, 1935, Vol. 6: 26; PC 224, July 26, 1935, Vol. 6: 60. For quote on editorial decisions, see ibid., PC 260-A, December 27, 1935, Vol. 6: 369.

60. Ashmun Brown, "The Roosevelt Myth," *American Mercury,* April 1936, p. 391; George Wolfskill and John A. Hudson, *All but the People: Franklin D. Roosevelt and His Critics, 1933–1939* (Toronto: Macmillan, 1969), p. 179 and chapter 7.

61. For a general discussion, see Frank Luther Mott, "Newspapers in Presidential Campaigns," *Public Opinion Quarterly* 8 (Fall 1944): 362. The press conferences by year and total pages of transcript were: 1933, 82 press conferences and 825 pages; 1934, 86 press conferences and 745 pages; 1935, 91 press conferences and 767 pages; 1936, 70 press conferences and 520 pages; 1937, 87 press conferences and 910 pages; 1938, 91 press conferences and 796 pages; 1939, 97 press conferences and 1,169 pages; 1940, 94 press conferences and 1,000 pages; 1941, 89 press conferences and 826 pages; 1942, 74 press conferences and 714 pages; 1943, 58 press conferences and 670 pages; 1944, 55 press conferences and 560 pages; 1945, 25 press conferences and 121 pages.

62. Jim Wright to Stephen T. Early, February 12, 1938, OF 36, FDRL. In Bascom N. Timmons, "This Is How It Used to Be," in *Dateline: Washington, the Story of National Affairs Journalism in the Life and Times of the Washington Press Club,* Cabell Phillips et al., eds. (Garden City, N.Y.: Doubleday, 1949), pp. 53–54, Timmons gives the peak newsproducing period as the first three years.

63. Burns, *Roosevelt: The Lion and the Fox,* p. 491.; Elmer E. Cornwell, Jr., "The Presidential Press Conference: A Study in Institutionalization," *Midwest Journal of Political Science* 4 (November 1960): 388; Walter Davenport, "The President and the Press," *Collier's,* January 27, 1945, p. 11. Raymond Clapper, "Why Reporters Like Roosevelt," *Review of Reviews,* June 1934, p. 17.

Roosevelt knew that he had great skill in determining the news. He once wrote Felix

Frankfurter in 1942 that he was about to "think of resigning this job and taking on the job of Public Relations man for the Government." Venkataramani, *The Sunny Side of FDR,* p. 15; reference to Roosevelt's letter to Frankfurter of May 1, 1942 as found in Max Freedman's *Roosevelt and Frankfurter: Their Correspondence—1928–1945,* (Boston: Little, Brown, 1967), p. 658.

"Like neighbors invited in for potluck." Picnic at Val-Kill Cottage in Hyde Park, July 4, 1939. Reporters taking notes, with Eleanor Roosevelt and FDR's mother, Sara Delano Roosevelt, in the background. Courtesy of AP/Wide World Photos.

4

Roosevelt and the Washington Correspondents

> To picture this little group of a dozen sprawled around the floor of the vast east room, talking this way, with us horning in and banter, etc. feeling of complete ease, freedom, just like a group around at any newspaper man's house. Never been anybody in White House like this I suppose.
>
> —Raymond Clapper, Diary, May 16, 1937

Correspondents recounted it was easy to talk to Franklin D. Roosevelt because "it was a personal relationship." In fact, Roosevelt's access system may have been part of the secret to his excellent press relations. The journalists were so dependent on the White House for news that FDR's personal relations could influence the news stories, especially with the new journalistic demands for interpretation.[1]

Interpretative journalism had been created by the correspondents as a method of explaining the New Deal's political-social-economic revolution. According to journalism historians Edwin Emery and Michael Emery, "The rise of interpretative reporting was the most important press development of the 1930s and 1940s." This new reporting style challenged the old-style objective of sticking to a factual account of what had been said or done. "Why" and "how" became especially important because readers wanted background information and context about the new government agencies and the flurry of New Deal activity.[2]

Many Washington correspondents reacted by writing interpretive columns to give the motivations and probable consequences of governmental acts. Syndicates sold popular columns written by Raymond Clapper, David Lawrence, Paul Mallon, Mark Sullivan, and Drew Pearson and Robert S. Allen, who wrote the "Daily Washington Merry-Go-Round." Interpretation also extended to John Gunther's "inside" books, which were best-sellers, and interpretive popular newsmagazines, such as *Time* and *Newsweek,* which increased their circulation in the 1930s.[3]

Franklin D. Roosevelt was hostile to this journalistic change, which he called "one of the most difficult problems we have." The day after the Democratic party's smashing victory in 1934, the president and the correspondents had a lively exchange on the topic. One correspondent asked, "If you were in our position, called upon to write an interpretative piece, would you interpret the verdict as an approval of what had happened or as a mandate to proceed further?" Roosevelt's answer was evasive: "You must have got to bed early to talk about interpreting stories today. . . ." He then remarked that "it must be hell to have to interpret." He acknowledged that "the press associations had got away from it pretty well," but said, "I think it is a mistake for newspapers to go over into that field in the news stories," mainly because people were beginning to lose their confidence in the news. FDR then explained his view about what the journalist should do: "Give them the facts and nothing else. In other words, reductio ad absurdum. That is the substance, because if I take Henry Morgenthau from Washington back to Dutchess County, there isn't anything behind the fact. But the story that says, 'In all probability this means that foreign debt was discussed,' or something like that, this is not news, that is just a wild stab in the dark, which is wrong, 99 per cent wrong at times." During the discussion, one correspondent retorted that the public will "want the best opinion they can get, even if they read three or four in order to get different interpretations, on the ground that they want it from competent observers, particularly at a time like this when there is so much doubt." When Appointments Secretary Marvin McIntyre suggested that the president "give the boys that write these stories a little more leads," Roosevelt cracked, "By God, I give them all the leads I can think of. I don't want to get into the dissertation stage." When another reporter said, "Of course, Mr. President, our job is always finding out what you are going to do," Roosevelt answered, "About two-thirds of the time I do not know."[4]

Roosevelt might say he did not know what he was going to do, but the correspondents continued discussing his options, the background of his possibilities, and the context of his actions. The White House carefully tried to get the right news interpretation. This became especially crucial in foreign affairs. In 1941, when asked about what interpretation the correspondents should put on his policy speech, FDR responded, "I wouldn't try to interpret, because you know it is a grave question as to whether interpretation is news." Later that same month when Roosevelt was asked if he gave any credence to the rumored withdrawal of marines from China, he evaded the question: "I am going to have a sign—I am going to place it right behind me: 'Don't Interpret.' " The "Don't Interpret" admonition did not deter the correspondents.[5]

Roosevelt himself knew that no two observers would present the same version of an event and no two judgments about the nature of a political controversy would necessarily be similar. Journalists usually described political change in subjective terms, impressionistic rather than analytical. Political stories, by their very nature, were interpretative. Roosevelt adjusted his news management methods accordingly. His numerous background press sessions, his carefully planned press conference explanations, and Steve Early's daily briefings for the correspondents were all designed to generate favorable interpretations.[6]

The president's personal relations were also important in influencing how news would be written. Members of his family and some of his closest friends were journalists. His wife Eleanor was a newspaper columnist and a member of the American Newspaper Guild. His only daughter, Anna, eventually married *Chicago Tribune* correspondent John Boettiger. After 1936 they both held editorial positions at the *Seattle Post-Intelligencer*. The godparents of their child, John Roosevelt Boettiger, were Betty Grimes Lindley, wife of *New York Herald-Tribune* correspondent Ernest K. Lindley, and Eddie Roddan of Universal News Service. FDR's White House secretarial staff included old newspaper friends, including Louis Howe, Stephen Early, Marvin McIntyre, and William Hassett.[7]

Those journalists who came into the greatest personal contact with the president were a special group. Of the 504 accredited Washington correspondents during the New Deal and some 750 during World War II, only 100 to 200 would cover the president at any one time. The White House made a great effort to accommodate them. When the White House office wing was extensively rebuilt in 1934, the president made sure that the press quarters were enlarged and included card and chess tables as well as the usual desks and direct telephone connections to the telegraphic press associations. When a correspondent first arrived in the capital, the president and other officials invited the journalist and a guest to teas and receptions. *New York Times* correspondent Delbert Clark recalled that while the number of invitations varied in direct ratio to the importance of the represented newspaper, such special attention could inevitably affect the correspondents' response to the president.[8]

As the Roosevelt press meetings became the "show" of Washington, many people wanted to go. For the most part, regular admission to the president's press conferences required "correspondent" status, which depended on admission to the congressional press galleries as "bona fide correspondents of a reputable standing who represent daily newspapers or newspaper associations requiring telegraphic service." Steve Early gave limited attendance privileges to foreign correspondents and visitor status to other groups. Although he granted a "one-shot" visit to the baseball writers, he made no provisions for journalists' wives, American artists, cartoonists, or photographers. Until the third term, the White House excluded radio correspondents. White House photographers were not admitted. It all depended on the president's whim.[9]

The White House correspondents, a smaller contingent of the Washington journalists, for the most part were a tightly knit group of mostly white males.

Southern-born Early did nothing to encourage qualified blacks who met the congressional gallery requirements of being journalists from daily newspapers. As early as 1933 Frederick S. Weaver of the *Atlanta Daily World* met the qualifications, yet he could not gain admission to the congressional press galleries or the White House. When a black daily was published in 1943, Early referred black journalists' admission requests to the Congressional Standing Committee of Correspondents, which did not budge until after the war. Although black editors and leaders complained about the lack of direct access to the president, particularly since most black newspapers continued to be favorable to Roosevelt's New Deal programs, Steve Early refused to change until 1944.[10]

The press office did make exceptions for regular admission when it chose to. Strickland Gillilan, a personal friend of Appointments Secretary Marvin McIntyre, was given regular attendance status through the White House Correspondents' Association although he was not admitted to the congressional press galleries. Gillilan's *Atlantic City Press Union* did not have daily newspaper status or a telegraphic news service. Nonetheless, Early urged approval of Gillilan's application, and Gillilan's name appeared on the 1934 Official Membership List (see Appendix).[11]

There were very few women among the White House correspondents. Although women had been in the press galleries since 1850, only a small number were political writers and Washington correspondents. Still fewer covered the White House. The 1934 White House correspondents' roster of 363 included only 15 women. In general, women were more readily accepted by the politicians than by their press gallery colleagues. The National Press Club denied women membership, which meant that women could not attend its annual banquets. Nor could they attend the White House Correspondents' Association's dinners where they did have membership and the president was the guest of honor.[12]

Most correspondents in the capital were not regularly assigned to the White House except for the semiweekly conferences. A small, elite group who had the presidential beat usually spent eight to ten hours a day in their own White House quarters. FDR called them by their first names, joked with them, swam and played water polo with them, and even discussed with them the details of the most confidential policies. These insiders included representatives of the wire services and the high-circulation newspapers who also traveled with the president. In 1933 only about eight newspapers could afford to keep a reporter with the president on trips, but so much news took place away from the White House that the numbers quickly more than doubled and sometimes grew to as many as thirty-one regulars. The president tried to limit the traveling corps to a wire service pool, but the correspondents complained so much that it was not reduced until his overseas trips during World War II.[13]

Roosevelt treated those reporters who were assigned to the White House on a full-time basis as members of his family. Several, like Ernest K. Lindley and Frederick A. Storm and their wives, were even invited to the Christmas evening meal, along with some twenty to twenty-five close family members and friends. Whenever a death or illness occurred in their families, the Roosevelts sent flowers and Mrs. Roosevelt made a personal call. Once, just as a correspondent was about to be married and go on a brief honeymoon, Roosevelt suddenly announced his plans for a holiday on a ship out of Coral Gables, Florida. When the president learned of the correspondent's predicament, he arranged for passes to permit the bride to board the Florida-bound special train. The president's cruise, lasting more than two weeks, provided a Florida honeymoon period, broken only by a light daily working routine.[14]

The president was especially relaxed with the insiders. *Time* magazine reported one June 1933 example. While the Roosevelts were chatting informally with the White House correspondents, one journalist asked Mrs. Roosevelt, "How would it be if we grabbed our racquets and got out on the White House tennis courts sometime?" She was said to have replied, "Why, most certainly. Any time you boys want to play, those courts are there for you." When a second correspondent asked the president, "What about the swimming pool some of these hot afternoons?" he was said to have shot back, "Yes, and there's also those sand boxes we've put out there for the children. You might try them, too."[15]

Besides providing camaraderie, these informal functions were valuable to correspondents because the president often launched into anecdotes and stories that gave them extra background information on such newsworthy topics as the 1933 Treasury Department's refinancing program and the Justice Department's plans to curb racketeering and kidnapping. *New York Times* correspondent Charles Hurd recalled that whether the conversation was planned in advance by Roosevelt, as one might think, or was spontaneous, "it was one of those no-direct-quote-but-for-background-only pieces that made up a larger part of our dispatches." At the small, informal Sunday night suppers, a tradition carried over from Roosevelt's Albany days, the journalists felt like "neighbors invited in for potluck." While Eleanor Roosevelt scrambled eggs in a chafing dish and daughter Anna "bustled around the table seeing that everyone had enough to eat," the journalists joined in the conversation with cabinet members, members of Congress, and presidential advisers. After supper, the party would adjourn to the second floor to see a popular movie and the newsreels of the day. Hurd said, "Covering Roosevelt was somewhat like an assignment to the City Hospital; one never knew when something important would turn up. We always had to count on the unexpected and prepare for it, even in such an informal atmosphere as an afternoon picnic."[16]

Such informality extended to White House square dance sessions, organized by Eleanor Roosevelt, who was interested in preserving American folk dance. The president joked with the dancers, who included the Raymond Clappers, Ernest Lindleys, Jay Haydens, Fred Essarys, James Wrights, Ulric Bells, as well as sons James and Elliott and their wives. Clapper wrote in his diary that these were relaxed, informal evenings, when the conversation ranged "all over the place," with the president talking easily about Hitler and Goering, fascism, and American tax-dodging methods.[17]

The informal functions gave the correspondents an unofficial press conference even with the "news lid on." On June 30, 1933, while FDR was vacationing at Campobello Island during the London Economic Conference, he gave the correspondents a "bombshell message" in the middle of a hand of cut-in-bridge. Hurd remembered FDR's "spontaneous conversation" about currency stabilization: "The American investors had trusted the debtor countries as they did their own, and yet they had wound up with worthless or depreciated bonds at the time they needed their savings most. He dwelt at some length on this feeling of resentment by the American public and furthermore indicated that he agreed with it." This was a major story. Although the president's words had been labeled "off the record," he obviously wanted to release the story without taking responsibility. He told the reporters, "How you handle anything you write is up to you. But isn't a Campobello dateline a pretty good hedge?" Together the correspondents reconstructed the account and sent in the story. When Hurd's dispatch appeared in the next morning's *New York Times,* the lead sentence read, "President Roosevelt will not obligate the United States at this time for any form of stabilization of the dollar, it was learned on high authority." The Associated Press story that followed attributed the statement directly to the president. Within twenty-four hours, words that had been unofficially spoken and unofficially reported helped doom the international conference, even though the president had not taken any formal action or issued a formal statement.[18]

The president used this informal technique for solving high-level problems. Hurd said that the "little White Houses," Hyde Park and Warm Springs, as well as other places used for similar purposes became a special force in the conduct of the president's office. Away from his official residence and with the cooperation of the press, Roosevelt could employ a type of "trial balloon" for actions that would be awkward or impossible within the limits of Washington's more formal procedure.[19]

Given such a cooperative relationship with the press, it was easy for the president and his staff to ask favors, whether it was for planting press conference questions or using an errand boy, such as Earl Godwin. Besides his work for the *Washington Times-Herald,* Godwin gave radio commentary and often did the White House bidding, as he did when Steve Early had him counteract Walter Winchell's 1939 commentary that the president was planning to run for a third term.[20]

Roosevelt's personal relations extended to the correspondents en masse. He regularly entertained the Washington correspondents. Within his first hundred days in office, FDR began holding what became an annual party for the correspondents, cabinet officials, and their spouses. During that first 1933 steamy, Washington summer evening, the reporters sweltered in dinner jackets before the affair became, as the *Washington Post* reported, "as informal as a barn dance." John O'Donnell and "the friendly Sons of St. Patrick" chanted Irish ditties and Eleanor Roosevelt and her son Elliott danced to the "Merry Widow Waltz." Raymond Clapper quoted the president as saying that this was the liveliest White House party since the wedding of Alice Roosevelt and Nick Longsworth. So too were the other annual press dances, where "the entire first floor of the mansion, as well as the garden, is thrown open, beer barrels set up in the main lobby, and fruit punch available at strategic locations," according to Delbert Clark of the *New York Times*. Clark recounted that while the journalists danced to a good jazz band, Mrs. Roosevelt and her children mingled with the dancers before serving a midnight supper and then continuing the dancing for an hour thereafter.[21]

The Roosevelts improved the Washington correspondents' general social standing. Previous administrations had given the press a mingling status only at important White House functions. During the Roosevelt years, the correspondents were guests, made to feel equal to diplomats and leaders at state dinners. Steve Early asked the first lady to divide the complete list of correspondents in the *Congressional Directory* by the number of official receptions held, so that by the time the season had ended, all journalists and their spouses would have been invited to at least one reception.[22]

The White House made other friendly gestures too. In response to the Washington Newspaper Guild's request, Secretary Early promised that the president would try to avoid any unnecessary extra working hours on Sundays. Early also arranged for reporters to see the president at lunches and breakfasts and after press conferences. In April 1933 when beer was legalized, Roosevelt acknowledged the cheering crowd of eight hundred who followed a truck with a large sign proclaiming, "President Roosevelt, the first real beer is yours." Roosevelt gave away those first cases to the National Press Club, which greatly appreciated his generosity.[23]

Roosevelt was especially solicitous to reporters assigned to Europe, often arranging for letters of introduction and discussing their pending trip. When the *New York Times* reassigned Charles Hurd to the *Times'* London bureau in 1937, the president invited both Hurd and his wife to the White House for tea. He wanted to explain the political situation in London as well as chat about the city. Hurd remembered, "It was the first occasion that we realized he thought of either of us as persons, as distinct from faces. He went into detail in discussing public figures I might encounter and was equally solicitous in giving some homely hints about London for my Eleanor." When Roosevelt sent the autographed pictures of himself and three letters of introduction to political figures, Hurd and his wife decided to keep the signed letters written on White House notepaper as souvenirs. Several months later, Hurd was admonished by the British Labour leader Arthur Murray, rasping over the telephone in his gruff and burry Scottish voice, "Hurd, this is Murray. Where the hell have you been? Franklin has written three times asking about you."[24]

The president and the journalists enjoyed themselves in other ways. On one warm, May evening two months after the first inauguration, several correspondents, among them Fred Storm of the United Press and Thomas Stokes of the *New York World-Telegram,* joined Appointments Secretary McIntyre and stood on the White House portico harmonizing "Home on the Range" while waiting for a conference communique. The following night the Roosevelts had the group at a White House "command performance." When NBC persuaded them to repeat their accomplishment over the airwaves, the president, obviously a showman, called the studio, disguised his voice, and offered them a contract. When their spokesman asked who was calling, he replied, "I'm the advertising manager for the Cascarets," a famous laxative. Roosevelt thought so well of the joke that at his next press conference he announced the correspondents would resign because "they had a very handsome offer to sing on the Cascaret Hour."[25]

Roosevelt cultivated the correspondents' personal goodwill. Until the war years, he attended their annual National Press Club dinners and the White House Correspondents' Association banquets as well as the Radio Correspondents' annual dinners. He also appeared at the spring and winter functions of the Gridiron, a select group of a hundred male Washington correspondents. On the same night Eleanor Roosevelt would entertain the female correspondents and the Gridiron widows at a White House dinner. FDR openly complained about the Gridiron Club's white-tie dress code and referred to the dignified group as the "stuffed, oops . . . I mean stiff shirt club." He especially disliked the Gridiron's skits that needled him and his policies, even though he could needle back and engage in one-upmanship. At the 1934 Gridiron dinner, he shocked the correspondents when he launched into a scathing attack on the self-righteous American press. After those first few surprising minutes, the Gridiron guests realized that his speech was actually a long quote from Henry Mencken's 1927 essay "Journalism in America." The hostile Mencken, seated at a nearby table, was furious. At the 1936 December dinner, FDR taunted the assembled publishers, editors, and correspondents for their interpretative journalism, particularly their viciously anti-Roosevelt front-page editorializing during the fall election. He delivered the first paragraph of his speech in Spanish, and then he scornfully noted that the South American republics were limited to reading nothing but actual news since they lacked the North American habit of news interpretation. He added that "perhaps in the days to come you can offer your services."[26]

FDR preferred to interact with a more fun-loving group, such as the J. Russell Young School of Expression. The club, named after the beloved elderly *Washington Star* correspondent and well-known service club speaker, John Russell Young, a Roosevelt favorite, was to use satire and have fun with those initiates who could earn "the Silver Tongue." The "school" had the president as a graduate, the White House as a campus, J. Russell Young as the dean, and Steve Early on its board of regents. The student body, made up of the White House press corps and "carefully screened outsiders," held an annual convocation at the Mayflower Hotel, complete with dinner and speeches. In 1940 the "Daisy Chain Parade" was led by such officials as Jesse Jones, Jim Farley, and Homer Cummings. The evening had the "usual class songs," "reunions," "class tree planting," and, above all, several "try-outs" for next year's diplomas. CBS even made a recording of the "school's hymn" and the "school's class song." Roosevelt always enjoyed the school's merriment. This informal blending of the executive branch and the fourth estate was clearly useful to both the president and the correspondents. In 1940 Roosevelt appointed John Russell Young as commissioner of the District of Columbia.[27]

Roosevelt had an informal reward system that to some extent depended on his personal relations. Because Herbert Hoover's habit of playing favorites had created difficulties with the press, Steve Early told reporters from the beginning that the president would grant no exclusive interviews and that all questions would be taken care of at press conferences. Yet bits of information, sometimes in exclusive form, were given to reporters. Scripps-Howard correspondent Ruth Finney remembered lingering with others after the press conferences to ask the president specific questions concerning southwest public power plans. Raymond Clapper received exclusive background information from the beginning, when Early told him and a few others about the proposed press conference arrangements. Clapper also came to the White House early on May 15, 1933, to preview the president's Geneva disarmament message.[28]

For at least part of the time, Clapper had a special relationship with the White House, serving as a conduit for the president. Such friendly relations with Clapper and others helped to suppress unfavorable stories. Clapper wrote in his diary in 1933 that the story of Roosevelt and Lucy Mercer Rutherford during World War I "buzzed around Washington." Yet Clapper and others never mentioned it publicly. Clapper and other journalists also did not mention the president's fall just before he was to give his acceptance speech at the 1936 Democratic National Convention. Early once asked Clapper to do an article boosting Joe Davies, who was greatly disappointed that he was not named ambassador to England in 1937. At Early's press briefing, the press secretary praised Clapper's column as accurately representing the attitude of the administration. Early gave Clapper exclusive background information on the controversial 1937 Court-packing proposal, including the president's reasons for advocating the bill and the strategy for passage. When Clapper wrote a favorable article on the president for the March 1937 *McCall's,* he even gave Early the advance sheets to read at Roosevelt's birthday dinner and pass along to Mrs. Roosevelt to use in her column.[29]

Before and after his inauguration, Roosevelt maintained close ties with *Collier's,* the large-circulation magazine. He had Thomas Beck of *Collier's* telegraph representative farm organizations for their suggestions for secretary of agriculture. He continued to give one of its chief journalists the type of favoritism that he and Steve Early claimed they avoided. *Collier's* political writer George Creel, the World War I chair of the Committee on Public Information, recounted that among the reasons the White House doors opened to him was FDR's connection with *Collier's.* Creel interviewed Roosevelt for a 1933 prophecy, "What Roosevelt Intends To Do," without direct quotations or other evidence of exclusiveness for that March issue. In the 1935 "Looking Ahead with Roosevelt," Creel wrote that the president actually dictated this article right after the Supreme Court ruled against the NRA. In another 1935 article, "The Amateur Touch," Creel satirized the party "old wheel horses," who had called Roosevelt "the poorest politician that ever sat in the presidential chair." Shortly after the 1936 election, Creel wrote another prophecy, "Roosevelt's Plans and Purposes," proposing an enlarged Supreme Court as a trial balloon. Creel recounted in his memoirs that the president dictated whole paragraphs for this December article as well as suggested the title. Yet Creel's exclusive interviews stopped when he became *Collier's* Washington editor during Roosevelt's second term.[30]

The president seriously considered becoming a journalist himself by joining *Collier's* editorial board after he left the White House. In January 1940 FDR signed a secret contract with *Collier's* to become a contributing editor with a minimum of twenty-six articles a year. The contract was to be voided only if the president returned to government service or official life. Four years later, editor William Chenery asked for an appointment to talk about the project again.[31]

The White House also gave exclusive information to Washington columnists Joseph Alsop and Robert Kintner of "The Capital Parade" and helped them write a 1940 pamphlet on American foreign policy, *The American White Paper.* Its publication was contingent on the president's approval. Early reported to FDR that "by correcting, eliminating and inserting, Joe Alsop has much improved his previous drafts and has given the final manuscript a fairer and much better 'balance.' " Such covert White House efforts fooled one reviewer. Professor R. B. Mowat assured his British audience that this was "not an official, white paper, but the work of two young Washington journalists who are obviously extremely well-informed and who have made a careful documentation of Mr. Roosevelt's policy."[32]

New York Times columnist Anne O'Hare McCormick had yearly "conversations" with the president in which he would set forth his philosophy, especially concerning foreign affairs. From her first talk in March 1933, "'Let's Try It,' Says Roosevelt," McCormick discussed without quotations what the president "foresees," "feels," and "thinks," with only an intimation that the author talked to the president. Such "tea and comprehensive talks," averaging one a year throughout the New Deal period, were a successful device for letting the president expound freely. The president expressed his appreciation, too, writing such comments as "nice letter" and "mention making another appointment to see her." McCormick's skill and special access to the president resulted in a Pulitzer prize in 1937 for her "general correspondence."[33]

Roosevelt usually did not give such interviews to Washington-based journalists. *New York Times* bureau chief Arthur Krock, who wanted the president's view of how the 1937 Supreme Court plan "fits into his conception of democracy," referred to McCormick's method in an interview request. Although Roosevelt granted him an exclusive interview, an interview the president probably needed during the intense furor over his plan to pack the Supreme Court, the White House imposed conditions. Both Early and Assistant Press Secretary William Hassett edited the article, after which Early wrote Krock, "I have taken the liberty of making a few penciled notations and also suggesting two inserts and an 'add.' I hope what I have done will be acceptable to you." Krock incorporated the "inserts and add" in the *Times* front-page article on February 28. According to Richard Strout of the *Christian Science Monitor,* the effort gave Krock the 1938 Pulitzer prize, his second in four years.[34]

The Washington correspondents knew that Krock had a sensational story. Although they had not openly complained about the McCormick interviews, they were most upset about Krock's privileges. They vented their anger to both Krock and Early the day after the *Times* article appeared. When the president held his next regular press conference two days later, Fred Essary of the *Baltimore Sun* immediately brought up favoritism. Roosevelt answered, "Fred, off the record, Steve laid his head on the block and so did I. It won't happen again." It did not happen again, at least with Washington-based correspondents. While McCormick did continue her yearly conversations with the president, White House correspondents competing with each other and under the gun from their editors did not have exclusive interviews with the president.[35]

Besides giving rewards that sometimes led to Pulitzer prizes, Roosevelt could also punish those whose interpretations he did not like. He went through a number of newspapers daily. According to his personal secretary Grace Tully, he covered the morning editions of the *New York Times, New York Herald-Tribune, Baltimore Sun, Washington Post, Washington Times-*

Herald, and *Chicago Tribune* and the evening editions of the *Washington Evening Star, Washington Daily News, New York World-Telegram, New York Journal American,* and *New York Sun.* Administration officials sent the president many other clippings. Louis Howe compiled a digest of coverage as well as a summary of how editors handled their correspondents' dispatches, and Steve Early followed the United Press and Associated Press dispatches carefully. Roosevelt wrote responses for the secretaries to relay.[36]

Roosevelt would react with anger over erroneous budget interpretations and what he labeled biased news stories. He especially disliked stories that appeared to have been written from an "insider's" viewpoint. When Congress was considering a repeal of the embargo acts a month after France and England had declared war on Germany in 1939, Ernest K. Lindley, a close personal friend, wrote in his October 19 *Washington Post* column that Roosevelt's foreign affairs background was based on his education, his travels in Europe, and his experience in the Navy Department during the Wilson administration, all of which gave him a pro-English bias. Roosevelt disagreed and immediately sent Steve Early a two-page memorandum with a point-by-point response to use. He concluded, "Tell Ernest that I forgive him. . . . It might be useful if Ernest would check with me." Within a week, Lindley published a twenty-three-inch retraction.[37]

Lindley later said, "I was pretty much running *straight news* in those days." He considered Roosevelt's interpretation straight news. Lindley, who had been a *New York Herald-Tribune* correspondent, had helped write Roosevelt's 1932 campaign speeches and campaign biography (from which FDR deleted several personal anecdotes). As a sympathetic journalist who later became an ABC broadcaster, Lindley received many exclusive news tips. The president once said that as "an old friend he has a right to check with me first on newspaper information." Lindley did not always do so, and he recalled being in conflict with Roosevelt many times when he did use stories. In the midst of the defeat of the Supreme Court Reform Bill and the controversial appointment of Hugo Black in 1937, Lindley's column infuriated the president. FDR was under pressure. At his August 9 Hyde Park press conference, Roosevelt spent forty minutes disagreeing with Lindley and others about their speculations that Boss Ed Flynn's visit was a presidential intercession in the heated New York mayor's race. According to Roosevelt, their interpretations were wrong:

> Remember, Ernest (Lindley), this has happened before. "It is reported" or "it is assumed." I know your difficulties. You have to turn out so much stuff a day. When you have no news you are still supposed to turn in so much news. I appreciate your difficulties but what the hell can you do when there isn't any news? You know, I can lock the gates. What are we going to do about it in the future? We are going to be here quite a lot from now on.

Q. (Mr. Lindley) I am under no compulsion to write news for my paper. . . .
THE PRESIDENT: Not a social visit, when you were told before that it was a social visit. There is no news interest in it then unless you fabricate news, which is in direct contravention of what I told you.

Several years later when Roosevelt refused to confirm Lindley's March 1940 inside story that he would run for a third term, Lindley became so upset that he stayed away from the White House until the annual Christmas family dinner. Yet Lindley continued to act as a handmaiden. During the war years, he published the president's version of the lend-lease program in Great Britain in *Newsweek*.[38]

The president and practically all the correspondents read the trend-setting *New York Times*. Most of the time Roosevelt allocated to morning newspapers was devoted to examining the accuracy, interpretations, and emphases of this newspaper because it was so influential. Both he and the correspondents closely watched the writings of the head of the *Times* Washington bureau, Arthur Krock. Krock was too important to ignore. By the end of FDR's first year, Krock recalled that the president began making critical remarks about his columns and the *New York Times* dispatches. When the correspondents asked about one of Krock's stories that appeared to be based on privileged information, because "it has embarrassed lots of us and it seems rather authentic," FDR was evasive: "I will have to read it; I will learn a lot about the Government." The correspondents, jealous of Krock and the *New York Times*, would laugh about Krock's falling for what appeared to be an erroneous story. When Roosevelt referred to Arthur's story, one correspondent brought down the house with his retort, "Little Arthur?"[39]

Although he helped frame questions for the *New York Times*, Krock did not attend Roosevelt's press conferences. Krock said that he tried to maintain a professional distance from FDR. He was cautious in his personal dealings with the president and for good reason. When the president wondered about his absences, Krock recalled replying that he could not keep his "objectivity when I'm close to you and watching you in action. You charm me so much that when I go back to write comment on the proceedings, I can't keep it in balance."[40]

By the end of 1934 Roosevelt thought that Krock's interpretations were definitely wrong. In August, when Krock gave an overly detailed account of Lewis Douglas's resignation as budget director, Krock learned that he was in "FDR's little black book." In October the president exploded after reading the *New York Times* account of the consolidation of the Executive Council and the National Emergency Council. Roosevelt found the *Times* reference to Chairman Donald Richberg as "an assistant President" especially odious, and he reacted: "Get hold of Krock and tell him . . . that this kind of thing is not only a lie but that it is a deception and a fraud on the public." By November

Krock was doing "much to hinder the friendly progress of negotiations" because of his article on British foreign minister Sir John Simon and the faltering World Disarmament Conference. Roosevelt said that the remarks appeared to be a personal attack on Simon, and he complained to *Times* publisher Adolph Ochs: "I may add that this article was carried in full by many British papers and coming from the *New York Times* was widely believed to be true." The president told Ochs that "the Times is so widely accepted because of the general fairness of its news stories" that "the interpretive articles such as Mr. Krock writes are accepted as statements of news facts." He complained that "this is not the first occasion in which Mr. Krock has rendered a real disservice." Ochs replied that if the president would discuss the article with Krock, he would "enlighten you with respect to other details." The president did not. Krock saw his role in this particular situation as a responsible and independent journalist. In reference to his interpretation, he wrote Early, "I am not conscious of having done any more or less than my duty in what I have written about the administration; certainly there has been no unfriendly motive on my part."[41]

Two months later, on January 26, 1935, Krock publicly reacted in a speech before the National Republican Club. Krock accused the "administration of more ruthlessness, intelligence and subtlety in trying to suppress legitimate, unfavorable comment than any other I have known." Krock then assured his audience that he spoke as one "on whom for some time, the President has not turned the warmth of his smile." Krock even sent Steve Early a copy of the speech.[42]

Whether there was the warmth of a smile or not, Krock and the president continued to depend on each other. Roosevelt was the foremost news source, and Krock relished the scoop. During a visit to Hyde Park in August 1936, Krock wrote that he heard Roosevelt outline his "great design" for dissipating the gathering war clouds. There could be a meeting of European leaders: King Edward, Stalin, Mussolini, Hitler, and Lebrun of France. Krock informed the president through his secretary Marguerite Le Hand that he would write a dispatch on the "design," if *it would not be denied*. Le Hand's return message only asked that Krock emphasize "a small committee." He had a sensational front-page story, which the other correspondents clamored for the president to label a fabrication. Roosevelt kept his word and refused to comment. The dispatch, a trial balloon to gauge the direction of national and international political winds, showed that the president's timing was wrong. When Roosevelt had Secretary of Agriculture Henry Wallace refute the story, Krock was furious. He knew he had been used. The article had been the test. Five months later, the president wrote Ambassador William E. Dodd, "That story by Arthur Krock was not wholly crazy. . . . a useful agreement might result."[43]

Their relationship continued to be rocky. Krock accused the administration of retaliating against unfavorable articles by eliminating news sources. Krock once wrote that he tried to check on Finland's concessions to Russia in October 1939, only to find that "Mr. Early—as often before—was not to be reached by telephone throughout the evening." Early quickly replied that he had, in fact, been at home. Krock's accusations, Early said, reminded him of the story of the proud mother who stood watching the parade and declared when she saw the men of her son's company passing by, "Everybody is out of step, *except* my son, John." Krock was out of step. He wrote that the president preferred to give inside information tips to *Times* correspondent Turner Catledge so that he would then acquire the reputation of being "well-informed; whereas the head of the Bureau was not." Krock was indignant that the president granted yearly interviews to Anne O'Hare McCormick, also of the *Times* editorial staff, and he was jealous of the president's close access to his publisher. While his ability to gather news might have been frustrated, Krock, ever grumbling, continued his efforts and maintained his independent position as "one of the best-informed correspondents in Washington" throughout the New Deal era.[44]

Franklin D. Roosevelt's public outbursts about critical newspaper stories were so rare that correspondents remembered those few incidents as forms of presidential punishment. Such an outburst occurred at the first press conference after the 1940 election. Appointments Secretary Marvin McIntyre told King Features columnist Paul Mallon, a longtime critic of the president, that he would not be welcome at future press meetings because of "inaccuracies in his column." When the *New York Times* and other newspapers requested information about this unprecedented action, the White House press offices backed down. Assistant Press Secretary William Hassett called both Mallon and the *Times* to say that Mallon had been "misinformed" and that he was not barred. Roosevelt then decided to punish all the correspondents by canceling his next press conference because he had "no news to offer." The *Christian Science Monitor* immediately labeled the incident as part of a new lack of access: "The function of the White House press conference in view of Washington correspondents who have seen many Presidents come and go, is not merely for the President to 'offer news,' but for the correspondents to question the President on matters of public interest." By the end of the month, Roosevelt resumed his regular press contacts.[45]

Another third-term incident in which a journalist was punished, one often cited, involved John O'Donnell of the hostile *New York Daily News*. O'Donnell, previously a Washington bureau chief, had been in enough favor to obtain a White House letter of introduction to the ambassador to France in 1939. Yet in 1941, when O'Donnell was suing the *Philadelphia Record* for libel, Steve Early gave a deposition in favor of the *Record*. Right after the bombing of Pearl Harbor, Roosevelt used the FBI to check secretly for those leaks giving the exact losses in Hawaii that John O'Donnell and others used in their stories. O'Donnell was threatened with the closure of "all privileges that go with the relationship between the press and government and direct appeals to their subscribers." By 1942 O'Donnell was an especially critical war correspondent in the Pacific. In writing a satirical column on the new wartime role of journalists, O'Donnell referred to Jack Turiott of the *Daily News* and George Druno of the International News Service as Pacific show stars, who were turning to "flutes and piccolos just to keep their fingers nimble for a time when censorship lets them beat the keys of their portable typewriters and turn out a tell-all story." FDR was livid. O'Donnell's succession of irritations had become too much. The war had been going badly, the pressure was great, and Roosevelt reacted. At his December 18 press conference, Roosevelt shocked the correspondents when he handed Earl Godwin the German Iron Cross to give to the absent O'Donnell. The Iron Cross was a symbol of O'Donnell's aid to the enemy. The incident did not stop there. When O'Donnell returned from the war in 1945 and along with another Patterson-McCormick correspondent asked for credentials to attend White House press conferences, the president said no because of "their isolationist, anti-British, anti-Russian pens." The response became public when the *Philadelphia Record* reported that Steve Early threatened resignation before Roosevelt finally yielded.[46]

Such public confrontations and "punishments" were rare during Roosevelt's twelve years of personal interaction with the Washington correspondents. FDR usually adopted more subtle methods for influencing an interpretation. The dunce hat award is an example. At his June 29, 1937, press conference, the president gave an imaginary dunce hat to Robert "Bob" Post of the *New York Times*, who had asked the president about a possible third term: "Getting back to what Governor Earle said the other day, can you tell us or would you say whether you would accept the nomination?" Roosevelt responded, "Oh, my God. This hot weather. (Laughter) Bob (Post) go into the corner over there (indicating) and put on the dunce cap and stand with your back to the crowd. (Laughter)." This method culminated in a resolution to dissolve the Dunce Hat Club as the 1940 Democratic Convention began.[47]

FDR had a lively sense of humor, and he frequently employed it for the correspondents' amusement. He entertained the correspondents, invited them into his home even while he was on vacation, and charmed them with his informal manner, his jesting, and his confidence. He liked journalists and considered himself one of them. Good personal relations could lead to favorable news stories, especially interpretative news stories, which were dependent on the background of many policies. While giving out the details, FDR could reinforce his own viewpoint and define exactly what was news, especially if he happened to be the only news source, as in some of the Clapper columns, the Creel *Collier's* articles, and the McCormick conversations. Moreover, as Arthur Krock once declared in reference to Roosevelt's efforts, those numerous small private hospitalities "have won him a regard among the reporters which . . . impels many of them to give him and his plans the best of it when there is a best that can be given without violence to the fact." If the correspondents had been swimming with the president, had dined at his table, had been charmed by his manner while playing a hand of bridge, then, as Krock suggested, they would probably be very careful about their choice of words and their interpretation concerning their friend the president. The working press tended to judge presidents as men, and Roosevelt gained their respect because of his pleas for the forgotten people. Reporters in general considered themselves among those forgotten men.[48]

The White House correspondents were an exclusive fraternal club, as club-like as Franklin Roosevelt's Hasty Pudding Club at Harvard. The president liked referring to his clubs: positive clubs like the J. Russell Young School of Expression and negative clubs such as the Dunce Hat Club and the "stiff shirt club." The White House correspondents' group was also a club, with definite admission requirements and unwritten codes, including "no blacks admitted" and "no females at formal functions and in the special clubs."

The White House correspondents followed another set of rules. The members expected to be treated equally, with no obvious news favors for any individual. A "dog-eat-dog" competition existed for getting the stories. Roosevelt made their lives a little happier and their work a little easier by using the press conference as a method of giving out information to the group en masse. Under great pressure from their editors, those correspondents were judged day by day, not necessarily by the quality of their news reporting or by the spot news they produced but by the production rate of their principal rivals. When President Roosevelt gave the *Times* bureau chief Arthur Krock an exclusive interview after submitting the sensational bill to pack the Supreme Court, it was almost more than the correspondents could stomach. Roosevelt realized his "mistake." Although he continued to talk to Anne O'Hare McCormick without complaint, he did not give any more exclusive interviews to those journalists based in Washington.[49]

When the president's warm personal relations did not work, he complained about inaccuracy and unfairness—as he did with the Krock and Lindley stories. He attempted to exclude one correspondent, only to incur the wrath of the group; the goodwill of the group was important, as he and his press secretary knew. His most extreme action involved John O'Donnell and the Iron Cross. Yet this outburst was unusual; it was dramatic; it was remembered. His scoldings and extreme actions were in contrast to his usual warm relations with the correspondents. By relying on his personality, his humor, and his adroit news skills, he could relay his viewpoints. He might complain about an interpretative news emphasis, yet he earnestly and successfully used this new journalistic form to his own advantage.

Notes

1. Charles Hurd refers to the "personal relationship" in *When the New Deal Was Young and Gay* (New York: Harper, 1965), p. 163.

2. Edwin Emery and Michael Emery, *The Press and America: An Interpretative History of the Mass Media,* 5th ed. (Englewood Cliffs, N.J.: Prentice-Hall, 1984), p. 435. The spelling of "interpretive" journalism was also used, for example, by Marquis W. Childs, "The Interpretive Reporter's Role in a Troubled World," *Journalism Quarterly* 27 (Spring 1950): 134–40. A classic textbook, Curtis Daniel MacDougall's *Reporting for Beginners* (New York: Macmillan, 1932), was renamed *Interpretative Reporting* (New York: Macmillan, 1938) six years later.

3. References to interpretation and column writing by Edward Folliard (writer for the *Washington Herald* and *Washington Post* and president of the White House Correspondents' Association in 1945), interview at his home, Washington, D.C., June 3, 1976; Richard L. Strout (of the *Christian Science Monitor*), interview, Washington, D.C., June 2, 1976; Robert S. Allen (writer for the *Philadelphia Record* and columnist of the "Daily Washington Merry-Go-Round" with Drew Pearson), interview, National Press Club, Washington, D.C., June 8, 1976; Arthur Krock, "The Press and Government," *Annals of the American Academy of Political and Social Science* 180 (July 1935): 163–64; *New York Times,* May 5, 1935, p. 1; Raymond Clapper, *Watching the World* (New York and London: Whittlesey House, McGraw-Hill, 1944), p. 22; Leo C. Rosten, *The Washington Correspondents* (New York: Harcourt, Brace, 1937), pp. 115, 144; A. Merriman Smith, *Thank You, Mr. President: A White House Notebook* (New York: Harper and Row, 1946), p. 3; Bascom N. Timmons, "This Is How It Used to Be," in *Dateline: Washington, the Story of National Affairs Journalism in the Life and Times of the National Press Club,* Cabell Phillips et al., eds. (Garden City, N.Y.: Doubleday, 1949), pp. 58–59. The "Merry-Go-Round" and Mark Sullivan's columns were published in 400 newspapers with a potential reading audience of 13 million.

4. Franklin D. Roosevelt, *Complete Presidential Press Conferences of Franklin D. Roosevelt* (New York: Da Capo Press, 1972), Press Conference (henceforth PC) 156, November 7, 1934, Vol. 4: 166–70.

5. Ibid., PC 782, November 7, 1941, Vol. 18: 292; PC 783, November 14, 1941, Vol. 18: 303.

6. In reference to political news coverage, see Raymond P. Brandt, "The President's Press Conference," *Survey Graphic,* July 1939, p. 449; Leo C. Rosten, "Political Leadership and the Press," in *The Future of Government in the United States,* Leonard White, ed. (Chicago: University of Chicago Press, 1942), pp. 91–92.

7. Ernest K. Lindley, interview, Cosmos Club, Washington, D.C., June 4, 1976. Universal News Service was a morning news agency of William Randolph Hearst. Louis Howe, who had covered Albany for the *New York Herald,* was the president's secretary until his death in 1936. Stephen Early had been with the Associated Press, United Press, and Paramount Newsreel Company until his appointment as the president's secretary in charge of the press. Former newspaperman Marvin McIntyre had been in public relations for the Navy Department during Roosevelt's tenure in the Wilson administration and was Roosevelt's appointments secretary. Formerly a *Washington Post,* Associate Press, and *Philadelphia Public Ledger* journalist, William Hassett was appointments secretary after McIntyre's death in 1943.

8. Many Washington correspondents had the title "correspondent" or "journalist" after their names in the Washington, D.C., phone book. For references to the numbers,

see Roosevelt, *Complete Press Conferences,* PC 149, October 10, 1934, Vol. 3: 420–21; PC 162, December 4, 1934, Vol. 4: 260, PC 163, December 7, 1934, Vol. 4: 263; F. B. Marbut, *News from the Capital: The Story of Washington Reporting* (Carbondale: Southern Illinois University Press, 1971), p. 179.

After the bombing of Pearl Harbor, the number of correspondents increased so much that the Secret Service had to limit the press associations to no more than fifteen journalists each and large metropolitan papers and radio chains to no more than five. See Michael Reilly, *Reilly of the White House* (New York: Simon and Schuster, 1947), p. 91.

In reference to the enlarged press quarters, see Henry F. Pringle, "Profiles: The President, III," *The New Yorker,* June 30, 1934, p. 21. In reference to invitations, see Delbert Clark, *Washington Dateline* (New York: Frederick A. Stokes, 1941), p. 21.

9. Steve Early explained these rules to Senator Theodore Bilbo, March 7, 1935, Official File (henceforth OF) 36, Franklin D. Roosevelt Library (henceforth FDRL); Steve Early Memo, January 12, 1934, OF 36, FDRL.

Requests and permissions were granted for Dr. Wilhelm Cohnstaedt of the *Frankfurter Zeitung* and Anna Louise Strong of the *Moscow Daily News.* Other visitor-status requests were mentioned in Early Memo to Marvin McIntyre, October 6, 1933, OF 36, FDRL; Early to George L. Edmunds, January 18, 1934, OF 36, FDRL; Early to Joseph Ness, November 15, 1933, OF 36, FDRL.

The exclusion of photographers probably had to do with the control over the president's pictorial image (see chapter 6 herein). In 1936 photographers were still excluded, although the White House News Photographers Association was included in the *Congressional Directory* in 1936. See *Congressional Directory,* 74th Congress, 2d session, p. 636; "Radio Galleries," in *Congressional Directory,* 76th Congress, 3rd session, pp. 703–5; "Rules Governing Press Galleries," in *Congressional Directory,* 73rd Congress, 3rd session, p. 679. The rules remained the same, and the Radio Correspondents Association listed their rules governing the radio correspondents' galleries in 1940, which were under control of the Executive Committee of the Radio Correspondents Association. See Marbut, *News from the Capital,* pp. 172–73; Rosten, *Washington Correspondents,* p. 86. Correspondents for periodicals were admitted to congressional galleries in 1941. See *Congressional Directory,* 77th Congress, 1st session, p. 739; White House Correspondents, Stephen T. Early Papers (henceforth STEP) 21, FDRL. Author has been unable to obtain membership lists from the White House Correspondents' Association, except for two, 1934 and 1941 from the Roosevelt Library.

10. Rosten, *Washington Correspondents,* p. 86. Requests concerning qualified blacks were from Trezzant W. Anderson to Steve Early, October 25, 1933, OF 36, FDRL; Frederick Weaver to Franklin D. Roosevelt, November 6, 1933, and Early to Frederick Weaver, November 15, 1933, OF 36, FDRL; Frederick Weaver to George Curno, President of the White House Correspondents' Association, November 23, 1940, OF 36, FDRL; Claude A. Barnett to Steve Early, November 10, 1943, OF 36, FDRL; Steve Early to Eustace Gay, December 7, 1940, OF 36, FDRL.

It should be noted that no anti-lynching bill passed Congress during the Roosevelt administrations, although it was proposed numerous times. According to George W. Bain, Steve Early was an important factor in this situation, since he feared southern voter alienation during the major elections. See Bain, "How Negro Editors Viewed the New Deal," *Journalism Quarterly* 44 (Autumn 1967): 554. See also Patrick S. Washburn, *A Question of Sedition: The Federal Government's Investigation of the Black Press during World War II* (New York: Oxford University Press, 1986), pp. 198–201.

11. "Press Galleries," *Congressional Directory,* 73rd, 74th, 75th, 76th Congresses, 1934, 1936, 1938, 1940. Strickland Gillilan to Marvin McIntyre, March 14, 1933, and Steve Early to Strickland Gillilan, March 18, 1933, OF 36, FDRL.

12. Jane Gray Swissholm broke the previous ban when she sent Washington news to Horace Greeley's *New York Tribune* in 1850. See Ishbel Ross, "Invading the Press Gallery," in her *Ladies of the Press: The Story of Women in Journalism by an Insider* (New York: Harper and Brothers, 1936), pp. 323–28.

Journalists had been admitted in Congress since 1801, according to Marbut, *News from the Capital,* p. 20; Drew Pearson and Robert S. Allen, *Washington Merry-Go-Round* (New York: Horace Liveright, 1931), p. 337; Ross, *Ladies of the Press,* pp. 336–37.

13. Raymond Clapper, "Why Reporters Like Roosevelt," *Review of Reviews,* June 1934, p. 16; Ernest K. Lindley, interview with author, Cosmos Club, Washington, D.C., June 4, 1976; Early to Francis Whiting, Managing Editor, *Cosmopolitan,* December 10, 1941, STEP, FDRL; Hurd, *When the New Deal Was Young and Gay,* p. 10; Grace Tully, *F.D.R., My Boss* (New York: Charles Scribner's Sons, 1949), pp. 266, 290–91. Concerning limitations, see letter to the president from the White House Correspondents' Association, February 14, 1940, signed by Felix Belair, Jr., of the *New York Herald-Tribune,* Doris Fleeson of the *New York Daily News,* Walter Trohan of the *Chicago Tribune,* and W. C. Murphy, Jr., of the *Philadelphia Inquirer,* OF 36, FDRL.

World War II changes meant that only representatives of the three largest press associations—Associated Press, United Press, and International News Service—covered the president's trips and no advance announcement was given as to departure or destination.

14. Hurd, *When the New Deal Was Young and Gay,* pp. 241–42; Clark, *Washington Dateline,* p. 87.

15. "The Presidency," *Time,* June 19, 1933, p. 11.

16. Hurd, *When the New Deal Was Young and Gay,* p. 267. See also Raymond Clapper Diary, 1933, Box 8, Raymond Clapper Papers (henceforth RCP), Manuscripts Division, Library of Congress (henceforth LofC); John Herrick, "With Reporters at the Summer White House," *Literary Digest,* August 12, 1933, p. 5; Kenneth G. Crawford to Betty H. Winfield, May 18, 1976. Hurd (p. 253) also mentions that $25,000 was appropriated annually for the president's travel and entertainment during the New Deal period.

Grace Tully notes that unless the suppers could be classified as "official," the costs for entertaining even for those Sunday night dinners came out of the normal household expenses, which the president had to pay out of his own pocket. An "official" designation meant that the function had to have guests of honor or congressional members of the opposition party or had to be a formal White House affair. See Tully, *F.D.R., My Boss,* p. 146.

According to Walter Davenport, by the fourth term the president was holding the supersecret "Sunday" suppers for the huge-circulation columnists, foreign correspondents, and commentators, who would all sneak in quietly by the side entrances to the White House. See "The President and the Press," *Collier's,* January 27, 1945, p. 49.

17. Clapper Diary, May 16, 1937, Box 8, RCP, LofC. Others talked about the informality: Ruth Finney Allen, Scripps-Howard Newspaper Alliance, interview at her home, Washington, D.C., June 8, 1976, and Ernest K. Lindley, interview, Washington, D.C., June 4, 1976.

18. Hurd, *When the New Deal Was Young and Gay,* pp. 169–71. Information was based on the *New York Times,* July 1, 1933. See also Frank Freidel, *Launching the New Deal,* Vol. 4 of *Franklin D. Roosevelt* (Boston: Little, Brown, 1973), p. 480.

19. Hurd, *When the New Deal Was Young and Gay,* p. 164.

20. Godwin begins appearing in the *Official Congressional Directory,* press gallery lists in January 1935. This means he was admitted as of December 20, 1934. For the example, see Steve Early to Marvin McIntyre, June 20, 1939, STEP, FDRL. Godwin kept the press secretary's office informed as to Hearst's editorial plans during the fight over the Supreme Court reforms. See WDH [William D. Hassett] Confidential Memorandum for Steve Early, February 15, 1937, President's Secretary's File (henceforth PSF), FDRL.

21. *Washington Post,* June 4, 1933, Clapper Reference File, Censorship, Box 110, RCP, LofC; Clapper Diary, June 3, 1933, Box 5, RCP, LofC.

22. For the difference, see Hurd, *When the New Deal Was Young and Gay,* p. 241. Early Memo to Mrs. Helm, November 15, 1933, OF 36, FDRL; Dinner Lists, 1933–45, PSF, FDRL.

23. Concerning the extra working hours, see J. D. Secrest to Steve Early, December 23, 1935, and Early to Secrest, January 2, 1936, OF 36, FDRL. Secrest was secretary of the Washington Newspaper Guild. For lunches or breakfasts or quick questions, see Early Memo to Franklin D. Roosevelt, October 6, 1938, OF 36, FDRL; Ruth Finney Allen, interview, Washington, D.C., June 8, 1976; Roosevelt, *Complete Press Conferences,* PC 85, January 5, 1934, Vol. 3: 47, and PC 254, December 3, 1935, Vol. 6: 325, where the stenographer did mention in parenthesis the post-conference discussion. For reference to the beer, see "Writers Will Get White House Beer," undated clipping, Clapper Reference File, Box 8, RCP, LofC.

24. Hurd, *When the New Deal Was Young and Gay,* p. 243–44. Colonel Arthur Murray, a prominent member of the British Labour party, was an old Roosevelt friend from World War I days. He had served as parliamentary undersecretary to Sir Edward Grey at the Foreign Ministry and had been an assistant military attaché in Washington, D.C., in 1917, 1918, and 1919. See explanatory notes in *F.D.R.: His Personal Letters, 1928–1945,* Vol. 1, Elliott Roosevelt, ed. (New York: Duell, Sloan and Pearce, 1950), p. 198.

See also Steve Early to William Bullitt, n.d., OF 36, FDRL, concerning the trip of John O'Donnell and his wife Doris Fleeson to France and Germany.

25. Thomas L. Stokes, *Chip Off My Shoulder* (Princeton, N.J.: Princeton University Press, 1940), p. 361; Clapper also refers to the incident in his diary, May 16, 1933, Box 5, RCP, LofC; Roosevelt, *Complete Press Conferences,* PC 21, May 16, 1933, Vol. 1: 264.

26. For comments about FDR's goodwill, see Leo C. Rosten, "President Roosevelt and the Washington Correspondents," *Public Opinion Quarterly* 1 (January 1937): 40; Marbut, *News from the Capital,* p. 177; Ruth Finney Allen, interview, Washington,

D.C., June 8, 1976. For the stiff shirt club, see Smith, *Thank you, Mr. President,* pp. 277–78; Clapper Diary, February 9, 1937, Box 8, RCP, LofC.

The 1934 Roosevelt Gridiron speech was in George Wolfskill and John A. Hudson, *All but the People: Franklin D. Roosevelt and His Critics, 1933–1939* (Toronto: Macmillan, 1969), pp. 172–73, and his 1936 speech was in Tully, *F.D.R., My Boss,* pp. 219–22. See also William Hassett, *Off the Record with F.D.R., 1942–1945* (New Brunswick, N.J.: Rutgers University Press, 1958), pp. 71–72. Roosevelt's complaints must have been initially effective since Secretary of Interior Ickes recorded in his diary in 1938 that the skits were "less savage" than they had been. See *The Secret Diary of Harold L. Ickes,* Vol. 2 (New York: Simon and Schuster, 1954), pp. 364–65.

27. Ruth Finney Allen, interview, Washington, D.C., June 8, 1976; Ernest K. Lindley, interview, Washington, D.C., June 4, 1976. The correspondents teased Young about his inspirational talks to the CCC and the Kiwanis in Roosevelt, *Complete Press Conferences,* PC 162, December 4, 1934, Vol. 5: 259; PC 253, November 26, 1935, Vol. 6: 318; PC 313, August 7, 1936, Vol. 8: 55.

For information on the school, see J. Russell Young to Steve Early, April 8, 1941, January 28, 1942, February 6, 1942, January 18, 1945, STEP, FDRL; Clapper Reference File, 1940 Folder, Box 9, RCP, LofC; Franklin D. Roosevelt to J. Russell Young, January 28, 1938, President's Personal File (henceforth PPF), FDRL. Concerning the appointment, see Early Memo to Franklin D. Roosevelt, March 27, 1940, PSF, FDRL.

28. Concerning the boundaries, see Marvin McIntyre Confidential Memorandum to Steve Early, April 3, 1933, OF 36, FDRL; M. A. Le Hand to Arthur Krock, May 3, 1933, PPF, FDRL; Early Memo to J. C. Dunn, State Department, October 5, 1933, and Arthur S. Draper to Louis McHenry Howe, July 18, 1933, OF 36, FDRL; Tully, *F.D.R., My Boss,* p. 151. Concerning special requests, see Rudolphe de Zappe to Steve Early, July 14, 1933, OF 36, FDRL. Ruth Finney Allen in an interview, Washington, D.C., June 8, 1976, mentioned lingering to ask special regional questions. Clapper's exclusive background information was mentioned in Clapper to Bob Bender, March 1, 1933, Clapper Personal File, Letters 1933, Box 8, RCP, LofC; Clapper Diary, May 15, 1933, Box 5, RCP, LofC.

29. In reference to Lucy Mercer Rutherford, see Clapper Diary, July 13, 1933, Box 6, RCP, LofC. For his fall at the convention in Philadelphia, see Clapper Diary, July 29, 1936, Box 8, RCP, LofC. Clapper headed this entry with "returning from vacation—catching up on notes" and said Roosevelt mentioned on his Georgia trip that the press had missed the story at Philadelphia.

For praise about Clapper, see "Clapper Gives a Truer Picture," Early Memorandum to the President, June 4, 1934, OF 36, FDRL.

For the Court-packing plan, see Clapper Diary, entries for January 20, January 28, February 2, and December 21, 1937, Box 8, RCP, LofC; Clapper's article, "Who Is This Man," *McCall's,* March 1937, p. 7.

Despite this close relationship, Clapper supported Wendell Wilkie for president in 1940 because of the third-term issue. See Clapper, *Watching the World,* p. 94.

30. *Collier's* circulation in 1936 was 2.4 million, just behind that of the *Saturday Evening Post.* See N. W. Ayer and Sons, *Directory of Newspapers and Periodicals* (Philadelphia: N. W. Ayer and Sons, 1936), p. 1188. Roosevelt also remained close to *Liberty* magazine by continuing to see and write Fulton Ouster, the editor. See Early Press Conference, July 17, 1940, STEP, FDRL.

George Creel, *Rebel at Large: Recollections of Fifty Crowded Years* (New York: G. P. Putnam's Sons, 1947) pp. 271–74, 290–95.

For articles, see Creel, "What Roosevelt Intends to Do," *Collier's,* March 11, 1933, pp. 7–9, 34, 36; "Looking Ahead with Roosevelt," *Collier's,* September 7, 1935, pp. 7–8, 45–46; "The Amateur Touch," *Collier's,* August 3, 1935, pp. 12–13, 34; "Roosevelt's Plans and Purposes," *Collier's,* December 26, 1937, pp. 7–9, 39, 49.

31. Steve Early, Confidential File Memorandum, January 7, 1940, STEP, FDRL. No memorandum or answer has been found to this letter. William Chenery to Stephen Early, January 6, 1944, STEP, FDRL.

32. "The Capital Parade" was syndicated by the North American Newspaper Alliance. Joseph Alsop was Eleanor Roosevelt's second cousin, and his mother was in the Roosevelt wedding as a bridesmaid.

Alsop and Kintner to Steve Early, February 21, 1940, Early Memorandum to Roosevelt, March 23, 1940, and Early Memorandum to Roosevelt, March 25, 1940, STEP, FDRL; R. B. Mowat, "The White Paper," *Fortnightly,* July 1, 1940, p. 43.

33. *The World at Home: Selections from the Writings of Anne O'Hare McCormick,* Marion Turner Sheehan, ed. (New York: Alfred A. Knopf, 1956), columns are on pp. 183–95; 278–88; 300–320; 311–36. Concerning requests for the talks and responses, see Marguerite Le Hand telegram to Anne O'Hare McCormick, May 26, 1936; McCormick telegram to Marguerite Le Hand, July 12, 1937, arranging for a talk on July 13, 1937; McCormick to Franklin D. Roosevelt, July 28, 1937; Marguerite Le Hand telegram to McCormick, August 2, 1937, arranging for talk on August 3, 1937; McCormick to Franklin D. Roosevelt, October 13, 1938; McCormick to Marguerite Le Hand, June 7, 1939, for the June 22, 1939 talk; McCormick to Grace Tully, January 11, 1940, for January 12, 1940; Emmett Watson to McCormick, n.d., arranging for an appointment on February 17, 1941; Roosevelt to McCormick, May 27, 1941, arranging for an appointment on June 11, 1941; McCormick to Tully, December 21, 1942, all in Selected Documents of Anne O'Hare McCormick, FDRL. Among her articles were "Still 'A Little Left of Center' " in 1936; "An Unchanging Roosevelt Drives On" in 1937; "As He Sees Himself" in 1938; "At 60 He is Still a Happy Warrior" in 1942; and "His 'Unfinished Business'—and Ours" after his death in 1945.

34. Arthur Krock to Steve Early, February 16, 1937, Early to Krock, February 16, 1937, William Hassett Memo to Early re Krock, February 24, 1937, Early to Krock, February 24, 1937, Krock to Early, February 26, 1937, STEP, FDRL. The article was in the *New York Times,* February 28, 1937, p. 1.

Krock had also asked for an exclusive interview right after the president was first inaugurated. See Marvin McIntyre Conference Memorandum to Steve Early, April 3, 1933, OF 36, FDRL; Arthur Krock to Marguerite Le Hand, May 2, 1933, PPF, FDRL. Richard Strout, interview, Washington, D.C., June 2, 1976.

35. Krock to Early, March 1, 1937, STEP, FDRL; Roosevelt, *Complete Press Conferences,* PC 349, March 2, 1937, Vol. 9: 190–91.

Hurd, *When the New Deal Was Young and Gay,* p. 230, contends Roosevelt did not have exclusives, and if writers gained exclusive information, they received it from outside sources. This seems incredible since Hurd, like Krock and McCormick, was from the *New York Times.*

36. Steve Early to Allen L. Appleton, March 4, 1935, PPF, FDRL; Tully, *F.D.R.,*

My Boss, pp. 76–77. Tully could have been confused about the New York newspapers, since the *New York Post* was pro-Roosevelt and it is hard to imagine that he did not look at it. Rudolph Forster, executive clerk and administrative officer in charge of the executive papers, sent Early the headlines to check the press conference questions while the president was traveling. See Forster to Steve Early, Care of President's Special, September 28, 1935, OF 36A, FDRL; Steve Early to Allen L. Appleton, March 4, 1935, PPF, FDRL. Howe's *Daily Bugle* gave the president a broader view of the press. White House Scrapbooks, FDRL; Arthur Brisbane to Marguerite Le Hand, March 16, 1934, and Roosevelt to Arthur Brisbane, March 21, 1934, OF 36, FDRL; Theodore Joslin's March 4, 1935, *Washington Star* article in Franklin D. Roosevelt, *The Public Papers and Addresses of Franklin D. Roosevelt,* Vol. 2, Samuel I. Rosenman, ed. (New York: Random House, 1938–50), pp. 40–41.

37. Franklin D. Roosevelt Memorandum to Steve Early, October 19, 1939, plus clippings, STEP, FDRL.

38. Ernest K. Lindley, interview, Washington, D.C., June 4, 1976. Lindley's books include *Franklin D. Roosevelt: A Career in Progressive Democracy* (1931); *The Roosevelt Revolution: First Phase* (1933); *A New Deal for Youth,* with Betty Grimes Lindley (1938); *Half Way with Roosevelt* (1937); and *How the War Came* (1942). By 1938 Lindley was doing columns for the *Washington Post.* Delbert Clark in *Washington Dateline* (p. 195) referred to Lindley's dissatisfaction with the anti–New Deal attitude of the *New York Herald-Tribune* and said he gave up his job because of it.

Roosevelt Memo to Steve Early, October 19, 1939, STEP, FDRL; Franklin D. Roosevelt to William Phillips, February 6, 1937, *F.D.R.: His Personal Letters, 1928–1945,* Vol. 1, p. 656, refers to talking to Lindley about a proposed article "on our European policy." In reference to Lindley's column in August, see Roosevelt, *Complete Press Conferences,* PC 389, August 9, 1937, Vol. 10: 109–39, quote on pp. 117–18.

In reference to the third-term issue, see Roosevelt, *Complete Press Conferences,* PC 628, March 5, 1940, Vol. 15: 182; PC 630, March 19, 1940, Vol. 15: 205. Lindley disagreed with James E. Pollard's version of the issue in *The Presidents and the Press* (New York: Macmillan, 1947), p. 814. Pollard wrote that Roosevelt broke with Lindley over this column. Jim Farley wrote that the president deliberately inspired the story and that when Roosevelt did not answer the question on Lindley's column at the March 5 press conference, Early had the question planted at the March 19 conference. See James A. Farley, *Jim Farley's Story: The Roosevelt Years* (New York: McGraw-Hill, 1948), pp. 226, 228. Concerning other tips to Lindley, see TRB [Thomas R. Blake] Memorandum to Mr. Hassett, December 9, 1941, and STE Memorandum for Hassett, December 9, 1941, STEP, FDRL.

39. For the trend-setter reference, see Rosten, *The Washington Correspondents,* pp. 94–95; Frank Freidel, *Launching the New Deal,* Vol. 4 of *Franklin D. Roosevelt,* (Boston: Little, Brown, 1973), pp. 274–75. For conflicts, see Arthur Krock, *Memoirs: Sixty Years on the Firing Line* (New York: Funk and Wagnalls, 1968), p. 159. Press conference references to Krock are in Roosevelt, *Complete Press Conferences,* PC 12, April 14, 1933, Vol. 1: 140–41; PC 17, May 3, 1933, Vol. 1: 207; the Arthur story reference was in PC 19, May 10, 1933, Vol. 1: 241–42.

40. Krock, *Memoirs,* pp. 179–180.

41. Ibid., pp. 159–60, 182–83; Arthur M. Schlesinger, Jr., *The Coming of the New*

Deal, Vol. 2 of *The Age of Roosevelt* (Boston: Houghton Mifflin, 1959), p. 546; Roosevelt Memorandum to Early, November 3, 1934, Roosevelt to Adolph S. Ochs, November 26, 1934, and Ochs to Franklin D. Roosevelt, November 30, 1934, PPF, FDRL. Note that the incident took place in November 1934 and not in 1935 as Krock remembers. In reference to his interpretation, Krock to Early, December 26, 1934, STEP, FDRL.

42. Arthur Krock Speech to the National Republican Club, New York City, January 26, 1935, Arthur Krock Papers, Princeton University Manuscript Collection; Steve Early to Arthur Krock, January 30, 1935, STEP, FDRL.

43. Krock, *Memoirs,* pp. 183–4; Clapper Diary, September 10, 1936, Box 8, RCP, LofC. Clapper substantiates that the Krock story came from Joe Alsop and said that the originator of the idea was British Labour leader George Lansbury, although British Ambassador Sir Ronald Lindsay was sour on it. Franklin Roosevelt to William E. Dodd, January 9, 1937, *F.D.R.: His Personal Letters, 1928–1945,* Vol. 1, pp. 648–49.

44. Krock, *Memoirs,* pp. 179–81; Steve Early to Arthur Krock, October 13, 1939, Krock to Early, October 16, 1939, and Early to Krock, October 17, 1939, STEP, FDRL; notes in *F.D.R.: His Personal Letters, 1928–1945,* Vol. 2, p. 744.

James MacGregor Burns, *Roosevelt: The Soldier of Freedom* (New York: Harcourt, Brace, 1970), p. 453, mentions that Catledge did become a Roosevelt confidant during the war.

45. Robert S. Allen, Ruth Finney Allen, Edward Folliard, Ernest K. Lindley, Richard Strout, interviews, Washington, D.C., June 1976; "White House Bars Reporter, Awhile," *New York Times,* November 9, 1940, and *Christian Science Monitor,* November 12, 1940, Early Scrapbooks, STEP, FDRL.

46. Early to William C. "Bill" Bullitt, July 6, 1939, STEP, FDRL; Early to Herbert Lyons, Jr., December 5, 1941, STEP, FDRL; in reference to the leaks, see Early to J. Edgar Hoover, December 12, 1941, and J. Edgar Hoover to Early, December 29, 1941, STEP, FDRL, concerning John O'Donnell's *New York Daily News* column, December 29, 1941, which was also carried in the *Washington Times-Herald.*

The iron cross incident is in Roosevelt, *Complete Press Conferences,* PC 869, December 18, 1942, Vol. 20: 309. The press conference transcript includes an addendum with the excerpt of O'Donnell's "Capital Stuff" column, *Washington Times-Herald,* December 16, 1942. For the threatened press conference exclusion, see *Philadelphia Record,* January 9, 1945, Early Scrapbook, STEP, FDRL.

47. Roosevelt, *Complete Press Conferences,* PC 377, June 29, 1937, Vol. 9: 466; for resolution, see ibid., PC 660, July 12, 1940, Vol. 16: 34–35.

48. Clapper, "Why Reporters Like Roosevelt," p. 16; Krock, Speech to the National Republican Club, January 26, 1935.

49. Clark wrote in 1941 that if correspondents were "scooped" by a rival, they should obtain an official denial, which they could use as alibis for the home office. If correspondents could "quote" the denial, then they could be absolved until it happened again. More often than not, the story would be one the official would rather not see in print. Since technical denials were not considered "dishonorable," they were not hard to obtain. Clark noted that it was a frequent practice to distort the story sufficiently while angling for a denial to ensure obtaining one. See Clark, *Washington Dateline,* pp. 24–25.

"The White House slant on the current news of the day." FDR meeting
with Edwin "Pa" Watson, military aide and secretary to the president,
and Stephen T. Early, the president's press secretary, August 25, 1939.
Courtesy of AP/Wide World Photos.

5

The New Deal Publicity System

It's a game here in Washington. The Executive has the sheep and we are the stealers—we're the poachers. We're trying to get the news and they are trying to keep it from us or select the news we get. And it's a game. They realize what we're trying to do and up to a point it's mutual, we help each other.

— Richard Strout, interview, June 2, 1976

During the Roosevelt administration so much news was happening that by 1934 the United Press wires were carrying three times more Washington, D.C., news than in 1930; one-fourth of all Associated Press news was originating in Washington. William E. Berchtold of the *New Outlook* said that prior to 1933 there had been a tendency to trim the Washington news bureaus, but in 1934 the capital was "the world's most important news center." Berchtold added that "the New Deal with its use of press agents and its surfeit of news . . . pumped new life into the Washington press corps."[1]

The news turnabout came in large part because of several unique conditions centering around the emergency legislation for the new agencies that specifically earmarked funds for information. Many competent, unemployed journalists were now available to work as publicity agents. Moreover, during FDR's first hundred days in office, new agencies were popping up like springtime dandelions—so fast that there was unprecedented public interest. Everything had become "hot news," from Treasury Department statistics to State Department announcements. Leo Rosten wrote in 1937 that "the public's demand for news in the dramatic days of 1933 was literally insatiable."[2]

The administration had many spokesmen for that hot news. The most preeminent and closest to the president were two members of his secretariat and his wife. The secretariat initially included Louis Howe as the ranking secretary, Steven Early as the press secretary, and Marvin McIntyre as the appointments secretary—all former newspapermen who had been members of

another one of Roosevelt's groups, the Cuff Links Club. Made up of close
personal aides who had been with Roosevelt during the 1920 campaign for
vice president and who had been given souvenir cuff links, the club preserved
its social bonds through special birthday reunions each January 30.[3]

After his election, Roosevelt appointed Louis McHenry Howe as *the*
secretary to the president. Howe, who knew FDR so well, could frequently
see FDR in private to discuss anything. As the preeminent publicity agent,
Howe helped shape both the president's and the New Deal's image. He insisted, for example, that every letter have an individual reply from a personal,
caring president. Howe carefully followed the national media coverage and
helped correct politically dangerous headlines.[4]

Howe fulfilled several media expectations, such as the press's demands for
an *éminence grise,* a behind-the-scenes adviser, much like Woodrow Wilson's
Colonel Edward House. He also could be portrayed as a Machiavellian figure,
an administrative mastermind, an image Roosevelt did not dispel. With his
twenty-three years of intimacy with the president, Howe was not a behind-the-
scenes adviser but an important and skillful administrative spokesman. When
the press's questions or topics became awkward, the secretary would respond
with folksy FDR stories. For example, during a news lull at the end of the first
hundred days, Howe gave the public the rundown on Roosevelt's summer
cruise: the antiaircraft practice; the crew's songs, dancing, and boxing; the
Sunday church services; and a dignified picture of a deeply worried president
putting "the position of our country beyond question."[5]

Howe used all the available media to communicate the administration's
message. He broadcast a number of Sunday radio programs, which were
useful trial balloons on some specific administration proposal. He criticized
the current laws and gave an inside story of the administration's actions. He
also wrote articles for the *Saturday Evening Post, Liberty, American Magazine,* and *Cosmopolitan* on such topics as national crime— "Uncle Sam Starts
after Crime"—and economic recovery— "Balanced Government, the Next
Step." Howe added to the growing Roosevelt folklore with pieces entitled
"Behind the Scenes with the President" and "The Winner," which portrayed
the president as a "perfectly impossible young man" who, refusing to bow to
the political bosses, had carried the noble banner of popular government
relentlessly for twenty-two years.[6]

Howe set up an organized press intelligence bulletin—informally called
"Howe's Daily Bugle"—as a kind of public seismograph. The secretary
supervised the combing of hundreds of the country's daily newspapers. In an
era before refined public opinion polling and reliance on survey statistics,
Howe made sure that twenty-five or so research workers summarized by topic
the major editorial issues of the day. To give the administration the nation's
state of mind, he included a synopsis of the public's letters to the president.

The "Bugle," sometimes as long as 125 single-spaced, typewritten pages, went not only to the president but also to every important government official. This prototype of the current White House daily news summary was consolidated with the Office of War Information bulletins in 1942 before temporarily going out of business in 1947.[7]

Although ill by 1935, Howe kept toying with several motion picture ideas for the 160th anniversary of the signing of the Declaration of Independence that would be in keeping with the "New Dealish" theme for the 1936 campaign. After Howe's death in April 1936, columnist Raymond Clapper quoted Ernest K. Lindley's overall assessment that Howe was "an idea man, a publicity stunt man more than a censor." Although his greatest impact had been as FDR's political mentor and press adviser during the pre-presidential days, Howe's communication lessons continued to blend with the president's own astute ability. Howe also encouraged Eleanor Roosevelt's press conference activities and her Gridiron-widow's parties and acted as her literary agent.[8]

Eleanor Roosevelt played a far more active publicity role than had other first ladies. As the president's roving emissary, she functioned as FDR's physical contact with the outside world and as information gatherer. More than any other administration spokesperson, she became a public figure in her own right with her unusual activities.[9]

One of her most innovative steps was to hold her own weekly press meetings. When her traveling companion and White House guest, Lorena Hickok of the Associated Press, originated the idea of regular press conferences that would be limited to women reporters, Louis Howe was delighted and gave Mrs. Roosevelt pointers on handling "loaded questions." She later recalled, "I was able to detect the implication of the questions and avoided any direct answer. Louis Howe trained me well."[10]

Two days before the president began his first press conferences, she met with female correspondents in the Red Room of the White House for what became mutually beneficial meetings. These were usually held on Mondays at 11 A.M. Eleanor Roosevelt at first had no special headline-making items, and, unlike the president, she readily allowed direct quotations. If she could not answer a particular question, she often obtained the information in time for the next press conference.[11]

The dynamic first lady was so newsworthy that the journalists wanted access to her. Since she limited the meetings to women only, such all-male Washington press bureaus as the Associated Press were forced to hire women to cover her. Initially, journalists labeled those early meetings as "girlish," where the White House menus, the social events, and the children were discussed. She soon changed the focus to political news by holding joint press conferences with female governmental officials, such as Secretary of Labor Frances Perkins. She also gave political insights into the president's new programs and her own current pet projects. Newspaperwomen traveled with her on her inspection tours, such as to the capital's depressed areas. Her exposure of problems set a news agenda, and Washington correspondents were then forced to ask the president about the situation at his press conference.[12]

Although FDR did not attend her meetings, she would sit knitting and then comment at some of his press conferences, especially those held in Hyde Park. There, she would give greetings, answer the president's questions directed at her, make remarks to correct a potentially erroneous impression, and even ask FDR questions herself.[13]

Eleanor Roosevelt further promoted the administration and herself by being a journalist. With her magazine articles, books, newspaper columns, and radio speeches, she assisted the president as a public extension of the administration. When she was asked to do a newspaper series on White House customs for both the McNaught and the Columbia syndicates, she included remarks about federal housing, health, and other agency work. Begun in 1935, her popular "My Day" column grew from 40 to 135 newspaper members by 1940. The column recounted her daily events and occasionally commented on administrative affairs. Sometimes she responded to rumors, such as the time she denied the government was paying rent to the president's mother while he was at Hyde Park in the summer. She also tested public opinion on various issues, such as wage and price controls in 1941. When reporters questioned the president, he admitted that the subject was indeed being considered.[14]

In 1940 her radio series became a campaign issue, not because of what she discussed—life in the White House and other family topics—but because she received money for doing so. The political charges of being a "money-grubber" included accusations that she had not paid her fair share of federal income taxes on those fees. She insisted that her radio pay went directly to the American Friends' Service Committee.[15]

Steve Early, the president's press secretary, who also oversaw Eleanor Roosevelt's press relations, tried to lessen the embarrassing stories about her radio and lecture fees. He also placated those news reporters who worried about the First Lady's scoops on the Roosevelt children's weddings or other newsworthy events. At the same time, he encouraged the correspondents to use Mrs. Roosevelt's expertise on social programs, such as subsistence homesteads. Once he wired McIntyre, who was aboard the president's train, that "she is an expert authority on Arthurdale and I am sure her comment will be of great value to the newspaper members of the party."[16]

Early's status within the administration was based on his long-term friendship with the Roosevelts as well as his ability. His relationship went back to Roosevelt's navy days and the 1920 election campaign, when Early had been FDR's campaign advance man. As an Associated Press correspondent, Early scooped all other journalists by reporting President Warren G. Harding's death in San Francisco. He gained a reputation as one of the top reporters in the country. He also had visual experience, having worked with the newly formed Paramount Newsreel Company as its Washington editor from 1927 until 1932. The day after FDR's election, the president-elect asked Early to join his administration as his secretary in charge of press relations.[17]

Early was the first presidential "press secretary," the first secretary whose title and duties meant a singular devotion to news. Journalists began using longer versions of the title on March 5, 1933, when the AP story in the *Washington Star* called Early "President Roosevelt's press liaison secretary" to distinguish him from other secretaries. By 1934 newspapers such as the *Toledo News-Bee* began using the expression the "President's press relations secretary."[18]

Early became both the director and the producer of Roosevelt's publicity. He had closely followed Howe's public relations techniques during the pre-presidential days, and when Howe died, Early moved into his office. Roosevelt described Early's duties: "He has also arranged to have a scheduled time each morning at which to meet members of the press for the purpose of giving them the White House background, or, in the parlance of the newspaper, the 'White House slant' on the current news of the day." The president also referred to Early's role as being "able to give the information necessary to keep the correspondents from printing inaccurate stories."[19]

While Early directed New Deal publicity, he focused on the president's press conferences as important for setting the executive branch's news agenda. He banished the ten-year-old indirect attribution, "the White House spokesman," and the twelve-year-old written-question requirement. He was the one who suggested that the president hold special press seminars on the budget, treaties, and governmental reorganization. On press conference days, he chatted with the president "on possible subjects for discussion by him" and "went over material for his afternoon conferences with the press," which he collected from various administrative units. Although Early rarely recorded these discussions, an occasional memorandum to the president, such as this one on October 28, 1941, indicates his carefully thought-out preparation:

1. You might tell the Press today that you have agreed to address the international labor organization on Wed., Nov. 5, in East Room of White House. Lubin thinks such an announcement by you to the Press would stimulate interest in meetings the delegates are now holding.
2. State Department wants comment on the fact one year ago Mussolini attacked Greece.
3. You may be asked this afternoon what you consider to be the most important current issue question now before the country. I told the Press this morning that you consider increased production to be the paramount question.

That afternoon, the president followed Early's suggestions.[20]

Early also assisted during the press conferences. Roosevelt would ask him to look up something or give out material, or he might point out that "Steve wanted me to stress that all this is in confidence until the Message is released and that nothing is to be said in advance of the release." At the same time, Early carefully monitored FDR's answers, clarified his statements, and sometimes even answered for him. Ever conscious of the final news product, Early even changed the mode of questioning and set a new agenda. After the correspondents kept asking abut the growing European confrontation, Early privately suggested to the president that he give out a family story about his sons' induction into the Shriners. If the most senior wire service man did not end a press meeting soon enough to stop a line of questioning, Early would shout, "Let's go." Once in 1938 Early committed the unprecedented act of filling in for the president at a scheduled presidential press conference. During the war Early increasingly spoke for the president (see chapter 10).[21]

As a careful listener and strict keeper of the press conference rules, Early sometimes intervened to label the president's statements with a quip, "the latter part is off the record." As mentioned, at the first press conference, he had warned the correspondents that he would make an example of anyone who violated the president's confidence. As noted in chapter 4, he was also quick to remind journalists about a rule infraction with a letter and a request for an article revision. Correspondent Ruth Finney remembered he "would wreak vengeance upon you if you broke the rule and would not answer questions at the daily press conferences and refuse to answer your calls." The *New York Times* often was in trouble about premature releases, and Early used the Secret Service to investigate its budget disclosures.[22]

As the White House gatekeeper of information, Early rarely traveled with the president. While Early "minded the store," Appointments Secretary Marvin McIntyre or Early's assistant, William Hassett, filled in as press secretary on the road. Early still kept a close watch on the president's news, and during one news lull he wrote to Hassett, "Thought this would make a story for you to give the newspaper men with you since there probably would be little else to give them." Neither McIntyre nor Hassett had Early's refined publicity acumen, however. In fact, the appointments secretary had some White House coordination problems; both Early and the president counseled McIntyre on what to say at his press briefings.[23]

Early followed a regular schedule of breakfast with the president to discuss his daily plans. About 10:30 the press secretary met with the White House correspondents and related the president's appointments, congressional messages, executive orders, conferences, signed documents, and upcoming speeches. Although much of what was to happen was given out in press releases at the daily press briefings, the reporters usually asked Early five or six questions, with at least one concerning another correspondent's or columnist's story.[24]

Early used other news management techniques as well. While he enforced an unwritten rule that the correspondents could not use information overheard in the secretaries' offices, especially the presidential reception room, he did arrange interviews with the president's visitors. He also suggested editorial material on dull news days and a story "slant," particularly for his friend Raymond Clapper. After seeing Roy Howard's negative editorials about the defense buildup, he suggested that Roosevelt appeal to Howard's vanity with an offer to be unofficial Latin American ambassador. Sensing a human interest story, Early once secretly arranged for a former slave of President Andrew Johnson to visit Washington and meet the president, and then he "leaked" the story.[25]

Both Early and the president carefully followed such news management efforts. When Roosevelt traveled, Early sent a compilation of the front-page headlines about the administration. He checked the news with the United Press daily bulletins coming into his office from 9 A.M. to 9 P.M. As the one individual with responsibility for overall press coverage, Early would have "to take it on the chin" from FDR when the stories were unfavorable, as they were in 1937 when Roosevelt proposed packing the Supreme Court.[26]

Early added to the favorable news coverage of the president and the administration by making sure that especially good editorials complimenting the administration were used as speech material or published in the *Congressional Record*. In addition, after Howe's death, Early wrote articles for such popular magazines as the *Saturday Evening Post, Cosmopolitan,* and *Redbook* about how the president worked, the mistaken fears about propaganda, and his "Below the Belt" file of "biased" stories. He edited important documents before they were released and proposed changes in the National Emergency Council report, which had used tables and statistics to imply that economic recovery had begun as early as 1932.[27]

With his knack for public relations, he could "play" a story and daily build a front-page headline and an audience for presidential speeches and radio addresses. He scheduled the radio time for FDR's broadcasts, dribbled the publicity to build a large audience, and kept charts to show the fluctuations in the audience sizes. Samual Rosenman, one of FDR's speech writers, recalled that Early "never hesitated to tell the President or us what he thought of a speech or any part of it." Just as he followed the newspaper accounts, Early monitored other political leaders' broadcasts. Ever jealous of any competition with Roosevelt's radio prestige, Early resented Churchill's ability in the medium that his chief had so long monopolized.[28]

Because of his previous work with Paramount films, Early knew how to monitor FDR's visual image. He would not allow photographs to be taken in the White House without permission. Upholding the strong taboo against any pictorial depiction of the president's physical handicap, he granted permission only for ceremonial occasions, speeches, or formal group portraits. He gave the news photographers tips on forthcoming events and carefully planned the newsreel coverage of selected portions of the president's speeches to avoid an oversaturation of the medium. He favored Paramount with inside information, and the company in turn gave the president a film copy of every presidential story it released.[29]

Steve Early was intensely opposed to any direct press censorship, right up to Pearl Harbor. The press secretary frequently tried to convince the president that American journalism should not be judged by its most partisan units, but Grace Tully recounted that Early thought Roosevelt often ignored his advice. Once, when Donald Richberg of the Executive Council proposed that some kind of regular government bulletin on official information bypass the press and directly transmit information to the public, Early vehemently argued against it: "To date I have been but a mild zephyr, moving gently and creating only a slight and occasional disturbance. If the government is to publish officially 'the Federal Register,' my barometer would drop immediately to new lows, registering in the cyclone or hurricane areas. In brief, I shall oppose the project with every ounce of energy and power I have." Early continued opposing such a bulletin, even during the war.[30]

Although Franklin D. Roosevelt might have determined much of his own good relationship with the White House reporters, Steve Early was immensely helpful to the busy president. His public influence became so effective that he was recognized as an administrative spokesman. The country came to accept stories attributed to "Stephen T. Early, Press Secretary to the President." Given the authority of his daily briefings, correspondents gave his word almost as much importance as that credited to Franklin Roosevelt himself.[31]

As press secretary, Early was also the overseer of executive department and agency publicity. Right after the 1932 election, Early began coordinating the administration's entire press relations by studying previous publicity methods, going over the record of a department's press officer, drawing up plans for revision, and replacing many press officers with the more energetic and imaginative members of the press corps. By January 1933 Early was sending such memoranda as "How to Call a Press Conference" to nominated administrators. On January 12, 1933, he sent Frank Walker these directions:

> Have a notice posted on the Bulletin board of the Press Club.
> Telephone Mr. Donalds, Superintendent of the House Press Gallery and ask him to put a notice on the Bulletin Board of the House Press Gallery.
> Telephone Mr. Collins, Superintendent of the Senate Press Gallery and ask him to put a notice on the Bulletin Board of the Senate Press Gallery.

Telephone the Press Room at the White House and ask one of the newspapermen there to announce it, or telephone Mr. Early's office and ask that it
advise the newspapermen there.

Telephone the Press Room of the Treasury Department and ask that one of the
newspapermen there put a notice on the Bulletin Board. For your information,
Mr. Robert Thornberg is the President of the Treasury Department Correspondents' Association.[32]

Breaking with the previous presidential policy of employing party hacks for
information officers, Early put in experienced journalists who enjoyed the
confidence of their colleagues. Although the press secretary took some journalists directly from newspapers, he hired mostly victims of depression lay-
offs, newspaper closures, and management changes. Early had great empathy
for the jobless reporters and even created a number of new $1,500-a-year
positions for them. Journalists appreciated such efforts, which in many cases
meant that they were hired on an emergency basis just to "tide them over."
Early directed, "Do your job just like you were working for a newspaper."[33]

The Roosevelt administration was not starting something new with information officers and an organized publicity program. It just revived a public
relations effort that had been coordinated by the World War I Committee on
Public Information. The system had expanded during the 1920s, when so many
news releases, clipsheets, and boiler-plate items went out that the Hoover
administration was spending over $3 million a year on handouts alone. Early
refined the system to the point that, as Delbert Clark wrote, "the White House
relations with the correspondents were put on a really systematic basis."[34]

The Roosevelt administration needed professional information officers who
could formulate, dramatize, and communicate information for the departments. Since the success of the New Deal programs demanded the widest
possible public support, the executive branch had to have an aggressive campaign of public information to advertise the agencies' services, to justify the
bureau's usefulness to the citizen, and to garner support from Congress.[35]

Individual press agents ran miniature news operations based on Steve Early's White House format. Early wanted to coordinate the president's public
utterances with others in the executive branch to create an overall positive
effect. The publicity agents from various bureaus attended FDR's press conferences, and they in turn informed their chiefs on the tack the president had
taken on various pertinent issues. These public information officers coordinated the information flow of each agency to follow the White House model.
To maximize personal contact with the press, each department arranged press
conferences for cabinet chiefs and agency officials and had someone available
to answer reporters' questions. The officers wrote speeches and magazine
articles for the department chiefs, determined publicity strategy for support,
and designed campaigns to cover negative actions. Like Steve Early, they sent

complaints to the managing editors about recalcitrant reporters who wrote "unfair" stories. They released a flood of mimeographed press material, "handouts," consisting of advance copies of addresses, texts of public announcements, statistics, official reports, rationalizations, and the necessary "inside stuff." Their handouts became so much a part of the information process that once after the president began his press conference with the usual "What is the news?" the correspondents retorted with "What is the handout?" The president's reply was, "There isn't any. I have to work it out."[36]

Roosevelt and Early experimented with one overall coordinating agency after another. In August 1933 the National Recovery Administration established the Division of Press Intelligence to compile a newspaper and magazine clipping service on national reaction to government. In July 1935 the Division of Press Intelligence was transferred to the National Emergency Council (NEC), which encompassed all cabinet members, agency chiefs, and their information officers. One of its divisions became the United States Information Service, an information clearinghouse for answering the public's questions on emergency activities. After the NEC was abolished July 1, 1939, all its information functions were transferred to the Office of Government Reports (OGR) as part of the newly created Executive Office of the President.[37]

Still experimenting, the president appointed Lowell Mellett, chief of the Office of Government Reports and former editor of the *Washington Daily News,* as one of his six assistants. Roosevelt called him a "general handy man" at an October 1940 press conference. News releases were not a function of OGR, yet Mellett did take over some of Early's former duties by appointing information officers and by formulating an overall information policy. Mellett's role was not to be so public. When the correspondents asked Roosevelt if Mellett would "have any connections with press relations," the president retorted, "I don't know. I haven't the faintest idea." He later admitted at that same press conference that Mellett would still keep a "fatherly eye" on the OGR. Mellett and the OGR were later absorbed into the Office of War Information.[38]

Agency information was distributed not only through the NEC but also through congressional channels. In practice, the White House used Congress for flooding the country with New Deal activities. The press secretary would have friendly members of Congress place material in the *Congressional Record* to mail later with their franking privileges. Sympathetic congressional representatives also sent out postcards with brief messages, reprints of the fireside chats, and other important statements. On May 19, 1938, Early wrote Colonel Edwin A. Halsey, secretary of the Senate, "You did such noble work last year with the summaries which we furnished you concerning activities and accomplishments of various government agencies that I am having similar material prepared this year. Here is the first installment—T.V.A. accomplishments. I will leave it to you to handle this in the way in which you are so adapt."[39]

The White House also coordinated and publicized administrators' speeches to sell the administration's proposals. Early requested and edited the major officials' articles and speeches and made numerous publicity suggestions. He once stopped Interior Secretary Harold Ickes from making a forceful attack against Congressman Martin Dies with a speech entitled "Playing with Loaded Dies." Early wanted the clipsheets of signed articles distributed by the Democratic National Committee to small-town and rural newspapers for lazy editors. Roosevelt often became involved during crises, such as the furor over the bill to pack the Supreme Court. Ickes noted in his diary that the president "outlined several things that he would like to have me say when I speak before the joint session of the Texas Legislature on Friday."[40]

Roosevelt's usual style of open, regular press conferences influenced the rest of the administration. Secretary of Labor Frances Perkins contended that the president had set a tone of openness for keeping the press informed about everything that was going on. By seeing the press regularly, "he whetted its appetite." Cabinet members and agency heads held their own regular press conferences, each suited to the official's own personality. Secretary of State Cordell Hull's daily dignified soirees contrasted with Jim Farley's weekly first-name informality. Attorney General Cummings gave out cigars, while Secretary of Labor Perkins gave out mimeographed statements which she read. When Roosevelt reduced his press conferences in 1936, the officials frequently canceled their press meetings too.[41]

When the president was open, the expectation was that the cabinet officers would be too. When Acting Secretary of the Treasury Henry Morgenthau, Jr., tried to limit access to his meetings and gave a general order that all departmental news must come only from him or his press agent, he created a furor. The correspondents protested to the president about the "rigid restrictions," and the gag order was immediately rescinded. There was a similar outcry when Ickes issued a similar closure, which he soon retracted.[42]

Ickes, who was also the public works administrator, expanded his press contacts and met with numerous regional correspondents at his twice-a-week press meetings. Those same reporters also covered federal relief administrator Harry Hopkins's press conferences, which were held immediately after Ickes's sessions. The timing of these two press meetings, the overlapping of both officials' jobs, and their inexperience in answering press questions did much to keep alive the famous Ickes-Hopkins feud. Reporters invariably began Hopkins's press conferences with "Secretary Ickes just said. . . ." Hopkins would give a quick retort, usually mixed with quotable spicy comments and an often unprintable profanity. Hopkins's remarks made splashy headlines, such as when he said the critics were "too damn dumb" to understand the

Public Works Administration activities. At the same time, the journalists' interpretations of these clashes of opinion raised vital public-policy questions concerning the possible solutions to the depression.[43]

Most government officials, uninitiated in the ways of the journalists, found meeting with the press a difficult task. Frances Perkins had problems in coping with the reporters' speculative nature and their thirst for background information. She once complained that if an official refused to tell the correspondents what he was thinking, "he was described in terms such as 'Secretary Refuses to Deal with Unemployment,' " and then she recounted that if the official "told the press the pros and cons not yet assembled, much less explained, the tendency was to report something like 'Secretary Planning All-Insurance,' which alarmed many readers." It was a difficult situation for any neophyte.[44]

President Roosevelt, ever cognizant of the officials' press relations problems, was soon advising his department chiefs and their press officers on the fundamental techniques of news management. During one National Emergency Council meeting, he warned,

> If some reporter says to you, "Mr. so-and-so makes such and such a remark (referring to somebody in another department); what do you think of it?", the practice had been to comment upon it in the past, in altogether too many instances. There is a definite reason why you should not, and a definite rule not to comment on it at all. In the first place, it catches you cold; you haven't studied it. In the second place, the quotation that is made to you by this member of the press is so phrased, in many cases, as not to represent what the other department actually said. There are many phases of those questions, many trick ways of putting things.

Roosevelt then cautioned against the "loose talk" around Washington and said that a news leak "was spread either by amiable people who are friends of the Drew Pearsons and Arthur Krocks, or it is paid for by them."[45]

Such news management lessons were important. With the press demands for information, the publicity bureaus of the new agencies were sending out thousands of press releases and other information yearly. The National Recovery Administration (NRA) and Agriculture Adjustment Administration (AAA) had so many people that they organized their press sections like the city room of a metropolitan newspaper. Publicity agents, like managing editors, directed the policy and supervised reporters, rewrite people, copyreaders, statisticians, researchers, and special writers. In less than one year, the NRA issued 5,200 handouts and the AAA almost 5,000. Other complete staffs prepared radio programs and produced motion pictures.[46]

The efforts could be effective. The country, greatly interested in the New Deal activities, wanted the legitimate news story. The administration set an effective "news agenda." There were numerous studies on such efforts. In the

1939 study *Government Publicity,* James L. McCamy found that during a seven-week period in 1937 the *New York Times* printed 1,281 items which appeared to have been released or influenced by administration publicity offices. Some 15 per cent of all "wire" items outside New York City referred to federal administrative matters. During a seven-week period in 1937, all of the *New York Times* news stories had a strikingly similar news style, according to McCamy. Moreover, the Washington, D.C., news bureaus could not ignore the extensive official information. Bryant Putney found in his 1940 study of federal publicity that during a typical three-day March period the Washington bureau of the *St. Louis Post-Dispatch* received 219 pieces of federal publicity in the mail, an average of 73 pieces a day, with 50 Labor Relations Board releases and 32 Department of Agriculture handouts.[47]

Many correspondents found the administration's efforts quite useful. So much was happening so fast with the administration's new agencies and emergency boards that it was hard for reporters to keep track of it. The agency press conferences and news releases cut down the pressures of newsgathering. Because of the depression, news bureaus in general could not afford to expand enough to meet the new demands. Correspondents who covered more than one agency or department needed those press handouts to explain quickly the changes. With facts at "an elbow," reporters could gain information in minutes without having to telephone different officials, locate knowledgeable people, and gain access. Raymond P. Brandt saw such handouts as efficient aids for assembling the news and as "tips" for stories, and Arthur Krock recounted that the Roosevelt administrative methods improved the quality of technical information.[48]

Yet the administration's efforts did not completely control the output. Many correspondents sought more, especially the popular columnists who tried to gather behind-the-scenes information from other sources, sometimes unauthorized ones. Robert S. Allen, coauthor of the "Daily Washington Merry-Go-Round," recalled that he relied on other officials for his news sources, such as Assistant Secretary of Labor Ed McGrady, Hopkins's economic adviser Leon Henderson, and White House aides Tommy Corcoran and Ben Cohen. He said that "one of my great sources" was Postmaster General James Farley. To get information efficiently, Allen would take the train with Farley, who commuted back to New York City on weekends, and then receive a "big fill-in" before getting off in Baltimore. Allen's partner, Drew Pearson, used the Diplomatic Corps, Interior Secretary Ickes, and Assistant Secretary of State Sumner Welles.[49]

Since the White House knew about the journalists' reliance on these unofficial news sources, Early and others would leak information that had been filtered down from the president. For example, Ickes noted in his diary that during the 1939 controversy over a concert hall for black contralto Marian

Anderson, the president outlined exactly what Ickes should tell Pearson and Allen to refute a story that the vice-president had ignored invitations to hear Miss Anderson sing at the Lincoln Memorial.[50]

Such administrative efforts generated a great deal of criticism. Senators publicly questioned such news management. In a 1934 radio address, Senator Thomas Schall accused the president of censoring economic data and general information concerning the executive branch. Critics both in and out of Congress began to question the size of the press staffs as well as their budgets. Senator Carter Glass suggested that his Committee on Appropriations examine the costs of the noticeable expansion, because "there are more newspapermen now employed in the various bureaus of the Government than are employed on the newspapers themselves." Glass, and others, immediately referred to the 1913 Publicity Act (Title 5, U.S. Code) forbidding appropriations "for the compensation of any publicity expert unless specifically appropriated for that purpose." He said that the administration circumvented "a publicity expert" with the appointments of "editors, editorial assistants, clerks, educational directors, information service representatives" and a dozen other euphemistic titles, even though Congress authorized the new agencies' educational and informational services. Glass asked for inquiries into the "house organs"—such as the NRA's weekly newspaper, *The Blue Eagles,* the AAA's *News Digest,* and the *Consumer Guide.* Such complaints themselves became newsworthy.[51]

During the 1937 congressional debates over the executive branch reorganization plan, the Senate hired the Brookings Institute to investigate such publicity efforts. The institute found that thirteen of the government's major agencies had spent $78,972 a month for 312 press relations employees a year. Following the drop after World War I, the number of Government Printing Office employees had increased from a peak of 5,307 during the war to the current 5,594. Besides raising the question of the administration's possible news advantage, Republican senators publicly complained that the payroll increases and free mailings greatly added to the Post Office Department's losses. In eight years the Post Office postage revenue losses more than quadrupled, increasing from $9.1 million in 1932 to $38.2 million in 1939. The criticism became so hostile that Congress failed to recognize the OGR formally for two years.[52]

Opposition publishers and their organizations labeled the administration's information efforts as "propaganda," especially because the results were spot-news stories. The attorney for the American Newspaper Publishers Association, Elisha Hanson, warned editors in 1935 that the departments had centralized news to the point that most of the spot news could be obtained only from established information divisions and nearly always became the front-page stories. Hansen said that the opinion pieces, the syndicated columns, and the editorials could be found only in the lesser-read inside pages. The administration was counteracting the publishers' biases.[53]

Journalists also complained. During 1936 Owen Scott of the *Washington Post* accused publicity agents of designing campaigns to cover the executives' trails. Newspapers such as the *Philadelphia Evening Bulletin* complained that there was no elbow room for taking notes at the president's press conferences in 1937 because so many press agents attended. The *Christian Science Monitor*'s bureau chief, Erwin D. Canham, noted that "the Washington correspondent has to keep his eyes open against new floods of material issued by press agents on the government payrolls," although he went on to add that "if we can't do that we deserve to lose our jobs."[54]

During World War II, Joseph H. Mader of Marquette University wrote that the administration's publicity efforts closed off hitherto open news sources. According to many correspondents, the only news access was through the press officers. Mader argued that the effect was to siphon away all the inconvenient, embarrassing, and unfavorable news, resulting in what might be called a dictatorship over the minds of Americans. Two retired correspondents, Robert Allen and Eddie Folliard, later remembered that the press had been less critical of this administration than of any other. Folliard labeled Roosevelt "the Master Manipulator."[55]

The old manner of "covering" Washington was out of style, out of date, and out of step during the Roosevelt years. An expanded federal government made the task of reporting so complicated that the average correspondent needed to be able to go to an appropriate official without spending days or wasting the time of others in aimless inquiry. Roosevelt and his spokespeople, such as Louis Howe, Eleanor Roosevelt, and especially his chief press secretary Steve Early, all helped both the administration and the reporters by making their newsgathering easier. The White House's coordinated informational efforts were an efficient means for disseminating information about the official facts and official versions of events.

While it might have been necessary for the Roosevelt administration to interpret and justify its programs, to publicize its achievements, and even to dramatize policies, these needs ran squarely into the traditional skepticism about political power and a too cozy relationship with the press. There was indeed an incentive for the press to accept the official version of what was happening, as noted by the McCamy study. The administration's press system could conceal government acts of which the public was not apprised. By controlling the news access, the administration could also rob the correspondents of other sources and influence their mental processes and approaches to public questions. As Arthur Krock wrote in 1935, "The channel system would completely substitute the dead printed leaflet—what we call the handout—for the warm and living speech of public men. Since governments are

made up of men and not of acts, the system defeats to this degree the legitimate will of the people to know the kind of men and women to whom they
have entrusted the conduct of affairs."[56]

With so many former journalists now employed as public information
officers speaking for the government, there was a symbiotic relationship between the government and the press: journalists were explaining the Roosevelt
administration by talking to fellow journalists. The correspondents not only
were acquainted with the new information officers but also were, at least
initially, sympathetic because the administration offered so many unemployed
newsmen jobs. Republicans had valid concerns that journalists would present
the Roosevelt administration in a favorable light, and they voiced their fears in
no uncertain terms.[57]

The administration's critics correctly feared possible propaganda. The
propaganda of the Nazis and the Communists and the demagoguery of Huey
P. Long and Father Coughlin received a great deal of coverage in American
newspapers of the 1930s. The falsity of their statements did not keep such
demagoguery from being published, especially with a press interested in
startling as well as informing. In fact, the American press had few effective
techniques for preventing skillful propagandists from bending the newspapers
to their own strategy.

Despite the president's own statement—"I have not tried to create a publicity bureau for the administration or to 'plant' stories on its behalf. . . ."—
Franklin D. Roosevelt and Stephen T. Early did just that. They and others in
the Roosevelt administration certainly made an attempt to play the Washington game well. By aiding the press in their work and particularly by aiding
the journalists personally, they maximized positive results for the administration. Despite the efforts of some correspondents to look beyond the official
versions to other news sources, the McCamy analysis showed that the president's attempts to coordinate information and set the news agenda worked
well. Indeed, Franklin D. Roosevelt made every attempt to control those
"sheep to be poached."[58]

Notes

1. Arthur M. Schlesinger, Jr., *The Coming of the New Deal,* Vol. 2 of *The Age of
Roosevelt* (Boston: Houghlin Mifflin, 1959), p. 526; William E. Berchtold, "Press
Agents of the New Deal," *New Outlook,* July 26, 1934, p. 24.

2. Leo C. Rosten, *The Washington Correspondents* (New York: Harcourt, Brace,
1937), p. 70.

3. The cuff links had the initials of F.D.R. on one side and the initials of the
individual recipient on the other. Besides Howe, Early, and McIntyre, the original
members were Charles H. McCarthy, Thomas Lynch, Kirke L. Simpson, Stanley

Prenosil, and James P. Sullivan. Then others included Samuel I. Rosenman, Henry Morgenthau, Jr., Basil O'Connor, and Henry Hooker. The following close associates were added during the White House years: Harry Hopkins, Ross McIntire, Edwin "Pa" Watson, and Robert Sherwood. Robert E. Sherwood, *Roosevelt and Hopkins: An Intimate History* (New York: Harper and Brothers, 1948), p. 941, n. 206.

4. References to Howe's important role include Grace Tully, *F.D.R., My Boss* (New York: Charles Scribner's Sons, 1949), pp. 136–37; Leila A. Sussman, "F.D.R. and White House Mail," *Public Opinion Quarterly* 20 (Spring 1956): 5–16; and Alfred B. Rollins, Jr., *Roosevelt and Howe* (New York: Knopf, 1962), p. 404.

5. Rollins, *Roosevelt and Howe*, pp. 424, plus 369, 376. Howe was aware of the funny figure he cut, and he often joked with reporters that he and Mrs. Roosevelt were running a contest to see which of them could find their ugliest newsphoto. For those press questions at the end of the hundred days, Rollins uses the radio script, July 8, 1933, Official File (henceforth OF) 36, Franklin D. Roosevelt Library (henceforth FDRL).

6. Rollins, *Roosevelt and Howe*, pp. 421, 423. Howe cleared many of the scripts with the president himself. See references in Frank Freidel, *Launching the New Deal*, Vol. 4 of *Franklin D. Roosevelt* (Boston: Little, Brown, 1973), p. 281. Louis M. Howe, "Uncle Sam Starts after Crime," *Saturday Evening Post*, July 29, 1933, pp. 5–6, 71–72, and "Balanced Government, the Next Step," *American Magazine*, June 1933, pp. 11–12, 84–86.

7. Slight references were made to the "Bugle" in Lela Stiles, *The Man behind Roosevelt* (Cleveland and New York: World Publishing, 1954), p. 249; and Cedric Larson, "How Much Federal Publicity Is There?" *Public Opinion Quarterly* 2 (October 1938): 638. For examples of these news summaries, see Guy T. Helvering to Howe, April 19, 1934, and the report of 234 newspaper editorial opinions on one FDR veto, Louis M. Howe Papers, FDRL.

8. Raymond Clapper Diary, May 10, 1936, Raymond Clapper Papers (henceforth RCP), Manuscripts Division, Library of Congress (henceforth LofC). See Rollins, *Roosevelt and Howe*, p. 426, and Stiles, *The Man behind Roosevelt*, pp. 297, 448, for Howe's motion picture ideas. Undoubtedly, Louis Howe had some effect on the determination of administrative policy at first, but certainly not a fraction of what journalists ascribed to him at the time. See Freidel, *Launching the New Deal*, p. 65.

9. Betty Houchin Winfield, "Anna Eleanor Roosevelt's White House Legacy: The Public First Lady," *Presidential Studies Quarterly* 13 (Spring 1988): 331–45.

10. Steve Early to Mrs. Charles Bond, February 7, 1934, OF 36, FDRL; Stiles, *The Man behind Roosevelt*, p. 264. See also as a summary, Tully, *F.D.R., My Boss*, p. 146; Ruby Black, *Eleanor Roosevelt: A Biography* (New York: Duell, Sloan and Pearce, 1940), pp. 161, 296.

11. Hickok made technical reports on her investigative trips. Betty H. Winfield, "Mrs. Roosevelt's Press Conference Association: The First Lady Shines a Light," *Journalism History* 8 (Summer 1981): 54–55, 63–67.

12. Winfield, "Mrs. Roosevelt's Press Conference Association"; Ruth Finney Allen, interview at her home in Washington, D.C., June 8, 1976; Maurine Beasley, *The White House Press Conferences of Eleanor Roosevelt* (New York: Garland, 1983); Black, *Eleanor Roosevelt*, p. 163; Franklin D. Roosevelt, *Complete Presidential Press*

Conferences of Franklin D. Roosevelt (New York: Da Capo, 1972), Press Conference (henceforth PC) 622, February 9, 1940, Vol. 15: 146–47.

13. For examples, see Roosevelt, *Complete Press Conferences*, PC 132, June 22, 1934, Vol. 3: 429; PC 140, August 29, 1934, Vol. 4: 34, 38; PC 160, November 23, 1934, Vol. 4: 230.

14. As a journalist, Eleanor Roosevelt joined the American Newspaper Guild, the first first lady ever to belong to a labor union. Her books included *A Trip to Washington with Bobby and Betty* (1935), *It's Up to the Women* (1933), *This Is My Story* (1937), and *This Troubled World* (1938). Black, *Eleanor Roosevelt*, pp. 112–15, 167; Marquis W. Childs, *I Write from Washington* (New York: Harper and Brothers, 1942), p. 233. For a full discussion, see Maurine H. Beasley's *Eleanor Roosevelt and the Media: A Public Quest for Self-Fulfillment* (Urbana: University of Illinois Press, 1987).

15. Black, *Eleanor Roosevelt*, pp. 111–12. For news control of the issue, see Steven E. Schoenherr, "Selling the New Deal: Stephen T. Early's Role as Press Secretary to Franklin D. Roosevelt" (Ph.D. dissertation, University of Delaware, 1976), pp. 30–31.

16. Concerning potentially embarrassing stories, see Early to Mrs. Roosevelt, June 23, 1937, November 2, 1937, and October 21, 1940, Stephen T. Early Papers (henceforth STEP), FDRL. For the Arthurdale suggestion, see Early Memorandum to Marvin McIntyre, May 26, 1938, STEP, FDRL.

17. Schoenherr, "Selling the New Deal," pp. 33, 35, 37.

18. For a general reference to being the "first designated press secretary," see F. B. Marbut, *News from the Capital: The Story of Washington Reporting* (Carbondale: Southern Illinois University Press, 1971), p. 178. Exact references to the title were found in the *Washington Star*, March 5, 1933, *Toledo News-Bee*, (n.d.) July 1934, and *Washington Times-Herald*, March 5, 1941, White House Scrapbooks, STEP, FDRL.

19. Franklin D. Roosevelt, *The Public Papers and Addresses of Franklin D. Roosevelt*, Vol. 2, Samuel I. Rosenman, ed. (New York: Random House, 1938–50), p. 39. See also "Office of Howe Ready for Early," *Washington Post*, December 16, 1936, White House Newspaper Scrapbooks, Vols. 13–16, FDRL.

20. Early Diary, in particular the entries of March 7, 1934, and February 15, 1935, STEP, FDRL. For the quotation, see Steve Early Memorandum to Franklin D. Roosevelt, October 28, 1941, STEP, FDRL; Roosevelt, *Complete Press Conferences*, PC 779, October 28, 1941, Vol. 18: 260.

For other compilations, see Nancy Foler to Early, October 10, 1937, OF 36, FDRL. For suggestions used at the president's press conferences, see STE to the President, March 3, 1938, STEP, FDRL; Roosevelt, *Complete Press Conferences*, PC 439, March 4, 1938, Vol. 11: 208–12; STE to the President, n.d., 1938, STEP, FDRL; and Roosevelt, *Complete Press Conferences*, PC 448, June 21, 1938, Vol. 11: 476–77.

21. In order of text reference, Roosevelt, *Complete Press Conferences*, PC 300, June 2, 1936, Vol. 7: 281–82; PC 148, October 5, 1934, Vol. 4: 104; PC 88, January 15, 1934, Vol. 3: 65; PC 266, January 14, 1937, Vol. 7: 72; PC 307, July 10, 1936, Vol. 8: 15; PC 313, August 7, 1936, Vol. 8: 62. For other examples, see ibid., PC 246, November 6, 1935, Vol. 6: 250; PC 86, January 10, 1934, Vol. 3: 58. As a substitute, Early filled in for PC 485-A, September 23, 1938, Vol. 12: 100–105.

Raymond Clapper's Reference File includes a clipping noting that Early signaled the senior wire service man to close the conference with "Thank You, Mr. President." See James Butler, "Turning Point in Press Relations of FDR Seen," n.d., Clapper Reference File, Box 110, RCP, LofC.

22. Roosevelt, *Complete Press Conferences,* PC 685, October 1, 1940, Vol. 16: 244. For the first press meeting, see Clapper Diary, March 8, 1933, Box 8, RCP, LofC. For warnings, Early to Byron Price, June 3, 1935, OF 36, FDRL; FDR Memorandum to Early, September 4, 1939, President's Secretary's File (henceforth PSF), FDRL; Ruth Finney Allen, interview, June 8, 1976. For difficulties with the *New York Times,* see OF 144b re Scotty Reston, October 12, 1943, FDRL; Krock to Early, February 23, 1942, STEP, FDRL; Early to Krock, and Krock to Early, January 27, 1942, STEP, FDRL; Early PC, January 27, 1942, STEP, FDRL. Early had Colonel Starling of the Secret Service undertake an investigation concerning confidential budget documents that had been published. See Early Memorandum to Colonel Starling, December 31, 1940, STEP, FDRL.

23. STE Memoranda for Bill Hassett, January 10, 1941, STEP, FDRL. "Mac" held his briefings in Poughkeepsie when the president was at Hyde Park, eight miles away.

Clipping from Thomas W. Phelps, "Reporters' Friend," *Wall Street Journal,* September 11, 1934, OF 36, FDRL, stated that McIntyre was slated for Early's job initially, but that at the last moment "wiser councils prevailed." See Paul W. Ward, "Roosevelt Keeps His Vow," *The Nation,* September 25, 1935, p. 348.

For suggestions to McIntyre, see FDR Memorandum to McIntyre, July 1933, *F.D.R., His Personal Letters, 1928–1945,* Vol. 1, Elliott Roosevelt, ed. (New York: Duell, Sloan and Pearce, 1950), p. 356–57; Russell Young et al. Memorandum to McIntyre, April 9, 1934, OF 36, FDRL. McIntyre was on leave for two years when he contracted tuberculosis in 1941, and he died in 1943.

24. See Early to Nan Pavey, May 14, 1937, OF 36, FDRL; Stephen T. Early Press Conferences, STEP, FDRL. For daily briefings, see Delbert Clark, "Steve Takes Care of It," *New York Times Magazine,* July 27, 1941, p. 11.

25. In reference to overheard information, see Early to Jerome B. Cowden, October 27, 1933, OF 36, FDRL; Early to Logan C. Harding, March 10, 1936, President's Personal File (henceforth PPF), FDRL. Clapper Diary, October 26, 1933, Box 8, RCP, LofC. Or, for other examples, see Early to I. A. Fulharty, n.d., November-December 1936, OF 300, FDRL; Early to Dorothy Dunbar Bromley, June 2, 1933, PPF, FDRL. For handling Howard's vanity, see Early Memorandum for the President, May 23, 1940, PSF, FDRL. In reference to the former slave, see Harold L. Ickes, *The Secret Diary of Harold L. Ickes,* Vol. 2 (New York: Simon and Schuster, 1954), entry for February 14, 1937, p. 72.

Others who have written about Early's work include George Michael, *Handout* (New York: G. P. Putnam's Sons, 1935), pp. 23, 31–32; Sherwood, *Roosevelt and Hopkins,* p. 207; Douglas MacArthur Bloomfield, "The Presidential Press Secretaries" (M.A. thesis, Ohio State University, 1963), p. 69; and Schoenherr, "Selling the New Deal."

26. Early Memorandum to the President, February 2, 1938, STEP, FDRL; Early to Allen L. Appleton, March 4, 1935, PPF, FDRL; Fauneil J. Rinn, "The Presidential

Press Conference" (Ph.D. dissertation, University of Chicago, 1960), p. 19. Concerning the Court-packing stories, see Ickes, *Secret Diary,* Vol. 2, entry for July 21, 1937, p. 165.

27. For examples of Early's efforts, see Early Memorandum to the President, July 23, 1940, STEP, FDRL; Early to Samuel I. Rosenman, October 2, 1940, STEP, FDRL; Early to Tom Corcoran, February 19, 1937, STEP, FDRL. In particular, see Early's article "Below the Belt," *Saturday Evening Post,* June 10, 1939, pp. 7, 111–12; James MacGregor Burns, *Roosevelt: The Lion and the Fox* (New York: Harcourt, Brace, 1956), p. 269. Early's articles are found in the Reference File, Magazine Articles, STEP, FDRL, and include: "Hobgoblins, 1935 Model," *Redbook,* April 1935; "Supreme Court," *Liberty,* February 24, 1940; "Around the Clock with F.D.R.," *Cosmopolitan,* November 1940; "How the President Works," *Redbook,* July 1943, and "So You Want to See the President," *Saturday Evening Post,* November 13, 1943.

28. Samuel I. Rosenman, *Working with Roosevelt* (New York: Harper and Brothers, 1952), p. 453; Schoenherr, "Selling the New Deal," pp. 109, 113; Bloomfield, "Presidential Press Secretaries," pp. 62, 71; Sherwood, *Roosevelt and Hopkins,* p. 444. In reference to Churchill's radio ability, see Early to McIntyre, June 20, 1939, STEP, FDRL.

29. Richard L. Strout, interview, Washington, D.C., June 2, 1976; Early's instructions to photographers are found in memoranda on January 30, February 2, February 8, and May 15, 1934, OF 36, FDRL, and Montague to Early, August 30, 1933, STEP, FDRL; William E. Leuchtenburg, *Franklin D. Roosevelt and the New Deal, 1932–1940* (New York: Harper and Brothers, 1963), p. 169, n. 3; Rosenman, *Working with Roosevelt,* p. 453. See chapter 6 herein on use of other media.

30. For general information, see Roosevelt, *Complete Press Conferences,* PC 26, June 2, 1933, Vol. 1: 345; Rosenman, *Working with Roosevelt,* pp. 453–54.

Early attempted to keep Roosevelt from dressing down the entire press corps over the column of one writer, according to Tully, *F.D.R., My Boss,* p. 87. In reference to an official information bypass, see Early Memorandum to Louis Howe, November 2, 1934, OF 788, FDRL, as found in Elmer E. Cornwell, Jr., *Presidential Leadership of Public Opinion* (Bloomington: Indiana University Press, 1965), p. 212.

31. Marbut, *News from the Capital,* p. 178.

32. Clark, "Steve Takes Care Of It," p. 11. For calling a press conference, see Early Memorandum for Frank Walker, January 12, 1933, STEP, FDRL.

33. Marvin McIntyre Memorandum to Steve Early, November 1, 1933, and Early to McIntyre, November 2, 1933, OF 36, FDRL; Raymond Clapper, "Telling the World," undated clipping, Clapper Reference File, Censorship, 1934–36, Box 110, RCP, LofC.

34. Delbert Clark, *Washington Dateline* (New York: Frederick A. Stokes, 1941), p. 81. See also Rosten, *The Washington Correspondents,* p. 68; Bryant Putney, "Federal Publicity," *Editorial Research Reports* 11 (March 18, 1940): 208.

35. Leo C. Rosten, "Political Leadership and the Press," in *The Future of Government in the United States,* Leonard D. White, ed. (Chicago: University of Chicago Press, 1942), p. 95; E. Pendleton Herring, "Official Publicity under the New Deal,"

Annals of the American Academy of Political and Social Science 179 (May 1935): 169–70.

36. Owen L. Scott, "Publicity and the New Deal," *Washington Post*, May 3, 1936, Clapper Reference File, Censorship, 1936–38, Box 111, RCP, LofC; Eugene A. Kelly, "Distorting the News," *American Mercury*, March 1935, p. 308; for quote, see Roosevelt, *Complete Press Conferences*, PC 267, January 17, 1936, Vol. 7: 78.

37. Cornwell, *Presidential Leadership of Public Opinion*, p. 224.

38. Ibid., p. 225. The Brookings Institute had recommended to the Senate Committee on Reorganization "budgetary and administrative control by a superior executive authority as the most feasible method of keeping publicity agencies within reasonable limits." See Margaret Hicks Williams, "The President's Office of Government Reports," *Public Opinion Quarterly* 5 (Fall 1941): 548–62.
At the end of Early's September 9, 1939, press conference, the press secretary mentioned Mellett's new job, Early Press Conferences, STEP, FDRL. FDR also referred to Mellett in Roosevelt, *Complete Press Conferences*, PC 685, October 1, 1940, Vol. 16: 239–241.

39. Early to Secretary Wallace, August 24, 1938, OF 180, FDRL. Early urged Wallace to take advantage of reprints at a cost of $62.26 and $40.11 respectively per 10,000 copies. See also Larson, "How Much Federal Publicity Is There?" p. 641. In reference to congressional franking mail, see Early to Colonel Edwin A. Halsey, May 19, 1938, OF 180, FDRL, as cited in Cornwell, *Presidential Leadership of Public Opinion*, pp. 223–24.

40. Early to Charles Michelson, July 16 and 31, 1935, OF 36, FDRL; Berchtold, "Press Agents of the New Deal," p. 23. In reference to Martin Dies, see Ickes, *Secret Diary*, Vol. 2, entry for January 7, 1939, pp. 546–47, and February 4, 1939, p. 573. For the Texas legislature, see Ickes, *Secret Diary*, Vol. 2, entry for February 16, 1937, p. 75.

41. Frances Perkins, *The Roosevelt I Knew* (New York: Viking Press, 1946), pp. 279–80. For references to other cabinet officer press meetings, see James K. Martel, "Washington Press Conference," *American Mercury*, February 1938, pp. 201–3; Rosten, *Washington Correspondents*, p. 19.

42. William L. Bruckart and Fred Essary on behalf of the Treasury Newspaper Correspondents to President Roosevelt, November 21, 1933, OF 36, FDRL. Morgenthau wanted admission only for those already admitted to the congressional galleries, which did not include the weekly business magazine and business newsletter writers. For others, see Clapper, "Telling the World," p. 67.

43. Martel, "Washington Press Conference," pp. 199–200.

44. Perkins, *The Roosevelt I Knew*, p. 280.

45. The National Emergency Council was made up of the cabinet members and the heads of the recovery agencies and their information officers. See Lester G. Seligman and Elmer E. Cornwell, Jr., eds., *New Deal Mosaic: Proceedings of the National Emergency Council* (Eugene: University of Oregon, 1964), pp. 378–80.

46. Rosten, *Washington Correspondents*, p. 71. For example, the Agriculture Department emphasized two information activities: publicity for new programs and the usual crop, weather, and market reports. This department extensively used radio, with

greatest allocations for the daily "National Farm and Home Hour" and the crop and market reports for the national networks and three hundred independent stations. The department also produced over three hundred motion pictures. See Putney, "Federal Publicity," p. 213.

47. James L. McCamy, *Federal Publicity: Its Practice in Federal Administration* (Chicago: University of Chicago Press, 1939), pp. 60, 64, 139–44; Putney, "Federal Publicity," p. 210. The administration's releases to magazines were less effective and comprised only 4.3 percent of the total articles.

48. Mentioning the usefulness of the efforts were Ruth Finney Allen, interview, June 8, 1976, and Clapper, "Telling the World." Raymond P. Brandt, "The Washington Correspondents," *Journalism Quarterly* 13 (June 1936): 175–76; Arthur Krock, "The Press and Government," *Annals of the American Academy of Political and Social Science* 180 (July 1935): 164.

49. Robert S. Allen, interview, National Press Club, Washington, D.C., June 8, 1976. Kenneth Crawford, United Press bureau chief until World War II, also recalled that Corcoran and Cohen were good off-the-record news sources. See Crawford, "Presidents and the Press," in *The Making of the New Deal: The Insiders Speak,* Katie Louchheim, ed. (Cambridge: Harvard University Press, 1983), p. 17.

50. Ickes, *Secret Diary,* Vol. 2, entry for April 15, 1939, p. 616.

51. Senator Schall to Franklin D. Roosevelt, August 24, 1934, in Roosevelt, *Public Papers and Addresses,* Vol. 3, pp. 377–78, 384–85. Senator Glass's criticisms and others were in Raymond Clapper's collected clippings from the *New York Herald-Tribune,* May 7, 1935, and *Washington Post,* April 17, 1935, Censorship, Box 110, RCP, LofC; "Government Spends Millions for Publicity, Survey Shows," *Baltimore Sun,* June 13, 1937, Censorship, Box 111, RCP, LofC; Larson, "How Much Federal Publicity Is There?" p. 637; Paul Mallon, "Has the New Deal Colored the News?" *New York Times Magazine,* November 17, 1935, p. 22.

52. For a suggested single executive agency over public information, see Turner Catledge, "Federal Bureau for Press Urged," *New York Times,* December 29, 1936. The Senate Committee to Investigate the Executive Agencies of the Government was under the chairmanship of Senator Harry Flood Byrd of Virginia and included Joseph T. Robinson (Arkansas), Joseph C. O'Mahoney (Wyoming), Charles L. McNary (Oregon), and John G. Townsend (Delaware). See Larson, "How Much Federal Publicity Is There?" p. 636; Clapper Reference File, newspaper clippings, Censorship, Box 112, RCP, LofC; *Washington Post,* January 17, 1937, which cited a total number of 312 public information officers costing $78,972 monthly, *New York Herald-Tribune* clippings, July 28, 1936, and March 9, 1938, Censorship, Box 111, RCP, LofC; Putney, "Federal Publicity," p. 203–4, which cites the "Postmaster General 1939 Annual Report"; *New York Herald-Tribune,* June 11, 1935, Clapper Reference File, Box 111, RCP, LofC, over second-class rates given to state publications aiding agriculture.

It was rather ironic that the conservative senators did not criticize the FBI media activities. Both Roosevelt and Attorney General Homer Cummings began doing so by 1936 and made attempts to cut the bureau's budget, which had doubled since 1933. See Kenneth O'Reilly, "A New Deal for the FBI: The Roosevelt Administration,

Crime Control, and National Security," *Journal of American History* 69 (December 1982): 639, n. 5; 645; 647, n. 32.

53. Even the usually favorable *New York Times* ran an article entitled "Official Propaganda and the New Deal," April 7, 1935. Elisha Hanson, "Official Propaganda and the New Deal," *Annals of the American Academy of Political and Social Science* 179 (May 1935): 176.

54. Owen L. Scott, "Publicity and the New Deal," *Washington Post,* May 3, 1936, Clapper Reference File, Box 111, RCP, LofC; *St. Louis Post-Dispatch Symposium on Freedom of the Press* (*St. Louis Post-Dispatch,* 1938 reprint), p. 19.

55. Joseph H. Mader, "Government Press Bureaus and Reporting Public Affairs," *Journalism Quarterly* 10 (June 1942): 194–95; Robert S. Allen, interview, June 8, 1976; Eddie Folliard, interview, at his Washington, D.C., home, June 3, 1976.

56. Krock, "The Press and Government," p. 163.

57. Herring, "Official Publicity under the New Deal," pp. 168–69.

58. Roosevelt, *Public Papers and Addresses,* Vol. 2, p. 39.

"Freedom of the Seas," fireside chat from the White House, September 11, 1941.
FDR's black armband was a sign of mourning after the death of his mother, Sara
Delano Roosevelt. Courtesy the Franklin D. Roosevelt Library.

6

Other Mass Media

When Cicero had finished speaking the People said, "How well he spoke." When Demosthenes had finished speaking, the People said, "Let us march against Philip."
—Plutarch, "Demosthenes and Cicero," 105–15 A.D.

Five years of fierce discussion and debate, five years of information through radio and moving pictures, have taken the whole nation to school in the nation's business. Even those who have most attacked our objectives have, by their very criticism, encouraged the mass of our citizens to think about and understand the issues involved, and understanding, to approve.
—Franklin D. Roosevelt, Fireside Chat, October 12, 1937

With technology, Franklin D. Roosevelt's public-speaking skill could surpass both Cicero and Demosthenes. His radio-speaking ability might be considered a technological extension of Cicero, the master Roman orator. Cicero presented a most favorable image—the image of one greater than Romulus, the founder of Rome. Roosevelt also presented a most favorable image—the strong rescuer of a depressed, beleaguered nation. Roosevelt's efforts to soothe a crippled nation and gain his New Deal objectives were as vigorous as Demosthenes' leadership. Demosthenes combined his great rhetorical skill with fluid, simple language when he spoke to the Greek people. Roosevelt used simple, fluid language and reached the American people with the most direct, technologically efficient means then available for both words and images—radio, photography, and newsreels. James Madison had advocated a popular government through popular information; FDR gave that popular information by making use of those twentieth-century technological advances. This chapter will show that with radio, photojournalism, and newsreels, Roosevelt could reassure the country and give progress reports, as well as portray an active, caring president.

Franklin D. Roosevelt was not the first president to use radio. Woodrow Wilson had spoken on radio in its infancy. Although hampered by the unfamiliar microphone and an underdeveloped radio network, Warren G. Harding broadcast periodically. Calvin Coolidge, who spoke an average of once a month to a growing radio audience, was "probably heard by more people than ever heard the voice of all our [previous] Presidents combined," according to speech scholar Samuel Becker. Herbert Hoover spoke on the radio to a national audience twenty-seven times in 1930, although he did not enjoy the task and was not an effective speaker. Roosevelt, who had used this "aerial speech" for gubernatorial broadcast appeals to counteract legislative impasses and Republican press reports, came into the presidency as an experienced broadcaster.[1]

Roosevelt had said that radio "tends . . . to restore direct contact between the masses and their chosen leaders." With radio, FDR could be the newsgatherer, the reporter, as well as the editor. He could control exactly what was said on the air and give his point of view and overall impressions without any intermediate journalistic filter to interpret or change his words. Radio would be his most direct means of communication. When Roosevelt gave his inaugural address on March 4, 1933, he not only spoke to the large crowd in front of the Capitol but also broadcast to the whole nation: "The only thing we have to fear is fear itself—nameless, unreasoning, unjustified terror which paralyzes needed efforts to convert retreat into advance."[2]

Radio was to be a major way to eliminate that fear. Although Roosevelt spoke twice on the radio during his first week in office, it was his first presidential fireside chat that made a difference. Given just eight days after his inauguration, the president's informal talk was an effort to calm the nation's panic over the bank closings. After that March 12 talk, the *New York Times* cautioned, "His use of this new instrument of political discussion is a plain hint to Congress of a recourse which the President may employ if it proves necessary to rally support for legislation which he asks and which the lawmakers might be reluctant to give him."[3]

After the president's broadcast on May 7, the manager of the CBS Washington bureau, Harry Butcher, coined the words "fireside chat" to refer to the president's particular radio-speaking style. Butcher referred to Steve Early's description, "the President likes to think of the audience as being a few people around his fireside," and he wrote the phrase into the advance press releases and into the CBS introduction. The public could then imagine the president sitting comfortably at his desk in front of the fireplace of his quiet study and talking easily, just as if he were physically present in their homes or they in his. As correspondent Richard Strout remembered, "You felt he was there talking to you, not to 50 million others, but to you personally."[4]

The fireside chats had a number of other specific characteristics that distinguished them from Roosevelt's regular radio speeches. They were foremost informal and short, usually less than thirty minutes. Traditionally, when a president spoke to the people, it was an address, an exhortation, an apologia, or a lecture. With his chats, Roosevelt discussed in a casual way his policy or gave a general accounting to the nation. As Steve Early told reporters, "It will be a report by the President to the country, and they usually call those fireside talks" for the general audience, not for a specific audience or special interest group.[5]

A great deal of Roosevelt's radio success had to do with his voice. After his inaugural address, speech textbook authors Alma Johnson Sarett, Lew Sarett, and William Trufant Foster explained such assets: "The clues in Franklin D. Roosevelt's voice—the voice alone—inspired confidence. . . . If Herbert Hoover had spoken the same words into the microphone . . . the stock market would have fallen another notch and public confidence with it." The president's voice was described with such adjectives as "fresh," "brilliant," "pleasant," "rich," and "melodious." Even critic John T. Flynn admitted, "Roosevelt possessed a golden voice and a seductive and challenging radio technique."[6]

Part of that seductive technique was the slow way in which Roosevelt relayed his personality through his voice. Eleanor Roosevelt recalled, "My husband had the very remarkable ability to project his personality through his speeches and he certainly had the ability to put into understandable English even quite difficult thoughts. He gave his listeners a feeling of gracious friendly familiarity and sincere concern." Roosevelt could identify with individuals on any level and convey his empathy in such phrases as "you and I know," "together we cannot fail," and "when your neighbor's house is on fire." Even "my friends" did not sound phony, because when he said the phrase, as John Sharon recounted, "he sounded like he thought that they were—or soon would be—'his friends.' " In using these analogies, associations, and intimate appeals, FDR relied on 75 to 80 percent of the thousand most commonly used words. Those words were also spoken at a comparatively slow rate. At 100 words per minute, Roosevelt's normal speaking rate was somewhat slower than most superior speakers, who clipped along at 105–110 words per minute.[7]

FDR's fireside chats became memorable because there were so few, so very few, that they became special events. During that crisis year of 1933, Roosevelt gave at least twenty broadcast addresses, but he gave only four fireside chats. In fact, during his first eight years in office, FDR broadcast only sixteen fireside chats. Roosevelt wrote that "the one thing I dread is that my talks would be so frequent as to lose their effectiveness." Later he explained, "I ought not to appear oftener than once every five or six weeks. I am inclined to think that in England, Churchill, for a while, talked too much and I don't want to do that."[8]

The fireside chats became so popular that people even asked for them.

Answering one 1935 request, FDR maintained that "if I had tried to keep up the pace of 1933 and 1934, the inevitable histrionics of the new actors, Long and Coughlin and Johnson, would have turned the eyes of the audience away from the main drama itself!" He was even more cautious when he answered Frank Walker's suggestion that he use such a method to respond to the 1936 Supreme Court decision against the Agricultural Adjustment Act: "I hope to make one or possibly two fireside talks between now and May, but there must be a logical occasion and I am looking for one." Apparently, he did not find that logical occasion since he did not make a fireside chat then.[9]

The president's talks, while appearing to be casual, were actually polished products and took extensive preparation. In 1936 he told of asking different people for advice and assistance:

> I have received drafts and memoranda from different people, varying from short suggestions as to a sentence here and there, to long memoranda of factual material, and in some cases, complete addresses.
>
> In addition to such suggestions, I make it a practice to keep a "speech material file." . . . Whenever anything catches my eye, either in the mail or in the press or in the course of reading articles, memoranda, or books, which I think will be of value in the preparation of a speech, I ask her to put it away in the speech material file.
>
> In preparing a speech usually I take the various office drafts and suggestions which have been submitted to me and also the material which has accumulated in the speech file on various subjects, read them carefully, lay them aside, and then dictate my own draft, usually to Miss Tully. Naturally, the final speech will contain some of the thoughts and even some of the sentences which appeared in some of the drafts or suggestions submitted.[10]

Roosevelt drew upon the full resources of the executive branch and sometimes a dozen different people, including members of the cabinet. For his first fireside chat, he had the assistance of Attorney General Homer Cummings, Secretary of the Treasury William Woodin, Under Secretary of the Treasury Arthur A. Ballantine, and publicist Charles Michelson. He worked side by side with his ghostwriters, such as Raymond Moley from 1932–36 and Harry Hopkins and Samuel Rosenman afterwards. Hopkins would furnish ideas, Rosenman would put them into logical sequence, and playwright Robert Sherwood would give them the necessary polish. Sherwood explained:

> When he wanted to give a speech for some important purpose, whether it was connected with a special occasion or not, he would discuss it first at length with Hopkins, Rosenman, and me, telling us what particular points he wanted to make, what sort of audience he wished primarily to reach and what the maximum word limit was to be (he generally put it far too low). He would dictate pages and pages, approaching his main topic, sometimes hitting it squarely on the nose with terrific impact, sometimes rambling so far away from it that he couldn't get back, in which case he would say, "Well—something along those lines—you boys can fix it up."[11]

Each speech went through numerous drafts (usually three to ten, with a record of twenty-two) as Roosevelt sought the most understandable terms. Sherwood remembered that Roosevelt, who disliked long words, would sometimes read "the speech out loud, to see how it sounded, for every word was judged not by its appearance in print but by its effectiveness over the radio." He would relate issues as individual problems. For example, rather than citing figures, prices indices, employment statistics, and bank deposits in his June 28, 1934, fireside chat, Roosevelt said, "But the simplest way for each of you to judge recovery lies in the plain facts of your own individual economic situation. Are you better off than you were last year? Are your debts less burdensome? Is your bank account more secure? Are your working conditions better? Is your faith in your own individual future more firmly grounded?"[12]

The final phraseology after the president's editing made the addresses peculiarly "Rooseveltian." As Samuel Rosenman wrote, "The speeches as finally delivered were his—and his alone—no matter who the collaborators were. He had gone over every point, every word, time and again. He had studied, reviewed, and read aloud each draft, and had changed it again and again, either in his own handwriting, by dictating inserts, or making deletions. Because of the many hours he spent in its preparation, by the time he delivered a speech he knew it almost by heart." One study of seventeen of his major international affairs speeches showed that the president himself was the primary source of the ideas, arguments, and language.[13]

Roosevelt prepared for his delivery just as carefully. He rehearsed each address several times. To vary his speaking rate and to meet the rigid radio schedules, he often marked off the final reading copy into five minute sections. Thus, he seldom had trouble making his speaking rate conform to any changes necessitated by applause or by his own impromptu insertions. For variety, he frequently divided sentences into short phrases of four or six words, relieved by occasional long phrases or entire sentences with no pauses. He made sure that he gave equal stress to important passages and paused between words and sentences. Robert Sherwood was quoted as saying, "I never saw a better actor than F.D.R."[14]

Roosevelt also paid attention to the microphone angle and sound. Few listeners were aware that the president added a false tooth for his radio speeches. With the separation between his front two lower teeth, he would whistle slightly on certain words, a most noticeable broadcast sound. Grace Tully recalled that when he would occasionally forget to bring down the removable bridge there would be a last minute dash to rescue the tooth in its little silver box on his bedside table.[15]

The White House paid just as careful attention to broadcast schedules. During the New Deal period, the president's talks were usually on Sunday evening around 10 P.M. eastern standard time. At that peak time, the public was relaxed, "in a benevolent mood." Eastern listeners would still be awake, and the western listeners were just ready to listen.[16]

When the three networks had been scheduled for a specific date and time, Early began his coordination with the press. He gave special advertising to the fireside chats that he did not give to any other Roosevelt speeches. He did not initially tell reporters the subject of the talks. Until 1942, Early would announce that there would be a fireside talk sometimes as much as three weeks in advance in a press release, similar to the format used for the fireside chat on September 11, 1941:

> The President will deliver a nationwide broadcast Monday evening at 9:00 p.m., E.S.T. He will speak from the White House in Washington. The three American major radio systems—NBC, CBS and Mutual—have offered their facilities. His remarks also will be translated into fourteen foreign languages and will be sent out by short wave, thereby giving the broadcast a world wide coverage.
>
> Although of great importance, the President will not require more than fifteen minutes for the delivery of this address. It is not possible at this time to disclose the subject of his remarks.[17]

The unknown speech topic would fill newspaper column after column with free publicity, speculations about the speech, and trial balloons on various possible subjects. As the announced date grew nearer, Early would then release a little more information, dribbling the news until finally the transcript was released. Once in 1941, when asked whether a particular speech would have "a little fireworks," Early retorted with an answer guaranteed to build headlines: "I don't want to say anything about the speech. *Off the Record,* I think it will be considerable."[18]

Just before a broadcast, Early would try to circulate advance copies of the speech, with a release date and time to insure press publication of the text and next-day commentaries. However, many times the president did not finish changing and rehearsing the speech until only a few hours before air time. Then, typing, mimeographing, and distributing the copies to reporters went down to the wire. Without time to read or study the speech, reporters depended on Early to point out the significant parts. He would highlight the speech and even say, "I think you will find your lead on about the 4th or 5th page, under the figures 1, 2, 3, 4, 5 and maybe 6." Because of Roosevelt's tendency to improvise during the broadcast, these advance copies could often be inaccurate. After the second fireside chat, the *New York Times* recorded and then printed a transcript of the recording rather than relying on the advance text.[19]

Roosevelt and Early would always check the radio audience reactions and size by the number of telegrams and the ratings. Although scientific public opinion polling was still in its infancy during the 1930s, organizations measuring radio audiences, such as the accurate and quick C. E. Hooper "Hooperatings," would send Roosevelt their results. Knowing FDR's interest in the audience size, Hooper began presenting a large colored chart to illustrate the dramatic rise in audience from almost 10 percent to 79 percent for fireside chats and regular speeches in 1936.[20]

Early would relay those Hooper statistics to the press. Following FDR's May 27, 1941, speech on national security and war supplies to Great Britain, Early exaggerated the estimate of 53,800,000 listeners: ". . . a 70 percent rating which is an all time high for any radio program ever carried by any network or system. Broken down into terms of population, that means that within the continental United States a minimum of 65,650,000 people heard him; that is only in the continental United States." The *Washington Star* cited Early's figures with a subhead, "Response to Speech Reaches All-Time High, Early Says."[21]

During those embryonic radio days, the networks tried to please the administration by donating time for administration speeches and supporting the New Deal recovery efforts. The day after Roosevelt's first fireside chat, CBS devoted three midday hours to congressional views of Roosevelt's emergency policies. During the president's first week in office, NBC donated over twelve hours of air time for executive branch discussions. At the same time, the networks chose their Washington staffs carefully. CBS appointed as head of the Washington bureau Henry Bellows, Roosevelt's Harvard classmate and a former federal radio commissioner. NBC appointed as its Washington news commentator George Holmes, brother-in-law of Steve Early.[22]

Roosevelt reciprocated. He gave careful thought to Federal Communications Commission (FCC) appointments. When the FCC replaced the Radio Commission in 1934, the president reappointed most of the old commissioners, who were also friends of industry. In 1940, when the radio correspondents had their own congressional galleries and rules, Roosevelt made sure they could also officially attend his press conferences. By July 1943 the president renamed his press meetings "Radio and Press Conferences." FDR participated in the opening of NBC's new Washington headquarters, and on the twenty-fifth anniversary of RCA in 1944, he wrote a congratulatory letter to his old friend David Sarnoff, head of RCA.[23]

The White House greatly valued radio's directness and speed, for good reasons. As Early explained, "It cannot misrepresent nor misquote. It is far reaching and simultaneous in releasing messages given it for transmission to the nation or for international consumption." Radio was especially important during the elections. Unless the speeches were labeled campaign addresses, the networks and stations usually provided the air time. When they did not, Early retaliated. After two Los Angeles stations refused to carry the president's "nonpolitical" September 6, 1936, fireside address on the drought, Early wrote Charles Michelson to suggest a reallocation of radio campaign spending: "We can afford to eliminate KFI and KECA. I hope we will and that we also will announce when the next program goes out over the chain of which these stations are members, that the Committee had requested their elimination. As far as I am able to ascertain, these are the only two, of all the stations in the United States, that refused to carry the President's 'fireside' chat."[24]

The White House also monitored the award of radio licenses. Roosevelt became increasingly concerned as more and more of his adversaries, in particular newspaper publishers, bought radio stations. He especially did not approve of the manner in which the FCC commissioners seemed to grant licenses almost automatically. In 1936 FDR urged Early to "get busy at once with Prall and tell him that Machold is the Power Trust." In 1938 he urged Early to "get in touch with McNinch and ask him if there is something we can do to keep the Wichita Falls papers, who are opposing Congressman McFarlane, from getting control of the radio." In a 1941 memo concerning the FCC actions, Roosevelt wrote, "Be sure to get a stopper with Fly on any action taking away the University of Georgia radio station." When the president heard a rumor in 1943 that the McCormick-Patterson group had offered $10 million for the NBC Blue Network, he immediately urged, "I think that this ought to be stopped without any question. It is bad enough to have them on Mutual."[25]

By 1940 newspaper publishers owned as much as one-third of the airwaves. Roosevelt was outraged. His adversaries could control two kinds of news media. FDR urged the FCC to make a policy statement on "divorcing press and radio." James Fly, chair of the FCC, sent out a questionnaire to radio stations to discern the relationship between radio and the press. Although he never acted on the undisclosed results, he did hold hearings on the networks' broadcast monopoly. He wrote Roosevelt, "Two men (Sarnoff and Paley) can say more than half of what people may or may not hear. NBC and Columbia networks control 86 percent of the total night-time radio power in the country. With their close affiliation with the newspapers they can measurably influence what the people may read. Democracy cannot rest upon so frail a reed." Roosevelt was not concerned about Sarnoff and Paley, and Early attempted to stop this particular investigation. After all, FDR could use the networks easily. The FCC commissioners, however, approved Fly's report, which ordered RCA to sell one of its NBC networks and took away CBS's control over affiliate station time. When reporters asked the president about the report at a press conference during a period of the Luftwaffe's heavy bombing of London, Roosevelt retorted that he had not read the regulations: "It is an awful thing to have to say, but there have been more important things in the last two or three weeks."[26]

During World War II, Roosevelt's radio concerns went beyond media ownership and network controls. The Axis twice captured American headlines away from the president's broadcast addresses. On the night of his December 29, 1940, fireside chat on lend-lease, the Germans subjected London to the heaviest bombing of the war. Later, in the depths of the wartime tragedies of 1942, the president attempted to rally morale with his February 23, 1942, address, "The Allies on the Offensive Soon." While he was speaking, a Japanese submarine surfaced off the California coast near Santa Barbara and fired at a ranch. Roosevelt's press conference response acknowledged that his speech had caused a reaction in the "opposite direction from which it was intended." Such news challenges were unusual for Roosevelt and that golden era of radio. The president controlled the medium, just as he controlled his image.[27]

Roosevelt took great care to control his pictorial image. With new flash attachments, new miniature cameras with wide-angle lenses and fast shutters, and prepackaged daylight-loading 35 mm. cartridges, photographers had a greater ability to take candid snapshots. At the same time, newspapers began printing more pictures. With the introduction of the Associated Press Wirephoto Service in late 1934, any AP-affiliated newspaper could immediately receive and publish pictures from across the country.[28]

The White House News Photographers Association had existed for a decade, but it took on a new life during the Roosevelt era. Because Roosevelt loved the dramatic and the unusual, he gave the photographers something newsworthy to shoot. FDR's informality and ever-changing facial expressions sharply contrasted to the stoic and deadpan Herbert Hoover. Photographers, both still and newsreel, went on his inspection tours, his many trips to Hyde Park and Warm Springs, and his travels to the Pacific and the Panama Canal. Franklin D. Roosevelt's image seemed to dominate the Sunday rotogravure section of the newspapers as well as the front pages.[29]

William L. Rivers once suggested that more attention should be given to Roosevelt's shrewd use of his own expressive features. Although Rivers recognized that FDR had rules forbidding photographs showing him in pain or discomfort, Rivers wrote that "otherwise, anything went," photowise. However, not "anything went," even before Roosevelt was inaugurated. FDR was not as willing as previous presidents to be photographed. At his February 1933 Miami speech he refused to repeat a few lines for still photographers and newsreel sound tracks. In addition, he would not wave to suit the cameramen's demands for a pre-inaugural posed gesture.[30]

During his second month in office, Roosevelt opened international meetings to American photographers, a contrast to the closure rules by the previous four administrations, but he controlled the number and access of the photographers. Steve Early set the rules: "One photographer only from each of the four major picture syndicates being admitted, with each of the local Washington papers being assured coverage from the respective syndicates serving them regularly."[31]

With his Paramount Newsreel experience, Early knew how to avoid over-saturation of the president's image during speeches and trips. Early's rules included no exclusive photographs, just as he had decreed no exclusive interviews. All photo coverage was to be pooled, since there were some eighty-five members of the White House News Photographers Association. When the White House cut the news coverage even more during World War II, the syndicates drew lots for special White House assignments. Early would give friendly photographers newsworthy photo tips about the administration. He set the boundaries for photographing dignitaries: the president could be pictured with his guests in proper poses only.[32]

There were other photography rules, even for candid shots. Early limited the distance to the president, depending on the size of the entourage and the crowd. In his 1946 survey, William McKinley Moore found that several photographers gave the usual minimum distance as twelve feet; when large crowds gathered, the estimate rose to thirty feet. This rule was not only to guard against possible assassins but also to equalize the opportunities for photographers to get pictures, limit the nearness of the blinding photo flashes, and give the crowd a dramatic open space around the president and a few carefully selected notables.[33]

No candid pictures were to be taken in the White House, not even at the press conferences, without special permission. Photographers were usually limited to ceremonial occasions, speeches, and formal group portraits. Early specified the place for the cameras to click, with such comments as "Still pictures may be made of the President with the Swedish Minister and Mr. Ostberg in the Green Room immediately before they enter the East Room for the actual presentation." For the president's safety and privacy, the photographers could only take pictures in the public areas of the White House, not in the living quarters. The same rule held for the Warm Springs and Hyde Park residence, the president's railway car, and his yacht. Early carefully specified the possible interior shots and the content for a pictorial layout. During the 1940 campaign, Early wanted images of a relaxed president at his farm: "If the President will get in his car and go out to the stables, have them lead a riding horse or two up to him so that he can be petting them while he is photographed; pictures of the President's little cubbyhole office; picture of the President with any of the children that may be there; with his mother; with Mrs. Roosevelt; around the fireplace; on the porch; out in the yard." Early's explicit instructions would cover even the exact equipment, down to the tripods.[34]

Despite Early's 1935 assurance that no permission was required for any "publication of the President's photograph provided it is not used for commercial advertising purposes," both photographing and publication did indeed require permission. After 1935 Early began to require that photos be made only *when* he gave the word to shoot, so they would illustrate no more than the intended story. He specified this additional rule following the misuse of a photo of the president, who had taken off his glasses to rub his eyes after withstanding the flash bulbs used for his birthday portrait. Early was furious when that picture was published with the captions, "Thinking Over the Farm Problem" and "President Roosevelt Meditates, Remarkable Study Snapped Soon After He Conferred on the Troublesome Agricultural Question."[35]

In June 1935, when "some decidedly poor photographs" were taken aboard the yacht *Sequoia* where "heretofore pictures had been barred," Early sent special instructions to Colonel Starling of the Secret Service about photographs. Cameramen, their number already limited for presidential trips, could snap their shots *only* at the precise instant the Secret Service announced. If the photographers missed that chance, they were permitted no second attempts, even if individual photographers failed to get their shutter clicked.[36]

The Secret Service helped Early control the White House photographers' access. Yet the press secretary could not stop others from taking candid snapshots and then distributing them to photo services, even though the official White House staff's pictures were to remain private and unpublished. Nor could Early stop Democratic congressmen who snapped pictures of the president eating lunch and in various informal situations while they were meeting with him at Jefferson Island during the weekend of June 25, 1937. Although Early had specifically requested that no photographs be taken on this trip, Acme News Pictures and the Associated Press Picture Service obtained copies of those snapshots and published them as exclusives. When the other four pictures services vehemently protested, Early immediately allowed all photography representatives to visit the island and take pictures. Early disciplined the offending agencies by placing a temporary ban on their taking any pictures of the president's next weekend visit to Hyde Park. When the British king and queen visited the president during the summer of 1939, Early prohibited newspaper photographers from the Hyde Park informal picnic, but he could not stop the staff from taking snapshots of the famous "hot dog party." They later sold or gave them to the press.[37]

By the fall of 1940, Early's attempts to control photographic access created extremely stormy relations between the White House and the photographers. During that fall campaign, Early decided there was room for only one photographer to record Frank Walker's oath-taking as the new postmaster general. The White House photographers demanded "all or none!" No one would move. Early called the Associated Press bureau offices which ordered Charles Gory to take the pictures. Roosevelt was so amused that he had Early snap a shot of the new postmaster general, the president, and the lone "brave cameraman." Even so, the White House photographers made their point. Early promised more space for all regularly accredited photographers, except under emergency conditions.[38]

For photographers, the greatest taboo was to depict the president's legs or reminders of his lameness. The only exception included those photos showing Roosevelt's physical comeback when he walked with crutches to the podium at the 1924 Democratic National Convention. As noted in chapter 2, prior to his presidential years, Roosevelt had had an unwritten rule about camera shots depicting his crippled condition. In one 1946 study, Johnny Thompson of Acme recounted "photographs were never taken of the President walking, by gentlemen's agreement with the Secret Service." White House rules also prohibited shots taken of the president handling crutches or photos implying he had crutches or was being wheeled in his wheelchair. Myron Hoff Davis, a *Life* photographer, remembered the "Secret Service requested that members of the White House Photography Association refrain from taking pictures when the President was getting in and out of wheelchairs or being transported in a wheel chair." All such pictures of Roosevelt in a wheelchair were to be voluntarily withheld and destroyed. Photographers were also requested not to take pictures of the president getting aboard his special railway car, although photos could be taken of the specially constructed ramps the president used.[39]

Nevertheless, some of Roosevelt's media adversaries did publish photographs of him with braces or other walking aids. *Life, Look, Fortune,* the *Chicago Tribune,* and the *New York Herald-Tribune* were among the publications that carried such pictures. In October 1937 the *Chicago Tribune* printed an Associated Press picture showing the president in braces. The *New York Times* carried the same photograph, but, like so many other newspapers that retouched such photographs, it cropped the picture below the trouser cuffs and thus kept the president's braces out of pictorial attention.[40]

In 1937, following the Supreme Court fight, *Life* printed the rarest of all photographs, that of Roosevelt being pushed along in a wheelchair. The photograph was taken when the president was on the way to visit a sick cabinet member and included the group of guards, the porter, and the wheelchair. The figures are so distant that no one could be identified without a caption. Steve Early was furious. He wrote the president's physician Ross McIntire: "Here is a picture of the President in his wheelchair—a scene we have never permitted to be photographed. The photographer evidently made his way into the Naval Hospital grounds to do this job or someone at the Hospital made the picture for him or supplied him with a print of the picture they made. I do think this should be investigated and steps taken to prevent any repetition."[41] By 1937 *Life* publisher Henry Luce had become very antagonistic toward Roosevelt's power, his plan to pack the Supreme Court, and the administration's rhetoric, ostensibly hostile to free enterprise.

Although Early mentioned an investigation, no evidence has yet been found on what steps, if any, Early or the Secret Service took in this instance or others. When Steve Early was asked at a press briefing about what the administration might do about a politically critical, retouched photograph showing the president behind bars, with the caption "Third Term Hell!! I'm in for Life," Early's response was, "I do not think that violates any law. Hence, my answer to your question 'what?' is 'nothing.' "[42]

Early's continual efforts to stop the publication of shots of the president's lameness met other defeats. Luce, McCormick, and other Republican publications would occasionally publish such photographs. After the president was in Chicago for the dedication of the new Outer Drive in 1937, *Life, Fortune, Look,* and the *New York Herald-Tribune* all published shots of the president walking with crutches to Cardinal Mundelein's residence. The *Chicago Tribune* continued publishing such photographs as the one of FDR holding the arms of both a Secret Service man and his chauffeur as he went into a voting booth in 1944.[43]

Still, these were only a few infractions depicting the president's lameness. Most photographers complied with Early's requests. Seldom did the American public see pictorial reminders of Roosevelt's crippled legs, although he was sometimes shown with a cane. Even cartoonists went along with the president's wishes. When Roosevelt fell full-length on the ramp of the speakers' platform at the 1936 Democratic National Convention at Franklin Field in Philadelphia, not a single picture or cartoon was published. In fact, there was no public mention of the incident, even though many people knew and many photographers were around the president.[44]

Although writers did describe how FDR was mobile via his wheelchair, cane, and crutches, the American public apparently did not like graphic references to the president's crippled condition. When *Time* used such terms as "shriveled legs" and "hobbled" before FDR's inauguration, indignant letter writers resented such descriptives in reference to their president. *Time* attempted to answer critics by stating that it would "contrive to regard Mr. Roosevelt's legs as mentionable—unless a great majority of *Time* readers have commanded otherwise." A great majority of *Time* readers must have deemed otherwise. References to Roosevelt's lameness were not frequently found after that January 2, 1933, issue. Instead, *Time* began emphasizing FDR's comeback from infantile paralysis.[45]

The president seemed so vigorous in so many other ways that most Americans never thought much about the fact that Roosevelt remained a cripple in a wheelchair. Not only did Early's photography rules reinforce that image, but many writers gave the impression that Roosevelt had fully conquered his infirmity. Certainly, his active administration belied any image of incapacity. Moreover, Roosevelt's nonchalant air about his legs and his carefree remarks like "Really, it's as funny as a crutch" or "I'm sorry, but I have to run now" all masked an image of paralysis. Even when an occasional magazine or newspaper referred to his lameness, the readers could not believe that that active, handsome man with his big jaw thrust forward and a cigarette holder clenched in his teeth at a jaunty angle could possibly be a cripple in a wheelchair. Such a systematic set of rules for managing his image was, for the most part, a friendly conspiracy with photographers. Thousands of seemingly candid pictures of Franklin D. Roosevelt showed his most expressive features and his mobile and animated face. The president was eating hot dogs, munching peanuts at a baseball game, kissing his wife, playing with his Scotch terrier, waving to the crowds, and smiling his infectious grin.[46]

Roosevelt also used motion pictures to enhance his image. By encompassing both the visual qualities of photography and the sound dimensions of radio, newsreels gave audiences what appeared to be pictorial fact, complete with image and interpretation. As Early once expressed it, "The newsreel brings to a modern world a truer picture of itself, and of its people, than any other agency heretofore known to mankind." He also contended that "people like the *big news* newsreel." The audiences could see and hear the president of the United States in action, and that was the big news.[47]

With rules concerning camera proximity, the inclusion of motion pictures, and the use of kleig lights, the president could present a "truer picture" of himself. He had the same rules as he had with still photography: he was never to be photographed walking with a crippled gait or riding along in a wheelchair. Unlike the still photographers, the newsreel photographers did not try to challenge Early's rules, since they had been trying for years to have representatives regularly cover the Oval Office.[48]

Early again controlled the content and guarded against oversaturation. He also knew what would make the most positive "big news newsreel." Just before FDR's dedication of the Great Smokey National Park in 1940, Early specified the focus he wanted in a memorandum to William Hassett: "It is all right for still pictures at the Moses Smith party . . . but as far as newsreels go, if it is in the evening, cut them out. No newsreels on that party. I want the newsreel for Chattanooga and the Smokies."[49]

As with still photographers, no newsreel company had exclusive access to the president, although Early favored his old company with news tips and inside information on the administration. William Montague of Paramount thanked Early for his help in getting exclusive film on Ambassador-at-Large Norman Davis before he left for the 1933 Geneva Disarmament Conference: "Just as you guessed, we piled around to his home, got a good story on him there and delayed him so long that the other newsreels did not get him at the boat." The grateful newsreel company made sure that Roosevelt had a copy of every presidential story released.[50]

The coverage could not be live either, for good reasons. The glare of the newsreel lights was so intense that Roosevelt had difficulty reading his manuscript. During a 1936 campaign address, Early wrote the newsreel cameramen, "It is respectfully requested that, if the lights and the camera are to work for the opening of the address, also for the closing and for the high spot of news feature of the remarks, that this be considered full and complete coverage." Early then noted that a copy of this request was being given to Colonel Starling of the Secret Service for access control.[51]

Newsreel reproductions of the fireside chats were done separately from the radio productions. On the day of the first fireside chat, Early sent a telegram to the newsreel companies: "President Roosevelt is giving your newsreel a five hundred word ringing appeal for confidence of the people and support of the nation's banking system. Respectfully request that his statement be released in full at earliest possible moment." The cameramen filmed only a short, staged excerpt after each broadcast. George Dorsey, manager of the Washington bureau of Pathe News, recalled the moment: "We would stand by until the broadcast was over. The President would relax a few minutes and enjoy a smoke and conversation with his aides and then do the highlights of the talk for the newsreels."[52]

The newsreel companies would occasionally film a speech a few days before the actual delivery, if all the rewriting had been finished. For example, the cameramen filmed summary of Roosevelt's address on unemployment six days before the November 14, 1937, broadcast. The newsreels were thus able to release the speech to the theaters at the same time as the actual radio broadcast.[53]

The release timing of the film was another detail Early supervised. The film producers agreed to make a 1936 campaign film of the president and his family at Hyde Park on October 3. In exchange for the access to the president's home, they agreed to hold the release of any of the film until the end of the month, October 23, for last minute personal contact.[54]

Early's tight control of film coverage produced positive results. In his content analysis of the Universal Newsreel Company's coverage of Roosevelt's first two terms, Steven E. Schoenherr concluded that the newsreels emphasized the president's character and appearances and not the controversial topics of his administration. The newsreels focused on the more personal and colorful aspects of his presidency, with the largest percentage covering his vacation or cross-country tours and the next largest capturing his ceremonial, nonpolitical appearances. By emphasizing his travels, his personality, and human-interest situations, the newsreels projected an image of an active, vigorous president.[55]

During the Roosevelt era, newsreels were an early version of televised news. When the dishes had been washed, average Americans went to one of their small neighborhood theaters to relax and enjoy a "first-run" picture, after it had appeared downtown. For twenty-five cents Americans saw films and also the "talking newspaper of the screen," which featured President Roosevelt's delivery of those same words they had heard on their radios. The president's visual presence added to the impact: the Roosevelt smile, the old-fashioned pince-nez, and the loose shirt collar. The president's seemingly informal speech was superb theater. A partner in a New York newsreel house in 1934, W. French Githens, wrote that announcements of FDR's fireside chats brought in hundreds of patrons: "We soon discovered that in Franklin Delano Roosevelt we had the greatest single attraction." [56]

Roosevelt was a star. He was the master of the technological media changes of the 1930s and 1940s. Such advances would take "the whole nation to school in the nation's business." He said in 1939, "You are, I believe, the most enlightened and the best informed people in all the world at this moment. You are subject to no censorship of news, and I want to add that your Government has no information which it withholds or which it has any thought of withholding from you." [57]

Because his voice and his image were so effective, FDR was also the political star. With media controls, he excelled in getting across his message. With radio's emphasis on a voice, the presidential voice, and newsreels' emphasis on an image, the president's image, the public had a singular, recognizable voice and a singular, recognizable image. When FDR spoke, the people listened. When he wanted access, he got it. Broadcasting companies could hardly refuse when the president's office called to request thirty minutes at 10 P.M. on a Sunday night. As the most prominent political figure in the country, he was the most newsworthy. With his words and his image, he not only spoke well, as had Cicero, but he could elicit action, just as Demosthenes. With these media technological advances, the president mastered the possibilities, using a combination of Cicero's ability to present a favorable image and Demosthenes' skill to soothe a troubled nation.

Notes

1. Samuel L. Becker, "Presidential Power: The Influence of Broadcasting," *Quarterly Journal of Speech* 47 (February 1961): 11–14; Ralph D. Casey, "Republican Propaganda in the 1936 Campaign," *Public Opinion Quarterly* 1 (April 1937): 35. For further discussion, see Edwin Diamond, "President Carter on the Airwaves—Echoes of F.D.R.," *New York Times*, March 20, 1977; Thomas H. Greer, *What Roosevelt Thought: The Social and Political Ideas of Franklin D. Roosevelt* (East Lansing: Michigan State University Press, 1958), p. 111.

2. The first quotation is taken from Arthur M. Schlesinger, Jr., *The Coming of the New Deal*, Vol. 2 of *The Age of Roosevelt* (Boston: Houghton Mifflin, 1959), p. 559. The second quote is in Lester G. Seligman and Elmer E. Cornwell, Jr., eds., *The New*

Deal Mosaic: Proceedings of the National Emergency Council (Eugene: University of Oregon Press, 1964), pp. 378–70. For other discussion of FDR and the radio, see Frank Freidel, *Launching the New Deal,* Vol. 4 of *Franklin D. Roosevelt* (Little, Brown, 1973), p. 202; Becker, "Presidential Power," p. 14.

3. *New York Times,* March 14, 1933.

4. Butcher reference is in Steven E. Schoenherr, "Selling the New Deal: Stephen T. Early's Role as Press Secretary to Franklin D. Roosevelt" (Ph.D. dissertation, University of Delaware, 1976), p. 110, and John H. Sharon, "The Psychology of the Fireside Chat" (Senior honors thesis, Princeton University, 1949), pp. 104–5; Richard Lee Strout, "The President and the Press," in *The Making of the New Deal: The Insiders Speak,* Katie Louchheim, ed. (Cambridge: Harvard University Press, 1983), p. 13.

5. Stephen T. Early's Press Conference (henceforth STE PC), May 23, 1940, Early 1940 Scrapbook, Stephen T. Early Papers (henceforth STEP), Franklin D. Roosevelt Library (henceforth FDRL).

6. Alma Johnson Sarett, Lew Sarett, and William Trufant Foster, *Basic Principles of Speech* (Boston: Houghton Mifflin, 1936), pp. 193–94; John T. Flynn, *The Roosevelt Myth* (New York: Devin-Adair, 1948), p. 283.

7. Eleanor Roosevelt, "Introduction" for "F.D.R. Speaks," which accompanied "Franklin D. Roosevelt's Authorized Speeches, 1933–1945," RCA Record; Becker, "Presidential Power," pp. 26–27; *New York Times,* May 16, 1937; Sharon, "The Psychology of the Fireside Chat," pp. 87–88, 116.

8. Franklin D. Roosevelt to Russell C. Leffingwell, March 16, 1942, *Franklin D. Roosevelt Reader: Selected Speeches, Messages, Press Conferences and Letters,* Basil Rauch, ed. (New York: Rinehart, 1957), p. 310; FDR to Mary T. Norton, March 24, 1942, *F.D.R.: His Personal Letters, 1928–1945,* Vol. 2, Elliott Roosevelt, ed. (New York: Duell, Sloan and Pearce, 1950), pp. 1300–1301. As a summation, see Schoenherr, "Selling the New Deal," pp. 104, 108, 110, 123.

Schoenherr and Sharon list the following addresses as fireside chats. Those with an * are among Schoenherr's 31, an addition to the 25 listed in Sharon's "The Psychology of the Fireside Chat," p. 107. The Franklin D. Roosevelt Library's Speech Index lists 21 chats. The discrepancies are because neither Early nor the president officially classified the talks; the press and radio labeled them as such.

1. March 12, 1933, The Bank Crisis
2. May 7, 1933, Outlining the New Deal Program
3. July 24, 1933, The Recovery Program
4. October 22, 1933, The Currency Situation
5. June 28, 1934, The Achievements of the 73rd Congress
6. September 30, 1934, Freedom and Security
7. April 28, 1935, The Works Relief Program
8. September 6, 1936, The Drought
9. March 9, 1937, The Reorganization of the Judiciary
10. October 23, 1937, The Unemployment Census
11. November 14, 1937, The Unemployment Census
12. April 14, 1938, Economic Conditions

13. June 24, 1938, Party Primaries
14. September 3, 1939, The European War
15. May 26, 1940, National Defense
16. December 29, 1940, The Arsenal of Democracy
17. May 27, 1941, Unlimited National Security
18. September 11, 1941, Maintaining the Freedom of the Seas
19. December 9, 1941, The Congress and the People Have Accepted the Challenge
20. February 23, 1942, The Allies on the Offensive Soon
21. April 28, 1942, National Economic Policy
22. September 7, 1942, Inflation and Progress of the War
*23. October 12, 1942, The Home Front
24. May 2, 1943, The Coal Crisis
25. July 28, 1943, The First Crack in the Axis
*26. September 8, 1943, The Third War Loan Drive
*27. December 24, 1943, The Teheran and Cairo Conferences
*28. January 11, 1944, The State of the Union
29. June 5, 1944, The Fall of Rome
*30. June 12, 1944, Opening the Fifth War Loan Drive
*31. January 6, 1945, The War Loan Drive

9. Roosevelt to Ray Stannard Baker, March 20, 1935, *F.D.R.: His Personal Letters, 1928–1945,* Vol. 1, pp. 466–67; Roosevelt to Frank C. Walker, February 13, 1936, ibid., p. 554.

10. Franklin D. Roosevelt, *The Public Papers and Addresses of Franklin D. Roosevelt,* Vol. 5, Samuel I. Rosenman, ed. (New York: Random House, 1938–50), pp. 391–92.

11. Sharon, "The Psychology of the Fireside Chat," pp. 91, 129; Robert E. Sherwood, *Roosevelt and Hopkins: An Intimate History* (New York: Harper and Brothers, 1948), p. 213. For specific talks, see Samuel I. Rosenman, *Working with Roosevelt* (New York: Harper and Brothers, 1952), pp. 2–15, 124–27, 226–29, 297–302, 492–94; "Speech Material," President's Secretary's File (henceforth PSF), FDRL.

Moley's relationship with FDR deteriorated and finally ended after a collaboration on the president's 1936 acceptance speech. See Elliot A. Rosen, "Raymond Moley," in *Franklin D. Roosevelt, His Life and Times: An Encyclopedic View,* Otis L. Graham, Jr., and Meghan Robinson Wander, eds. (Boston: G. K. Hall, 1985), p. 261.

12. Sherwood, *Roosevelt and Hopkins,* p. 215; Greer, *What Roosevelt Thought,* pp. 110–11.

13. Rosenman, *Working with Roosevelt,* p. 11; Ernest Brandenburg, "The Preparation of Franklin D. Roosevelt's Speeches," *Quarterly Journal of Speech* 24 (1949): 214–15.

14. James F. Ragland, "Franklin D. Roosevelt and Public Opinion, 1933–1940" (Ph.D. dissertation, Stanford University, 1954), p. 679; Becker, "Presidential Power," pp. 25–26; Sharon, "The Psychology of the Fireside Chat," pp. 87, 111. For reference to Sherwood, see Lewie V. Gilpin, "Ladies and Gentlemen, the President . . ." *Broadcasting,* August 15, 1940, pp. 19, 64, found in Early 1940 Scrapbook, STEP, FDRL.

15. Grace Tully, *F.D.R., My Boss* (New York: Charles Scribner's Sons, 1949), p. 100.

16. Sharon, "The Psychology of the Fireside Chat," pp. 95–103.

17. Early Telegram to William Hassett, September 6, 1941, STEP, FDRL. For other reference to Early's role, see Sharon, "The Psychology of the Fireside Chat," p. 95; Schoenherr, "Selling the New Deal," p. 114.

18. In reference to the "Maintaining Freedom of the Seas" speech, September 11, 1941, see Early Telegraph to William Hassett, September 6, 1941, STEP, FDRL.

19. Schoenherr, "Selling the New Deal," p. 118.

20. In reference to Hooper ratings, see Early Memorandum to Harry Butcher, January 20, 1942, and Early to Butcher, April 2, 1942, STEP, FDRL. The Hooper chart in the Franklin D. Roosevelt Library, accession 42-102-22, shows these ratings:

Speech Date	Homes Listening	Percent of Total Homes
June 10, 1936	6,300,000	9.7
October 10, 1936	13,700,000	20.1
October 21, 1936	10,900,000	16.2
January 8, 1938	16,400,000	23.8
November 4, 1938	15,000,000	22.2
January 8, 1940	19,100,000	27.5
March 7, 1940	10,300,000	15.4
June 10, 1940	42,500,000	57.0
October 12, 1940	21,900,000	31.4
December 29, 1940*	43,900,000	59.0
May 27, 1941*	53,800,000	69.8
September 11, 1941*	50,100,000	67.0
December 9, 1941*	62,100,000	79.0
February 23, 1942*	61,365,000	78.1

*Denotes fireside chats only

21. STE PC, May 28, 1941, and *Washington Star,* May 29, 1941, Early 1941 Scrapbook, STEP, FDRL.

22. Schoenherr, "Selling the New Deal," p. 128.

23. Ibid., pp. 128, 190; *Congressional Directory,* 76th Congress, 3rd Session, January 1940, pp. 703–5; Early to Walt Dennis, July 1, 1943, and Dennis to Early, June 29, 1943, Official File (henceforth OF) 144, FDRL. Early responded to Dennis of the National Association of Broadcasters, "who had suggested a name change," and wrote, "Hereafter, at the White House they will designate the President's stated message with the news gatherers as 'press and radio conferences.' " See the resulting change in Franklin D. Roosevelt, *Complete Presidential Press Conferences of Franklin D. Roosevelt* (New York: Da Capo Press, 1972), Press Conference (henceforth PC) 907, July 9, 1943, Vol. 22: 1; also note in ibid., PC 669, August 10, 1940, Vol. 16: 669, that the president responded to a press conference question about a radio rumor with "Oh, that is all right. (Turning to a representative of the Columbia Broadcasting Company.) You heard that?" For reference to the Sarnoff letter, see STE Memorandum for Bill Hassett, October 12, 1944, STEP, FDRL.

24. For first Early quote, see Early to Merlin Aylesworth, President of NBC, May 18, 1933, OF 228, FDRL. Lazarsfeld found some 70 percent of those surveyed in October 1938 preferred radio as a news source. See American Institute of Public Opinion poll of October 17, 1938, as reported in Paul Lazarsfeld, *Radio and the Printed Page: An Introduction to the Study of Radio and Its Role in the Community of Ideas* (New York: Duell, Sloan and Pearce, 1941), p. 259. See also Schoenherr, "Selling the New Deal," p. 129.

Early Memorandum for Charles Michelson, September 15, 1936, STEP, FDRL, concerning KFI and KECA, Los Angeles, which wanted payment for carrying fireside chats in 1936. See also unlabeled AP report, September 10, 1936, Clapper Reference File, Censorship, Box 111, Raymond Clapper Papers (henceforth RCP), Manuscripts Division, Library of Congress (henceforth LofC).

Early used radio speakers to counteract critics. For example, he wrote McIntyre in 1939 that he had Earl Godwin answer Walter Winchell twice in one day. Early to McIntyre, June 20, 1939, STEP, FDRL. Early reprimanded other broadcasters as well. See James G. Crowley to William D. Hassett, October 25, 1941, OF 36, FDRL.

25. Roosevelt Memorandum for Early, October 16, 1936, Early Confidential Memorandum for Miss Le Hand, October 20, 1936, and Walter T. Brown to Marguerite Le Hand, October 3, 1936, PSF, FDRL. Machold was Henry Edmund Machold, former speaker of the New York assembly and a partner of Floyd L. Carlisle, the "power baron" of northeast New York state. Prall was FCC Chairman Anning S. Prall.

Roosevelt Memorandum for STE, April 30, 1938, PSF, FDRL. Handwritten notation on the letter was "Done S.E." McNinch was FCC Commissioner Frank R. McNinch.

Roosevelt Memorandum for Early, September 8, 1941, STEP, FDRL. Fly was FCC Chairman James L. Fly. FDR Memorandum for Mac, May 13, 1943, PSF, FDRL.

26. FDR's anger was expressed in Roosevelt Memorandum for Morris L. Ernst, February 7, 1941, PSF, FDRL; James Fly letter to Franklin D. Roosevelt and "Re: Broadcasting Monopoly," May 5, 1941, PSF, FDRL.

For Early's attempts, see Early Memorandum to Edwin "Pa" Watson, March 15, 1941, and May 3, 1941, STEP, FDRL; "NBC Ordered to Drop Out One of Networks," UP Dispatch, May 3, 1941, OF 36, FDRL.

Roosevelt, *Complete Press Conferences,* PC 741, May 16, 1941, Vol. 17: 316.

27. Sherwood, *Roosevelt and Hopkins,* pp. 228, 504; William D. Hassett, *Off the Record with F.D.R., 1942–1945* (New Brunswick, N.J.: Rutgers University Press, 1958), p. 18; Roosevelt, *Complete Press Conferences,* PC 807, February 24, 1942, Vol. 19: 57.

28. Kalton C. Lahue and Joseph A. Bailey, *Glass, Brass and Chrome: The 35mm* (Norman: University of Oklahoma Press, 1972), pp. 77–81; Aaron J. Erickson, *Get That Picture!* (New York: National Library Press, 1938), pp. 30, 104; Howard L. Kany and William C. Bourne, "Just One More Please," in *Dateline: Washington, the Story of National Affairs Journalism in the Life and Times of the National Press Club,* Cabell Phillips et al., eds. (Garden City, N.Y.: Doubleday, 1949), pp. 141–52.

29. William L. Rivers, Theodore Peterson, and Jay W. Jensen, *The Mass Media and Modern Society,* 2d ed. (San Francisco: Rinehart Press, 1971), p. 26.

30. William L. Rivers, *The Opinionmakers: The Washington Press Corps* (Boston: Beacon Press, 1967), p. 137; *New York Times,* March 3, 1933.

31. Early Memorandum to Al Nesensohn, April 11, 1933, STEP, FDRL.

32. Early Memorandum for the Photographers, April 27, 1933, OF 36, FDRL; Early to A. B. Bottini, August 26, 1936, and Bottini to Franklin D. Roosevelt, August 15, 1936, OF 72, FDRL. See also Early Memorandum for the Photographers, May 1, 1933, OF 36, FDRL; Stephen T. Early Diary, June 9, 1939, STEP, FDRL. As examples, Early instructions to the photographers were in the following memoranda: January 30, February 2 and 8, May 15, 1934, OF 36, FDRL; Early to George T. Bye, September 25, 1941, OF 72, FDRL. See also White House Photographers Association, OF 36, FDRL.

33. The Secret Service took particular care after the February 1933 assassination attempt on Roosevelt's life. They would not allow trains or cars to pass the president. See William McKinley Moore, "F.D.R.'s Image: A Study in Pictorial Symbols" (Ph.D. dissertation, University of Wisconsin, 1946), pp. 474, 476–77.

34. Early Memorandum for the Photographers, January 30, February 2 and 8, and May 15, 1934, OF 36, FDRL; Early Memorandum for the Photographers, May 1 and 20, 1933, OF 36, FDRL; Early Memorandum for the Photographers, January 30, 1934, OF 36, FDRL; Charles Hurd, *When the New Deal Was Young and Gay* (New York: Harper, 1965), p. 231; Early Telegram to McIntyre, September 1, 1937, OF 72-N, FDRL; Early Memorandum, May 25, 1939, OF 171, FDRL: Early Diary, October 28, 1937, and April 4, 1939, STEP, FDRL; Early Memorandum for William Hassett, August 27, 1940, STEP, FDRL.

35. Early Night Letter to George B. Freeman, May 24, 1935, OF 36, FDRL; Kany and Bourne, "Just One More, Please," p. 150; undated, unlabeled clippings concerning the 1935 farm problem found in Clapper Reference File, Censorship, Box 110, RCP, LofC.

As another incident, William Hassett mentions being furious when an unnamed movie star managed to sit next to the president at Warm Springs and photographers snapped pictures. Hassett wrote, "We suppressed all the pictures." See November 28, 1944, *Off the Record with F.D.R.,* pp. 300–301.

36. Early Memorandum to Colonel Starling, June 9, 1935, STEP, FDRL. Early notation "Fix with S.S. No pictures of the President. S.T.E.," written from phone memo from Eleanor Ragsdale of *Life,* June 12, 1943, STEP, FDRL.

37. Moore, "F.D.R.'s Image," pp. 484–85; *New York Tribune,* July 20, 1937, plus three other clippings, unlabeled, found in Clapper Reference File, Censorship, Box 111, RCP, LofC. Early's 1937 Scrapbook, STEP, FDRL, is full of clippings about the incident.

When Eleanor Roosevelt's bodyguard Earl Miller wanted to sell his snapshots of the "hot dog party" to the Associated Press, Early attempted to stop him. See Early Memorandum to Miller, June 20, 1939, OF 171, FDRL.

38. Thomas S. Bills to Dorothy Jones, September 25, 1940, OF 36, FDRL; *Time,* September 23, 1940, *Washington Star,* September 12, 1940, *Washington Times-Herald,* September 12, 1940, Early 1940 Scrapbook, STEP, FDRL. See also Kany and Bourne, "Just One More, Please," p. 151.

This was not the first boycott of photographing FDR. Moore wrote that there was a pre-inauguration boycott in January 1933 when Roosevelt stipulated that the pictures of himself must be as he was speaking at the opening of the Theodore Roosevelt Memorial Hall in Manhattan's American Museum of National History. The photographers turned in no pictures. Moore, "F.D.R.'s Image," p. 467. The same reference was in the undated *Washington Times-Herald* article found in Clapper Reference File, Censorship, Box 111, RCP, LofC.

39. Moore, "F.D.R.'s Image," pp. 477–78, 510–11, 639; Hugh Gregory Gallapher, *FDR's Splendid Deception* (New York: Dodd, Mead, 1985), pp. 93–94.

40. Moore, "F.D.R.'s Image," pp. 511, 637; Compton MacKenzie, *Mr. Roosevelt* (London: John Lane, 1944), p. 136; *Fortune,* October 1932, p. 40, for one of the few photographs showing Roosevelt with a cane; *Fortune,* August 1932, p. 24, for a caricature of Roosevelt with a cane; *New York Times,* October 6, 1937.

41. "The President's Album," *Life,* August 6, 1937, p. 27; Early Confidential Memorandum for Dr. McIntire, August 23, 1937, STEP, FDRL. For more on Luce's break with FDR, see James L. Baughman, *Henry R. Luce and the Rise of the American News Media* (Boston: Twayne Publishers, 1987), pp. 106–7.

42. STE PC, March 11, 1937, White House Scrapbook, STEP, FDRL. See also Stephen Early Memorandum for the Attorney General, February 10, 1938, OF 10B, FDRL.

Edmund William Starling does not mention any stopping or policing of photographers in *Starling of the White House* (New York: Simon and Schuster, 1946).

43. Moore, "F.D.R.'s Image," p. 638.

44. Raymond Clapper Diary, July 29, 1936, Box 8, RCP, LofC; James M. Mac-Gregor Burns, *Roosevelt: The Lion and the Fox* (New York: Harcourt, Brace, 1956), p. 273.

45. *Time,* January 2, 1933, pp. 2–4. The comeback image references were in Moore, "F.D.R.'s Image," pp. 642–43. Henry F. Pringle did describe FDR's mobility in "Profiles: The President, II," *The New Yorker,* June 23, 1934, p. 20.

46. William E. Leuchtenburg, *Franklin D. Roosevelt and the New Deal, 1932–1940* (New York: Harper and Brothers, 1963), p. 169; Rivers, *The Opinionmakers,* p. 137; Clark Kinnaird, *The Real F.D.R.* (New York: Harper and Brothers, 1945), p. 36.

47. Early, "The Newsreels," script for broadcast, October 15, 1954, Broadcast on Station WOL, STEP, FDRL. For other motion picture discussion of the era, see Raymond Fielding, *The American Newsreel, 1911–1967* (Norman: University of Oklahoma Press, 1972), p. 311.

48. Early to George M. Dorsey, n.d., OF 36, FDRL; Schoenherr, "Selling the New Deal," p. 145.

49. Early Memorandum to William Hassett, August 27, 1940, STEP, FDRL.

50. William P. Montague to Stephen T. Early, August 30, 1933, STEP; Early Memorandum for Marvin McIntyre, March 8, 1938, STEP; Early to John S. Martin, editor of the *March of Time,* January 14, 1936, STEP, FDRL; Schoenherr, "Selling the New Deal," p. 157.

51. Stephen Early Memorandum for J. C. Brown of Metro Goldwyn Mayer, September 12, 1935, STEP, FDRL.

52. Early Telegram to Editor of Universal Newsreel and to Pathe, Paramount, Fox, and MGM, March 12, 1933, OF 73, FDRL; Ragland, "Franklin D. Roosevelt and Public Opinion, 1933–1940," p. 251. Ragland interviewed and quoted George Dorsey, manager of the Washington bureau of Pathe News.

53. Early Diary, November 8, 1937, STEP, FDRL.

54. Ibid., September 29, 1936.

55. Schoenherr, "Selling the New Deal," pp. 153–55.

56. "FDR Statement," May 2, 1943, STEP, FDRL.

57. Roosevelt, *Public Papers and Addresses,* Vol. 1, p. 430; Roosevelt, *Franklin D. Roosevelt Reader,* pp. 222–23.

"All about us are threats of new aggression—military and economic."
The president's State of the Union Message to Congress, January 4,
1939. Courtesy of the Franklin D. Roosevelt Library.

7

Second-Term Crises and a Lack of Newspaper Support

Verily, the freedom of the press is in jeopardy, not from the Government but from certain types of newspaper owners.
—Franklin D. Roosevelt to Cleveland Rogers of the
Brooklyn Daily Eagle, August 11, 1936

Franklin Delano Roosevelt wanted not only unfiltered news about himself and his administrations but also an American press to mirror the popular will. The newspapers, however, did not mirror what seemed to be public opinion, especially because of the tremendous gap between his election returns and the editorial support of his opponents. When journalists asked about press freedoms, the president was quick to retort that freedom of the press was in danger from the editorial biases of newspaper owners. Such a lack of newspaper editorial support existed not only while FDR was running for office but also while he was trying to lead the country and set new policies. Indeed, this condition may have been a major factor in determining Roosevelt's news management tactics, especially during several crucial crises from 1936 to 1940: his 1936 reelection campaign, the Court-packing plan, Justice Hugo Black's appointment, the 1937–38 recession, the 1938 congressional election, the growing international war, and his 1940 reelection campaign. This chapter will cover Roosevelt's media actions and reactions to these crises.[1]

With each election year, Roosevelt had less and less newspaper editorial support. When Roosevelt was elected in 1932, he had 57 percent of the popular vote but the editorial support of only 41 percent of the American dailies and 45 percent of the weeklies. In 1936 when the American public reelected Roosevelt by 60 percent of the popular vote, his newspaper support dropped to 37 percent of the dailies and a little over 40 percent of the weeklies. The president then lost William Randolph Hearst's endorsement and split the Patterson-McCormick chain, with the *New York Daily News* supporting him and the *Chicago Tribune* continuing its animosity. According to Frank Luther Mott's findings, the 1940 presidential election revealed one of the largest gaps between newspaper and popular support since the days of Thomas Jefferson. Roosevelt had 55 percent of the popular vote but the support of only 25 percent of the daily newspapers and 33 percent of the weekly newspapers. No longer did the president have the endorsements of the *New York Daily News,* the *New York Times,* or the Scripps-Howard papers, which had a close association with the United Press Association. The *New York Times* came back in 1944, but other major newspapers did not. Roosevelt's progressive decline in newspaper support also indicated that the opinion pieces and editorial slants of the American press did not have strong persuasive powers.[2]

During Roosevelt's first year, several major American daily publishers, such as William Randolph Hearst and Robert McCormick, had begun a frontal attack on those New Deal social and economic changes which aimed for a redistribution of national income and challenged their own "vested interests." In particular, they and other publishers were angry about the National Recovery Administration Codes: section 7 (a), which gave employees the right of collective bargaining, and section 4 (b), which specified maximum hours, minimum wages, and restrictions on the employment of children. To the publishers, the code enforcement was especially onerous, since it would give the president a type of licensing power; to the publishers it would be a blow to freedom of the press.[3]

Hearst instructed his *New York American* editor, Edmund Coblentz, to tell the president that he would fight the NRA—that "Nonsensical, Ridiculous, Asinine interference"—"with every means at my command . . . even if it costs me every nickel I possess." When the *Chicago Tribune's* correspondent questioned the president about freedom of the press, Roosevelt retorted, "You tell Bert McCormick that he is seeing things under the bed." After the publishers insisted on an additional section to guarantee freedom of the press, Roosevelt in disagreeing with their demand told the correspondents, "The recitation of the freedom of the press clause in the code . . . has no more place here than would the recitation of the whole Constitution or of the Ten Commandments. The freedom guaranteed by the Constitution is freedom of expression and that will be scrupulously respected—but it is not freedom to work children, or do business in a firetrap or violate the laws against obscenity, libel or lewdness."[4]

Initially, Roosevelt's method for treating such opposition was to go over the heads of the publishers and use his personal charm. While he did not meet with the American Newspaper Publishers Association (ANPA) in the White House, he did hold annual press meetings for the National Conference of Business Editors (NCBE) and for the American Society of Newspaper Editors

(ASNE), where many editors were also the publishers. Roosevelt sent congratulatory letters on their anniversaries, acknowledged favorable editorials, and wished their conventions and press association meetings well. Yet in January 1936 he wrote Roving Ambassador Norman Davis, "Things here are going well in spite of the Supreme Court majority opinions and Hearst and Alfred E. Smith, and an 85 percent newspaper opposition."[5]

Roosevelt's concern was understandable, especially given the opposition of the Hearst papers, the *Chicago Tribune,* the *New York Herald-Tribune,* the *New York Sun,* the *Detroit Free Press,* and the *Los Angeles Times.* A newspaper's editorial stand could affect the news interpretation. According to Leo Rosten's study on the Washington correspondents, reporters from the large Hearst chain and the *Chicago Tribune* were "stopped from writing anything that even suggested the possibility of Roosevelt's reelection."[6]

FDR used knowledgeable publicists for the 1936 campaign. In July they had Eleanor Roosevelt do an analysis much like Louis Howe used to do. Charlie Michelson had responsibility for the publicity, while Early, White House assistant Stanley High, and correspondent Henry Suydam of the *Brooklyn Daily Eagle* were part of the steering committee. They suggested press answers to the Republican charges and also arranged for a regular supply of news, feature stories, pictures, mats, and boiler-plate items. To make sure the president received fair coverage by the country's largest press association, Roosevelt wrote Ambassador Robert Bingham, a former president of the Associated Press and publisher of the *Louisville Courier-Journal,* "I am delighted that you are coming back the first of June and I think that if you can plan to be here through June and perhaps over the fourth of July before returning to London, you will be able to lay a lot of groundwork in the Associated Press organization looking toward complete fairness by them."[7]

FDR and his press advisers wanted to project an image that was above politics. The president opened the Cleveland Exposition, inspected restoration in the flood-damaged Midwest, viewed public works projects, and took "look-see" trips through the drought-striken Plains states. Roosevelt's strategy was to appear as an active president, touring and speaking for a few minutes without referring to the opposition by name or to the campaign. He pursued the strategy so relentlessly that in August, United Press correspondent Fred Storm asked Early, "Say, Steve, is this going to be a nonpolitical campaign?"[8]

In all his travels and speeches, Roosevelt made the same points over and over again: that March 1936 was certainly different from March 1933 and that the New Deal was playing the role of getting the country out of the depression. The opposition papers had to print such spot news, along with the explanatory news releases about these official trips, since they were institutionally dependent on the wire services. As public relations expert Carl Byoir wrote Marvin McIntyre, "Someone in this connection has handled the personal contact problem with the press association representatives so well that the regular wire dispatches hit the editor from the source he is accustomed to regard as a real news source, and so it gets printed largely without editing."9

At the same time, many journalists helped the committee. Roy Howard, head of the Scripps-Howard League, suggested a synopsis of the president's speeches to give the afternoon papers a break. Both the *Chicago Times* and the *New York Daily News* distributed campaign buttons. The *Daily News* donated full pages opposite the editorial page to both the Republican and the Democratic committees to print their own "Battle Pages," which were also syndicated throughout the country. When Arthur Krock asked in a *New York Times* column, "Can the New Deal Credits Be Itemized?" Secretary of the Treasury Henry Morgenthau, Jr., obtained the necessary data and on September 20 the *New York Times* ran "Uncle Sam's Ledger for Four New Deal Years."10

Yet anti-Roosevelt publishers were unceasing in their attacks. The *Washington Times-Herald* wrote that "this administration has been marked by the transparent encouragement of left-wing agitators and plotters against our government." The *New York Herald-Tribune* played up Democrat Henry Breckinridge's radio speech, "Roosevelt, a Sponsor of Hate," which insisted that "no President ever stirred more rancor." The Hearst papers and the *Chicago Tribune* accused the New Deal of Communist party connections and wrote that Moscow ordered the American Communists to back FDR. When the *Chicago Daily Times* offered a $5,000 reward for proof of the *Tribune's* accusation, no one responded.11

In the meantime, Robert McCormick was doing more than "seeing things under the bed." From the beginning of August, the *Tribune* telephone operators answered the telephone with "Good Afternoon," followed by the *Tribune's* daily box and changing numbers: "Only 92 days remain to save your country. What are you doing to save it?" After the president spoke in Chicago, the *Tribune* staged a picture of a man sweeping up discarded Roosevelt buttons from Chicago's streets. The *Chicago Times* discovered that McCormick had paid the sweeper and donated the buttons.12

While the anti-Roosevelt publishers continued to attack, the publicity steering committee used various defensive tactics. When the *New York Herald-Tribune* changed a wire service story and wrote misleading headlines, Early suggested to Charlie Michelson that "some very prominent New Yorker be found who will write the editor of the *Herald Tribune* a letter along the lines of the attached draft." When the GOP sent a circular to editors offering them campaign writings, Michelson made sure that they also received a clipsheet naming columnists David Lawrence, Mark Sullivan, and Frank R. Kent as "the three musketeers of anti-administration." To answer the Hearst communist charges, Early prepared a memorandum full of possible editorial quotations and references from Ferdinand Lundberg's *The Imperial Hearst* and Henry Cabot Lodge's and Theodore Roosevelt's published correspondence.[13]

The committee also relied on dissension within the Hearst ranks. Hearst's chief columnist Arthur Brisbane wrote Roosevelt in March that he could not "see any great change in the (election) situation." Eddie Roddan, formerly Hearst's International News Service White House correspondent, prepared the "Battle Page" campaign material. Hearst correspondents passed along every move of the publisher to the Democratic leaders well in advance. When the administration learned of Hearst's plan to charge in Hearst papers across the country that Roosevelt had the support of the Russian Communists, Early had enough time to counter with a press statement: "My attention has been called to a planned attempt by a certain notorious newspaper owner to make it appear that the President passively accepts the support of alien organizations hostile to the American form of government. The President does not want and does not welcome the vote or support of any individual or groups taking orders from alien sources. The American people will not permit their attention to be diverted from the real issues to fake issues which no patriotic, honorable, decent citizen would purposely inject into American affairs."[14]

The president and his national committee used the radio to a great extent. Their largest publicity expense was $840,000 for radio, an increase of $500,000 from 1932. In fact, radio was so much a part of the campaign that Stanley High worried in September that the committee was using it too much, at the expense of platform campaigning. To gain free broadcast time, Roosevelt would speak in his official capacity as president. No complaints were filed about such presidential "educational" addresses until the fall, when Roosevelt's September fireside chat on the drought was cut by two Los Angeles stations, as noted in chapter 6.[15]

The Republicans also relied heavily on radio, but their candidate was no oratorical match for FDR. Alf Landon's attempts appeared "painful," or as Marquis Childs wrote, "You could be homely and homespun but if you didn't know how to put it across, you looked merely inept and foolish." The GOP tried to use various dramatic series to stress points. On October 17 Senator Arthur Vandenberg conducted a "Mystery Fireside Chat," with edited sections of Roosevelt's recorded speeches. The senator then debated the excerpts. Once CBS realized what was happening, it cut off one-third of the eastern stations and deleted program portions from the western area. In the ensuing uproar the press and some members of Congress demanded an investigation, although the FCC did nothing.[16]

The president's campaign tactics were effective in what many people called "one of the most slanderous campaigns in the entire history of American journalism." By mid-October the *New York Times* announced in its survey of twenty national political newswriters that the president was the obvious win-

ner. At the end of October Heywood Broun wrote, "The working newspaperman who has been close to the campaign is utterly convinced that Roosevelt
will win, and that he will win easily . . . no man in the White House has ever
succeeded in converting so many correspondents to his cause. . . . There
never was any President who could charm the newspaperman down from the
trees as Franklin Delano Roosevelt."[17]

In November Roosevelt's win swept the country like a tidal wave, the
biggest popular plurality recorded to date. He carried every state but Vermont
and Maine. FDR referred to the lack of newspaper editorial support in a letter
to his former boss, Ambassador Josephus Daniels: "Thank the Lord it was not
a close vote. . . . One of the most amazing of the undoubted facts was the
discrediting not only of the Hearst papers, but the Chicago Tribune, the New
York Herald Tribune and the Sun and The Boston Herald, but also of dozens
of smaller papers which aped the others. . . . I think that this type of newspaper so overdid things that the public saw through it at least by September
and since then the attacks gained us votes."[18]

Pro-Roosevelt commentators wrote of the irony of such a large FDR win
given so little press support. A *New York Post* editorial warned that the
president's extraordinary victory was serious, not only because Roosevelt's
biggest majorities were in cities where the bulk of the press was against him
but also "because it bespeaks a sharp decline of public confidence in the
nation's major channels of information, the newspapers."[19]

At the December Gridiron dinner, FDR could not resist a satirical barb
about the newspapers' campaign coverage:

> This character Roosevelt was a villain. He combined the worst features of Ivan
> the Terrible, Machiavelli, Judas Iscariot, Henry VIII, Charlotte Corday and Jesse
> James. . . . I began to believe it myself. Didn't I read it in the columns of our
> great papers? These papers had been awarded prizes for their artistic make-up
> and sometimes even for their enterprise in ferreting out facts. . . .
>
> Yet some people . . . speak of the danger of the regimentation of our press. . . .
> Suppose the Government required newspapers to purchase and print some of the
> canned editorial features dealing with national affairs that now fill our Press! The
> outcries of editors present here tonight would be heard around the world. Gen-
> tlemen, it needs no Government to regiment the American press. Any regimenting
> of the American press which is present today or looms in the offing comes from
> regimenting of it by the Press itself.[20]

Two weeks after his second inauguration, Roosevelt planned to ensure his
New Deal programs legally. He proposed a judicial reform bill to permit the
president to appoint a new Supreme Court justice for every justice who failed
to retire by the age of seventy. Although there was no provision for the
number of Supreme Court justices in the Constitution, as many as six new
justices could be appointed. With statutory changes, the original six justices

had increased to as many as ten in 1863. Roosevelt's public rationale was the Supreme Court's inefficiency, congestion, and judicial delay—all due to the justices' advanced ages. Indeed, the bill pointedly referred to the Court's inefficiency and age rather than to its philosophy, which led to the voiding of the National Recovery Act and other New Deal legislation, or to the fact that Roosevelt had not been able to make a single Supreme Court appointment.[21]

Roosevelt did not follow his usual method of consulting with his advisers and congressional leaders before he presented this major piece of legislation. After his overwhelming reelection, the president seemed to toss all political caution to the winds. Although FDR had secretly dictated George Creel's December *Collier's* article, "Roosevelt's Plans and Purposes," the Court plan as a trial balloon had been ignored. FDR surprised the country, including his own leaders in Congress, when he broke the news of the Court proposal to the press first.[22]

On February 5 the president called a special news conference to read his message. The correspondents found the "air tense" when they arrived at a meeting that they thought concerned "wages and hours legislation." Raymond Clapper noted the unusual conference began with "nothing casual, no joking with the men on the front row while others were assembling, high pitched excitement." Clapper wrote that while the president explained his proposals, "he betrayed his keyed up, tense voice and seemed a little breathless as he read and talked." He paused and received laughs with his references to the justices' advanced ages: "The congestion of the courts and litigation had now become a life-long adventure." As Roosevelt continued, Thomas Stokes of the United Press felt the tension increase in the room: "What a story!"[23]

Not all journalists were impressed. Mark Sullivan, suspicious of Roosevelt's motive, wondered if the president was trying to take the limelight away from the five-week-long General Motors strike, which involved other industries and half a million workers. He also questioned whether this was Roosevelt's warning to the Supreme Court since it was scheduled to consider the Wagner Labor Act.[24]

The Court reform bill had tremendous public and newspaper opposition. The public responded with letters and telegrams to Congress running nine to one against the plan. Within a month, the American Institute of Public Opinion showed only 38 percent of the people supported the bill. The bill also fed previous editorial accusations that Roosevelt was trying to subvert institutions and overturn the Constitution. Within two weeks, newspapers such as the *New York Times* and the *Washington Post* began running two pages of critical letters. In addition, the *Washington Post, New York Herald-Tribune,* and *Portland Oregonian* began printing pages of comments from other newspapers. Frank E. Gannett collected considerable sums of money for his National

Committee to Uphold Constitutional Government and sent out hundreds of reprints of the opposition's addresses, such as those by Senator Carter Glass.[25]

Eleven days after Congress received the plan, Harold Ickes wrote in his diary that he did "not recall any single issue affecting the Government that has caused the spilling of so much printer's ink or led to so many fervent discussions. The President has a first-class fight on his hands. Practically all the newspapers are against him, even those in the Scripps-Howard chain which supported him during the election."[26]

After the Scripps-Howard papers came out against the Court plan, Roosevelt and presidential assistants Tom Corcoran and Ben Cohen tried to win over Washington bureau chief George "Deac" Parker. Although he began to tone his editorials down a bit, Parker still wrote that the plan was "too clever," "a little too ingenious," and "too slick." Parker argued that it would have been better to have made the proposition straight out on its merits of changing the Court's philosophy rather than "dressing it up" in the guise of overage justices and inefficiency.[27]

When the oratorical barrage from both sides became more strident amid public rumblings, Roosevelt tried an unprecedented press action. He gave his only exclusive interview to a Washington correspondent. To get his viewpoint on the front pages of the major trend-setting newspaper and possibly garner editorial support, the president explained his philosophy and his purposes for the Court reform bill to *New York Times* bureau chief Arthur Krock. As noted in chapter 4, this interview backfired with the other correspondents.[28]

The White House then decided to "sell the court plan to the country" through the Democratic National Committee (DNC). Much as they did during the election, Jim Farley and Charlie Michelson wrote speeches and then arranged for them to be inserted in the *Congressional Record,* so that they might be printed and distributed in conveniently franked envelopes. But these efforts were half-hearted, fumbling, and weak compared with the opposition's efforts in Congress.[29]

Roosevelt waited until March 4 before speaking. His election victory celebration speech before 1,300 Democrats was broadcast to thousands more at 1,100 other victory dinners elsewhere. He was determined, and he wanted to rally support. He had a public mandate and had carried with him a huge Democratic majority in Congress. Roosevelt came out fighting with a vengeance: "I say we must act—now!"[30]

As his ultimate tactic, Roosevelt gave a fireside chat on March 9. He compared the highest court to an obstinate horse which refused to pull together with the other horses in the "three horse team" of the national government. The president then defended his Court plan at length and pointed to his own record of devotion to civil and religious liberty. Yet his frank appeal failed to move Congress or the people.[31]

In the meantime, the Supreme Court knocked the props out from under

Roosevelt's actual reasons for reform by delivering a series of pro-New Deal decisions. In January the Court had upheld the Silver Purchase Bill and the Washington state minimum wage law. By the end of March the Court ruled in favor of the Railway Labor Act and the revised Frazier-Lemke farm mortgage moratorium. The most obvious change of the Court's philosophy came on April 12 when it upheld the Wagner Labor Relations Act. Justice Owen Roberts, who had voted with the Court conservatives, now switched to the liberal side. In addition, Justice Willis Van Devanter, who had kept secret his plans to retire, aided the bill's opponents by timing his resignation on May 18 to coincide with the expected vote of the Judiciary Committee against the Court bill.[32]

At 4:15 P.M. that same day, when Franklin D. Roosevelt held his regularly scheduled press conference, he acknowledged the large expectant crowd. J. Russell Young quickly retorted, "They are just curious today." Before anyone could ask about the most newsworthy happenings—Justice Van Devanter's resignation and the Senate committee's veto—FDR quickly launched another topic. He went into an off-the-record discussion of the McClure Syndicate's confidential pink sheets that went out to 270 editors and read two items from the May 12–13 and May 14–15 editions: that the president was found in a coma with a "neck rash which is typical of certain disturbing symptoms" and that an American Cyanide official asserted at a recent banquet that a "couple of well-placed bullets would be the best thing for the country." Roosevelt kept on this topic as the correspondents asked many questions about the "pink sheets" and editor Richard Waldo. Finally, someone commented, "There seems to be a strange temerity here today, about asking about the Supreme Court." Only eight questions followed that particular remark. When a correspondent inquired, "Will Justice Van Devanter's retirement affect your program in connection with the court program?" Roosevelt's response gave away his tactic, "I don't think there is any news in that" to close the issue.[33]

Such timing was perfect. The McClure sheets vied with Justice Van Devanter's retirement and the Senate Judiciary Committee's veto for headline news. In the ensuing uproar over the McClure sheets, the National Press Club expelled Richard Waldo. The White House Correspondents' Association posted additional rules to bar from membership those reporters who made a business of selling confidential information.[34]

Despite intense news management efforts, the proposal to reform the Supreme Court was essentially dead. The Court had switched its votes; one member had resigned. All hope for a further congressional fight was lost after Senate Majority Leader Joe T. Robinson's sudden death on July 14. Nothing had worked to pass the Roosevelt Supreme Court reform measure—not the Democratic National Committee's publicity efforts, not the talks with bureau chief "Deac" Parker, not the *New York Times* exclusive interview, not even the special fireside chat. After the Court had embarked on a new course, the opposition was too great. The crescendo of protest by patriotic groups, bar associations, and town meetings constituted a public denouncement of the president's plan. The issue became not "efficiency," as Roosevelt had emphasized, but rather the president's disingenuous way of meeting the Court's conservative philosophy. Moreover, Roosevelt's surprise announcement to Congress, to the cabinet, and to the people alienated many potential supporters and prevented a broad coalition of support. The Court fight as a logical extension of the president's personal campaign victory in 1936 did not work in 1937. All Roosevelt's publicity efforts failed. This time the people were not behind him. All he could do was set another news agenda with the Waldo incident.[35]

The Court battle story ended, but an epilogue remained. The president now had a chance to make his first Supreme Court appointment. FDR again surprised everyone by nominating Alabama Senator Hugo Black. Again, he acted quickly without consulting with his advisers and Senate leaders or carefully checking on Black's credentials. As a respected colleague, Black received Senate confirmation before Congress adjourned in August. The new justice then left for a European vacation, and the president went fishing. In the meantime, Paul Block of the *Pittsburgh Post-Gazette* produced categorical proof that Black had been a Ku Klux Klan member in the 1920s. Such membership created a news roar during the summer news void.[36]

On September 14 Roosevelt said in his first press conference after his vacation: "Anticipating what you are going to ask and in order to save time (laughter)—I know approximately what is on your minds and I want to be helpful if I can. Therefore I am going to give you this statement for direct quotation. Get out your pencils." The president then successfully closed the topic by stating that he only knew what he read in the newspapers, and "until such time as he [Black] returns there is no further comment to be made." The topic was still newsworthy. No record was kept about what happened at the next press conference a week later when the president was again asked about Black, because the transcript was surprisingly deleted: "By instructions, no notes were taken of about five minutes of discussion off the record" during the questioning about Senator Black's Klan affiliation. This action was unprecedented in the record of Roosevelt's press conferences.[37]

The Black story, as a "hot" news item, prevailed even after Black returned from Europe and defended himself on the radio October 1. Newspapers responded, especially the opposition press. The *New York Post* called the Black statement "inadequate and disappointing"; the *Washington Times-Herald* used a page of other newspaper clips which showed almost unanimous condemnation of Black's speech. FDR sat tight. In the midst of the furor, Black took his bench seat while the Supreme Court considered and then tabled two petitions on the legality of his appointment.[38]

In the meantime, the European war was raging, and the president tried to signal that news. FDR's October 5 Chicago speech was a warning that the epidemic of world lawlessness was spreading. Although Roosevelt had had such a foreign affairs speech in mind ever since the Japanese September assault on northern China, the press accused him of deliberately timing the "quarantine speech" to coincide with Justice Black's return from Europe and the ensuing furor. The press had expected an explanation about Justice Black, and Roosevelt had surprised them again. In fact, Grace Tully remembered that there had been much press speculation on what the president might say in Chicago over Justice Black's KKK connection.[39]

The next day the correspondents tried to pin down the president on the Black appointment at the press conference. After rereading the president's September 14 statement, "until such time as he returns there is no further comment to be made," Bob Anderson of the Associated Press remarked, "Now he is back" and "that probably implied that there would be a comment, did it not?" The president emphatically insisted:

No, it strongly implied that there was a possibility, that is all; not that it would be.
I know my English.
Q. Until?
THE PRESIDENT: No.

Roosevelt refused to discuss Justice Black's Ku Klux Klan affiliation any further no matter how interested the reporters were.[40]

World events switched public attention away from the Court appointment. The significance of Roosevelt's quarantine speech was not lost on publishers. Even the hostile *Chicago Tribune* acknowledged that the president's words "may well prove the most important speech Roosevelt ever made." On the other hand, many papers, such as those run by Hearst, screamed, "We are being precipitated into war." Yet the expression "quarantine," the key word in the speech, appeared in the titles of editorials and cartoons and gave the American people something to think about while the Spanish Civil War was raging, the Germans and Italians were arming, and the Japanese were pushing into China. The *Washington Herald* and the *New York Post* named Roosevelt the "figure of the week" and the "man of the week." World events and the president's efforts diverted the public once again from an embarrassing matter.[41]

One other event did overwhelm the president's news management ability. Roosevelt lost even more popular confidence with the 1937–38 "Roosevelt Recession." The administration had allowed the Federal Reserve Board to restrict monetary expansion and attempt to balance the budget. By mid-November the 1937 economic decline was so severe that it could not be ignored. Roosevelt called Congress into a special session for new legislation. Despite the Supreme Court's new decisions giving the federal government the right to shape economic policy, Congress remained independent and did not pass a single Roosevelt bill. The nation's unemployment figures grew rapidly, and small businesses began folding. Roosevelt needed to explain his proposals and actions.[42]

Although the correspondents had been asking about the economy since mid-October, Roosevelt remained evasive and testy through November. In December, responding to one correspondent's double question about the worsening recession and his plans to check it, the president answered:

On number one, it is an assumption and, number two, don't tie my hands.

Q. You think it is an assumption?

THE PRESIDENT: Well, people argue it both ways.[43]

In his January 1938 special press seminar on the budget, Roosevelt finally publicly acknowledged the severe economic decline and stated that he expected "approval of Congress and the public for additional appropriations if they become necessary to save thousands of American families from dire need." By the middle of February the issue was so pressing that Roosevelt had to announce federal action. He came to his press conference with a long press statement and a series of agency charts to explain the problem.[44]

In April the president completely reversed his previous plans for a balanced budget. At a special press conference of editors and publishers of trade papers, Roosevelt went into a long explanation of the benefits of economic "pump priming," his proposed relief and public works appropriations. Not only did he maintain the money would immediately put people to work but he said the public works would include flood control and soil erosion projects.[45]

At the same time, Roosevelt began blaming the recession on the press, in particular the American newspaper editors. While Congress was discussing his proposals, the president accused the editors of unfair editorials, inaccurate leads, and misleading headlines and said that the country's newspapers "have been more responsible for the inciting of fear in the community than any other factor." He then challenged the editors to change, as "the press can be largely responsible for cutting out the petty stuff and getting their shoulders in behind national recovery." By fall he assured the correspondents that government expenditures, including deficit spending for economic recovery and monetary expansion with pump priming, would not reach their maximum until the next spring.[46]

The legislative battles over the Supreme Court and the recession resulted in a division of the Democratic party officeholders. Conservative Democrats lined up with conservative Republicans to protest expansions of executive power and to thwart Roosevelt's proposals. By the spring of 1938 it was not certain whether a liberal wing of the Democratic party could nominate a 1940 ticket. Within the New Deal, there was a cry for vengeance. An opportunity was at hand when some of the senators were up for reelection. Tom Stokes of the Scripps-Howard Newspaper Alliance later wrote that a "'purge'. . . flowered slowly from the rank and poisonous hatred generated as passions were aroused by the fight over the Supreme Court." Although the president sought party realignment along the ideological lines of his liberal programs, the administration's efforts were severely limited in scope. Roosevelt's "purge," however, had great symbolic importance for serving notice that the president would not support those candidates whose overall record had not been for the New Deal principles.[47]

Roosevelt, who found the conservative tactics undemocratic and intolerable, embarked on his cleansing campaign with a fireside chat on June 24. In the broadcast, FDR identified himself as the leader of the Democratic party charged with the responsibility of seeing that its candidates remain faithful to their platform pledges. He announced his intentions to campaign for liberal congressional candidates as Democratic party leaders. He said, "I feel I have every right to speak in those few instances where there may be a clear issue between candidates for the nomination involving those principles, or involving a clear misuse of my name."[48]

Ever mindful of the power of words, Roosevelt abhorred the newspaper reference to "purge," and he chided the correspondents for using such "an immature word" in headlines and leads. Rather, the president preferred statements entitled "Why the President 'Interferes.' " He also defended himself against what he called the "Tory Press" accusations that he should remain silent.[49]

FDR's endorsement may have helped several faithful senators such as Alben Barkley of Kentucky win renomination, but his opposition to southern conservatives such as Senator Walter George of Georgia and Senator "Cotton Ed" Smith of South Carolina came too late to be effective. In one New York congressional race, his supporters campaigned successfully to stop the renomination of the obstructionist chair of the House Rules Committee, John J. O'Connor. FDR used his special assistant, Eugene Casey, to go on the radio every night for fifteen minutes during the Lewis-Tydings primary election campaign in Maryland to deflate what the *Baltimore Sun* papers said, but FDR's preference, David Lewis, lost.[50]

The 1938 election resulted in the first important Republican gains in a decade: eighty-one new House seats, eight new Senate positions, and thirteen new governorships. More than any other issue, the recession hurt the Democrats and resuscitated the Republicans. For all of his efforts, Roosevelt's political power appeared to be diminishing. Raymond Clapper wrote, "Clearly, I think, that President Roosevelt could not run for a third term even if he so desired."[51]

International events would change the script. In 1938, while Roosevelt struggled with the recession, the Nazis engulfed Austria. As he lectured to the

American Newspaper Editors that spring about their unfair editorials, inaccurate leads, and misleading headlines, the Japanese, who were convinced of American apathy after the bombing of the *USS Panay,* two Standard Oil tankers, and American missions along the Yangtse, prepared for another assault on China. During the midterm election campaigns, Hitler pushed into Sudetenland. While Roosevelt endeavored to protect the New Deal from an aggressive Congress, the Germans were swallowing up the rest of Czechoslovakia and looking over the map of Europe. When the president tried to alert the country to the Nazi dangers and sought to rebuild American defenses, critics hooted that he was trying to cover up domestic failures by embroiling the country in foreign adventures.[52]

As the European events grew more critical, the president had to move cautiously, in part because he was manacled by the isolationists and public opinion. The majority of the American people and newspapers wanted to stay out of the 1939 European war, despite the Nazis' actions on the continent. When France and Great Britain quietly began purchasing munitions in 1939 as part of the American program of increased arms production, Roosevelt insisted on secrecy. After an American bomber with a French official aboard crashed in California in January, the president at first equivocated when correspondents asked if planes also went to England: "I do not know. I don't think they are actually after any planes at this time; not that I know of." Yet four days later in a press conference, FDR referred to the French and British controversial plane orders.[53]

When the president met with the Senate Military Affairs Committee in February, a "storm" surfaced after someone leaked the president's words that the American frontier "lay on the Rhine." Roosevelt responded that "some boob got that off; I don't think it was a member of the press." While enroute to Florida two weeks later, the president used the opportunity to explain to the traveling reporters how nations were dependent on each other, as an attempt to define the much publicized phrase. Although he refused to state the extent of U.S. interests, Roosevelt discussed the economic and political interdependence of Europe and the United States. He then suggested the news interpretation to the journalists: "Having told you all this off the record, I think that unconsciously, in the writing of future stories, not in the next two weeks but in the next few months, now that you have the low-down, that you will subconsciously infiltrate the idea into your stories. This is an honest, polite way of putting it." When one correspondent asked, "In other words, bend over forwards back?" the president retorted, "What they call subconscious infiltration."[54]

Even with such infiltration, the journalists had to be amenable. The international danger directly affected the correspondents' access to the White House. After Hitler moved into Czechoslovakia, Roosevelt suggested that everybody in the White House be fingerprinted, including the correspondents. By March

21 the Secret Service was carefully checking the fingerprinted correspondents as they came into the press conference.[55]

The president personally campaigned the American editors to support the lifting of the arms embargo. He talked to the American Society of Newspaper Editors in an April off-the-record press conference about his need to alert the country to the dangers of the European situation. He ended the meeting with "God knows, we do not want to get into a war and again, on the doctrine of chances of our getting into a war, it is an extremely long-range bet. I think we want to keep out but, on the other hand, I think we want to do everything we can to keep the survival of democracy."[56]

As Roosevelt moved cautiously in his foreign policy, he also returned to his customary preparation for a major policy change. He sought to unify the Democrats in Congress for a repeal of the arms embargo in the rigid 1935 neutrality bill. He told congressional leaders that a repeal would make an Axis victory less likely. Yet when he called Senate leaders to the White House late that summer to explain that war might be imminent in Europe, Congress would not budge. In their prepared press statement, the senators accepted responsibility for a postponement of any repeal until January and prayed that there would not be another crisis.[57]

By fall the rest of Europe reacted to the Axis onslaught. On September 1 when the Nazis invaded Poland, France and Great Britain both declared war on Germany. The president, in discussing the gravity of the situation with correspondents, asked for "full cooperation of the Press throughout the country in sticking as closely as possible to the facts. . . . I particularly hope that there won't be unsubstantiated rumors put out, whether they originate here or elsewhere, without checking." The crisis was great, and journalists knew it. Roosevelt's words were effective too, because nine days later Steve Early commended the journalists "for the accurate and factual reporting" of the news.[58]

At the same time, Steve Early had Eddie Roddan and Lowell Mellett launch a publicity campaign to bring public pressure on Congress to revise the neutrality act. The plan was for individuals and groups outside the administration to generate much of the publicity, thus making the campaign a public expression. They prepared for prominent key speakers, such as Republicans Alf Landon and Frank Knox, to respond to Senator William Borah's isolationist speeches. Knox, the publisher of the *Chicago Daily News* and Landon's running mate in 1936, ran an editorial against Borah's stand on his front page. Interventionist groups such as the Committee for Repeal of the Embargo attempted to assist the administration's efforts.[59]

The administration's publicity campaign, coupled with the shocking successes of the German armies in Poland, persuaded Congress to repeal the embargo and to allow cash-and-carry trade with England and France. For two more years, Early continued the aid campaign by scheduling speakers and arranging for book publications and magazine articles. To support the president, he used such radio and motion picture stars and writers as Humphrey Bogart, Groucho Marx, and Leonard Levinson, writer for the popular "Fibber McGee and Molly" radio show.[60]

The number of correspondents at the president's press conferences increased with each new German invasion. The war was certainly newsworthy, but the right emphasis and interpretation were crucial. During the German blitzkrieg through Belgium and Holland into France, Roosevelt worked hard to explain the context of the war in terms of the danger to world democracies. At his special off-the-record press conference for the American Society of Newspaper Editors in April 1940, the president commended the American newspapers for carrying more foreign news. Yet, he said, "I do not know that I can say that this is real accomplishment, because I think the American public, the best informed in the world, is still very badly informed about the world. In other words, it has a long ways to go."[61]

One other issue competed as a speculative news story: the possibility of an unprecedented third-term president. There appeared to be no other choice but Roosevelt during such an international conflict. Following the 1936 election, Raymond Clapper had Steve Early's assurances that "this was his (Roosevelt's) last campaign." In June 1937, when correspondent Bob Post asked about a possible third term, the president jokingly told the *New York Times* reporter to go to the corner and put on a dunce hat. Yet that same summer, Fulton Oursler of *Liberty* magazine sent Roosevelt his survey of editors, industrialists, and business and labor leaders, which concluded that FDR would be the 1940 nominee and the first third-term president. After a May 1938 dinner party, Clapper acknowledge that "none could name anybody they wanted for President in either party to succeed rvt. [Roosevelt]. Dearth of material."[62]

Even as late as January 1940, the president seriously considered leaving office. As noted in chapter 3, he signed a secret contract to be a contributing editor for *Collier's,* to be voided only if he should return to government service or official life. Yet Steve Early must have considered the distinct possibility of a third term because he wrote of the wavering in January 1940: "And so it came about that Franklin D. Roosevelt, unless he is the first President of the United States to be elected for a third term in office, shall become contributing editor of Collier's, the National Weekly, at the expiration of his second term—January 20, 1941."[63]

In March 1940 Ernest K. Lindley floated the president's trial balloon about the election. He quoted the president as saying that he did not expect to run for a third term, that Secretary of State Hull would make a good nominee, but that it would be inexpedient to nominate Postmaster General James Farley for vice-president. When asked about Lindley's column at his next press conference, Roosevelt responded with his usual evasive answer, "I have not seen that."

Two weeks later, time enough for the president to gauge the political winds, Roosevelt brought up the Lindley story himself: "Of course I never said such a thing about Jim Farley, and the rest of the story was equally false." Farley was furious and broke with the president. Lindley was so upset that he stayed away from the White House until Christmas.[64]

By the end of May the president must have decided to run for reelection. The monumental European crisis influenced his decision. The Germans had already raged through Denmark and Norway and had launched a blitzkrieg against the Low Countries and France. Roosevelt confided in no one, including the press, gave no overt instructions or final plans, and waited for the party to summon him. When the Democratic party began its convention in July, the correspondents guessed the outcome and reminded the president about the Dunce Hat Club: The Dunce Hat Club, "which you formed a few years ago and which has a large membership of reporters who have asked third term questions, will hold a meeting in Chicago to dissolve the organization and turn in their dunce caps. (Laughter)."[65]

Even when the Democratic National Convention met and shouted, "We want Roosevelt," accompanied by an hour-long demonstration, Roosevelt said nothing. Indeed, he had wanted his New Deal programs to continue and waited to accept the nomination until he pushed through his choice for vice-president, liberal Henry Wallace. FDR's indirect tactics were rewarded. The seemingly spontaneous acclamation lessened the onerous third-term issue. Roosevelt was overwhelmingly nominated on the first ballot. When Roosevelt addressed the convention by telephone, he justified his acceptance: "Like most men of my age, I have made plans for myself, plans for a private life of my own choice. . . . Today all private plans, all private lives, have been in a sense repealed by an overriding public danger."[66]

The European war was the overriding public danger. The underlying issue became "not to change horses in midstream" because of the war. The president strengthened his position by appointing two eminent Republicans as cabinet members: Henry Stimson, who had been a cabinet member under both presidents Taft and Hoover, became the secretary of war, and Frank Knox, publisher of the *Chicago Daily News* and the 1936 Republican vice-presidential candidate, became the secretary of navy. Again, Roosevelt's timing created the ultimate news effect. His announcement came on the eve of the Republican National Convention and competed for front-page headlines. The angry GOP delegates cried, "Dirty Politics."[67]

Even more widely opposed to Roosevelt than in 1936, the newspapers were overwhelmingly for Wendell Willkie. Former election supporters such as the *New York Times,* Henry Luce, Joe Patterson and the *New York Daily News,* and Roy Howard and the Scripps-Howard chain now came out for Roosevelt's opponent. In his press conferences, FDR complained again about the inaccurate newspaper columns and biased press associations. With Ambassador

Bingham's death, Roosevelt had no close ties with the Associated Press as he did in 1936. With Roy Howard's support of Willkie, he did not have a close connection with United Press either. In fact, citizens sent letters to the White House protesting the newspapers' tendencies to minimize or even to suppress news favorable to Roosevelt while running headlines, columns, editorials, and cartoons favorable to Willkie. There also were accusations of radio bias. *New York Times* reporter Charles Hurd later accused some radio commentators of openly slanting their reports against the president.[68]

Rather than campaign openly, Roosevelt relied on his commander in chief status during the Battle of Britain. The timing was perfect. FDR toured defense installations and gave his response to the international events. In September, after Roosevelt signed the Selective Service Act and became vulnerable to Willkie's hysterical accusations of "warmonger," Roosevelt initiated his proclamation to bypass Congress and trade fifty reconditioned destroyers to the frantic British in return for the lease of military bases. The Republicans and their supporting newspapers were outraged. The once pro-FDR *St. Louis Post-Dispatch* declared that not only had "Mr. Roosevelt today committed an act of war" but also he had become "America's first dictator." So sensitive was the president to a correct press interpretation of the destroyer-armament agreement that he allowed the White House correspondents a chance to check their notes with the press conference stenographic copy, not just for quotations but for facts.[69]

Preoccupied with the European crisis, Roosevelt did not officially open his campaign until the very last weeks before the election. On October 23 he gave a rousing broadcast speech in Philadelphia, where he declared that he welcomed the opportunity to answer the Republican falsifications with facts. He proclaimed, "I am an old campaigner and I love a good fight." FDR put on a great show with his mocking statements against the GOP and their press supporters. The crowd loved it. He refuted Willkie's charge that the New Deal had failed to bring about recovery by comparing the *New York Times* financial pages with the *Times* editorial section, which supported Willkie. He remarked, "Wouldn't it be nice, if the editorial writers of *The New York Times* could get acquainted with their own business experts?"[70]

Edward Flynn, a consistent FDR supporter who had replaced Farley as the chair of the Democratic National Committee, became the party spokesman against the press. He stressed that rather than the president's being a dictator as charged, the newspapers of the country "are under a real dictatorship, a financial dictatorship of their advertisers and stockholders." When one reporter asked Flynn if there was not a free press in this country, Flynn answered, "No, . . . it is dominated by the financial interests of the country."[71]

Again, the president used his ultimate, unfiltered communication weapon—radio. For many Americans, radio had become the preferred news source since the beginning of the European war. Roosevelt once more had the advantage. His effective voice contrasted with Willkie's croaky voice. The president's reliance on radio seemed all the more urgent because of so many Republican newspapers. He and his cabinet officials directly reached the people. In fact, Early urged that adept speakers use the New York hookup for fifteen minutes each night to analyze and counteract the newspaper distortions, omissions, and unfairness. The Democrats earmarked over $350,000 for the October radio schedule alone. On election eve, the Democratic party broadcast a two-hour radio extravaganza from 10 P.M. to midnight, EST, featuring not only the president but also Secretary of State Cordell Hull, Carl Sandburg, Alexander Woollcott, and Dorothy Thompson—all mixed in with a great deal of entertainment from Broadway and Hollywood.[72]

On November 5 Franklin D. Roosevelt won an unprecedented third term with a 55 percent popular margin and 449 electoral votes. Only 25 percent of the American dailies supported Roosevelt. The president's major adversaries were not the opposition party and Congress but rather their mouthpieces, the American newspapers. Both he and his staff reacted immediately.[73]

As mentioned in chapter 4, the Friday after the election at the president's regular press conference, Hearst columnist Paul Mallon, who had been especially critical, was told he was unwelcome at future press conferences because of "the inaccuracies of his column." Roosevelt's antagonistic attitude toward the press was apparent. Rather than showing his usual jovial manner, FDR was easily irritated. When Fred Perkins of the *Pittsburgh Press* asked him about campaign inferences that he would not accept a fourth term, without the humor of the "dunce hat," Roosevelt retorted, "Well, the question is this: Oughtn't you go back to grade school and learn English? It was perfectly clear to me and to almost everybody else in this country."[74]

After cancelling his next press conferences with a statement of "No News," FDR waited eleven days before he met with the correspondents, and that was just before he left for his Hyde Park Thanksgiving break. Although FDR was also taking definitive steps to assist Great Britain, he gave out very little information, clipping his answers and refusing to elaborate on nearly all the questions. Roosevelt could not stay angry long, however. His personality and his need to educate the public would not allow it. He continued his press conferences on more or less a regular basis, and by the end of the month he returned to his familiar informality and good-humored jesting with the journalists.[75]

Rather than continue to vent his anger toward correspondents, the president cut off publishers' and the editors' access. He was too busy to meet personally with the American Society of Newspaper Editors until 1943. His advisers went after the print-media owners in earnest. His friend and speech writer Morris Ernst kept urging the president to keep publishers away from radio ownership. Presidential assistant Lowell Mellett took Henry Luce to task for *Time*'s lack of accuracy, especially in describing the president on election night: "I was offended by this story, as a newspaperman with a fetish for accuracy, as a supporter of the President who felt that the latter had been put in an unfair light before your readers, and finally, as a citizen who believes it is terribly important that journalists shall not knowingly and willingly abuse the freedom of the press." Luce maintained Mellett disliked the news magazine and was obviously unable to "understand the entire theory and practice of TIME."[76]

Right after the election, Secretary of Interior Harold L. Ickes, a longtime vocal critic of the press, issued an accountability challenge to the daily news-papers: "Last Tuesday we elected a President who was supported by less than 23 percent of our daily press. This reveals an unprecedented and progressively perilous situation requiring public consideration. Although we are fortunate in having free communication over the air, I am convinced that our democracy needs more than ever before, a truly free press that represents no class or economic group and that will rewin the confidence of our citizens because it is worthy of re-winning their confidence." Ickes's implicit accusations were part of his two-year public debate with newspaper editors over the advertising and financial bias of news.[77]

From 1936 through 1940 Franklin D. Roosevelt had to contend with the increasing animosity of American newspapers. He and his advisers worried that newspapers' biases would affect the news columns and rightly so; the election campaigns were crucial. FDR's news tactics included his astute sense of timing. He could skillfully deflect embarrassing controversies and attract public attention to himself, as he did by introducing the Waldo "pink sheets" on the heels of the Senate Judiciary Committee's veto of his Supreme Court proposal and by appointing Republican cabinet members during the GOP convention. While he could not stop the loss of public confidence concerning the recession, he used evasive tactics when questioned about the extent of the problem. With all his Dutch stubbornness, Roosevelt refused to answer ques-tions on a possible third term and successfully avoided the question up to his nomination. When the European war became one devastating Allied defeat after another, FDR very much wanted the American press to explain the events in terms of the overriding international dangers and suggested that the correspondents "subconsciously infiltrate" the interdependence of nations in their stories.

The president's tactics were not perfect. In winning so handily in 1936, the president had scaled the peak of public support to a previously unknown height. In his euphoria, Roosevelt tried to surmount another summit, the antagonistic Supreme Court. Roosevelt forgot about his successful first-term political tactics of timing, garnering advice, compromising, and gauging pub-lic opinion. Without them, his publicity methods of an astounding announce-ment, a news conference full of charm and wit, a radio address, a fireside chat, and even an exclusive interview were no longer successful. The people did not support the Court plan. He slid even lower down an abyss of lost public confidence with the unwieldy recession, until he pulled himself up with pump priming. When he tried to purge the Congress of recalcitrant members, most people were unreceptive. Only the European war and the president's return to his usual method of planning a publicity campaign to accompany his policy proposals enabled him to push his legislation through Congress. In 1940, 55 percent of the American people gave him a vote of confidence and an unprecedented third term. The public did not follow the newspapers' advice. During the crises of those four years, the president had tried to lead; yet he knew his failures. He once told Judge Samuel Rosenman, "It is a terrible thing to look over your shoulder when you are trying to lead—and to find no one there." When no one was there, even the president's most astute publicity efforts did not work.[78]

Notes

1. The Commission on Freedom of the Press, 1947, saw newspaper concentration of ownership as the new menace to freedom. See the commission's report, *A Free and Responsible Press, a General Report on Mass Communication: Newspapers, Radio, and Books* (Chicago: University of Chicago Press, 1947), pp. 17–19. See also Jerilyn S. McIntyre, "Repositing a Landmark: The Hutchins Commission and Freedom of the Press," *Critical Studies in Mass Communication* 4, no. 2 (1987): 136–60.

2. Frank Luther Mott, "Newspapers in Presidential Campaigns," *Public Opinion Quarterly* 8 (Fall 1944): 357–58, 362. While he did not cover the 1944 election, Mott found the editorial support of successful candidates within 10 percent of the popular vote in every election since Abraham Lincoln's 1860 election. E. W. Scripps merged three newsgathering agencies into the United Press Association in 1907 and had a clientele of 1,200 in 1933. For more on mergers and chains, see Alfred McClung Lee, *The Daily Newspaper in America* (New York: Octagon Books, 1933), pp. 536–37.

3. "President's 'Rebuke' Stirs Publishers' Ires," *Literary Digest*, March 3, 1934, p. 7; Elisha Hanson, "Official Propaganda and the New Deal," *Annals of the American Academy of Political and Social Science* 179 (May 1935): 178.

4. George Wolfskill and John A. Hudson, *All but the People: Franklin D. Roosevelt and His Critics, 1933–1939* (Toronto: Macmillan, 1969), p. 175; Franklin D. Roosevelt, *Complete Presidential Press Conferences of Franklin D. Roosevelt* (New York: Da Capo Press, 1972), Press Conference (henceforth PC) 64, October 27, 1933, Vol. 2: 383.

5. Meetings are indexed under "newspaper." After 1940, there were no meetings with editors except for one short visit in 1943. Even during the war years, FDR kept meeting with the National Conference of Business Magazines and Newspapers. Editors and publishers came to the semiannual Gridiron Club dinners, which the president continued to attend during the war. See President's Personal File (henceforth PPF), for the correspondence, and the President's Secretary's File (henceforth PSF) under Politics, Franklin D. Roosevelt Library (henceforth FDRL); Roosevelt to Norman Davis,

January 14, 1936, *F.D.R.: His Personal Letters, 1928–1945*, Vol. 1, Elliott Roosevelt, ed. (New York: Duell, Sloan and Pearce, 1950), p. 545.

6. William Weinfeld, "The Growth of Daily Newspaper Chains in the United States: 1923, 1926–1935," *Journalism Quarterly* 13 (December 1936): 364. Hearst also had thirteen magazines and eight radio stations. Leo C. Rosten, "President Roosevelt and the Washington Correspondents," *Public Opinion Quarterly* 1 (January 1937): 51. Rosten quotes *Time* magazine, November 2, 1936, which had a lengthy analysis of the 1936 campaign, and Paul Ward, "Farley Captures Labor," *The Nation*, October 31, 1936, p. 512.

7. For campaign responsibilities, see Eleanor Roosevelt to FDR and Others, July 16, 1936, *F.D.R.: His Personal Letters, 1928–1945*, Vol. 1, pp. 598–601; Jim Farley to Mrs. Roosevelt, July 25, 1936, PSF, FDRL. For quote, see Roosevelt to Robert W. Bingham, May 4, 1936, *F.D.R.: His Personal Letters, 1928–1945*, Vol. 1, p. 587.

8. Plans were in James Farley to Eleanor Roosevelt, July 25, 1936, PSF, FDRL. Raymond Clapper, "White House Ignorant of Fact Political Campaign Is Going On," *Washington Daily News*, August 13, 1936, Clapper Reference File, Censorship, Box 111, Raymond Clapper Papers (henceforth RCP), Manuscripts Division, Library of Congress (henceforth LofC).

9. For campaign theme, Drew Pearson and Robert S. Allen, "The Washington Merry-Go-Round," *Washington Times-Herald*, October 22, 1936, clippings in the White House Scrapbooks on microfilm, Vols. 13–16, FDRL; Carl Byoir to McIntyre, October 7, 1936, Stephen T. Early Papers (henceforth STEP), FDRL.

10. For Howard's suggestion, see Farley to Early, August 29, 1936, STEP, FDRL; Early Memorandum to Charles Michelson, March 13, 1936, STEP, FDRL. See also James L. Houghteling to Franklin Roosevelt, September 9, 1936, PSF, FDRL. Houghteling wrote that the *Chicago Times* advertised Roosevelt buttons and gave away 2,000,000 of them so fast that the Democratic National Committee asked it to hold back on account of the expense. See "National Affairs, Political Press," *Time*, November 2, 1936, pp. 12–14. In reference to Krock's column, see Roosevelt to Henry Morgenthau, Jr., September 9, 1936, *F.D.R.: His Personal Letters, 1928–1945*, Vol. 1, p. 612.

11. Clipping, *Washington Times-Herald*, October 3, 1936, and clipping, *New York Herald-Tribune*, October 4, 1936, White House Scrapbooks on microfilm, Vol. 13, FDRL; Wolfskill and Hudson, *All but the People*, p. 192.

12. Wolfskill and Hudson, *All but the People*, pp. 187–88. See also Mark Ethridge to Steve Early, October 19, 1942, with undated clipping from the *Louisville Courier-Journal*, Official File (henceforth OF) 36, FDRL.

13. For attacks, "National Affairs, Political Press," p. 14. *Time* listed the following newspapers as especially anti-Roosevelt: *Philadelphia Inquirer, Los Angeles Times, Detroit Free Press, Denver Post, San Francisco Chronicle, Portland Oregonian, Seattle Times, St. Louis Post-Dispatch*, and *Omaha World-Herald*. *Time* also mentioned that Paul Block's seven dailies followed Hearst.

Early Memorandum for Charles Michelson, September 21, 1936, STEP, FDRL; see Charles Michelson, "Dispelling the Fog," for release on April 4, 1936, Clapper Reference File, Censorship, Box 110, RCP, LofC. Boxed-in remarks include "To the Editor: This letter is not copyrighted; it comes to you without restriction for use, in whole or in part, and either with or without credit." See also Albert L. Warner, "Press

Critics Held Slurred," *New York Herald-Tribune,* April 22, 1936, Clapper Reference File, RCP, LofC.

For possible editorial quotations, see Early Memorandum for Charles Michelson, September 23, 1936, STEP, FDRL. Memo refers to an unnamed Scribner publication that gives the correspondence of Theodore Roosevelt and Henry Cabot Lodge.

14. For general dissension, Arthur M. Schlesinger, Jr., *The Politics of Upheaval,* Vol. 3 of *The Age of Roosevelt* (Boston: Houghton Mifflin, 1960), p. 573; Franklin D. Roosevelt to Arthur Brisbane, March 21, 1936, *F.D.R.: His Personal Letters, 1928–1945,* Vol. 1, p. 576; Wolfskill and Hudson, *All but the People,* who quote the press statement in the *New York Times,* September 20, 1936, p. 192.

15. Budget for Democratic National Campaign, PSF, FDRL. A fifteen-minute late evening slot on CBS cost a minimum of $5,208, and a full one-hour, coast-to-coast hookup of two hundred stations required $52,000, according to the *New York Times,* May 10, 1936; Stanley High to Franklin D. Roosevelt, September 14, 1936, PSF, FDRL. See also *Broadcasting,* October 1, 1936, p. 15; *Broadcasting,* October 15, 1936, p. 26.

16. Marquis W. Childs, *I Write from Washington* (New York: Harper and Brothers, 1942), p. 118; "F.C.C. Not to Act on Vandenberg Radio Debate," unnamed newspaper, October 30, 1935, *Washington Star,* October 20, 1936, and *New York Sun,* October 19, 1936, all in White House Scrapbooks on microfilm, Vols. 13–16, FDRL.

17. "The Press Loses the Election," *New Republic,* November 18, 1936, p. 63. "Washington Writers by 19–1 Pick Roosevelt, Give Him 374 Electoral Votes to 157," *New York Times,* October 15, 1936; Heywood Broun, "It Seems to Me," unlabeled column, October 26, 1936, White House Scrapbooks on microfilm, Vols. 13–16, FDRL.

18. Roosevelt to Josephus Daniels, November 9, 1936, *F.D.R.: His Personal Letters, 1928–1945,* Vol. 1, p. 626.

19. "The People vs. the Press," *New York Post,* November 7, 1936, White House Scrapbooks on microfilm, Vols. 13–16, FDRL.

20. Franklin D. Roosevelt, Gridiron Speech, December 21, 1936, *Franklin D. Roosevelt Reader: Selected Speeches, Messages, Press Conferences and Letters,* Basil Rauch, ed. (New York: Rinehart, 1957), pp. 165–66.

21. Roosevelt, *Complete Press Conferences,* PC 342, February 5, 1937, Vol. 9: 136; James MacGregor Burns, *Roosevelt: The Lion and the Fox* (New York: Harcourt, Brace, 1956), pp. 293–94; Joseph Alsop and Turner Catledge, *The 168 Days* (Garden City, N.Y.: Doubleday, Doran, 1938), p. 7.

22. Joseph P. Lash, *Dealers and Dreamers: A New Look at the New Deal* (New York: Doubleday, 1988), p. 291. See chapter 4 concerning Creel's *Collier's* article.

23. Raymond Clapper Diary, February 5, 1937, Box 8, RCP, LofC; Roosevelt, *Complete Press Conferences,* PC 342, February 5, 1937, Vol. 9: 130–47; Thomas L. Stokes, *Chip Off My Shoulder* (Princeton, N.J.: Princeton University Press, 1940), p. 463.

24. Mark Sullivan, "Roosevelt, a Zestful Dramatist," *New York Herald-Tribune,* February 6, 1937, White House Scrapbooks on microfilm, Vol. 15, FDRL.

25. For opposition, see *New York Times,* March 7, 1937; White House Newspaper Scrapbooks on microfilm, Vols. 14 and 15, FDRL; Clapper Diary, February 5 and 8, 1937, Box 8, RCP, LofC. See also Alsop and Catledge, *The 168 Days,* p. 72.

26. Harold L. Ickes, *The Secret Diary of Harold L. Ickes,* Vol. 2 (New York: Simon and Schuster, 1954), entry for February 16, 1937, pp. 74–75.

27. Clapper Diary, February 8, 1937, and undated clippings, 1937, Box 8, RCP, LofC.

28. Roosevelt, *Complete Press Conferences,* PC 349, March 2, 1937, Vol. 9: 191.

29. Alsop and Catledge, *The 168 Days,* pp. 109, 183.

30. Ibid., pp. 107, 112.

31. Burns, *Roosevelt: The Lion and the Fox,* p. 300; John H. Sharon, "The Psychology of the Fireside Chat" (Senior honors thesis, Princeton University, 1949), p. 118.

32. Alsop and Catledge, *The 168 Days,* pp. 3, 139, 144. See also Burns, *Roosevelt: The Lion and the Fox,* p. 306.

33. Roosevelt, *Complete Press Conferences,* PC 367, May 18, 1937, Vol. 9: 368–70; concerning "strange temerity," see ibid., p. 374; concerning Justice Van Devanter, see ibid., p. 375.

34. "Reporters Act to Ban Tipster at White House," *New York Herald-Tribune,* May 17, 1937, *Baltimore Sun,* May 28, 1937, and "R. H. Waldo Expelled by National Press Club," *Editor and Publisher,* June 7, 1937, p. 6, Clapper Reference File, Censorship, Box 110, RCP, LofC.

Early did write editor and publisher associations about the material. See Stephen T. Early to Alfred H. Kirchofer, President of American Society of Newspaper Editors, May 20, 1937, and Early to James G. Stahlman, President of the American Newspaper Publishers Association, May 24, 1937, OF 36, FDRL. See also Early's article, "Below the Belt," *Saturday Evening Post,* June 10, 1939, p. 113.

35. Burns, *Roosevelt: The Lion and the Fox,* pp. 291–315; William E. Leuchtenburg, *Franklin D. Roosevelt and the New Deal, 1932–1940* (New York: Harper and Brothers, 1963), pp. 231–38.

36. Burns, *Roosevelt: The Lion and the Fox,* pp. 208–10, 214, 321, 338.

37. Roosevelt, *Complete Press Conferences,* PC 398, September 14, 1937, Vol. 10: 208; PC 398, September 14, 1937, Vol. 10: 208–10, 213; PC 399, September 21, 1937, Vol. 10: 221.

38. Clippings of the *New York Post,* October 2, 1937, *Washington Times-Herald,* October 3, 1937, and *New York Times* and *Washington Post,* October 5, 1937, White House Scrapbooks on microfilm, Vols. 13–16, FDRL.

39. Lindsay Rogers, "President Roosevelt's Press Conferences," *Political Quarterly* 9 (July–September 1938): 366–67; Ickes, *Secret Diary,* Vol. 2, entry for October 9, 1937, p. 222; James A. Farley, *Jim Farley's Story: The Roosevelt Years* (New York: McGraw-Hill, 1948), p. 98; Leuchtenburg, *Franklin D. Roosevelt,* p. 226; Tully, *F.D.R., My Boss* (New York: Charles Scribner's Sons, 1949), pp. 230–31.

40. Roosevelt, *Complete Press Conferences,* PC 400, October 6, 1937, Vol. 10: 233–35.

41. Tully, *F.D.R., My Boss,* p. 233; Ickes, *Secret Diary,* Vol. 2, entry for October 9, 1937, pp. 226–27; clippings of the *Washington Times-Herald,* October 10, 1937, and *New York Post,* October 9, 1937, White House Scrapbooks on microfilm, Vols. 13–16, FDRL.

42. Robert E. Burke, "Election of 1940," in *History of American Presidential Elections, 1789–1968,* Vol. 4, Arthur M. Schlesinger, Jr., and Fred L. Israel, eds.

(New York: Chelsea House, 1971), p. 2918; Leuchtenburg, *Franklin D. Roosevelt,* pp. 244–51.

43. Roosevelt, *Complete Press Conferences,* PC 405, October 22, 1937, Vol. 10: 287; PC 411, November 23, 1937, Vol. 10: 363; PC 414, December 7, 1937, Vol. 10: 393.

44. Ibid., PC 421, January 4, 1938, Vol. 11: 11; PC 435, February 18, 1938, Vol. 11: 158–76.

45. Ibid., PC 449-A, April 8, 1938, Vol. 11: 290.

46. Ibid., PC 452-B, April 21, 1938, Vol. 11: 357, 362; PC 488, October 4, 1938, Vol. 12: 130. For another reference, see ibid., PC 506, December 6, 1938, Vol. 12: 281.

47. Burke, "Election of 1940," p. 2918; Stokes, *Chip Off My Shoulder,* pp. 487–88.

48. Stokes, *Chip Off My Shoulder,* pp. 487–88. See also David L. Porter, " 'Purge' of 1938," in *Franklin D. Roosevelt, His Life and Times,* Otis L. Graham, Jr., and Meghan Robinson Wander, eds. (Boston: G. K. Hall, 1985), pp. 338–39.

49. Roosevelt, *Complete Press Conferences,* PC 482, September 2, 1938, Vol. 12: 76; PC 476, August 16, 1938, Vol. 12: 24–25.

50. Burke, "Election of 1940," pp. 2918–19; Ickes, *Secret Diary,* Vol. 2, entry for September 24, 1938, p. 475; Jonathan Daniels, *White House Witness, 1942–1945* (Garden City: Doubleday, 1975), pp. 213–14.

51. Raymond Clapper, "Return of the Two-Party System," *Current History* 49 (December 1938): 14.

52. In reference to the international events, see Roosevelt, *Complete Press Conferences,* PC 452-B, April 21, 1938, Vol. 11: 357–59; Clapper Diary, April 21, 1938, Box 8, RCP, LofC; Leuchtenburg, *Franklin D. Roosevelt,* p. 284.

53. Leuchtenburg, *Franklin D. Roosevelt,* pp. 228–29; Roosevelt, *Complete Press Conferences,* PC 521, January 27, 1939, Vol. 13: 91; PC 522, January 31, 1939, Vol. 13: 102.

54. Roosevelt, *Complete Press Conferences,* PC 523, February 3, 1939, Vol. 13: 117; PC 525, February 17, 1939, Vol. 13: 149 for quotes, 132–51 for discussion. See also *New York Times,* February 4, 1939.

55. Roosevelt, *Complete Press Conferences,* PC 529, March 10, 1939, Vol. 13: 13, 180–81; PC 531, March 21, 1939, Vol. 13: 209. References to both fingerprinting and identification shots and cards were made in ibid., PC 716, February 7, 1941, Vol. 17: 109.

Kenneth O'Reilly points out that by 1935 the White House began to solicit FBI reports on FDR's critics and that in 1940 the FBI forwarded investigatory reports on the defense and lend-lease critics. See O'Reilly, "A New Deal for the FBI: The Roosevelt Administration, Crime Control, and National Security," *Journal of American History* 69 (December 1982): 646, 648.

56. Roosevelt, *Complete Press Conferences,* PC 540-A, April 20, 1939, Vol. 13: 324. See also ibid., pp. 299–324.

57. Ibid., PC 562, July 14, 1939, Vol. 14: 20; PC 563, July 18, 1939, Vol. 14: 29; PC 564, July 21, 1939, Vol. 14: 32, 34; Joseph Alsop and Robert Kintner, *The American White Paper* (1940 pamphlet), pp. 44–46. As noted in chapter 4, Roosevelt edited the Alsop and Kintner paper.

58. Roosevelt, *Complete Press Conferences,* PC 575, September 1, 1939, Vol. 14: 131; Early Press Conferences, September 9, 1939, STEP, FDRL.

59. Early Memorandum to Mellett, September 26, 1939, STEP, FDRL; Robert A. Divine, *The Illusion of Neutrality* (Chicago: University of Chicago Press, 1962), p. 302. Edward (Eddie) L. Roddan was on the staff of the Democratic National Committee. Lowell Mellett was an assistant to the president and head of the Office of Government Reports.

60. For Early's efforts, see Early Memorandum to Le Hand, January 4, 1940, STEP, FDRL; Early Letter to Cudahy, September 23, 1940, STEP, FDRL; Early Memorandum to Marshall, June 5, 1940, STEP, FDRL; Chiefs of Staff, Early Memorandum to Roosevelt, February 26, 1941, STEP, FDRL; Marquis Childs Letter to Early, March 14, 1941, STEP, FDRL; Early Memorandum to Roosevelt, May 22, 1941, STEP, FDRL. See also, Early Memorandum to Mellett, July 25, 1940, OF 36; Block Reports to Le Hand, November 16, 1940, PPF; Williams Letter to Roosevelt, July 18, 1939, OF 444-D, all at the FDRL.

61. See remarks in Roosevelt, *Complete Press Conferences,* PC 576, September 5, 1939, Vol. 14: 14, 36; PC 642, May 10, 1940, Vol. 15: 326; PC 636-A, April 18, 1940, Vol. 15: 267.

62. Clapper Diary, November 16, 1936, Box 7, RCP, LofC; Roosevelt, *Complete Press Conferences,* PC 377, June 29, 1937, Vol. 9: 466; Steve Early to Franklin D. Roosevelt, September 3, 1937, *F.D.R.: His Personal Letters, 1928–1945,* Vol. 1, pp. 710–11; Clapper Diary, May 2, 1938, Box 8, RCP, LofC.

63. Early File Memorandum, January 27, 1940, STEP, FDRL.

64. Farley, *Jim Farley's Story,* pp. 226, 228; Roosevelt, *Complete Press Conferences,* PC 628, March 5, 1940, Vol. 15: 182; PC 630, March 19, 1940, Vol. 15: 204; Ernest Lindley interview, June 4, 1976; chapter 4 herein.

65. Roosevelt, *Complete Press Conferences,* PC 660, July 12, 1940, Vol. 16: 35. As noted in the introduction, it has proved impossible to find evidence of other Dunce Hat Awards in the 1937, 1938, 1939, and 1940 press conferences. They could have been awarded in those press conferences not included which were given informally while the president was on trips. For more discussion, see Leuchtenburg, *Franklin D. Roosevelt,* pp. 315–17; Burns, *Roosevelt: The Lion and the Fox,* pp. 425–29.

66. Burns, *Roosevelt: The Lion and the Fox,* p. 430.

67. Burke, "Election of 1940," p. 2931; Childs, *I Write from Washington,* p. 202; Ickes, *Secret Diary,* Vol. 2, entry for September 9, 1939, p. 718.

68. Robert E. Sherwood, *Roosevelt and Hopkins: An Intimate History* (New York: Harper and Brothers, 1948), p. 186; Burns, *Roosevelt: The Lion and the Fox,* p. 445; Tully, *F.D.R., My Boss,* pp. 291–92. Sherwood, Burns, and Tully note that Joe Patterson broke with the president over the third-term issue and aid to the Allies. In Early's Memorandum to Roosevelt, October 9, 1940, Early mentions a $5,000 contribution to the national party and an equal amount to the state campaign from Joe Patterson. Perhaps, he did not "break" completely and followed the election public mood, as noted in Early Memorandum, October 9, 1940, STEP, FDRL.

For FDR's complaints, see Roosevelt, *Complete Press Conferences,* PC 666, August 2, 1940, Vol. 16: 85; PC 678, September 6, 1940, Vol. 16: 194; Sherwood, *Roosevelt and Hopkins,* p. 186.

Charles Hurd, *When the New Deal Was Young and Gay* (New York: Harper, 1965), pp. 238–39. David Holbrook Culbert argues that there was radio bias during the war. See Culbert, *News for Everyman: Radio and Foreign Affairs in Thirties America* (Westport, Conn.: Greenwood Press, 1976), pp. 26–27.

69. Leuchtenburg, *Franklin D. Roosevelt,* p. 305; Burns, *Roosevelt: The Lion and the Fox,* pp. 445, 441; Roosevelt, *Complete Press Conferences,* PC 678, September 6, 1940, Vol. 16: 198.

70. Burns, *Roosevelt: The Lion and the Fox,* pp. 446–47.

71. "Press Dictatorship Charged by Flynn," *New York Times,* October 17, 1940, Clapper Reference File, Censorship, Box 112, RCP, LofC.

72. For FDR's radio advantage, see Paul Lazarsfeld, *Radio and the Printed Page: An Introduction to the Study of Radio and Its Role in the Communication of Ideas* (New York: Duell, Sloan and Pearce, 1940), p. 259; Burns, *Roosevelt: The Lion and the Fox,* p. 446. For campaign efforts, see Michelson to McIntyre, October 10, 1940, and G. W. Johnson to Michelson, October 10, 1940, OF 300, FDRL; Early to Michelson, October 19, 1940, STEP, FDRL.

73. Mott, "Newspapers in Presidential Campaigns," p. 357.

74. "White House Bars Reporter Awhile," *New York Times,* November 9, 1940, Clapper Reference File, Censorship, Box 110, RCP, LofC. Mallon's name was given in *Editor and Publisher,* November 16, 1940, Clapper Reference File, Censorship, Box 110, RCP, LofC. Early was on vacation at the time when the Mallon incident took place; whether he could have stopped the incident remains conjecture. Roosevelt, *Complete Press Conferences,* PC 694, November 8, 1940, Vol. 16: 301–2.

75. "'No News' Reason for Press Conference Cancellation," *Editor and Publisher,* November 16, 1940, Clapper Reference File, Censorship, Box 110, RCP, LofC; Roosevelt, *Complete Press Conferences,* PC 695, November 19, 1940, Vol. 16: 308–13; PC 699, November 29, 1940, Vol. 16: 330–36.

76. Morris L. Ernst to Franklin D. Roosevelt, November 7, 1940, PSF, FDRL; Lowell Mellett to Henry R. Luce, December 7, 1940, PPF, FDRL; Henry R. Luce to Lowell Mellett, December 24, 1940, PPF, FDRL.

77. *Baltimore Sun,* editorial page, November 9, 1940, Clapper Reference File, Censorship, Box 110, RCP, LofC. Ickes debated Frank Gannett in January 1939 over radio's "Town Hall of the Air" on the topic "Have We a Free Press?" Ickes argued that while the press of the country was free from government regulation and control, it was not free from financial and advertising control. Both the president and Early were "enthusiastic over the prospect of this joint discussion," according to Ickes, *Secret Diary,* Vol. 2, entry for December 18, 1938, p. 527. Ickes also referred to the uproar the debate created and the great deal of newspaper comment, editorials, and letters to the editors. See ibid., entry for January 22, 1939, pp. 564–65, and entry for April 23, 1939, p. 622.

Ickes wrote *America's House of Lords: An Inquiry into Freedom of the Press* (New York: Harcourt, Brace, 1939) in which he accused most American newspaper owners of having a tendency to divert public opinion to their own uses. Ickes, in *Freedom of the Press* (New York: Vanguard Press, 1940), included twenty-eight articles discussing this issue from the various viewpoints of journalists, pollsters, and others. See also Mott, "Newspapers in Presidential Campaigns," p. 348.

78. Burns, *Roosevelt: The Lion and the Fox,* pp. 318–19.

"All of this and Churchill too." Sixteen days after Pearl Harbor, Roosevelt and Winston Churchill at a joint press conference, December 23, 1941, with Press Secretary Steve Early in the background and the stenographer to Roosevelt's left. Courtesy of the Franklin D. Roosevelt Library.

8

Publicity for a War Operation

This is the people's war, and to win it the people should know as much about it as they can. This Office will do its best to tell the truth and nothing but the truth, both at home and abroad. Military information that will aid the enemy must be withheld; but within that limitation we shall try to give the people a clear, complete and accurate picture.
—OWI poster, signed, Elmer Davis, Director, July 10, 1942

On the day of the Pearl Harbor bombing, Franklin D. Roosevelt continually issued information to the press through his press secretary. Although in October he had established the Office of Facts and Figures (OFF) as an independent information agency to answer war questions, Director Archibald MacLeish said that he knew no more than what he had heard on the radio. The OFF attempted to secure the release of information about the Pearl Harbor attack and the subsequent events, but it found itself up against the controlled silence of the president and the War and Navy departments. This was to be a continual pattern throughout the war.[1]

On December 7, 1941, the administration had neither a centralized information, propaganda, or censorship agency nor an overall commitment for one. FDR, in his usual fashion, had established four separate agencies for information. In addition to the OFF under MacLeish and his deputy director Robert Sherwood, the Office of Government Reports (OGR), directed by former Scripps-Howard editor Lowell Mellett, coordinated the government's motion picture program, compiled and analyzed press intelligence, and answered public inquiries. The Division of Information in the Office of Emergency Management, run by former Scripps-Howard reporter Robert Horton, conducted a day-by-day news operation. The Foreign Information Service in the Office of the Coordinator of Information (COI), under Colonel William J. Donovan, disseminated information to foreign centers. Even the director of the Office of Civilian Defense, New York City Mayor Fiorello La Guardia, had presented the president with propaganda plans for improving morale. Yet, when one agency did not function smoothly, there could always be another. If that approach caused confusion, Roosevelt was undisturbed. The method allowed the president to procrastinate, to watch his subordinates thrash out the details of an issue, and to intervene only when he felt the time was right. This method, however calculated, inhibited any coherent information program and meant that centralized control of information could only proceed with a series of very tentative steps.[2]

As a member of the Wilson administration during World War I, FDR was aware of the lingering suspicious hysteria generated by the Creel Committee on Public Information (CPI). Ever sensitive to public opinion, the president had no intention of allowing a formal government bureau the same latitude that the CPI had enjoyed in both releasing information and censoring material. At the same time, Roosevelt did not want any agency competing with his own information controls.[3]

Press Secretary Steve Early also resisted efforts to establish a single propaganda agency. At first, he counted on the regular department press bureaus to release war news. In the early aftermath of Pearl Harbor, however, Roosevelt ordered that the White House release all battle news. Even during the immediate Pearl Harbor shock, Early reassured reporters on December 10 that the White House hoped to return information to various bureaus and appropriate departments. He said, "There is a report in this morning from General MacArthur, the War Department will give it to you." When one correspondent asked, "There will be no central source of information?" Early replied, "No, and I hope there never will be." Early continued to do all he could to retain that hope.[4]

Nevertheless, the need for coordinated information became so great during the international crisis that in January FDR sent the director of the budget a memo suggesting that the Office of Facts and Figures simply be renamed the Office of War Information, rather than starting a new agency. Something had to be done immediately about a positive message—indeed propaganda—to counter the negative news of 1942. OGR Director Lowell Mellett, who wanted to head such an agency himself, found many earnest people asking for an American Goebbels "not exactly like Goebbels, but the same kind of thing, and just as effective."[5]

Although Steve Early remained steadfastly opposed to an outright propaganda agency, after Pearl Harbor even he acknowledged Mellett's suggestion for the need of "a man in such a key spot . . . whose habits of thinking are as nearly the same as the President's own as possible." Since Early's workload was tremendous at this time, he lessened his opposition somewhat, although he warned that he was against "the creation of any elaborate information or propaganda agency that would take this essential direction and control too far away from the White House." On June 13, 1942, Roosevelt signed Executive Order 9182 for just such a centralized agency, the Office of War Information (OWI). The White House dilemma then became what war information to release and what overall role Roosevelt would play. The president had no intention of letting the control of information, especially the vital information about the war, get too far away from his purview.[6]

In general, the public approved of Roosevelt's appointment of Elmer Davis, a popular broadcaster and a longtime newspaperman. With his ten years at the *New York Times* and three years as a CBS news analyst, he was what *Time* magazine called "one of the best newsmen in the business." The *New Republic* hailed him as "a liberal respected by conservatives."[7]

The new agency would assume the powers and duties of the previous information agencies, the Office of Facts and Figures (OFF), the Office of Government Reports (OGR), and the Division of Information Service of the Office of the Coordinator of Information (COI). The presidential directive mandated the agency to direct an accurate and consistent flow of information on the war policies, the activities and aims of the government, and the status and progress of the war effort. The OWI also was to review and approve all the government-sponsored radio and motion pictures and to maintain a liaison with the Allied nations' information agencies. Moreover, the OWI was to coordinate the news with the Office of Censorship.[8]

Davis said that the executive branch would issue all news and background information essential to a clear understanding of the war. He explained that the only information to be withheld was that which would give aid and comfort to the enemy. The implementation of that policy created continual conflict with the military. When he asked Associate Director Milton S. Eisenhower to coordinate the release of information from the War and Navy departments, he explained his own purpose: "I just don't have much faith that very much information being handed out is reliable . . . and that must change. This is the people's war and the people have a right to know what is going on. There must be no camouflaging of unfavorable information and no sitting on bad news until it can be offset by good news."[9]

To help him, Davis had an able group of assistants, most of whom already had strong connections with the president. His two deputy directors were part of Roosevelt's informal policy group. Archibald MacLeish became an assistant director for policy development and Robert Sherwood became the administrative director for overseas operations. Palmer Hoyt, publisher of the *Portland Oregonian,* took over as director of domestic operations. Lowell Mellett became the motion picture bureau director, the government's liaison officer for both civilian films and governmental efforts. Office of Emergency Management head Robert Horton moved into the news bureau group as the chief, until he went over to the Office of Price Administration and then finished the war as publicity director for the Maritime Commission. Over 2,000 employees from other information divisions in the executive branch moved into the OWI.[10]

Another key player was William J. "Wild Bill" Donovan, who had gained Roosevelt's confidence after his successful 25,000 mile, fact-finding mission for the Navy Department in 1940. As head of the new Office of Strategic Service, Donovan was to argue constantly with OWI overseas director Robert Sherwood about the release of war information. Sherwood, who feared that American credibility would be impaired by outright lies, was in continuous conflict with Donovan, who saw information as potential propaganda and another war weapon. In addition, Sherwood wanted civilian control, which might lose out to Donovan's military orientation and secret foreign informational activities.[11]

Within his first two months, Davis wrote Roosevelt that all agency and department informational activities, regardless of war connections, must now be coordinated to give the same message. The New Deal era of publicity about policy disagreements, such as the Ickes-Hopkins feuds mentioned in chapter 5, was to end. Davis explained that officials' public statements, "when they deal with matters touching more than one department or agency, do not always contribute to either the accuracy or the consistency of public information." He further maintained that the public might think that the government as a whole did not know its job and that administrators' quarrels diverted energy away from fighting the enemy. He asked, "Is it too much to hope that officials, pending such announcement of policy or the ascertainment of the facts in the case, could be instructed to think before they talk?"[12]

Roosevelt had Appointments Secretary Marvin McIntyre draft Davis's suggestion in a confidential letter to all departments and agencies. The president, under tremendous pressure because the war was not going well, agreed with the OWI director and added, "In my opinion, many of the present misconceptions held by the people with respect to the problems now being so widely discussed are in large measure due to these public squabbles among officials." He asked that differences be resolved in private conferences or, failing that, they immediately be brought to his attention. Roosevelt directed that his letter be passed along: "After such announcement, it is the duty of members of my administration to desist from public disavowal of such policy—or to resign."[13]

Yet from the beginning, the military, with Roosevelt's backing, hindered Davis's efforts to release information about the war. Even with the OWI's first major story, Davis's hands were tied. During the summer of 1942, eight Nazi saboteurs captured by the FBI on the East Coast were tried in Washington. The newspaper and press associations wanted to report all phases of the trial, which they contended did not damage the nation's wartime security. The Justice and War departments claimed that *any* publicity would compromise FBI counterespionage activities. The president appointed a special military commission to try the saboteurs behind closed doors. Davis sent veteran newspaperman Henry Paynter to try to open the session. After Paynter waited for an hour in the War Department anteroom, General John McCloy finally sent the message, "The General does not wish to see the gentlemen. The gentlemen need not wait."[14]

Davis did not wait either. He went with Secretary of War Stimson to the White House. Roosevelt deferred to the military commission, which had refused to allow access to the trial. Rather, the OWI could publish a brief, daily military communique about the proceedings. Davis's subsequent public statement put him into direct conflict with the president over the security question: "I think that insofar as the national security is not imperiled by disclosure of secret information, the public would feel better if proceedings at a military commission could be reported by outside observers." The OWI lost. Davis's organization took a beating over the release of this newsworthy information. The stage was set for future acts of disagreement between the OWI director and the president.[15]

There was also a limit on how much Roosevelt would listen to Davis's suggestions, even for tighter restrictions on the news. Before the Allied invasion of northern Europe, Davis suggested that the president request at his next press conference a suspension on news speculations, particularly those "dangerous" viewpoints about when the war would end. Early penned on Davis's memorandum: "Shown to the President. Did not use."[16]

The White House consistently failed to support the OWI in other ways. Roosevelt could not easily coordinate information with Davis or anyone else. He had always in effect issued material directly to the press, bypassing his own agencies. His reservations ensured that attempts to establish any kind of propaganda network would be halting and hesitant at best. In fact, his penchant for conflicting appointments allowed him to play off one assistant against another. As an example, Henry Paynter, a former Hearst man, working away at his new OWI job, was amazed when a stranger walked into his office and introduced himself as head of the United Nations news bureau. "That's interesting," said Paynter, "So am I."[17]

At the same time, the president's detachment, a characteristic of his administrative approach, was especially frustrating to Davis. Survival was the priority. As the nation's commander in chief, Roosevelt believed that winning the war took precedence over all else. He even assumed personal responsibility for the important diplomatic negotiations. Secretary of State Cordell Hull said that while he voiced America's foreign policy, he could not always play the key role in it. In fact, he once complained to Secretary of the Treasury

Henry Morgenthau, Jr., "The President runs foreign affairs; I don't know what's going on."[18]

With such a hands-on style, Roosevelt publicly and privately concentrated on victory first, with little postwar planning. Unlike Woodrow Wilson, he talked only in vague generalities about the future, despite the OWI's repeated requests for specific declarations of war aims. FDR discussed the Four Freedoms and the Atlantic Charter in general terms, and anything else could wait until after the war. He did not want to repeat Wilson's preoccupation with postwar goals. Partly because of the president's ambiguity and partly because of their own conflicting convictions, top OWI staffers decided not to sell one particular version of the war. Too, the OWI could say little as long as Roosevelt avoided committing himself to verbalizing specific peace aims or explaining the war. Despite Davis's demands for one from the administration, the OWI did not have a coordinated voice itself.[19]

There was a personal failure, too. Davis did not have the same access that George Creel had had to President Wilson. Davis had not known the president before he came to Washington, and Roosevelt did not make any great effort to know Davis better. Davis was on his own, without much support from FDR. He also had to take the barbs of administration critics that became part of the budget negotiations. Roosevelt further undermined Davis and the OWI by leaving him at home when he went to the Quebec conference in 1943, even though Brendan Bracken, the British minister of information, was there.[20]

No matter what the OWI or any agency did, Roosevelt had his own ideas about how to generate an image and release information. He once asked Lowell Mellett what he thought about preparing a series of editorials based on the Hearst method, "(Isn't that terrible for me to say?)." Such a Hearst style would have one word in large caps in every sentence and could have the length to fit a single page leaflet or handbill for the Democratic National Committee to issue during the winter and early spring before the 1944 election.[21]

During the periods of greatest crisis, FDR still took a hand in particular publicity efforts. For example, on December 18, 1941, he sent Archibald MacLeish a photostatic copy from a Bern publication showing a German eagle roosting on a swastika surmounting the globe, and he pointed out, "This has real news value which could well be disseminated throughout the papers, together with the photograph." In April 1942 Roosevelt asked MacLeish to distribute a William Allen White editorial entitled "Don't Kid Yourself," which referred to the Nazi propaganda being spread in the United States, and suggested that an organization should be working to see that warnings like this be broadcast throughout the country. He also proposed having a Lippmann editorial put over the air and then given to the press. He suggested that Canadian prime minister MacKenzie King's private encouragements be released. On another occasion, he recommended a letter as an introduction to a press statement on the 1944 International Labor Conference Report.[22]

Roosevelt received the numerous Bureau of Intelligence reports and the early public opinion polls on a regular basis. In critiquing OWI publications, the president would recommend changes. He sent Associate Director Milton Eisenhower to North Africa in 1942 to study the OWI's work and see if any improvements might be made. In a memorandum, Roosevelt chided the OWI for allowing any columnist to appear in the U.S. Army weekly: "I know of no column published in the United States which does not contained a very large percentage of 'facts' or 'news' which are simply not true. I see no reason for the Government to reprint to the soldiers news which is not correct."[23]

Within a year, the OWI's public efforts were controversial. Journalists viewed the agency's domestic news efforts with suspicion and its uncoordinated foreign efforts with alarm. By 1943 the propaganda seemed so overt that the *New York Times* began monitoring and reporting the OWI's output on a twenty-four-hour basis. During the July Italian campaign, Arthur Krock's front-page story and column berated OWI broadcasts, which were different from the administration's statements. "OWI Broadcast to Italy Calls Ruler 'Fascist' and 'Moronic Little King' " blazed across the headlines. Krock pointedly said that the labels would make it more difficult if the U.S. planned "to build a bridge to the democratic government in Italy." He asked if OWI actions imperiled both international negotiations and the lives of American soldiers abroad. When another reporter asked about these implications at FDR's July press conference, the president, unhappy about the OWI's insubordination and subsequent public controversy, said, "I think Bob Sherwood is raising Hell about it now. It ought never to have been done." The OWI's overseas interpretations were wrong, as Krock had indicated, since they conflicted with the president.[24]

Although Steve Early had needed assistance, he did not want a powerful, coordinated publicity agency competing with the White House. In fact, Davis never did receive full White House support. The note that Early had written Harry Hopkins within weeks after Pearl Harbor remained a consistent policy despite the president's directive. Early had urged that the White House alone control any propaganda activities: "The real directives in the war, including the directives of propaganda (should) come necessarily from the President. . . . . They could be given through you or through me—or both of us, but from us only when close communion with the President enables us to know beyond certainty what he wants done."[25]

After eight years of keeping FDR's name on the front pages, Early did not plan to stop, regardless of a new agency. The press secretary tried to have something newsworthy every day come from the White House and would often bypass the OWI and have the Army and Navy departments' press offices send him stories to release from the White House, which would emphasize the president's role as commander in chief of the armed forces.[26]

By its very nature and purpose, the overseas branch created additional problems. Davis's overall aim was propaganda to make the United States look good, but the overseas division recruited mostly foreign correspondents, who were an independent group and more at ease criticizing public policy than disseminating government propaganda. They had a difficult time speaking in unison for the country. In less than six months, their uncoordinated work became a public fight. During the fall of 1942, the president approved a temporary agreement with the Vichy admiral Jean François Darlan, who had collaborated with the Nazis. The OWI's Radio Moroc personnel, sympathetic to Free France, refused to accept the president's decision, even as a temporary arrangement. Their hostility was evident in their broadcasts, monitored in London and flashed by Reuters and the Associated Press until they were cut off. The OWI could not control its own personnel. The situation did not improve until C. D. Jackson, a leading *Time-Life* journalist, flew to North Africa and took full charge. Even after cable communications to the London office were restored, most dispatches written by American correspondents or reported by such independent broadcasters as Edward R. Murrow continued to reflect their hostility toward Darlan.[27]

The overseas branch had other personnel problems as well. Davis could not compete for quality overseas recruits. Davis complained to the president, who promised him that he "would get to it tonight, see Marshall tomorrow and ask him what about it," but Davis later noted that "it was two months more before final action was taken."[28]

Davis never could control the overseas branch's open criticisms. Such intrigue culminated in a showdown in 1944. In a letter to the president, Davis blamed an inner circle in the New York office, mostly COI members before Pearl Harbor. He said the New York top personnel were not in touch with changing OWI policies or with persons authorized to administer those policies. The group which exercised control through the regional editorial board took over many of the domestic branch functions and did them poorly. Davis told of a sloppy Norwegian edition of an OWI magazine published despite the protest of the Washington, D.C., Norwegian expert, who found 82 errors in 66 pages. Davis cited other problems, including insubordination, falsely signed cables, unanswered memos, unfinished reports, and dual assignments. When the director of the overseas branch, Robert Sherwood, refused to fire the errant subordinates, Davis asked the president for Sherwood's resignation because of "bad administration."[29]

Roosevelt refused to fire his close friend and speech writer Robert Sherwood. He delayed any action and hoped the two men would settle the matter. Nothing happened. By the end of the month, the press picked up the fight and speculated that Davis would be replaced. *Time* recounted, "As a friend and speech doctor to Franklin Roosevelt, Sherwood had easy entry to the White House. Davis presumably the nation's No. 1 news dispenser is not even close.

All the U.S. remembers that the President did not take Elmer Davis to Cairo and Teheran. In fact, Davis wasn't even invited to Quebec."[30]

The OWI's administrative chiefs were fighting in public. Roosevelt was furious, especially since it was understood from the beginning that no disagreements would be aired publicly. According to Davis, the president called Sherwood and Davis to the White House and "told us that he wished he had a good long ruler, the kind that school boys' hands used to be slapped with when he was in school; that he was good and God damned mad at both of us for letting a thing like this arise and get into the papers at a time when he had a war to think about." Roosevelt said he did not want to lose either of them because he was fond of them both and because it would take too much of his time to find a replacement. He emphasized that Davis was head of the agency and responsible for its operations, but he didn't want "Sherwood sent to Guam." He asked both men to go out in the cabinet room and get together.[31]

The chiefs held a fragile truce. The OWI was reorganized and Edward W. Barrett, Davis's choice, became the executive director of the overseas branch. He was to work under Sherwood but assumed all of Sherwood's authority at home. Barrett took Sherwood's title as well when Sherwood resigned from the OWI to work on Roosevelt's election campaign in September 1944. Davis won, but it was a hollow victory.[32]

The OWI chief continued to have problems with the military over the release of war information. The OWI had to take the army line as the government's official policy. The State Department cooperated only when and insofar as it chose. In spite of its announced goal of public education about the war, the administration came to look upon the war effort as something that had to be sold or manipulated as an informational product. The crisis was too great. In fact, there was an almost universal attempt to prevent the leakage of "unfavorable" news. The OWI mapped out an elaborate publicity campaign to "buttress the emotional appeal to patriotism." This meant, by necessity, an inflexible commitment to preserve things as they were. As Bruce Catton wrote, "More and more, as the war progressed, did the public officials who kept asking, 'What will the people think?' add the second question, the payoff question—'And how can we keep them from thinking it?' "[33]

Davis's originally stated purpose of openness and subsequent opposite actions created many of his problems. His most obvious attempts to curb and coordinate the writers and to make them stick to positive facts became public disasters. Before the end of his first year, thirty-eight writers quit during April and May 1943. One group resigned rather than alter the damaging statistics in the 1942 report on the potential food supply.[34]

About the same time, another writers' group resigned because advertisers and public relations experts had taken over the OWI. The writers resented their techniques, a "too-slick selling of the war." In a statement to the press,

Henry Pringle, Arthur M. Schlesinger, Jr., and others said, "No one denies that promotional techniques have a proper and powerful function in telling the story of the war. As we see it, the activities of OWI on the home front are now dominated by high pressure promotioners who prefer slick salesmanship to honest information." Schlesinger later recounted that they were greatly concerned that they would not be permitted to write the truth about domestic problems, such as race relations. At the time, Davis responded that the writers were insubordinate and that anyone entering the government service was part of a joint team with the president, who was the judge as to what truths would be expounded. "If each individual writer were to be the final judge of what might be put into a pamphlet," Davis said, "the public would be confused about what were the policies of the government." As independent thinkers, the writers were not about to be intimidated or herded by Davis. They resigned. Schlesinger, in retrospect, saw Davis as protective of the OWI's foreign activities and not wanting to fight a more conservative Congress, which was determined to keep the OWI from promoting domestic reform.[35]

The OWI was bound to fail in most instances. There was no way that Davis could keep his initial promise of a consistent, accurate flow of information about the war on both the domestic and international fronts. In a 1944 *Time* interview, former domestic branch director Palmer Hoyt likened the OWI to a beggar asking for alms; OWI information needs were at the mercy of the War and Navy departments' public relations officers. Davis did win a few skirmishes. After an appeal to the Army and Navy departments, Davis could publish the casualty lists by December 1942. The OWI chief justified this to the president: "We believe—and the public relations bureaus of the Army and Navy concur in this—that release of full casualty lists for publication not regionally, as at present, but by any paper that chose to print them all, would have a salutary effect on public understanding and public morale." Roosevelt agreed.[36]

No matter how vigorous, energetic, and noble Davis's efforts had been, critics continued to connect the OWI with a propaganda campaign. Davis was in a no-win situation. Even when he sought to take a more neutral war topic— whether "The Negro's Contribution to the War" or the president's leadership in the United States—he would offend one group or another. A cartoon booklet on the president's life, designed for overseas distribution, was "labeled purely political propaganda," according to New York Representative John Taber. Taber, also the ranking Republican on the House Appropriations Committee, asked, "How much longer are the American people going to have that kind of stuff pulled on them?"[37]

When the first issue of *Victory,* an OWI publication designed for overseas use, included an article "Roosevelt of America—President, Champion of Liberty, United States Leader in the War to Win Lasting and Worldwide

Peace," Senator Rufus Holman (Republican, Oregon) was incensed. The mostly pictorial magazine featured among other shots a large color photograph of Roosevelt against the background of the American flag. When Holman complained that the magazine and other OWI efforts were but a "window dressing" for another Roosevelt campaign, hostile Democrats joined in the fray. Senator Harry Byrd of Virginia indicated that his Joint Committee for the Reduction of Nonessential Federal Expenditures would investigate "all government propaganda ventures."[38]

Davis conceded that he had not read the Roosevelt story until the Holman speech, yet he insisted that *Victory* was aimed solely at foreign audiences. When Senator Joseph C. O'Mahoney (Democrat, Wyoming) called for a Senate committee investigation, Davis denied in *Newsweek* "that any of his publications were stumping for a Roosevelt fourth term—as some senators had charged—but admitted that some of his writers had been interspersing their facts with opinions," and he promised to "make them stick to the facts." Whatever Roosevelt's fourth-term intentions, the *Philadelphia Record* asked, "What are they afraid of—that the Democrats in 1944 will sweep the fifth ward in Casablanca?"[39]

The OWI had questionable congressional support before the end of Davis's first year. When Davis had to defend his budget, the president made it clear that he had no intention of going out of his way to protect the new agency. Uneasy about formal propaganda and unwilling to allow publicity to slip from his hands, Roosevelt accepted the OWI as a weak propaganda organization, a necessary but cumbersome addition to the war effort that demanded only his minimal support. Early in 1943 Roosevelt told Domestic Chief Gardner Cowles, Jr., that he would not intervene in what appeared to be a difficult struggle in Congress over the proposed 1944 OWI appropriation. Such a response was symbolic. FDR said that he simply was not willing to put his own credibility or credit on the line for an agency about which he cared very little.[40]

The OWI's budget became more and more controversial. Within the first six months, the OWI spent $3.9 million. Congressional suspicion of an overt American propaganda agency became so great that the House voted to eliminate the domestic branch altogether. Although the Senate rescued it, the result was a drastically reduced 1943 domestic agency budget. The OWI had to close twelve regional offices, its motion picture bureau, and its publications office. Congress, however, increased the OWI foreign branch budget by $24 million for psychological warfare. For the 1945 budget, the president requested $64.4 million, mostly for the overseas propaganda efforts. Since the OWI was a temporary war agency, it dissolved by August 31, 1945.[41]

Like the Creel Committee, the OWI's legacy left a lingering distaste for domestic propaganda. The OWI was but another public information agency, fraught with conflict. Its publicly stated purpose of disseminating truthful information conflicted with its actions. The task was impossible. Perhaps Roosevelt knew it all along. To tell the truth in a democracy during an all-out war would undercut the official wartime policy and possibly jeopardize the war effort. For the United States to wage a war successfully, it had to exert a singular authoritative effort. An authoritarian government by its very nature is not open and does not tolerate divergent viewpoints.

For the OWI, a middle road was too hard to follow, given the military thrust of government. Moreover, the OWI's major news source, the military, refused to cooperate in the OWI's pursuit of truth. The president as commander in chief set the example. In most conflicts over war information, Roosevelt backed the military. To wage war successfully, the country needed to speak in one voice rather than express divergent viewpoints, and information became another weapon.

Americans, in general, were used to being independent, to speaking their minds. It was impossible for OWI personnel, who were used to expressing diverse viewpoints, to speak in one voice. Such conflicts as the writers' resignations, the Sherwood and Donovan disagreements, and the hostilities toward the Darlan agreement only exemplified the OWI's dilemmas. A democratic system places limitations on overt national propaganda, whether for domestic or foreign consumption.

Underneath all the OWI efforts, it was impossible to fulfill Davis's original aim of telling nothing but the truth at home and abroad during this external crisis of an international war. Although Congress supported the OWI's overseas efforts, particularly in the area of psychological warfare, it used its control over the budget to stop any Goebbels-like domestic propaganda attempts. When the OWI published what it thought were safer topics, such as the president as an international leader, members of Congress complained. Unlike the World War I era, there was a presidential election and an incumbent as a candidate. Davis was bound to face an uproar.

As one of the greatest propagandists of the era, Roosevelt was not interested in any agency competing with his own publicity efforts. FDR might have thought that he needed an office of war information, yet he never really wanted a strong centralized one outside his office. His resulting ambiguity might have benefited the country.

Notes

1. Allan Winkler, *The Politics of Propaganda: The Office of War Information, 1942–1945* (New Haven, Conn.: Yale University Press, 1978), p. 24; Sidney Weinberg, "What to Tell America: The Writer's Quarrel in the Office of War Information," *Journal of American History* 55 (June 1968): 76; John Morton Blum, *V Was for Victory: Politics and American Culture during World War II* (New York: Harcourt Brace Jovanovich, 1976), pp. 22–23.

2. Winkler, *The Politics of Propaganda,* pp. 20–21; Richard W. Steele, "Preparing the Public for War: Efforts to Establish a National Propaganda Agency, 1940–1941," *American Historical Review* 75 (October 1970): 1649.

3. Steele, "Preparing the Public for War," p. 1653; Winkler, *The Politics of Propaganda,* p. 5; Blum, *V Was for Victory,* p. 21.

4. Early Memorandum to Surles et al., December 8, 1941, Stephen T. Early Papers (henceforth STEP), Franklin D. Roosevelt Library (henceforth FDRL); Early's Press Conference, December 10, 1941, STEP, FDRL.

5. Roosevelt Memorandum to the Director of the Budget, January 19, 1942, Official File (henceforth OF) 4619, FDRL; Bruce Catton quotes Mellett in *The War Lords of Washington* (New York: Harcourt, Brace, 1948), pp. 63–64.

6. Mellett Memorandum to Early, December 19, 1941, STEP, FDRL; STE Memorandum for Harry Hopkins, December 26, 1941, STEP, FDRL; Francis Biddle Memorandum for the President, April 22, 1942, OF 5015, FDRL; Hillier Krieghbaum, "The Office of War Information and Government News Policy," *Journalism Quarterly* 19 (September 1942): 242.

7. For general approval, see MacLeish to Roosevelt, June 16, 1942, OF 4619, FDRL, as found in Winkler, *The Politics of Propaganda,* p. 31; Catton, *The War Lords,* p. 190. *Time,* June 22, 1942, p. 21; "A Job for Elmer Davis," *New Republic,* June 22, 1942, p. 848.

8. "Office of War Information," in *Civilian Agencies,* Vol. 1 of *Federal Records of World War II* (Washington, D.C.: General Services Administration, National Archives and Records Service, 1950), p. 547.

9. Elmer Davis, "OWI Has a Job," *Public Opinion Quarterly* 7 (Spring 1943): 8; quote in Milton S. Eisenhower, *The President Is Calling* (Garden City, N.Y.: Doubleday, 1974), p. 128.

10. Krieghbaum, "The Office of War Information and Government News Policy," p. 243; FDR to Palmer Hoyt, May 4, 1943, penciled note about the stipulation of only six months, OF 5015, FDRL. See also *Newsweek,* April 26, 1943, p. 40. Franklin D. Roosevelt to Lowell Mellett, December 18, 1941, Lowell Mellett Papers, FDRL; Catton, *The War Lords,* p. 189; "Office of War Information," p. 547. As a general summary of what happened, see Elmer Davis, "OWI Report to the President, The Office of War Information, June 13, 1942 to September 15, 1945," p. 8, Elmer Davis Papers (henceforth EDP), Manuscripts Division, Library of Congress (henceforth LofC); Elmer Davis, "Report to the President," *Journalism Monographs,* August 7, 1968, p. 55.

11. Richard Harris Smith, *OSS: The Secret History of America's First Central Intelligence Agency* (Berkeley: University of California Press, 1972), p. 2.; Winkler, *The Politics of Propaganda,* pp. 25–27, 30.

12. Davis to the President, August 4, 1942, OF 5015, FDRL.

13. Draft of the Roosevelt letter, July 28, 1942, to all departments and agencies, OF 5015, FDRL.

14. Catton, *The War Lords,* p. 192; Winkler, *The Politics of Propaganda,* pp. 48–49.

15. "The Diary of Henry L. Stimson," July 9, 1942, as found in Winkler, *The Politics of Propaganda,* p. 48; Krieghbaum, "The Office of War Information and Government News Policy," p. 247.

16. STE Memorandum for the President, January 18, 1944, OF 5015, FDRL.

17. Winkler, *The Politics of Propaganda*, pp. 20–21, 34–35; Blum, *V Was for Victory*, p. 23. Paynter quote in *Time*, March 15, 1943, p. 14.

18. Henry Morgenthau, Jr., *From the Morgenthau Diaries*, Vol. 3, John Morton Blum, ed. (Boston: Houghton Mifflin, 1959–67), pp. 241–42.

19. For general discussions of the problems, see Gaddis Smith, *American Diplomacy during the Second World War, 1941–1945* (New York: Wiley, 1965), pp. 8, 10; Raymond G. O'Connor, *Diplomacy for Victory: FDR and Unconditional Surrender* (New York: W. W. Norton, 1971), pp. 33–34; Robert A. Divine, *Roosevelt and World War II* (Baltimore: Johns Hopkins Press, 1969), pp. 57–58; Robert A. Divine, *Second Chance: The Triumph of Internationalism in America during World War II* (New York: Random House, 1967), pp. 49, 83–84; Gabriel Kolko, *The Politics of War: The World and United States Foreign Policy, 1943–1945* (New York: Random House, 1968), pp. 4, 167, 242.

20. Winkler, *The Politics of Propaganda*, pp. 36, 70, 103; Eisenhower, *The President Is Calling*, p. 128; Weinberg, "What to Tell America," p. 83.

21. FDR Memorandum to Lowell Mellett, January 18, 1944, *F.D.R.: His Personal Letters, 1928–1945*, Vol. 2, Elliott Roosevelt, ed. (New York: Duell, Sloan and Pearce, 1950), p. 1487. No proof of the implementation of this suggestion has been found.

22. Presidential Memo to Archibald MacLeish, December 18, 1941, in reference to a letter from Tony Biddle to Franklin D. Roosevelt, December 11, 1941, OF 144, FDRL; Presidential Memo to MacLeish, April 3, 1942, OF 144, FDRL; FDR to Tully, August 17, 1944, OF 340, FDRL; Ambrose Leighton McCarthy to Tully, February 19, 1944, OF 340, FDRL; Roosevelt's note to Tully asking if the International Labor Conference Report might be given to the press, August 22, 1944, OF 340, FDRL.

23. Eisenhower, *The President Is Calling*, p. 139; R. Keith Kane, Chief, Bureau of Intelligence to Grace Tully, January 29, 1943, February 25, 1943, PSF, FDRL; FDR Memorandum to Adolf A. Berle, Jr., and Elmer Davis, October 5, 1943, *F.D.R.: His Personal Letters, 1928–1945*, Vol. 2, pp. 1450–51.

24. Winkler, *The Politics of Propaganda*, pp. 95, 98–99; Franklin D. Roosevelt, *Complete Presidential Press Conferences of Franklin D. Roosevelt* (New York: Da Capo Press, 1972), Press Conference 911, July 27, 1943, Vol. 22: 36.

25. In reference to the problem, see Dean Carl V. Ackerman to President Franklin D. Roosevelt, July 28, 1943, President's Personal File, FDRL; Early Memorandum to Hopkins, December 26, 1941, STEP, FDRL.

26. For Early's lack of enthusiasm for competition, see William Hassett to Stephen T. Early, February 25, 1944, STEP, FDRL. For Early's efforts to have a daily White House newsworthy item, see Stephen T. Early's Press Conferences, February 7, 20, and 24, 1942, Early Memorandum to MacLeish, February 19, 1942, and Early Memorandum to Roosevelt, May 25, 1942, STEP, FDRL.

27. Davis, "OWI Report to the President, The Office of War Information, June 13, 1942 to September 15, 1945," pp. 8–9, EDP, LofC; Eisenhower, *The President Is Calling*, p. 141; A. M. Sperber, *Murrow: His Life and Times* (New York: Freundlich Books, 1986), pp. 214–17.

28. Davis, "A Specimen Day in Washington," January 5, 1943, OWI, Japan to OWI, EDP, LofC.

29. Davis to the President, January 8, 1944, OWI, Japan to OWI, EDP, LofC; *New York Times,* January 26, 1944. See also Eisenhower, *The President Is Calling,* p. 145, who wrote that the new director, Edward Barrett, quickly got control of the operation.

The main overseas branch troublemakers were James Warburg, deputy OWI director for psychological warfare, Joseph Barnes, deputy director for the OWI's Atlantic operations, and Ed Johnson, chief of the overseas editorial board.

30. *Time,* February 7, 1944, p. 11.

31. Davis's "Notes on a Conversation with the President," February 2, 1944, OWI, June 13, 1942–September 15, 1945, EDP, LofC.

32. Davis to Sherwood, September 25, 1944, and Sherwood to Davis, September 22, 1944, OWI, EDP, LofC.

33. Hull to Davis, July 8, 1942, Records of the OWI, Box 4, EDP, LofC; Davis to Hull, July 10, 1942, Records of the OWI, Box 5, EDP, LofC; "OWI Report to the President," p. 237; Catton, *The War Lords,* pp. 74, 194.

34. MacLeish to Rosenman, June 4, 1943, Samuel I. Rosenman Papers, FDRL; Weinberg, "What to Tell America," pp. 86–87; Harold F. Gosnell, "Obstacles to Domestic Pamphleteering by OWI in World War II," *Journalism Quarterly* 23 (December 1946): 361.

35. Davis's Statement to the Press, April 14, 1943, MacLeish Papers, as found in Winkler, *The Politics of Propaganda,* pp. 64–66. See also Gosnell, "Obstacles to Domestic Pamphleteering by OWI in World War II," p. 362. Arthur M. Schlesinger, Jr., to Betty Houchin Winfield, September 22, 1989.

36. *Time,* January 17, 1944, p. 14; Elmer Davis to Franklin D. Roosevelt, December 19, 1942, President's Secretary's File, FDRL.

37. *Time,* March 15, 1943, p. 13.

38. "Congress Blast against OWI Portends Assault on New Deal," *Newsweek,* February 22, 1943, p. 25; "Roosevelt of America," *Victory* 1, no. 1 (1945): 25; *New York Times,* February 11, 1943. See also Winkler, *The Politics of Propaganda,* pp. 66–67.

39. *Newsweek,* February 22, 1943, p. 26; for *Record* quote, see *Newsweek,* May 3, 1943, p. 36.

40. In reference to Early, see Weinberg, "What to Tell America," pp. 79, 83; Lester G. Hawkins, Jr., and George S. Pettee, "OWI—Organization and Problems," *Public Opinion Quarterly* 7 (Spring 1943): 19.

41. The president initially requested $1.749 million on July 3, 1942, then another $2.185 million on September 17, with $75,000 to change buildings by December 15. See President to the Secretary of the Treasury, OF 5015, FDRL. By 1944 the president proposed $64.4 million for the fiscal year 1945. The overseas branch would receive the bulk, $59.6 million. See Press Release, March 29, 1944, OF 5015, FDRL.

"The American people want promptly all the news that can be told safely." Joseph Stalin, FDR, and Winston Churchill posing with both still and newsreel photographers at the Teheran, Iran, conference, November 29, 1943. Courtesy of the Franklin D. Roosevelt Library.

9

The Office of Censorship

All Americans abhor censorship, just as they abhor war. But the
experience of this and of all other nations has demonstrated that some
degree of censorship is essential in war time, and we are at war. The
important thing now is that such forms of censorship as are necessary
shall be administrated effectively and in harmony with the best interests
of our free institutions.
　　　—Franklin D. Roosevelt, Press Conference, December 16, 1941

While Americans may abhor censorship, World War II caused Franklin D. Roosevelt and his advisers to become more secretive. Information
about the war could be a tremendous strategic advantage and extremely dangerous. Even though freedom of expression generally precluded prior cen-
sorships, the Roosevelt administration placed restraints on particular publications, the newsgathering of military information, and the distribution of that
information during World War II. For those journalists who did not follow the
rules, the administration would punish, too.

Roosevelt already had within recent memory a foundation for censorship:
the World War I Committee on Public Information, the 1917 Espionage and
Trading-with-the-Enemy acts, the new 1940 Smith Sedition Act, as well as
several years of preliminary military planning. When Roosevelt had declared
a national emergency on September 1, 1939, with the outbreak of war in
Europe, army personnel had begun a training program for censoring the mail
entering and leaving the country. By June 1940, with the president's support,
a joint army and navy board had issued preparations for national censorship by
either law or executive order. Before Pearl Harbor, in March 1941, the Navy
Department had asked that newspapers voluntarily withhold information
about American shipyard repairs to damaged British ships. By August 1941,
the Navy Department had set up cable censorship headquarters and a training

school in Clarendon, Virginia, and had trained four hundred men by December 7, 1941.[1]

There also had been indirect warnings about pending war censorship in Roosevelt's mouthpiece, *Collier's* magazine. Citing the pressures on FDR to do something about the press, radio, mail, and cables that were far too candid for the nation's security, the magazine pointed to the 1916 National Defense Act and emergency clauses concerning radio broadcasting as legal censorship justifications. *Collier's* urged the president to call for a coalition of media owners; publishers representing the American Newspaper Publishers Association, major magazines, and newspaper chains; and radio representatives to formulate a voluntary censorship plan.[2]

With the bombing of Pearl Harbor, such censorship became more than a plan. American military chiefs, concerned about the enemy's knowledge and American morale, quickly stopped the transmission of any damaging details to keep the American public from learning the extent of the losses. The Office of Naval Intelligence immediately censored the radio-telephone communications, even in the middle of a United Press news alert being transmitted from Honolulu to Los Angeles. The War Department at once began censoring the mails crossing the borders. In fact, not until after the war did the public learn the extent of the Pearl Harbor damage. Four days after the disaster, the official communique said that, although there were 3,000 casualties, only one "old" battleship and a destroyer were sunk and other ships were damaged, while the Japanese suffered the heaviest casualties. In reality, the Americans had some 3,500 casualties and lost 200 airplanes, 8 battleships, 3 light cruisers, 3 destroyers, and 4 auxiliary crafts, which either sunk, capsized, or were heavily damaged. The Japanese Pacific Fleet must have known the extent of the damage because American intelligence sources learned that Japanese newspapers reported the damage. Yet, as the shocking details filtered back to the White House, officials were appalled by the catastrophic losses and American unreadiness. Secretary of the Treasury Henry Morgenthau, Jr., was said to have remarked, "They will never be able to explain it."[3]

They would not have to "explain it." Such vital information was immediately censored. In fact, the president ordered the FBI director J. Edgar Hoover to coordinate all censorship until the appointment of a censorship director. Hoover immediately sent Lowell Mellett, then director of the Office of Government Reports, a tentative draft of a censorship organization and its policies, the basis for what became the Office of Censorship. Hoover asked for a lot and, with the numbing shock of war, he got it. There would be a stop to all international communications having to do with the Allied forces, shipping, military operations, munitions productions, and the locations of war industries, as well as such internal information as economic news and intelligence reports. For Hoover, almost all war information could be dangerous.[4]

As the war crisis deepened, Hoover's powers within the administration grew and came to affect journalists. In the aftermath of Pearl Harbor, the director went after recalcitrant journalists, in particular columnists Drew Pearson and Robert S. Allen and their popular "Washington Merry-Go-Round." Pearson and Allen created a furor when they disclosed more specific details of the Hawaiian military losses in their syndicated column than had been given in the official reports. The FBI director, "in his capacity as temporary coordinator of censorship arrangements," not only talked to Allen but also proposed that the White House send a telegram to the two columnists. In an unprecedented action, Steve Early threatened to stop their column and bar their governmental access. Early used Hoover's exact words: "If they continue to print such inaccurate and unpatriotic statements, the Government will be compelled to appeal directly to their subscribers and to bar them from all privileges that go with the relationship between Press and Government."[5]

The Roosevelt administration went even further than their previously planned information restrictions as the shock of Pearl Harbor lessened and the reality of American vulnerability became known. In his January 29 morning briefing, Steve Early not only discussed the need for wiretapping but also acknowledged the FBI investigations. To the correspondents, he defended such expanded FBI powers: "The President's feeling is that handcuffs ought to be taken off the FBI and put somewhere else."[6]

Yet Early was careful to distinguish between the newly proposed censorship program and the World War I Creel Committee on Public Information (CPI). Early said that while a director would conduct the overall operation, a small interdepartmental committee would actually undertake the censorship. Early promised that there would be no delays and no censorship categories as had previously existed. Reporters would have access to the same information sources, and he added, "News has its value and I think the factor of great value in news is getting it from the sources to the reader in a minimum of time. This plan is designed to bring that about."[7]

The censorship mechanism was put in place on December 16, when Roosevelt established the Office of Censorship (OC) under the authority of the War Powers Act. He appointed Associated Press executive news director Byron Price as director, responsible directly to the president. He also set up the eight-member censorship policy board as the interdepartmental committee, consisting of Postmaster General Frank Walker, Archibald MacLeish, and six other government officials. In a press release, Roosevelt said that the director would censor "in his absolute discretion" all communications "through the medium of the mails, radio or cable transmission, or by any other means."[8]

Roosevelt explained that he had instructed Director Price "to coordinate the efforts of the domestic press and radio to withhold voluntarily from publication military and other information which should not be released in the interest of the effective prosecution of the war." Unlike the CPI, the OC would not release anything directly for publication; instead it would withhold information that would endanger the country.[9]

Initially, the press reaction was favorable, not only because the governmental news sources would continue to be the same but also because the agency would be more decentralized than the 1917 Creel operation. Right after the establishment of the OC, the *Milwaukee Journal* commented, "Roosevelt said that whatever censorship is necessary should be administered in harmony with democratic processes . . . [and] the nature of the [director's] appointment was regarded as encouraging by those who had favored overdrastic censorship."[10]

Byron Price also began with major administrative support. Since he was an Associated Press executive, the White House knew him. Steve Early supported his appointment, as did Attorney General Francis Biddle. Early wrote Harry Hopkins, "You know my high opinion of Byron Price. He is a man of complete integrity, and has the equipment for administering the censorship job better than anyone else I can think of." He also wrote the AP bureau chief Kent Cooper, "I believe his selection for the job was largely responsible for the attitude of the whole press, the radio, news photographers, etc."[11]

Some people did oppose Price for personal and political reasons. Lowell Mellett, who had wanted this position for himself, warned Early, "But you know also that Byron, with all his admiration and respect for the President, does not share the President's whole political philosophy." The newspaper guild representatives were not happy either. *P.M.* Washington correspondent Kenneth Crawford reminded Early that it was Price who had announced that he would rather resign than deal with the guild when the correspondents' hours were "endless and the pay disgracefully low in the AP." Crawford noted, "Thanks to the Guild and in spite of Price, decent conditions are now the rule in the AP as elsewhere." In fact, weeks later, the newspaper guild tried unsuccessfully to convince the president to establish a newspaper-industry advisory committee, equally composed of working newspapermen from the guild and editors.[12]

Early initially oversaw the direction of the OC. He publicly explained to the press the extent of the president's directives. Early said that all exclusives should go to Price. Otherwise, the chain of command meant that Price would serve as the court of appeals. Should the interdepartmental committee be in doubt, it could ask Price, who if unsure, "as he might be in the beginning, could check with Mellett." Early told the journalists, "If Mellett wants to, he can check with me; I will check the President, if necessary."[13]

Given all the censorship arrangements, Early was amazed that the press and radio cooperated so well, at times even asking for censorship. The guild pledged complete cooperation for wartime censorship. *Washington Star* columnist Raymond P. Brandt reminded his readers that FDR had told the American Society of Newspaper Editors in April 1941, "So far as I am concerned, there will be no governmental control of news unless it be of vital military information," and that war "requires censorship just as it requires propaganda."[14]

Brandt explained the OC in hopeful, positive terms. He said that the operation would have around 16,000 employees, "an exorbitant figure, yet it only indicates the comprehensive scope of this wartime activity." He noted that Price would have a far more efficient administrative organization than Creel's CPI, even though the board had similar representatives. Brandt acknowledged that realistic and fundamental objections could be leveled against "censorship at the source," but he assured his readers that the present self-censorship, the "voluntary censorship," would be better than that imposed during World War I. Discussing the possible longterm censorship effects, Brandt maintained that "with Price as censor there was little likelihood that mild censorship will be carried into the postwar era."[15]

What was Roosevelt's role in all of this? Attorney General Biddle wrote on December 19, 1941, that the president had no clear idea of what exact censorship there was to be. Biddle mused that Roosevelt "still believes that Price is going to censor newspapers—which of course, is not the fact, the President not even having that power under the revised Overman Act."[16]

The president and Price wanted to avoid the excesses of World War I—the arrest of thousands and post office controls over newspapers and magazines. Unlike the CPI, the OC emphasized voluntary cooperation. Price organized the office to censor any information that the enemy would like to have about defense matters, shipping data, weather conditions, and the details of war projects. The OC worked in two areas. Internally, it supervised the voluntary censorship effort on the part of newspapers and other publications and enforced the stringent radio-broadcasting controls prohibiting "the man on the street" interviews, special music requests, and audience-participation quizzes that might give the enemy agents prearranged coded messages. Externally, it monitored mail, cable, land-wire, radio-telegraph, radio-telephone, and all other means of communication between the United States and foreign countries. An interdepartmental committee, composed of representatives from the War Department (General Alexander Surles), the Navy Department (Admiral Ernest King), and the State Department (Michael McDermott), was established to assist Price. An advisory policy board met only infrequently that first year, while the more active interdepartmental operating board met often during those early months of 1942.[17]

Roosevelt acted as the final arbitrator in censorship controversies. He could and did clear access. For example, in 1944, when one AP correspondent tried to interview Yugoslavia's Marshal Tito for a political feature story, the Allied military authorities said no. Roosevelt intervened, and the story was distributed within a week.[18]

Roosevelt also intervened to censor information, especially those stories concerning sensitive international negotiations. For example, when the atrocity stories concerning the Japanese prisons began appearing in 1943, the president ordered the articles to be stopped at the source, the escaped prisoners. He directed that such stories be prevented until he had authorized the news release. The major justification for such censorship was the possibility of jeopardizing the missions of the prisoner-exchange ship *Gripsholm*.[19]

With Roosevelt's support, the OC budget grew by $7 million within six months with increasing support of Congress. By the time that the OC was abolished in November 1945, the budget had grown to $29.7 million. Director Price defended these early budget operations at the House Appropriations Committee hearings by emphasizing the OC's successes: "As to security, Censorship has discovered and enabled other agencies of the Government to forestall enemy plots. People have been arrested and in some cases executed as a result of the evidence that we produced." He also explained that the Treasury Department and other departments had profited by the discovery of plots to charge the government much more than military materials were worth: "We have returned to the United States treasury, several times over the appropriation you gave us, in actual case, because of the information we have found from censorship."[20]

Even though press censorship was voluntary and newspaper editors were their own censors, the censorship codes affected the press conferences and briefings immediately. In January 1942, when a reporter asked Early, "Steve, there are reports that Pat Hurley is going to New Zealand as our minister," the press secretary responded, "Well, Tom, I am sorry you asked the question. If you read your rules of censorship, you will see that diplomatic missions and movements of the military are not printable. . . . unless announced by the White House as the Senate receives such a nomination and CONFIDENTIALLY, by that time he will be there. Then we can announce it. In the meantime, it is OFF THE RECORD."[21]

There were constant code violations, and, as Frank Clough wrote in 1943, probably all areas were violated in minor instances. Most violations pertained to two areas: the publishing of military addresses that revealed certain units had gone overseas or the interviews with servicemen or civilians from war zones. Although servicemen had been instructed not to discuss military operations, they returned from the combat zones full of thrilling war tales, all newsworthy. Small-town newspaper editors especially did not always follow the code and clear such interviews. The OC learned of violations by reading the publications or by receiving clippings or whole newspapers from readers. Such editors then would receive a letter, telephone call, or telegram from the OC asking for their cooperation. As early as August 1942 Director Price began informing the president of enforcement problems. At the same time, Price noted the irony of no OC suppression of those interviews with ranking Allied officials, mostly because such a procedure "would have international repercussions and result in more harm than good."[22]

The roundup stories on military airplane accidents were another problem. Price agreed with Roosevelt that the press services should refrain from carrying these stories and try to confine the lesser accidents to regional publications. Price warned that these accidents had usually become known to some parts of the country and if they disappeared entirely from the newspapers, rumors of all kinds would result and then people would really worry about how much was being suppressed. The president went along with Price's suggestion that the Office of War Information publicize the small percentage of these accidents with no special blame.[23]

Price recommended that the military censor the source abroad instead of his office censoring so much. The armed forces already controlled journalists' access wherever American forces were stationed. The censorship machinery had already been put in place by the army in Australia and by the navy in New Zealand. Roosevelt, who agreed to cut off field news sources, became involved and offered suggestions from time to time. In September 1944 General George Marshall wrote General Dwight Eisenhower, "The President desires that I transmit the following message to you: There have appeared in the press photographs of American soldiers fraternizing with Germans in Germany. These photographs are considered objectionable by a number of our people. It is desired that steps be taken to discourage fraternizing by our troops with the inhabitants of Germany and that the publication of such photographs be effectively prohibited."[24]

Despite a policy of controlling access to war news, the White House was inconsistent, especially concerning publishers. When Arthur Sulzberger wanted to go to Moscow in 1943, Secretary of State Hull said that he would have no objection if Sulzberger did not write any articles and would go as a member of the Red Cross Central Committee to study future relief. When Frank Schroth, owner and publisher of the *Brooklyn Daily Eagle,* wanted to go to the British Isles, Early noted that while Schroth was an old friend, "he is an owner—publisher—one who comes within the policy prohibitions now enforced." When Henry Luce asked to go to Chungking in 1943, Early relayed Roosevelt's policy, "Not a single exception to this policy has been made, to my knowledge." Yet, exceptions were made. Luce cited the overseas trips of others and asked again in 1944. Early again refused, explaining that

Ogden Reid of the *New York Herald-Tribune* and Roy Howard of the United Press had been invited by the British to England only.[25]

Although the White House sometimes equivocated, the OC director was firm. For example, the office went after the *Washington Times-Herald* social columnist Igor Cassini, who wrote on May 29, 1942, "Uncle Sam is planning to open a branch of the War Department in London very soon. Two thousand one hundred U.S. officers will leave, in three shifts of 700 each, from the middle of June to the middle of July. . . ." Byron Price warned publisher Cissy Patterson that this column was forbidden. She responded that her newspaper had had no intention of violating the code, explaining that her newspaper had been terribly shorthanded because twelve men from the city room had gone to the armed services in the past few weeks and that an observant editor had killed the item in the last 100,000 copies of the issue. Cassini also wrote that he had not intended to violate the censorship regulations. Since army officers told him the story in a public place without asking that he not repeat the story, he said he did not think it was a guarded military secret. Price's response was indicative of his style. He emphasized he appreciated the newspapers' spirit of cooperation, but he had been disturbed by unintentional violations since "innocent mistakes may be just as damaging to the national interest as are deliberate violations."[26]

In contrast, the president could be unforgiving toward his critics, especially the *Tribune* publishing group. On December 4, just before Pearl Harbor, the *Tribune* group dared to publish the news that the Americans had extensive war plans after breaking the Japanese code. The headlines were "Secret War Plans Revealed." Secretary of Navy Frank Knox told the president that "we would be derelict in our duty if we let this flagrant case go by without at least an official attempt to uncover by a grand jury how much secret material got into the heads of newspaper reporters employed by newspaper publishers who were unscrupulous enough to publish it on the very eve of war." Knox suggested that "a few samples of this sort of reckless disregard of national security would do a lot" to improve the situation. Roosevelt was willing to stifle what he considered subversive, even pro-fascist propaganda.[27]

Convinced that the *Chicago Tribune*'s actions were seditious, FDR had Attorney General Biddle initiate a grand jury investigation in 1942. At the last minute the Navy Department refused to cooperate and forbade the Justice Department to disclose what harm had been done. The grand jury then refused to take the case seriously or to issue any indictments against the *Tribune*. As assistant William Mitchell reported to Biddle, "You may remember that at the very beginning . . . I became convinced that no progress could be made with the case at all unless the Navy was willing to have intelligence officers explain how the information collected at Pearl Harbor had been obtained and how the Japanese could make the necessary inference from the publication to enable them to take such action as would hamper further efforts of naval intelligence along the same lines."[28]

Although Mitchell had recommended that the case be dropped because of the Navy Department's half-hearted interest, Roosevelt had insisted upon continuing. Mitchell complained that the intractable Navy Department had lost the case: "They sort of sold me down the river and the Department of Justice as well." Unhampered, the *Tribune* continued the story. On June 4, 1942, the *Tribune* group published "U.S. Navy Knew In Advance All About the Jap Fleet." The Navy Department might have said that the story was dangerous, yet the Office of Censorship had released the information. Nothing further happened.[29]

Roosevelt was so sure that the *Tribune* group and Hearst newspapers were pro-fascist and publishing pro-German propaganda that he had the Justice Department do a content analysis of a sample of their editorials and news articles. Department coders tried to identify sixteen major Nazi radio themes in their newspapers from December 7, 1941, to May 1942. Although the readers did find criticism of the president, internal American conditions, and the United Nations, they did not find consistent Nazi themes, and the Justice Department dropped the study. No direct connection could be made.[30]

Still, Roosevelt remained unconvinced of the *Tribune* group's loyalty. He disliked Cissy Patterson and often talked about "Cissy's subversive mind." He had a surveillance put on her and Colonel Joseph Patterson of the *New York Daily News*. FDR once told Morris Ernst, who was representing a client against Cissy Patterson, "When you examine the woman down to her undies, do not invite me to be present. I have a weak stomach."[31]

When Joe Patterson tried a reconciliation with the president a few days after Pearl Harbor "to confess that he has been wrong in his isolationist policy," Roosevelt was far from gracious. According to Grace Tully, the president launched into a hard-hitting litany of Patterson's many wrongs, such as his editorials against lend-lease, the selective service act, and the destroyer deal. Roosevelt said that he could not remember "a single instance when Patterson's paper had supported any measure for defense against a potential enemy." The president then became relentless and caused Patterson to "cry like a baby," Grace Tully wrote. The president reportedly said that he wondered if "many more American boys had met their death just because Patterson had told his millions of readers . . . that America was not in any danger of attack," thus lulling the nation into inertia.[32]

Roosevelt might have tried to stifle the messages of his most vocal critics and the administration might have made some attempts to enforce the sedition acts, yet fewer people were prosecuted for sedition during World War II than in World War I. Attorney General Francis Biddle refused to allow charges to be brought without his personal approval. When some members of Congress proposed censorship of the foreign-language press, several members recounted the bad experience in World War I, and the plan was dropped. The government did use the Alien Registration Act, known as the Smith Act, in 1943 to convict a little group of Trotskyists for advocating violent overthrow of the government in their printed polemics. Moreover, the government used the 1917 Espionage Act to indict twenty-six fascists, including Gerald B. Winrod, Elizabeth Dilling, and Gerald L. K. Smith. Although the Justice Department easily showed that the defendants had engaged in mass propaganda and exhibited hatred against Jews, blacks, communists, and public officials, it was next to impossible to prove that these individuals conspired with one another or with the Germans or that their intent had been insubordination in the armed forces. The trial went on for more than seven months and became a public embarrassment, with the defendants acting unruly, the lawyers screaming, and the courtroom in tumult. After the judge died, the Justice Department moved for a dismissal and thus obtained no convictions.[33]

Rather than rely on legal means, the administration used the more effective behind-the-scenes and informal punishments. Such was the case with Father Charles Coughlin and his magazine *Social Justice,* with its circulation of 200,000. When Coughlin charged that Jews and communists had tricked America into war, Biddle did not want Coughlin to give grand jury testimony that might transform him into a martyr. Instead, he used the 1917 Espionage Act to revoke the *Social Justice*'s second-class mailing privileges and ordered the Cuneo Press and Express Company to stop deliveries. With Biddle's urging, Archbishop Mooney had Coughlin sign a detailed apology and cease *Social Justice* or any other publication. In the end, Coughlin's previous religious immunity crumbled, and he was silenced.[34]

Roosevelt received regular reports and news summaries on the OC's censorship efforts and American press disclosures. For example, there were news stories about American officers escaping from the Philippines, UP reports about the submarine sinkings of aircraft carriers, the March of Time films of troop departures, and General Douglas MacArthur's press releases which might indicate to the Japanese that the codes had been broken.[35]

When there were information conflicts between the military and journalists, Roosevelt usually backed the military. Navy Intelligence officers were far more stringent with the code requirements and war information in general than the civilian directors. Admiral Ernest King, in charge of all naval information, was reluctant to publish *any* negative information about the war, including the 1942 sinking of the battleship *Lexington* in the Coral Sea. Even when Roosevelt and Secretary of Navy Knox wanted to announce the loss as soon as the survivors reached shore, King said no. The catastrophe was too early in the war, when Americans were benumbed by the negative events.

According to Early, King said that he was willing to take full responsibility for any resentment the American people might feel when they learned the facts were kept secret for more than a month.[36]

Overall, the military censorship efforts were effective and lasting. What once would have been normal stories and newsgathering practices continued to be censored through 1944. To stop speculative stories about the war's end, Roosevelt asked that departments and agencies refrain from such disclosures, pending military announcement or White House authorization. When General Mark Clark returned to Washington to discuss with the president the impending European invasion, General Marshall ordered that the visit be kept secret. The White House did not mention Clark's appointment on the president's schedule during the daily press briefing. When Clark's apartment neighbor Constantine Brown of the *Washington Evening Star* broke the story, the wire service correspondents were furious. Press assistant Thomas Blake recounted that "they are still burning and feel that they are not in a position to tell their organizations based on what they are told in the White House that the President has or has not seen or done anything."[37]

For the White House correspondents, the biggest changes in covering the president concerned reporting his whereabouts. Before World War II, correspondents who traveled with Roosevelt reported his trips, the sites and the cities he visited. During the war, the president as commander in chief of the armed services used prohibitions against revealing officer or troop movements to keep his travels secret. It all came to a head in September 1942 during the congressional campaigns, when Roosevelt spent two weeks on a coast-to-coast military inspection trip. The OC had said that not one word of this trip could be printed until the president returned to the White House. Accompanied by only three privileged wire service correspondents and eight Navy Department photographers, the president inspected the tank and bomber assembly lines in the Midwest and the airplane plants and shipyards on the West Coast. To the journalists standing on the sidelines in Portland, it was infuriating to hear the president whisper into the portable mike, amidst the laughter of 14,000 shipyard workers, "You know, I'm not supposed to be here today. So you are possessors of a secret—a secret even the newspapers of the United States don't know. I hope you will keep it a secret. . . ."[38]

Such secrets became an immediate source of contention between the OC and the Washington correspondents. Even a small report on the controversy was a violation of the censorship code. Many newspapers strained to tell of the problem. The *Buffalo Evening News* reported that "it will not be long before this comes out into the open. . . . At present newspapers and radio have no right under the voluntary code, to explain what the dispute is about." When FDR returned to Washington, the *Washington Post* argued that this trip, no different from so many other trips taken by Roosevelt, was no secret to the hundreds of thousands of citizens who saw him in the teeming industrial centers and was "secret only to the great mass of patriotic citizens who read newspapers and listen to the radio and depend on them for information." Such a policy was both inadvisable and unnecessary, insinuating malicious rumor and distrust, said the *Post*. Moreover, the newspaper said that such a step could easily lead to abuse endangering a fundamental guarantee of the Bill of Rights. The *Post* wrote that there was no such parallel in Great Britain: "Whenever Mr. Churchill traveled to Russia or Egypt or to the front, the stories were printed before Mr. Churchill returned to London."[39]

Throughout the war, Roosevelt personally exploited this form of domestic censorship during his frequent train stops at Lucy Mercer Rutherford's Tranquility Farms estate near Newark, especially in 1944. When local newspapers pointed out the visits and tried to get publication permission through the OC, they were rebuffed, as were the traveling correspondents. Yet in 1943 there were references to the president's travels to international conferences. In January when the president left for Casablanca, Director Price sent out a confidential reminder to all editors and broadcasters that the code provision restricted any information regarding the movement of the commander in chief and any other ranking officials, but that the administration would release stories before the president returned. On January 26 Price reminded journalists that the release of Casablanca stories did not mean that the president had returned.[40]

When British journalists published information before their American counterparts, the correspondents were furious. During the 1943 Cairo and Teheran trips, Roosevelt bowed to the competitive pressures and told the army, navy, and the OWI, "The American people want promptly all the news which can be told safely, and they are entitled to have it without interposition of artificial barriers."[41]

As the war went on, some agencies asked the White House for a relaxation of the rules, especially concerning successes. By 1943 the War Shipping Administration was asking for a liberalization of news about the Merchant Marines. Roosevelt agreed with Emory Land's request to find some method to permit the press and radio to tell more fully those successful war activities.[42]

There was another kind of censorship—restrictions on the distribution of information to the troops. In its zeal, the military banned such books as *Under Cover* by John Roy Carlson. During the 1944 campaign, the Republicans wanted to stop distribution to those government tracts that referred to Roosevelt or the New Deal. Senator Robert Taft (Republican, Ohio) pressed for Title V of the Soldier Voting Act to limit the distribution of those books, magazines, newspapers, radio broadcasts, and motion pictures paid for or sponsored by the government. FDR, who termed the bill too narrow and "wholly inadequate and confusing," did not mention such a censorship provision when he allowed the bill to become law without his signature.[43]

Despite administration support for the separate Office of Censorship and a very capable director, Press Secretary Steve Early continued as the major information overseer, especially concerning information about the president. When Winston Churchill arrived on December 22, 1941, Early told the correspondents, "Preliminary publication of that story would certainly violate the Censorship Act."[44]

Roosevelt might have said that Americans abhor censorship, just as they abhor war, but war and censorship go together. The president's foremost priority was the nation's survival during wartime. As the government became more military-oriented, it became more authoritarian about information and placed limits on freedom of expression. The president could censor information legally under the War Powers Act, the Espionage Act, and the Smith Act. Yet he and the executive branch preferred to do so indirectly by controlling access to information and mail privileges.

The president preferred an information system that would make his job easier, allow him to proceed quickly and eliminate or minimize negative news stories. Roosevelt's method of controlling military information by censorship, direct and otherwise, was efficient. Whether direct or indirect, censorship of information is antithetical to democracy. The Roosevelt administration, however, thought that information during wartime was too vital a weapon to be entirely open to the public.

Such censorship efforts were formidable. The effect could not help but be chilling. The press had to contend with the president, the attorney general, the military, threats of punishment by prosecution, and FBI surveillance. Moreover, single critics, such as Father Coughlin, were silenced. Other critics, especially those of the *Tribune* group, had questions raised about their patriotism, their loyalty, and even the possibility of their committing treason.

Such World War II censorship also changed the role of the press in a sense. While one function of the news media is to transfer vital information, another important function is to put that information into a context, even a critical one. To make judgments, the press must have enough information to comment, whether through formal means or leaks or travel to battle zones. Newsgathering is but one step in writing a story. Without access to information, there cannot be a story. Censorship restricted access and cut off potential news stories before publications. Such censorship instituted a form of prior restraint. Since so much of the government's actions related to the war effort, the Roosevelt administration, as a military government, was able to keep secret a good deal of information about its activities. Thus, it became all the more difficult for journalists to criticize and to hold that government accountable.

The Office of Censorship undertook sweeping censorship efforts by inhibiting informational flow ahead of time and by halting the distribution of information. The OC operated under Roosevelt's guidelines, justified by war and national survival. When the OC censorship methods did not work well, the president used other agencies to stop information, whether by halting distribution or punishing after the fact. The military especially tried to stop war information, perhaps more information than necessary. The repercussions of such actions lingered long after World War II ended. The question remains, were these actions always "in harmony with the best interests of our free institutions," as Roosevelt said himself right after the Pearl Harbor attack?[45]

Notes

1. War Draft, June 10, 1940, President's Secretary's File (henceforth PSF), Franklin D. Roosevelt Library (henceforth FDRL); "Office of Censorship," in *Civilian Agencies,* Vol. 1 of *Federal Records of World War II* (Washington, D.C.: General Services Administration, National Archives and Records Service, 1950), pp. 318–19; Price testimony at the First Supplemental National Defense Appropriations, 1943, Hearings 77th Congress, 2d Session, Part 1, pp. 334–35, as found in Edward N. Doan, "Organization and Operation of the Office of Censorship," *Journalism Quarterly* 21 (September 1944): 208, 211. For the World War I precedents, see James R. Mock and Cedric Larson, *Words that Won the War: The Story of the Committee on Public Information, 1917–1918* (Princeton, N.J.: Princeton University Press, 1939), p. 341.

2. *Collier's,* February 1941, pp. 19, 62.

3. Philip Knightley, *The First Casualty; From the Crimea to Vietnam: The War Correspondent as Hero, Propagandist and Mythmaker* (New York: Harcourt Brace Jovanovich, 1975), pp. 272, 275. For losses, see Charles E. Neu, "Pearl Harbor," in *Franklin D. Roosevelt, His Life and Times: An Encyclopedic View,* Otis L. Graham, Jr., and Meghan Robinson Wander, eds. (Boston: G. K. Hall, 1985), p. 318. Robert Dallek's assessment is a little different: 2,405 Americans killed, 1,178 wounded, 7 battleships destroyed, and most of the navy and army aircraft at Oahu destroyed. See Robert Dallek, *Franklin D. Roosevelt and American Foreign Policy, 1932–1945* (New York: Oxford University Press, 1979). p. 312.

For the initial organization and operation, see "Office of Censorship," pp. 318–19; Doan, "Organization and Operation of the Office of Censorship," p. 211. Doan gave the actual date for operations as March 16, 1942.

4. "Draft of Tentative Objectives of Censorship of International Communications," December 9, 1941, and J. Edgar Hoover to Lowell Mellett, December 9, 1941, Lowell Mellett Papers, FDRL.

The FBI had been doing investigative work on espionage and subversive activities since Hitler's 1939 European expansions. Much work has been done to show that Hoover abused the authority he received from the president. See Kenneth O'Reilly, "A New Deal for the FBI: The Roosevelt Administration, Crime Control, and National

Security," *Journal of American History* 69 (December 1982): 638–58; Athan G. Theoharis, "The FBI's Stretching of Presidential Directives, 1936–1953," *Political Science Quarterly* 91 (Winter 1976–77): 649–72; Frank J. Donner, "Hoover's Legacy: A Nationwide System of Political Surveillance Based upon the Spurious Authority of a Press Release," *The Nation,* June 1, 1974, pp. 678–99.

5. J. Edgar Hoover to Stephen T. Early, December 12, 1941, and Early to Hoover, December 12, 1941, Stephen T. Early Papers (henceforth STEP), FDRL. By 1943 Pearson was broadcasting that he was being wiretapped and followed. See *Newsweek,* September 13, 1949, p. 49.

While Allen went to the army as an aide to General Patton, Drew Pearson continued his column and was under fire for his critical disclosures. Robert S. Allen, interview, Washington, D.C., Press Club, June 8, 1976.

Kenneth O'Reilly points out that the FBI launched a sweeping investigation against those who had spoken out against the lend-lease bill, used wiretaps, bugs, and physical surveillance in 1940, and carried these actions over into the war years. See O'Reilly, "A New Deal for the FBI," pp. 648–49.

6. Stephen T. Early Press Conference (henceforth STE PC), January 29, 1942, plus Early 1942 Scrapbook, STEP, FDRL; see chapter 4 herein as this also included John O'Donnell; J. Edgar Hoover to Steve Early, December 29, 1941, STEP, FDRL. See also Kenneth O'Reilly, *Hoover and the Un-Americans: The FBI, HUAC, and the Red Menace* (Philadelphia: Temple University Press, 1983), pp. 23–24.

7. STE PC, December 17, 1941, STEP, FDRL. See also Byron Price, "Sorry Restricted," in *Dateline: Washington, the Story of National Affairs Journalism in the Life and Times of the National Press Club,* Cabell Phillips et al., eds. (Garden City, N.Y.: Doubleday, 1949), pp. 211–20.

8. Press Release, December 16, 1941, Statement by the President, Official File (henceforth OF) 4695, FDRL; *Milwaukee Journal,* December 17, 1941, Early 1941 Scrapbook, STEP, FDRL. See also S.S. Statutes 840; Doan, "Organization and Operation of the Office of Censorship," p. 211.

9. Press Release, December 16, 1941, Statement of the President, OF 4695, FDRL. See also Doan, "Organization and Operation of the Office of Censorship," p. 211.

10. *Milwaukee Journal,* December 17, 1941, Early 1941 Scrapbook, STEP, FDRL.

11. Biddle Cabinet Meeting Diary, December 12, 1941, Francis Biddle Papers, FDRL; Early to Harry Hopkins, December 31, 1942, STEP, FDRL; Early to "K.C." [Kent Cooper], December 31, 1941, STEP, FDRL.

12. Mellett Memorandum to Stephen T. Early, December 19, 1941, STEP, FDRL; Crawford to Early, December 15, 1941, STEP, FDRL; Early to Price, January 22, 1942, OF 144, FDRL.

According to Walter Trohan, Mellett proposed himself as chief of the unit, and Early urged Trohan to write a story about it. The trial balloon created such a storm in Congress that it cost Mellett the job. See Trohan, *Political Animals: Memoirs of a Sentimental Cynic* (Garden City, N.Y.: Doubleday, 1975), p. 164.

For other reactions to Price, see W. P. Hobby to Early, January 8, 1942, Ralph

McGill to Early, December 17, 1941, and J. V. Connolly, December 16, 1942, OF 4695, FDRL.

13. STE PC, December 17, 1941, STEP, FDRL.

Price and his associates did not resign from the AP either, and the AP supplemented Price's $10,000 salary, as did Scripps-Howard for Assistant Director John Sorrells. Price defended the allowances to "have the highest type of personnel which we probably could not do otherwise." See Byron Price Memorandum for Early, January 20, 1942, STEP, FDRL.

14. Price Memorandum for Early, January 20, 1942, STEP, FDRL; Early to Price, January 22, 1942, OF 144, FDRL. Brandt wrote in the *Washington Star,* March 15, 1942, clippings in Early Diary, 1942, STEP, FDRL.

15. *Washington Star,* March 15, 1942.

16. Biddle Cabinet Meeting Diary, December 19, 1941, Francis Biddle Papers, FDRL. See also Doan, "Organization and Operation of the Office of Censorship," p. 205; Theodore F. Koop, *Weapon of Silence* (Chicago: University of Chicago Press, 1946), p. 45.

17. The Office of Censorship was authorized by Congress under Title III, Section 303 of the First War Powers Act of December 19, 1941. Doan, "Organization and Operation of the Office of Censorship," pp. 200, 203; STE PC, December 19, 1941, STEP, FDRL.

By 1944 the policy board had only met three or four times, and the operating board held four meetings, all in the first few months of 1942. Byron Price, "Government Censorship in War Time," *American Political Science Review* 36 (1942): 837–39; Byron Price, "The Censor Defends the Censorship," *New York Times Magazine,* February 11, 1946, p. 11. See also Paul. L. Murphy, "Office of Censorship," in *Franklin D. Roosevelt,* Graham and Wander, eds., p. 299.

18. Kent Cooper to Roosevelt, May 16, 1944, Roosevelt to the Secretary of War, May 18, 1944, Kent Cooper to Roosevelt, May 20, 1944, General Watson to the Secretary of War, May 22, 1944, and Roosevelt to Kent Cooper, May 25, 1944, OF 340, FDRL.

19. George C. Marshall to Douglas MacArthur, Mark Harmon, Jack J. Richardson, Delos Emmons, Simon Buckner, and Joseph Stillwell, December 6, 1943, Map Room (henceforth MR) 46, FDRL; Chester Hammon Memorandum for the President, October 7, 1943, MR 46, FDRL; Press Briefing, January 28, 1944, Early 1944 Scrapbook, STEP, FDRL; Doan, "Organization and Operation of the Office of Censorship," p. 201.

20. The OC budget went from the December 19, 1941, allotment of $1.5 million out of the president's emergency fund to another $4.15 million by February 6, 1942, to another $350,000 on March 3, 1942, and by May 25, 1942, another million. By June the president allocated another $484,152, and by July 11, 1942, another $780,000 for salaries for employees. See Budget, Office of Censorship, Director of the Budget to the Secretary of the Treasury, December 19, 1941, February 6, 1942, March 3, 1942, May 25, 1942, June 8, 1942, and July 11, 1942, OF 4695, FDRL. For Price quote, see First Supplemental National Defense Appropriation Bill for 1943, Hearings, 77th Congress, 2d Session, Part 1, pp. 334–35. See also Doan, "Organization and Operation of the Office of Censorship," p. 216; National War Agencies Appropriation Bill for 1944,

78th Congress, 1st Session, Part 1, pp. 73–74; Murphy, "Office of Censorship," pp. 299–300.

21. STE PC, January 24, 1942, STEP, FDRL. Frank Clough points out that more than 60,000 copies of each issue of the code were distributed to some 2,700 daily newspapers, 11,000 weeklies, 7,000 general periodicals, 5,000 trade, scientific, and professional journals, 11,000 business house organs, and about 9,000 miscellaneous publications, including church and lodge bulletins and newspapers. See Frank C. Clough, "Operations of the Press Division of the Office of Censorship," *Journalism Quarterly* 20 (September 1943): 220–22.

22. Clough, "Operations of the Press Division of the Office of Censorship," pp. 220–22. Price Memorandum for the President, August 28, 1942, PSF 161, FDRL.

23. Price Memorandum for the President, August 28, 1942, PSF 161, FDRL; Koop, *Weapon of Silence,* p. 168.

24. Executive Operations Division to Supreme Headquarters, November 21, 1944, MR 46, FDRL.

25. In reference to newspaper publishers, see Franklin D. Roosevelt Memorandum for the Secretary of State, May 11, 1943, OF 144, FDRL; William Stanley to Miss Tully, October 9, 1943, and FDR Memorandum to GGT [Tully], October 13, 1943, OF 144, FDRL; Early Memorandum from John J. McCloy of the War Department, August 26, 1943, and Early to John J. McCloy, OF 144, FDRL; TDB [Blake] Memorandum to Mr. Early, August 31, 1944, STEP, FDRL.

26. Frank C. Waldrop, Editor, *Washington Times-Herald* to Byron Price, June 4, 1942, Price to Patterson, May 29, 1942, Patterson Telegram to Byron Price, June 1, 1942, Price to Patterson, June 2, 1942, Frank C. Waldrop to Byron Price, June 4, 1942, and Price to Waldrop, June 6, 1942, STEP, FDRL.

27. Knox to the President, March 21, 1942, OF 144, FDRL.

28. Biddle Conference with the President, April 22, 1942, Francis Biddle Papers, FDRL; Phone Memorandum for Early, June 11, 1942, OF 4695, FDRL; William D. Mitchell to Francis Biddle, August 31, 1942, Francis Biddle Papers, FDRL.

29. William D. Mitchell to Francis Biddle, August 31, 1942, Francis Biddle Papers, FDRL.

30. Justice Department Content Analysis, December 7, 1941–May 12, 1942, as found in Francis Biddle Papers, FDRL.

31. Biddle Conference with the President, April 22, 1942, Francis Biddle Papers, FDRL; FDR Memorandum for Morris L. Ernst, March 23, 1942, *F.D.R.: His Personal Letters, 1928–1945,* Vol. 2, Elliott Roosevelt, ed. (New York: Duell, Sloan and Pearce, 1950), p. 1300.

Early was also quick to let Cissy Patterson know of any factual errors. See Early to Tully, June 11, 1943, with enclosed letter for the president in OF 144, FDRL.

32. ERW [Edwin R. Watson, White House aide] Memorandum for the President, December 10, 1942, PSF, FDRL; Grace Tully, *F.D.R., My Boss* (New York: Charles Scribner's Sons, 1949), pp. 292–93.

33. Richard Polenberg, *War and Society: The United States, 1941–1945* (Philadelphia: J. B. Lippincott, 1972), p. 48.

34. Conference with the President, April 22, 1942, and Biddle Diary, May 1, 1942, Francis Biddle Papers, FDRL. See also Polenberg, *War and Society,* pp. 47–48.

35. War Department to General MacArthur, November 15, 1942, MR 46, FDRL; CINPAC to COMINCH, August 8, 1942, MR 46, FDRL; COM 5 to OPNAV, May 28, 1942, MR 46, FDRL; Marshall to MacArthur, April 30, 1942, MR 46, FDRL; Censorship Reports, OF 3695, FDRL.

36. Robert Humphreys, "How Your News Is Censored," *Saturday Evening Post,* September 26, 1942, pp. 16–17.

37. Franklin D. Roosevelt to All Departments and Agencies, February 18, 1944, MR 163, FDRL; Blake Memorandum to Steve Early, May 12, 1944, STEP, FDRL.

38. James MacGregor Burns, *Roosevelt: The Soldier of Freedom* (New York: Harcourt, Brace, 1970), p. 269.

39. *Buffalo Evening News,* September 29, 1942, Early 1942 Diary, STEP, FDRL; *Washington Post* editorial, October 2, 1942, OF 144, FDRL.

Columnist John R. Covert wrote in the *Philadelphia Bulletin* "that in some part the complaint is justified would be obvious if it were permissible to disclose facts from which it grew." See *Philadelphia Bulletin,* October 1, 1942; and also Arthur Krock, "Censorship Conflict," *New York Times,* September 30, 1942, OF 144, FDRL.

40. Roosevelt exploited this censorship. When local newspapers pointed out the New Jersey visits and tried to get publication permission through the Office of Censorship, they were rebuffed, as were the correspondents. See Early Memorandum to Hassett, September 1, 1944, Clough to Blake, September 12, 1944, Blake Memorandum to Early, September 13, 1944, and Early to Blake, September 13, 1944, STEP, FDRL.

Price general letter to the editors and publishers, January 9, 1943, OF 144, FDRL; Price note to editors and broadcasters, January 26, 1943, OF 144, FDRL.

41. Roosevelt to Brendan Bracken, December 18, 1943, OF 340, FDRL; also copies to the secretary of war, the secretary of navy, Elmer Davis, and Byron Price.

42. Price Memorandum for the President, October 26, 1943, OF 144, FDRL; Roosevelt to Land, October 27, 1943, OF 144, FDRL; McIntyre to Price, October 28, 1943, OF 144, FDRL.

43. Presidential Memorandum for Honorable Jonathan Daniels, November 8, 1943, President's Personal File 2841, FDRL; William M. Leary, Jr., "Books, Soldiers and Censorship during the Second World War," *American Quarterly* 20 (Summer 1968): 237–45.

44. STE PC, December 22, 1941, STEP, FDRL; see also Early to Price, January 5, 1942, STEP, FDRL.

45. Franklin D. Roosevelt, *Complete Presidential Press Conferences of Franklin D. Roosevelt* (New York: Da Capo Press, 1972), Press Conference 792, December 16, 1941, Vol. 18: 369.

"Finally, a message!" FDR, MacKenzie King, and Winston Churchill meeting with reporters after the Quebec Conference at the Citadel, August 24, 1943. Courtesy of the Franklin D. Roosevelt Library.

10

World War II Press Relations

Q: Mr. President, what does constitute a national defense secret?
THE PRESIDENT: Well, I don't think we have ever had any trouble about that before. There has been mighty little that has been kept secret, and I don't think it has hurt anyone. . . .
—Press Conference, February 21, 1941

Mr. Early: Tremendous conference.
THE PRESIDENT: They will get damn little.
—Press Conference, December 9, 1941

"In a war, the first casualty is truth" was a phrase identified with World War I. In World War II, even before the United States had officially entered, some truths had already become casualties. With Pearl Harbor, the White House initially approved the release of general information, but it withheld the specifics, the total figures, the names, and the details—all symbolic information casualties of enemy actions.

When Franklin D. Roosevelt met with the correspondents two days after Pearl Harbor, he meant it when he muttered, "They will get damn little." His phrase signified an immediate wartime information change. Specifically, he asked the journalists not to print the lists of names and places of casualties: "You will get the totals, and the families will get the names." The details, the truth not only might give valuable information to the enemy but also might damage morale. Such "truth" also included the actual state of the American war involvement, the production figures, the weapons, the war itself, as well as the domestic efforts, all of which might be controversial and devisive. Thus, thousands of bits of information that the White House had formerly released to the press now would be withheld. The country's war condition as well as the president's reaction immediately affected the White House press relations.[1]

On that unforgettable day of December 7, 1941, Steve Early began releasing one statement after another for one of the greatest news stories of the century to the ever-increasing crowd of reporters. All the news management efforts of those previous eight years somehow flowed effortlessly that momentous afternoon. Beginning at 2:24 P.M. Early gave, bit by bit, each news fragment in the same manner that he had previously released information. At 3:10 he said, "So far as known now the attacks on Hawaii and Manila were made wholly without warning—when both Nations were at peace—and were delivered within an hour or so of the time the Japanese Ambassador and the Special Envoy, Mr. Kurusu, had gone to the State Department. . . ." At 3:15 Early told the sixty correspondents that the attacks were still in progress. At 3:20 he relayed the War Department's dispatch that an army transport carrying a load of lumber, not personnel, was torpedoed some 1,300 miles west of San Francisco. By 4:00 the press secretary began prefacing his remarks with "I am just trying to bring you to date." He then announced that the president would speak to the nation that evening and that he had called a cabinet meeting for 8:30 P.M. and the congressional leaders would join them at 9:00 P.M. For the reporters' interpretation, he suggested, "You can say, also, that the President is assembling all the facts as rapidly as possible and that in all probability he will, as quickly as possible, make a full informative report . . . in the form of a message from the President to Congress."[2]

Although Franklin D. Roosevelt did not immediately meet with the White House correspondents, he did give an informative report that evening to one trusted journalist, CBS London correspondent Edward R. Murrow. Murrow and FDR talked until after midnight about Churchill, Britain, and the air raids as well as the surprise attack, the casualties, the death count, the ships sunk at dockside, and the planes knocked out. Murrow's dilemma became the American journalist's dilemma: what to do with inside information during a major crisis. Although in this case the president had not labeled the evening "off the record," Murrow grappled the rest of the night about whether or not to tell *the* major behind-the-scenes story of the century. With an overwhelming, immediate sense of responsibility, Murrow essentially kept secret those war details.[3]

Murrow's dilemma about the release of information was also a White House problem. Steve Early continued to try to give newsworthy accounts and the specifics about the Hawaiian damage. In contrast, Franklin D. Roosevelt relied on his military advisers who tried to close the doors to information. The difference between these two men was all the more poignant the day after Pearl Harbor. At his December 8 press briefing, Early updated his Sunday reports: "The damage caused our forces in Oahu in yesterday's attack appears more serious than at first believed." He said that one old battleship had been capsized, several others were seriously damaged, one destroyer had been blown up, and other small ships had been seriously hit. He recounted that the bombing of army and navy fields had destroyed several hangars and that a large number of planes were put out of commission. While the damage was later found to be much larger, Early was close to being accurate when he said that the total number of Oahu casualties would probably amount to about three thousand, with nearly half of them fatalities.[4]

When asked the following morning if the specifics would be released, Early said, "Certainly, we intend to do it," adding that the reports must be sifted to find the truth and that "we are in a sifting process now." Asked if this was the worst naval disaster in American history, Early responded that he could not go beyond his statements, although he acknowledged, "First, the losses were heavy, and subsequent reports show those losses to be heavier than at first reported." Early assured the journalists, "I don't think you will be long in getting it after the government has it."[5]

When Roosevelt met the press two days after the disaster, the change to wartime press conferences was immediately noticeable. Referring to the tightened security for access, Maine newspaper correspondent May Craig commented, "You've got a new system out there" and "it's going to take a long time to get in." In contrast to what Early had promised, the president told the reporters who asked for more details on the attack, "Not yet. Not yet." When asked if he intended to give the public the benefit of the reports, FDR replied that two conditions now determined news and they ought to be put up in every office in Washington, "that includes newspaper offices as well as department offices." Those conditions were that the information must be accurate and would not give aid and comfort to the enemy. The president then made it clear that the military would filter and decide such conditions.[6]

Such qualifications brought an immediate response. Veteran correspondent Raymond "Pete" Brandt of the *St. Louis Post-Dispatch* recounted his newsgathering difficulties with the military and said that an official censor would be better, "someone there who can say whether it does conform [to the president's policy]." Roosevelt interrupted, stating that "that has got to be determined by the higher officers—the Army and Navy." When Brandt asked if these officers had instructions not to talk on any subject, FDR retorted, "I think that is probably correct." Brandt plaintively replied, "Where does that put us?" amidst the correspondents' laughter.[7]

For journalists, these new hinderances to newsgathering were most frustrating. The president insisted they all would have to wait until the information conformed to what the military approved. When Brandt told of having to spend as much as four hours getting information that was already a matter of record, the president responded, "Oh, but lots of these things may be matters of record. It does not mean that they conform." Roosevelt insisted that the release of information must be subject to military approval. He explained,

"Now you fellows can't determine that. The papers are not running the war. The Army and Navy have got to determine that."[8]

Brandt lamented, "We spent four hours on two paragraphs. All we want to know is if somebody in the Army can tell me whether they can or cannot give it out,—." The president interrupted, "There may be reasons," as Brandt continued with "rather than give us the run-around." When the highly respected Brandt noted that there was no reason why information could not be given out, the president reminded him that he must remember the psychological condition of the officers. Another journalist retorted, "What about our psychological condition?" Roosevelt responded, "Your toes haven't been stepped on, and theirs have." They were indeed uptight, and FDR had to deal with a military caught short in the rapidly expanding war. His preference in any kind of choice was obvious.[9]

More specifically, when Brandt explained that he had attempted to learn what happened with a congressional appropriation for Guam, Roosevelt said such an appropriation was a matter of public record—"no reason why you shouldn't have that"—and reminded Brandt that it was probably in his own office. Yet the president balked at publishing the details of the work done at Guam: "I don't think that that ought to be printed." When Brandt referred to that April appropriation for improving the Guam Harbor, Roosevelt discounted the possible news angle: "I think it is an awfully small matter, Pete, because really, dredging out the Harbor of Guam was not going to save that Island."[10]

As the correspondents were leaving, the president appeared to have asked for some reassurance about his new rules. He queried *New York Herald-Tribune* correspondent James Minifie, "Don't you think those two qualifications are pretty good?" Minifie answered, "Fundamental, sir—fundamental. We must have them." Roosevelt restated his intention: "What we want is to get the news out as soon as we can, subject to the two qualifications, and do it in the most convenient way." Minifie asked for someone, a censor, "who is responsible, [from whom] you can get a tip. The little man will kill it; but you can get the chief censor, and he usually lets it go." The president had asked, "You have been in London. . . . do you think their system was pretty good?" The correspondent agreed, "Very good. And then particularly—the best thing about it is they never cross up, and you can't get ahead of the Army and Navy about that." In this crisis, Minifie had summed up the wartime change when he said, "It sounds funny for a newspaperman to be advocating censorship."[11]

At his press briefing the following morning, Steve Early not only disagreed with the president's new closures on information but also refused to take responsibility for the changes. He emphasized, "I listened to Pete Brandt's report of his troubles yesterday and I want to tell you all . . . no orders have gone down from here." When another *St. Louis Post-Dispatch* correspondent asked if Brandt would be authorized to appeal or call should he have any more trouble, Early said, "Tell him to ring the alarm; sound the sirens."[12]

The press secretary tried to reassure the journalists: "We are rather hopeful of the returning of information to the bureaus in their various and appropriate departments." As mentioned earlier, when asked if there would be a "central source of information," Early vehemently asserted his viewpoint, "No. And I hope there never will be." Yet an Office of War Information was needed. As a symbolic end to an era of open information, Early closed his first World War II briefing with "Watch the War Department . . . they are going to give out the story."[13]

Even before Pearl Harbor Franklin D. Roosevelt had been extremely cautious in discussing foreign policy and war information. The change had not been abrupt but gradual. All during 1941 Roosevelt had been shutting off information in one instance after another. When Hitler's armies engulfed Europe and the United States began preparing for an inevitable involvement, the president raised what he called "ethical" issues concerning confidentiality about the defense of the country. In February 1941 he was already arguing that military information must be kept secret. One correspondent asked, "Isn't there a difference between what might be published in peacetime and what might be published in wartime?" and then questioned FDR's caution about the publication of congressional testimony: "Don't you think it is the function of the Press to keep the public informed?" Roosevelt's response was simply that the journalists should not publish military secrets involving the safety of the country.[14]

When the correspondents asked, "What *does* constitute a national defense secret?" Roosevelt asserted that it was the advice or recommendation of the Army and Navy departments on what would be harmful to the country's defense. The president emphasized that it was a question of *when* information would be disclosed and that the timing of news was crucial. Something that ought not to be made public on one day "might be perfectly all right to make . . . public a week hence." One correspondent pointed out, "Mr. President, you realize, of course, that we are up against a proposition; not being a Government-controlled press, we have to decide what really constitutes a dangerous secret." Referring to a military decision, another journalist suggested that "it may be . . . an attempt, under secrecy, to withhold information." Roosevelt retorted, "I don't think so." Deferring to the military some ten months before Pearl Harbor, FDR declared that "the only things that ought not to be printed that come out of a secret session of a committee are determined by the defense people, not by you, not by me."[15]

For years the president had complained about the correspondents' inaccuracy concerning foreign policy. By 1941 such overt mistakes could be devastating. When the president agreed that an erroneous report would do more damage than a true one, the journalist retorted, "I suggest that we have the truth!" amidst the correspondents' laughter. The evasive president retorted, "That's a little too slick!"[16]

Roosevelt's closure of information was protective. As the Axis engulfed both Europe and Asia in 1941, so too did a cloak of secrecy cover American reactions and actions. For the first time, the president lied to the press about his whereabouts. He even lied to his staff, the chief of the secret service, and his press secretary about his August 1941 "Atlantic fishing vacation," really an international conference with Winston Churchill. When three British journalists thinly disguised as historians broke the story, Steve Early was so furious, said Grace Tully, that he "blew his top" and threatened to quit. As a result, Tully said that the press secretary knew about all subsequent conferences in advance, and, while wartime regulations meant that the correspondents could not disclose the president's travels, at least they then knew where he was going and his purpose.[17]

The Atlantic Conference had been a dynamite news story, especially because it signaled a new American commitment to the British in its war with Germany. The resulting Atlantic Charter's eight points concerned territorial aims, free trade, open seas, and joint British and American economic development, all of which had been announced by the British first. Besides having been scooped, the American correspondents had had no chance to question the president or the prime minister on the charter's points or the new U.S. involvement.

After the furor, Roosevelt apologized to the correspondents and released the Navy's pictures of Churchill and himself. He assured the journalists he had demanded that these "literary gentlemen" give their story to the American press associations in London free of charge if they ever wrote anything about the conference within a year. Roosevelt was more sensitive to how the journalists worked, and in this instance he allowed the three press associations to leave his ship press meeting first. He also talked to them about who was at the meeting, but he warned the reporters about publishing the ships' exact location on the high seas, the dates, the length of the meetings, and the names of the two ships, even though he admitted that the British probably had published them. Although his meeting with Churchill had been an unsuccessful attempt at secrecy, it was but a prelude to other wartime information closures.[18]

During the Battle of the Atlantic in the fall of 1941, the White House was also cautious and secretive. When the U.S. Navy created an Atlantic fleet to serve as a convoy escort for British ships in U.S. waters, Early relayed the president's label of "a deliberate lie" concerning the *Washington Post*'s premature story. When isolationist Senator Burton Wheeler (Democrat, Montana) disclosed American troop occupation of Iceland along with the British, the journalists asked Early what power the president might have for this action. The press secretary retorted, " . . . why do you ask me?"[19]

Neither Early nor the president would give the correspondents much information about American ships being fired on that fall either. When asked about the position of the *U.S. Greer,* twice fired upon September 4, Roosevelt closed the subject with "The destroyer—it is a very, very fortunate thing that the destroyer was not hit in these attacks. And I think that is all that can be said on the subject today." He waited seven days before he issued a prepared statement on the attacks. When Germany torpedoed the destroyer *U.U.S. Kearny,* a convoy escort near Iceland, Roosevelt deferred comment "until the Navy established all the facts." When correspondent Tom Reynolds asked for the kind of navy regulations for hunting down the marauders, Roosevelt skillfully retorted, "Regular Navy orders. I don't know that I would say to hunt down the marauders. You ought to go into the Navy, Tom—really— honestly. Sea-faring—sea-faring—er—question. Why, Lord—we'll get you to Annapolis and put you on the Football team. You will be all right. We are turning them out—this is off the record—they are ninety-day wonders—over at—in Annapolis. It's a short course. You get paid for the taking of it, and graduate as an Ensign, and—(He laughs)." Reynolds interrupted and said, "I want a story, not a commission, Mr. President." An unnamed correspondent closed the line of questioning with "Let's throw him over the side."[20]

The president was all the more protective when American ships were being sunk in the Atlantic. On October 21, when the American merchant ship *Lehigh* was torpedoed and the correspondents asked who sunk it, FDR's tone was that of an exasperated parent, "Well, put on your 'thinking cap.' Who do you suppose? Certainly wasn't a British submarine. It certainly wasn't one of our submarines. And, certainly wasn't an Argentine submarine. It certainly wasn't a French submarine. So what kind of submarine was it? In other words, a process of elimination. Sometimes a very useful thing to do, even in—er—writing stories for newspapers. Of course, it is very rarely done. Leave that off the record. (Laughter)." On December 5 reporters asked for more details about such encounters between U.S. Navy ships and Axis submarines: "Does that mean a change in policy, and are we going to hear about such things from now on?" Roosevelt's answer was, "I don't know. I can't tell you anything else but what the Navy gave out."[21]

As American naval confrontations with the Germans increased and negotiations with the Japanese became more and more intense, the president increasingly evaded such press conference discussions. Employing his most evasive tactics, he refused to answer the correspondents' questions about diplomacy. In October, when the Germans were within sixty miles of Moscow and the Japanese militarists under War Minister Hideki Tojo gained power, Roosevelt responded to questions with "I don't think that I have any news at all." At the November 7 press conference, when reporters asked if the presence of the U.S. Marines in China had been the subject of the conversations between the Japanese and the Americans, the president only said, "No. Never has." By November 14, when the Japanese forced the U.S. Marines to leave China, the correspondents asked for clarification: Did the president think "anybody over-rates the seriousness of the Far Eastern situation?" Roosevelt retorted, "It's a difficult question to answer. What do you mean by 'seriously?' What do you mean by 'over-rate?'" When a journalist asked, "There is going to be a war?" Roosevelt declared, "I sincerely trust not." After the president read a statement about the withdrawal of U.S. Marine detachments from Peking, Tientsin, and Shanghai, one correspondent asked, "Can you tell where they will go?" Roosevelt only replied, "No," and he would not respond to guesses of "Singapore?" Another correspondent tried another tack: "Does the withdrawal of the Marines in any way affect our—." But Roosevelt interrupted with "The question and the answer are not worth putting down. It wouldn't mean anything."[22]

Despite the increasingly tense world situation, the president refused to disclose much of anything at his November 18 press conference. He explained to the correspondents that when he asked Early if he had anything, "he said he had nothing for me that I would be willing to talk about." To the next three pertinent questions—including the query, "Could you tell us anything about that conversation at the Executive Mansion yesterday with the two Japanese envoys?"—the president answered, "No. There isn't any news on that either." By November 21 the reporters were asking the president, "Have you any reasons to feel optimistic about the Japanese talks?" Roosevelt would only say, "Oh well, that's one of those 'are you beating your wife?' questions." When the reporter continued, "Is there anything you could tell us about them?" the president strongly emphasized, "No. No, no."[23]

Despite Roosevelt's lack of specific information, reporters sensed that war was imminent. One event after another pointed to it. Not only had the Germans sunk three American ships in a matter of weeks that fall, but by November 17 Congress had repealed sections of the U.S. Neutrality Act, which meant the country could arm merchant ships and enter combat zones. The Japanese Diet had approved a "resolution of hostility" against the United States. U.S. Navy commanders had been warned of the possibility of a surprise aggressive movement, including an attack on the Philippines or Guam. By November 26 Washington had rejected the Japanese "final" proposals of November 20. By November 27 all U.S. military forces were placed on a "final alert" status, with Pacific units receiving a "war warning." All this time, the president was supposed to be going to Warm Springs for a Thanksgiving vacation, but he kept postponing his travels with lame excuses to journalists.[24]

At his November 28 press conference, when a correspondent asked the president if there were any new developments in the Japanese talks, FDR finally acknowledged the situation was quite serious. For once he gave the reporters a much-needed background talk. He pointed out that while the American flag flew from the Philippines, the Japanese military was in control of the Chinese coasts and that "a study of the map would be advisable for all of us, because the Hitler method has always been aimed at a little move here and a little move there, by which complete encirclement, [was] a prelude to the extension of aggression to other places." Then he concluded the discussion: "I don't think that anything more can be said at this time." As if to warn the country, he said, "We—we are waiting."[25]

At his next press conference on Tuesday, December 2, the first question had to do with the Japanese march on Thailand and what the United States might do. The president, in no mood to give any more information, refused to speculate. When discussing the future intention of the Japanese government, FDR acknowledged that "we hope to get a reply to that very simple question shortly." When queried about his demands for an early reply to the secretary of state's proposals, Roosevelt appeared not to know about them and asked, "What proposals? And who was the State Department authority?" When the reporter refused to disclose his source, Roosevelt retorted, "Well then, I can't answer the question." On Friday, December 5, when the president was asked if he had any word as to the Japanese reply, he said that the Japanese were to see the secretary of state that morning and that Hull was coming to lunch. When Earl Godwin asked if there would be any announcement of the Japanese conversation, FDR only answered, "I don't know."[26]

On December 4, the *Chicago Tribune* gave the bombshell disclosure of the country's war plans to defeat Germany and its satellites by July 1, 1943. The correspondents' subsequent interchange with Steve Early and the president only amplified the press secretary's and the president's philosophical differences over openness and secrecy. While Early said that he had not talked with the president about the story and that he was "not in a position to confirm or deny" it, he acknowledged that both the army and the navy had war plans. "It is their duty, even in peacetime, to study and to devise plans for all possible emergencies." Early reminded the correspondents that "an unlimited national emergency had been declared" and that "if the military lacked plans to meet this emergency or any phase of it, they would be guilty of an inefficiency." He said, "If the President of the United States permitted them to face an emergency without a plan, he too would be guilty of negligence. I think that statement covers it." The reporters asked Early to learn from the president whether "this very important story" was true or not and if they published it, "would they also be guilty of any violation of the so-called voluntary censorship?" Early responded, "I don't think anyone would be correct in printing it . . . unless you attribute it to the papers that broke the story." He went on to say, "I consider that the Press is operating as a free press and the responsibility in this instance is more on the Government than on the Press—assuming the thing is genuine." Despite the subsequent Justice Department investigation, Early told the journalists no action would be taken as a result of the publication. He said, "Your right to print the news, I think, is unchallenged and unquestioned. It depends entirely on the publisher or editor or reporter whether in printing, it is patriotic or treason." One reporter pointedly reminded Early of the press's role in a democracy: "Of course, there is on the side of the paper which may publish it, the question whether the public has a right to know." Early's response to "the public's right to know," a phrase which became a rallying press cry of the 1950s, was "I just conceded that right to the editor."[27]

When Franklin D. Roosevelt was asked if he had "any comment to make on the story the *Chicago Tribune* had yesterday morning, regarding alleged war plans," the president's answer was, "I don't think I have any news on that. I think the Secretary of War is saying something about it today." Perhaps if the president had discussed the immediacy of war earlier than the November 28 backgrounder, the American public and their news messengers would not have been so surprised with contingent war plans or so shocked by Pearl Harbor.[28]

Roosevelt's wartime press conferences in many ways were similar to his New Deal meetings. He still planned for the meetings and some of the questions ahead of time. He used many of his same evasive tactics, refined during his previous administrations. He relied on his humor, his preconference kidding, his labeling devices, and his jawboning to turn aside those questions he did not like. With the war, he would evade questions with such new quips as "That is just what Hitler wants to know."[29]

The correspondents also had to contend with the confusing, ever-changing press conference rules. Just before Pearl Harbor, Roosevelt redefined the background rule when Steve Early suggested at the November 28 press conference, "For the benefit of the newcomers, will you do it again?" FDR explained, "'Background,' as I remember it, is that it is not to be attributed to me in any way, or to the White House in any way. But it is just so it will help you to write your stories." He further instructed, "And I don't think I would attribute it to 'high sources in the Administration,' but you call it, 'best information obtainable in Washington' or something like that."[30]

Early's interpretation was broader concerning limited attributions and quotations. He told the journalists they could use the "third person" and explained, "Newspaper reporters are not permitted to use it (material in the press conference) except in the third person." No direct quotes were to be used without permission, and he reminded the correspondents that "no permission was given to quote the President directly in this instance."[31]

Another example of rule change was the conference signal to close with "Thank you, Mr. President." The unwritten rule was that after those words there were to be no more questions. Jim Bishop wrote in *FDR's Last Year* that whenever the conferences droned on and the questions and the responses became more and more flippant and superficial, FDR would turn his eyes to the senior reporter present, who would cry out, "Thank you, Mr. President." Yet many times, especially during the war years, the conferences did not stop. Pertinent questions continued and so did the interviews, as did the quiet personal interchange with Anna O'Hare McCormick.[32]

The war added another dimension to what the White House released. The president, Prime Minister Churchill, and their aides planned the unprecedented joint press releases on submarine warfare, some of which were discussed at the press conferences. By July 1, 1943, Churchill proposed agreed-upon joint statements. By July 7 FDR said he liked the general idea, and by the end of the month, Churchill cabled, "The July Canaries to date number 35 making a total of 85 in the 91 days since May 1. Good hunting. Instead of making any announcement as agreed on August 10, let us settle together on the 12th what food our cats are to have." The press reacted favorably to such Anglo-American statements, and the *New York Times* entitled an article "To Issue Monthly Report."[33]

Even for these joint press releases, the military oversaw the final release. Roosevelt asked for reactions from the army and navy chiefs as well as from Elmer Davis of the Office of War Information. After the navy chief said there was no problem from the standpoint of security, the press release went out August 15. By September, when the mechanics for another public release were still being worked out, Rear Admiral Wilson Brown cautioned in a file memo that such releases should be conditional, issued from the two governments rather than from the president and the prime minister, and cabled from London with the time arranged by Elmer Davis and the Office of War Information and London.[34]

The military continued to be the ultimate filter for which news to release. Within the first six months after Pearl Harbor, Roosevelt went to the secretaries of the War and Navy departments with a statement about war production to boost the nation's morale. War Secretary Henry Stimson subsequently emphasized that "the press should not expect the issuance in the future of monthly production figures." He also said that as satisfactory as the figures were, the United States was only beginning to approach the peak of production. Following Stimson's lead, the president said in his statement to the press, "We ordinarily do not release production figures because they might give aid and comfort to the enemy. I am going to give today just a few which are definitely going to give the Axis just the opposite of 'aid and comfort.' "[35]

When the president gave out detailed information the following year on the expenditures for equipment, personnel, bombs, and gasoline used in the Bremen air raids, the press gave it a warm reception. After the release of such statistics that 5,000 American crew members took part and used 2.75 million rounds of ammunition, the *Washington Evening Star* noted that the president's information "illuminated the whole picture" and "educates the people as a whole and helps promote a sound national morale." The *Star* further said that "if this is to be a continuing White House policy, it will be universally welcomed, not by newspapermen alone but by a general public hungry for those significant little details that put flesh on the bare bones of official communiques and make them meaningful."[36]

Unfortunately, such significant little details were not regularly released by the president, who had a diminishing number of press meetings each year during the war. The president held 89 press conferences in 1941, 74 meetings in 1942, and 58 in 1943. In 1944, an election year, he had only 55 press conferences, while in 1945 he had 25. His meetings were also increasingly shorter, going from 826 pages of transcript in 1941 to 560 pages in 1944 and 121 pages in 1945. The reasons were many.[37]

By April 1942 the president began canceling press conferences. While many of the cancellations were due to his trips, FDR also began skipping conferences. He went three weeks in June without press conferences. From a news standpoint these were crucial newsworthy weeks: Tobruk and Sevastopol fell, Winston Churchill visited the country, the Japanese made more inroads into China, and American pilots had their first announced raids on German-held western Europe. The *Philadelphia Inquirer* Washington bureau staff complained, "If the normal procedure of two presidential press conferences each week had been followed, all of those events would have been talked over by the President and the newspapermen."[38]

The president had little that he wanted to tell. In fact, the correspondents began complaining that there was a lack of substance to the meetings. Because of censorship, FDR would not discuss many important stories, stories which pertained to the most newsworthy aspect of the period—the war. At the same time, the president became more and more sensitive to stories that implied conflict or told of divisiveness within the administration or between the United States and its allies. Political conflict, whether internal or external, had been and would continue to be an important news item. Reporters had access to the interdepartmental and intradepartmental disagreements during the New Deal, but the president and others attempted to stifle governmental conflicts during the war years, as noted in chapters 8 and 9.

When FDR finally did meet with the press on July 7, the first reporter's remark was, "Long time no see!" The conversation continued:

THE PRESIDENT: Long time.
Q: Three weeks.
THE PRESIDENT: I am afraid I am a bit rusty.
Q: So are we. . . .

THE PRESIDENT: I hope that you have all had a "happy holiday" in the last two
or three weeks. I have. (Laughter) I have no news, because I have been so
completely off the record during the short time passed.[39]

That press conference was also unproductive. FDR avoided telling the
journalists the exact nature of Ambassador William Phillips's new job. He made
the correspondents play twenty questions on what he might have discussed with
New York Representative Michael J. Kennedy that morning about the New
York governor's race. It was also a fruitless fishing expedition when the
correspondents asked about the other elections, negotiations to get French
warships out of Alexandria, the forthcoming dinner with Colombia's president-
elect, the possible increase in inflation with Little Steel's wage increase, and the
standards of the War Labor Board. Roosevelt would dismiss a question with
"Well you are getting to the kindergarten stage now." When the correspondents
asked about controversial gasoline rationing to solve the rubber problem, the
president's answer was, "I don't think there is any particular use in talking
about this subject because you talk—we can talk all day, and we would all be at
sixes and sevens." In his most protective manner, he added, "I couldn't write a
story on it, and I suppose I have as much information as anybody in the
room."[40]

The president waited ten days before having another press conference. In
fact, he would go for other ten-day intervals in August (August 11–21) and
then in September (September 1–11). He took a two-week, war-production
tour of the country from September 15 to October 1, which was off the record.
For the rest of 1942, however, the press conferences more or less followed the
normal twice-a-week schedule.[41]

Information crucial to the war was just too dangerous. The spring 1942
conferences were so unproductive that at the end of the May 5 meeting, after
the usual "Thank you, Mr. President," one journalist retorted, "For what?"
FDR said in return, "For what is right." Correspondent Earl Godwin left
mumbling, "Not much of a meeting, Mr. Early. Not much of a meeting." At
the end of the September 1 meeting after the "Thank you, Mr. President,"
Roosevelt responded with "Sorry. It just ain't," and Earl Godwin was quoted
as saying, "Things aren't good today."[42]

For much of 1942 the war was going badly, and the press conferences were
generally unproductive or not held at all. Frustrated correspondents were thus
quick to note any change for the better. On November 10, just after the off-
year elections, FDR was asked about long-range planning for the African
expedition. He finally spoke at length, discussing in detail the Allied landings on the Algerian and Moroccan coasts two days before. At the end of
that conference, Tom Reynolds said as he rushed out, "A little copy there,"
and "You made a few good stories."[43]

The reporters also lost access to the president when he traveled. As commander in chief of the armed forces whose movements were kept secret, FDR had few meetings with the three traveling wire service representatives. Even those conferences were all off the record until he returned, as was coverage by local reporters. With such travels, Roosevelt missed many 1943 meetings. He took ten days or more for each of four vacations and held a joint meeting with the Canadian and British prime ministers in August. He also missed over a month of press meetings during the Teheran Conference in November and December. The same type of pattern existed in 1944, when he canceled press conferences in January while he had the flu and in January, March, and April when he had bronchitis and then went to Bernard Baruch's Hobcaw Barony in South Carolina for recuperation. He also missed weeks at a time in June, July, and December of 1944 as well as a month during January and February of 1945 for the Yalta Conference.[44]

Such press exclusion became so critical by 1944 that five major newspaper correspondents wrote to Early and asked to know of the president's approximate whereabouts so that they might stay within a reasonable distance. They said they had been motivated in the last few months by such pertinent concerns as the president's health, which had not been good, the 1944 election year, and what was probably the most decisive year in the European war. The journalists argued that "if newspapers are to fulfill their responsibilities to the public, they must do everything possible to cover the President fully at all times, wherever he may be. We are mindful, of course, of the long-established precedent that the White House is wherever the President is." Steve Early must have agreed with the journalists since he at least began announcing the president's trips at his press briefings.[45]

The correspondents might also have had fresh in their memories their exclusion from the fall 1943 United Nations Conference on Food and Agriculture. The reporters had asked the president if he had "any comment at all on some of the reports that the restrictions on the press coverage at Hot Springs constitute restrictions on freedom of the press." Roosevelt answered, "I haven't . . . anything," and he proceeded to tell an anecdote about a journalist's suggestion that there be tiers of benches in the cabinet room for press observers. Someone interrupted, "What's wrong with that?" FDR responded, "A good idea," but added, "You will be asking to come in next to watch me take my bath. After all there are certain limits!" There were indeed wartime limits, limits on access and secrecy even for a food conference.[46]

Also limited was public knowledge about the president's health. By 1944 Franklin D. Roosevelt was seriously ill, which affected his press conference responses. He was not his former self. His hearing had deteriorated to the point that he had to have questions constantly repeated. FDR's once booming voice also became so weak that reporters could not hear his answers from the back of the Oval Office. By spring, correspondents were repeating the questions after Early would say, "He can't hear you" or "louder," and then reiterating his response, "Can't hear you, Mr. President," or "Would you mind speaking a little louder, Mr. President?" Moreover, he would have lapses in memory, and Early would have to fill in often, as shown in this July 11, 1944, interchange:

Q: Mr. President, is the text of the memorandum which you read available?
THE PRESIDENT: What?
Q: Is the text of the memorandum which you read available for—
THE PRESIDENT: (Interposing) No. I suppose the State Department has the—the tentative thing, which was done in London, and that is the—
MR. EARLY: (Interposing) The text of this memorandum—
THE PRESIDENT: (Interjecting) What?
MR. EARLY: (Continuing)—he refers to the memorandum you just read, Mr. President.
THE PRESIDENT: No, because it isn't—it isn't in shape.[47]

Steve Early's position became increasingly difficult as he took on additional roles to generate White House information. He said, "We try to have something interesting every day and especially do we strive to get material for the President to announce at his conferences." Also, the timing of news made Early's job a little harder. Before Pearl Harbor, Early had to think of only a three hour time difference between the East and West Coast. With the war and "Washington as the news center of the world," news had to be released once an hour to hit all the pertinent world areas as a story was breaking. Even speeches were more complicated. The text had to be ready in time to distribute to the country's newspapers before the president spoke so that the newspapers could be on the streets at the exact moment the first word was broadcast.[48]

During the war Early increasingly became known as "the White House Spokesman." Such a term, which had been used at the end of the Harding era and through the Coolidge years, actually indicated what a president had said without attribution. When Roosevelt said something off the record, the words "White House spokesman said . . ." were used. By 1939 the term began to be used in reference to Steve Early's information. The *Washington Star* entitled an article "The White House Spokesman 'Steve' Early is Adept in Handling Press Relations." At his April 1942 briefing, Early referred to such unnamed qualifiers: "I see that from one source or another attributed as 'authorized' or 'spokesman' or 'from informed quarters' or 'circles,' et cetera, there is a probability of some action by the President this week." Early went on to specify, "I should say that there is nothing definitely decided, but FOR YOUR GUIDANCE and without attribution to me, there is a distinct possibility that it will take the form of a message."[49]

After Pearl Harbor Early used more and more such qualifiers as "off the record," "for your guidance only," "just for your own information," or

"strictest of confidence." These stipulations often concerned background information about the president, particularly his trips, which took up much of
Early's briefing time and were the greatest sources of conflict between the
journalists and the White House. To be careful, Early now had three stenographers taking down his remarks at his daily briefings. For example, at a
February 1942 briefing, Early said, "Gentlemen, OFF THE RECORD ENTIRELY,
you will recall about two weeks ago that a certain situation prevailed with
respect to the President and his whereabouts. A similar situation again is
present and all I can do is to turn to the sign and say, 'We will Serve in Silence
for the Duration.' "50

During Roosevelt's Casablanca trip, the first time a president had left the
country during wartime, the correspondents had numerous complaints about
the lack of news. Thus, for the subsequent Quebec conference, FDR asked
Early to go along, and he in turn allowed reporters other than wire service
representatives to be there. Although Roosevelt would not release even a hint
of these discussions, Early gave out other information. He held background
sessions on the progress of the war, the arrivals and departures of American
and foreign officers, and the fact that Roosevelt and Churchill stayed up
talking until 2:30 A.M. He arranged with some difficulty a joint press conference with Churchill, Roosevelt, and the Canadian prime minister. While
this was not a question and answer session, there were at least the leaders'
appearances and statements. The journalists appreciated Early's role in getting
them news, and some twenty of them sent to the White House an unprecedented resolution from the White House Correspondents' Association. They
commended both the president and Steve Early for "GALLANTRY IN ACTION
ABOVE AND BEYOND THE CALL OF DUTY," for averting a catastrophe for the
"JUSTIFICATION OF QUEBEC EXPENSE ACCOUNTS. . . ."51

After the trips, Early made special outlines for the president to follow at his
press conferences since he had been away from the White House for a while.
Sometimes they were to placate the journalists who were disgruntled over
their lack of access. For example, after the Casablanca trip in 1943, Early
wrote a memorandum to the president suggesting a way to appease the correspondents who had been left at home: "Express thanks. . . ." Roosevelt
began his press conference that day with thanks to "the press and radio of the
United States for living up so very faithfully to the request of the Offices of
Censorship and Information" for keeping his movements secret. He also said,
"It was beautifully done, and I am very appreciative of it. . . ."52

Early's office had to be ever so mindful of possible questions at the conferences and leaks from the administration that might become bombshell
stories. For example, Early's assistant, Thomas Blake, warned the press secretary that Constantine Brown of the *Washington Star* had obtained a story
about a U.S. naval vessel being turned over to the Russians and suggested that

if FDR were questioned about specific ships and tonnage, he could say for reasons of military security the information was not available. Early's follow-up memorandum to the president suggested an answer: "This is a military matter. Nothing can be said about it now because we refuse to give the enemy information that will be of value to him." While the question did not come up at the next press conference, it did at the subsequent one. Roosevelt interrupted the query, "I wonder if you would . . . ," with "No. This is the thing you forgot to ask me last—last Friday," amid much laughter. The correspondent in defense said, "You gave us a little too much then." FDR retorted, "I will have to give you the same answer I would have given last Friday—it's all right: ask the Navy Department."[53]

Early's important role as center of White House news became more and more apparent. In June 1943 Roosevelt began one of his press conferences with "Steve (Early) and I are agreed we haven't either of us got a thing—not a thing." Early, who was rarely referred to during the 1941–43 meetings, became the president's overt question reminder, prodder, repeater, and answerer in almost every press conference after December 1943. By 1944 the Roosevelt press conferences became more and more joint Early-Roosevelt press conferences. He would remind the president of the budget summary and then prompt him to discuss it. Or he would jog the president's memory about such things as who attended cabinet meetings or who covered a story about Finland. Sometimes he would prompt the president by repeating the words in the questions: "Any comment, Mr. President, on the reported expulsion of British and American military missions from Bulgaria?" Other times Early would simply answer the questions himself, as he did in September 1944 when FDR was queried about the value of the German mark.[54]

Early increasingly filled in the gaps from early 1944 onward by correcting the president's retorts, answering for him, and serving as his sidekick for humor. As pointed out in chapter 3, Roosevelt held shorter meetings and fewer press conferences during this period. The president needed his assistant's help because he was out of touch with the day-to-day news and, more important, he was ill a great deal of the time.[55]

With the war correspondents' and publishers' increased complaints about so much censorship of the Allied invasion in Europe in 1944, Steve Early took on the new position as the administration's publicity troubleshooter. At the invitation of General Dwight Eisenhower's chief of press relations Harry Butcher, he went to Paris in February 1945 to examine the press system at the Supreme Headquarters. He found the same conflict concerning access that existed in the White House. The war correspondents sought the news, and the military tried to keep back anything that could be of value to the enemy. In their zeal, the overcautious censors held up stories and deleted unfavorable bits of news, especially those stories about their own blunders. Both the army and the war correspondents hoped Early would iron out some "of the wrinkles and wrangles of censorship." After a month's investigation, Early advised loosening censorship and increasing the flow of military news back to the United States. If a story was withheld, the military should at least release the reasons why.[56]

By 1945 Early was exhausted. He had had twelve years of the daily White House news grind. His last four years had been under intense fire as he had tried to release news from the White House. More and more frequently he had to substitute for the president at the press conferences. It was all too tiring. Early planned to enter private employment in June. Jonathan Daniels, son of Roosevelt's former boss when he was assistant secretary of the navy, became the new press secretary. The president asked Early to fill in as the secretary in charge of appointments until June.

Although Early had relinquished the title of press secretary, he took over again on April 12. In the midst of a benumbed staff that fateful day, it was Steve Early who told the correspondents about the president's death, called in Harry Truman, arranged the next Constitutional steps, and then flew to Georgia with Eleanor Roosevelt. Throughout it all, Early, bit by bit, released news about the president's death as he learned it, much as he had done with the Pearl Harbor announcements.[57]

To Steve Early, Franklin D. Roosevelt might have said "they will get damn little" news during World War II, but that was not necessarily true. Early tried to make sure that they would damn well get something. Truth might have been another war casualty, but it was not a fatality. The American military chiefs tried to block news of war blunders, "for the good of the country," while releasing news of war heroics. War information could be too potentially dangerous a weapon, even when close to a subsequent peace. Although the press secretary might have been the correspondents' White House news advocate, the president for the most part went along with the military. The news blackout, perhaps necessary for security reasons, allowed this president a greater freedom of movement and activity than that given any other modern president.

Notes

1. Franklin D. Roosevelt, *Complete Presidential Press Conferences of Franklin D. Roosevelt* (New York: Da Capo Press, 1972), Press Conference (henceforth PC) 790, December 9, 1941, Vol. 18: 343; PC 791, December 12, 1941, Vol. 18: 363.

2. Stephen T. Early Press Conferences (henceforth STE PC), July–December 1941, listed by dates and times about what happened on December 7, 1941, Stephen T. Early Papers (henceforth STEP), Franklin D. Roosevelt Library (henceforth FDRL); *New York Times*, December 8, 1941.

3. Grace Tully, *F.D.R., My Boss* (New York: Charles Scribner's Sons, 1949), p. 258; Alexander Kenderick, *Prime Time: The Life of Edward R. Murrow* (Boston: Little, Brown, 1969), p. 239; A. M. Sperber, *Murrow: His Life and Times* (New York: Freundlich Books, 1986), pp. 206–8. Sperber points out that Murrow and his wife had been invited for dinner on December 7, a dinner Eleanor Roosevelt hosted alone. At the president's request, Murrow waited afterwards until the cabinet and congressional leaders departed. Janet Murrow later said that she essentially agreed with Sperber's account, although she did not recollect that Bill Donovan had come that evening too. Telephone interview with Janet Murrow, July 7, 1986.

4. STE PC, December 8, 1941, STEP, FDRL. While Early was close to the total number of casualties according to Robert Dallek's account some thirty-nine years later, he was way off as to the extent of damage to the Pacific Fleet. Dallek wrote that the bombing killed 2,405 Americans, wounded an additional 1,178, and destroyed the bulk of the American fleet: seven battleships and most of the navy and army aircraft on Oahu. Whether Early actually knew the extent of damage cannot be said at this point. See Robert Dallek, *Franklin D. Roosevelt and American Foreign Policy, 1932–1945* (New York: Oxford University Press, 1979), p. 312.

5. STE PC, December 9, 1941, STEP, FDRL.

6. Roosevelt, *Complete Press Conferences*, PC 790, December 9, 1941, Vol. 18: 343, 348–51.

7. Ibid., pp. 349–50.

8. Ibid., pp. 350–51.

9. Ibid., pp. 352–53; Martin V. Melosi, *The Shadow of Pearl Harbor: Political Controversy over the Surprise Attack, 1941–1946* (College Station: Texas A & M Press, 1977), pp. 12, 14, 168, 265.

10. Roosevelt, *Complete Press Conferences*, PC 790, December 9, 1941, Vol. 18: 351–52. Guam became an issue again during the 1944 presidential campaign when Roosevelt said that Congress was to blame for the lack of defenses which enabled the Japanese to capture Guam. See *Washington Times-Herald,* September 6, 1944, Early White House 1944 Scrapbook, STEP, FDRL.

11. Roosevelt, *Complete Press Conferences*, PC 790, December 9, 1941, Vol. 18: 356.

12. STE PC, December 10, 1941, STEP, FDRL.

13. Ibid.

14. Roosevelt, *Complete Press Conferences,* PC 720, February 21, 1941, Vol. 17: 142–43.

15. Ibid., pp. 143–46.

16. Ibid., p. 143.

17. Tully, *F.D.R., My Boss*, pp. 132, 247.

18. Roosevelt, *Complete Press Conferences,* PC 761, August 16, 1941, Vol. 18: 82–83, 76–77.

19. Early had said, "The President of the United States this morning said, after reading the other morning paper, that he thought the author of the story had very cleverly woven a long time and historical policy of the United States into a story which is a deliberate lie." See STE PC, April 17, 1941, STEP, FDRL; *Washington Star,*

April 17, 1941, and *Washington Times-Herald,* April 17, 1941, Early 1941 Scrapbook, STEP, FDRL.

On February 1 the U.S. Navy had created the Atlantic Fleet essentially to act as a convoy escort. See STE PC, August 8, 1941, STEP, FDRL.

20. Roosevelt, *Complete Press Conferences,* PC 767, September 5, 1941, Vol. 18: 140–41; The President's Press Statement, September 11, 1941, STEP, FDRL; concerning the *U.U.S. Kearny,* see Roosevelt, *Complete Press Conferences,* PC 776, October 17, 1941, 18: 229–35. No matter what the correspondents asked, the president evaded the questions and summarized the session with "I don't think that I have any news at all," only to be asked, "Well, may I try this?" amid the correspondents' laughter. For the rest of the conference, the president would comment only on local issues. For the Tom Reynolds excerpt, see pp. 235–36.

21. Roosevelt, *Complete Press Conferences,* PC 777, October 21, 1941, Vol. 18: 240–41. In reference to that particular press conference, Raymond P. Brandt reported statements of Roosevelt's which were different from the press conference transcripts. See Brandt, "White House Puts on Pressure for Using U.S. Ships to Deliver Arms," *St. Louis Post-Dispatch,* October 22, 1941. For quote on encounters, see Roosevelt, *Complete Press Conferences,* PC 789, December 5, 1941, Vol. 18: 340–41.

22. Roosevelt, *Complete Press Conferences,* PC 776, October 17, 1941, Vol. 18: 230; PC 782, November 7, 1941, Vol. 18: 291; PC 783, November 14, 1941, Vol. 18: 299, 302–4.

23. Ibid., PC 784, November 18, 1941, Vol. 18: 306; PC 785, November 21, 1941, Vol. 18: 315.

24. Ibid., both previous press conferences.

25. Ibid., PC 787, November 28, 1941, Vol. 18: 325–26.

26. Ibid., PC 788, December 2, 1941, Vol. 18: 333–36; PC 789, December 5, 1941, Vol. 18: 339.

27. STE PC, December 4, 1941, STEP, FDRL. The *Tribune* story also embodied a letter reportedly written by the president to Secretary Stimson. When reporters asked Early about the published letter, Early reminded the journalists, "The rule is not to publish unless permission is given. Those who have gotten copies of the President's letters and have asked permission, usually have received it. In this instance, no request was received at the White House. . . ."

28. Roosevelt, *Complete Press Conferences,* PC 789, December 5, 1941, Vol. 18: 338. See Notes, December 6, 1941, Francis Biddle Papers, FDRL. By December 6, Attorney General Biddle went over to talk to the president about the leak to the *Chicago Tribune* concerning the expeditionary force. Biddle wrote in his diary that he reported to him about the preliminary report indicating "a high army officer and a leakage on the Hill." Later it was disclosed that an army captain who was isolationist stole the document from the War Plans Division and passed it on to Senator Burton K. Wheeler, who in turn gave it to *Tribune* correspondent Chesly Manly. Roosevelt suggested that Biddle "get help from Roy Howard and perhaps Patterson on the ground that now is an opportunity for doing a patriotic job." See chapters 8 and 9 herein.

29. Roosevelt, *Complete Press Conferences,* PC 745, May 24, 1941, Vol. 17: 369.

30. Ibid., PC 787, November 28, 1941, Vol. 18: 326–27.

31. Steve Early to Charles P. Shaeffer, June 11, 1943, Official File (henceforth OF) 144, FDRL. Early made a clear distinction between "off the record" and background at the next presidential conference. See Roosevelt, *Complete Press Conferences*, PC 905, July 25, 1943, Vol. 21: 407.

32. Jim Bishop, *FDR's Last Year, April 1944–April 1945* (New York: Morrow, 1974), p. 59. Two more questions were asked at PC 759, July 29, 1941, Vol. 18: 65–66; PC 789, January 13, 1941, Vol. 19: 79; and PC 804, February 10, 1942, Vol. 19: 131. Besides meeting with Anna O'Hare McCormick, Roosevelt had personal interchanges with Walter Winchell, PC 809, March 6, 1942, Vol. 19: 183; Sir Percival Philip Gibbs, PC 805, February 13, 1942, Vol. 19: 144; Irving Brandt, PC 798, January 13, 1942, 19: 144; and Brandt, PC 798, January 13, 1942, Vol 19: 79; PC 811, March 12, 1942, Vol. 19: 204. Fred Perkins even asked after the "Thank you," "Are questions barred now?" only to have other reporters say, "Everything is over," and "yes," although the president said, "They all tell you 'No.'" Perkins proceeded to ask about FDR's statement on the "need to adjourn politics" and said Senator Guffery charged that Attorney General Biddle was up to his neck in politics, to which the president answered, "I can't comment on any of those things, because I don't know." See ibid., PC 812, March 17, 1942, Vol. 19: 218. For others, see May Craig's remarks at PC 831, June 9, 1942, Vol. 19: 381, and the naming of the president's retreat as Shangri La and Earl Godwin's comments at PC 837, July 24, 1942, Vol. 20: 23, and PC 934, February 8, 1944, Vol. 23: 41.

33. Winston Churchill to Franklin D. Roosevelt, July 31, 1943, Map Room (henceforth MR) 30, FDRL; *New York Times*, "To Issue Monthly Report," July 10, 1943.

34. Joint Statement, September 9, 1943, MR 30, FDRL.

35. FDR to Winston Churchill, July 3, 1944, MR 30, FDRL; Submarine Memorandum for Director of Public Relations, Navy Department and Director, Office of War Information, July 8, 1944, MR 30, FDRL; *New York Times,* July 10, 1944, MR 30, FDRL; FDR Memorandum for the Secretary of War, the Secretary of the Navy, OF 340, FDRL; Henry L. Stimson Memorandum for the President, June 30, 1942, OF 340, FDRL; Statement by the President, June 25, 1942, OF 340, FDRL.

36. Roosevelt, *Complete Press Conferences*, PC 921, Vol. 22: 142–43. Lt. Colonel Chester Hammond of the general staff of the army had sent William Hassett the statistics authorized by the army air forces. See Chester Hammond Memorandum for Hassett, October 12, 1943, MR 46, FDRL. Hammond had also written, "The president might wish to use the tremendous expenditure of equipment, personnel, gasoline, etc., used in the raid mentioned above as an excellent reason for even greater support from the home front in such things as increased production, buying of war bonds, etc." See *Washington Evening Star*, October 15, 1943, clipping found in MR 46, FDRL.

37. See Roosevelt, *Complete Press Conferences,* Vols. 17–25, as well as chapter 3 herein.

38. "White House Cancels F.D.R.'s Press Parley," *Philadelphia Inquirer,* April 17, 1942, Early 1942 Scrapbook, STEP, FDRL.

39. Roosevelt, *Complete Press Conferences,* PC 834, July 7, 1942, Vol. 20: 1.

40. Ibid., pp. 2, 4–5, 7.

41. See ibid., Vol. 20.

42. Ibid., PC 824, May 5, 1942, Vol. 19: 321; PC 845, September 1, 1942, Vol. 20: 88.

43. Ibid., PC 859, November 10, 1942, Vol. 20: 236.

44. Winegar to Secret Service, February 11, 1943, OF 36, FDRL; see Roosevelt, *Complete Press Conferences,* Vols. 17–25. He vacationed February 26–March 12, April 9–19, June 15–25, and August 1–10. The Canadian meeting was August 11–14, 1943. The Teheran meeting was November 10–December 17, 1943. He missed press conferences during the following periods: December 28, 1943–January 18, 1944; January 19–February 1, March 28–April 7, 1944; April 7–28, June 14–23, July 11–29, November 27–December 19, 1944; December 22, 1944–January 2, 1945; and a month for the Yalta conference, January 20–February 19, 1945. The numbers of journalists were also limited, as pointed out in chapter 3 herein.

45. John H. Crider, *New York Times,* Thomas F. Reynolds, *Chicago Sun,* William C. Murphy, *Philadelphia Inquirer,* Bert Andrews, *New York Herald-Tribune,* Joseph A. Fox, *Washington Star,* to Steve Early, March 31, 1944, STEP, FDRL.

46. Roosevelt, *Complete Press Conferences,* PC 897, May 18, 1943, Vol. 21: 323.

47. Ibid., PC 961, July 11, 1944, Vol. 24: 14–15. Concerning FDR's hearing, see ibid., PC 943, March 17, 1944, Vol. 23: 107; PC 944, March 24, 1944, Vol. 23: 116–17; PC 964, Vol. 24: 54–55. In fact, in almost every press conference in 1944, Steve Early filled in the gaps and repeated questions or reminded the president of the answers.

48. Quote was found in William Hassett to Stephen T. Early, February 24, 1944, STEP, FDRL; see also STE PC, February 24, 1944, STEP, FDRL.

49. *Washington Star,* November 11, 1939; also found in *St. Louis Post-Dispatch,* November 19, 1939, Early 1939 Scrapbook, STEP, FDRL; Early was also identified as the White House spokesman and "government source" in the *London Evening Standard,* May 28, 1941, Early 1941 Scrapbook, STEP, FDRL; STE PC, April 13, 1942, STEP, FDRL.

50. STE PC, February 2, 1942, STEP, FDRL. Lowell Mellett took over much of the hiring of public information officers. See Margaret Hicks Williams, "The President's 'Office of Government Reports,' " *Public Opinion Quarterly* 5 (Winter 1941): 560.

51. Roosevelt, *Complete Press Conferences,* PC 914, August 24, 1943, Vol. 22: 57–75; PC 915, August 31, 1943, Vol. 22: 77–78.

52. Early Memorandum for the President, February 2, 1943, OF 36, FDRL; Roosevelt, *Complete Press Conferences,* PC 876, February 2, 1943, Vol. 21: 97.

53. TDB [Tom Blake] Memorandum to Early, May 22, 1944, STEP, FDRL; STE Memorandum for the President, May 26, 1944, STEP, FDRL; Roosevelt, *Complete Press Conferences,* PC 952, May 30, 1944, Vol. 23: 191.

54. Roosevelt, *Complete Press Conferences,* PC 904, June 15, 1943, Vol. 21: 392, and PC 950, May 16, 1944, Vol. 23: 169–70, in response to the budget; PC 943, March 17, 1944, Vol. 23: 101, about the cabinet attendees and connections; PC 934, February 8, 1944, Vol. 23: 37–38, concerning jogging FDR's memory about an AP story on Finland; PC 970, September 29, 1944, Vol. 24: 136, in response to the

question on Bulgaria; PC 970, September 29, 1944, Vol. 24: 136, in reference to the German mark.

For other examples of Early's prompting the president, see ibid., PC 930, January 18, 1944, Vol. 23: 3, 4; PC 937, February 18, 1944, Vol. 23: 60; PC 938, February 22, 1944, Vol. 23: 68. For an example of Early's providing the answer and FDR's merely repeating it, see ibid., PC 943, March 17, 1944, Vol. 23: 102.

55. See chapter 3, note 63, for yearly press conference numbers and pages. For references to Roosevelt's illness in 1944, see Roosevelt, *Complete Press Conferences*, PC 930, January 18, 1944, Vol. 23: 1, concerning the flu; PC 944, March 24, 1944, Vol. 23: 116, about his cold; PC 932, February 4, 1944, Vol. 23: 20–21, about surgery on the "wen" on the back of his head; PC 945, March 28, 1944, Vol. 23: 119–20, about his bronchitis; PC 947, April 28, 1944, Vol. 23: 141, about his month-long recuperation from bronchitis in North Carolina; PC 948, May 6, 1944, Vol. 23: 147, about bronchitis; PC 973, October 17, 1944, Vol. 24: 181, on his health in general; PC 983, November 27, 1944, Vol. 24: 257, about not smoking so much.

56. Henry L. Stimson Memorandum to the President, December 28, 1944, President's Secretary's File, FDRL; Neal Stanford, "Early's Mission to Europe Covers War-News Reports," *Christian Science Monitor*, January 15, 1945, STEP, FDRL; James Russell Wiggins to Early, January 26, 1945, STEP, FDRL; Harry Butcher, *My Three Years with Ike* (New York: Simon and Schuster, 1950), pp. 741, 751, 761, 773–76.

57. STE PC, April 12, 1945, STEP, FDRL; *New York Times*, April 13, 1945.

"I can speak as one who knows. . . ." FDR campaigning in Philadelphia, October 27, 1944. Courtesy of the Franklin D. Roosevelt Library.

11

Public Opinion Polling

A final stage in democracy would be attained if the will of the majority of the citizens were to be ascertainable at all times.
— James Bryce, *American Commonwealth*, 1913

To ascertain what the public is thinking is a tremendous political necessity. Initially, Franklin D. Roosevelt relied on the content of the American press, mail summaries, and information reports. After the daily newspapers' erroneous election predictions in 1936 and 1940, the president lost confidence in the press's ability to indicate national public opinion. Since it was imperative that the White House have an accurate gauge of public opinion during World War II, Roosevelt, ever flexible, tried the newest means of gathering such information—refined public opinion polling. Although he had used scientific surveys before, mostly for elections campaigns, by 1940 he and his advisers asked for statistical data for administrative planning. Roosevelt kept his newspaper clipping service, the Intelligence Bureau, but it became less and less important and moved from agency to agency until it finally died in 1943. Scientific polling appeared to be a better means of ascertaining public opinion. FDR also continued to receive his mail summaries as well as reports from his various information-seeking scouts, such as his wife, troubleshooter Morris Ernst, and journalist John Franklin Carter. Yet public opinion surveys more and more proved to be useful for election forecasting and news management.[1]

Public opinion polling did not begin during the Roosevelt era. Rather, it developed in the nineteenth century when American newspapers tried to learn election results. The *Boston Globe* sent reporters to gather the earliest returns from representative precincts. By the end of the century, front-page stories included sampled public opinion along with events. The editors knew that it was newsworthy to report what people thought as well as what they did. By the twentieth century, magazines began using an organized type of public opinion polling. The *Literary Digest,* among the first to do so, garnered the prestige for forecasting presidential elections. By 1920, after the *Digest* had predicted a Warren G. Harding win by three to one in six key states, Tammany Boss Murphy's men scarcely bothered to campaign in New York City. When the *Digest* successfully predicted Roosevelt's 1932 total popular vote within 1.4 percent, newspapers called such forecasting "uncanny" and "amazingly accurate."[2]

By the 1936 election the *Digest's* reputation as the nation's chief prognosticator was thought to be infallible. On the basis of its gigantic sample of 10 million ballots sent to one out of four in selected communities and one in every three registered Chicago voters, the *Digest* gave Republican Alf Landon a presidential victory by more than two to one. On October 31 the *Digest* confidently said, "So far, we have been right in every poll." When Roosevelt received a 62.5 percent plurality and an electoral win of all but two states, *Digest* pollsters and followers were stunned. Their methods had been flawed. As an explanation of its erroneous forecast, the *Digest* said, "We've always got too big a sampling of Republican voters." Indeed, their sample had been auto owners and telephone subscribers—chiefly the upper- and middle-income group of voters during a major depression.[3]

Other pollsters had long disagreed with the *Digest's* sampling methods and predictions. Chief among them was George Gallup of the American Institute of Public Opinion. Gallup used personal interviews in a population sample that included people from all income strata. Even before the magazine ballots had been sent out, Gallup had estimated the *Digest's* error within one percent and had warned his subscribers that the *Digest's* old-fashioned methods would point to the wrong man.[4]

Roosevelt himself did not appear to pay much attention to the early survey reports on issues. Rather, he and his advisers became more and more interested in election forecasting as polling became more statistically refined. They initially used expert survey analyst Emil Edward Hurja and the *Digest* predictions in 1932 and 1936. Hurja underestimated the electoral college vote by 40 percent in 1936, but Roosevelt's campaign manager James Farley publicly took full credit for correctly predicting the 1936 election, claiming that he alone had predicted the president would carry all states but Vermont and Maine.[5]

By 1940 the *Literary Digest's* errors and Emil Hurja's miscalculations gave way to more accurate predictions. Polling became another powerful political weapon, an advantageous aid to enhance or change an image or to get across a message or new policy, especially since the survey data distinguished important demographic aspects of the electorate. The "Monday morning quarterbacks" of sampling published their findings in the four-year-old *Public Opinion Quarterly.* An editor, Hadley Cantril of the Princeton American Institute of Public Opinion, included the writers who had said there was "little idea that Wendell Willkie would win."[6]

Election survey results assisted administration policies. After the 1942 Democratic party loss of forty-four House seats and seven Senate seats, FDR's advisers, armed with data from Hadley Cantril and his associates, suggested the president adopt a more conciliatory stance toward the new Congress and strengthen party unity. Cantril said in a memo to presidential assistant David Niles, "It is more necessary for the President to cooperate with Congress than for Congress to cooperate with the President." Cantril attributed the election results to the inability of most soldiers and war workers to vote. He advised, "Ways must be found to make it possible and easy . . . for men in the armed forces to vote both at home and abroad and . . . for defense workers to vote in any location to which they have moved and under any working conditions." By the time of the 1944 election, the Seventy-eighth Congress did just that. Depending on state legislation, it became fairly easy for soldiers to vote by absentee ballot.[7]

During that 1944 election, public opinion polling had been so perfected that the predictions were almost accurate. Cantril was within one-half of one percentage point of the election outcome. Gallup, who had been hired by Republican candidate Thomas Dewey, had the widest margin, with less than two percentage points. The pollsters sampled specific crucial items. In January Niles asked Cantril to survey the "Negro vote" in a possible Roosevelt versus Dewey contest. The pollster found that among black voters some 62 percent planned to vote for Roosevelt and 23 percent for Dewey. Cantril advised that the Negro vote could give Roosevelt the northern cities. He also suggested that the president reach out to particular constituents, such as women. According to Cantril, women were stronger supporters of the president than men were—53 percent of women favored Roosevelt and only 41 percent were for Dewey, whereas 48 percent of men favored Dewey and only 47 percent supported Roosevelt. In his one-page July 12 synopsis, he said to Niles, "You had better do all you can to get the ladies out to vote."[8]

Cantril's team also submitted other helpful survey data to the president. They found that twice as many people were interested in domestic affairs as in international affairs. Some two-thirds of the people thought the United States should not give aid to foreign countries after the war if it would result in a lower standard of living. Cantril recommended that the president avoid any public impression that foreign affairs would be carried on at the expense of domestic progress and that whenever possible all public statements should refer to the important connection between international cooperation and the public's self-interest at home. Cantril maintained that the major campaign emphasis should be on domestic issues. He stated that "the overwhelming majority of people believe the most important problems facing the next President . . . will be domestic, not international," mostly concerning jobs. Cantril wrote, "The major issue here was that while the public considered F.D.R. to be more able to handle the military and foreign policy, Dewey was more favored to cope with the general domestic problems." Roosevelt followed Cantril's advice. In his annual message to Congress in January 1944, he heavily stressed the home front, proposing an "economic bill of rights" that encompassed some sixty million jobs.[9]

In the fall *Public Opinion Quarterly,* Cantril referred to the polling differences between war and domestic election issues. As of June 1944, 5 percent more of those people with close relatives in the armed forces intended to vote for Roosevelt than those without a service connection. Cantril found that when people thought of the candidates as peacemakers and peaceplanners, the president at 63 percent came out far ahead of Dewey's 26 percent. Roosevelt's greatest possible weakness was when people were asked about who would run things at home more efficiently; Dewey had 43 percent to Roosevelt's 46 percent.[10]

From March on, Cantril sent reports to the president through his speech writer Samuel Rosenman. Although it is impossible to make a FDR campaign connection with the ending of the war and the resulting public opinion, Cantril made one. Cantril reported that some 69 percent of the public approved of the way FDR handled his job as president, but he also found some other interesting data. If the war were still going on, the vote would be 51 percent for Roosevelt and only 32 percent for Dewey. If the end were clearly in sight, the vote would be closer, 42 percent for the president and 41 percent for Dewey. Yet, if the war were over, Roosevelt would get only 30 percent as opposed to Dewey's 51 percent. After the Normandy landings in June, Cantril's polls showed 76 percent approved of FDR's job performance, his highest rate in over a year. Thus, by summer, Roosevelt pointedly adopted the political stance of being commander in chief.[11]

In that last Roosevelt election, FDR's poor health, as evidenced by the pictures of his haggard looks in the newsreels and the newspapers and his faltering speeches, had the pollsters searching for a solution. Elmo Roper wrote Roosevelt's advisers that the "worry over Roosevelt's health" was an important factor "helping to account for such defections as there are from Roosevelt support." The Democratic National Committee (DNC) had Cantril search in all Republican polls for possible returns on the president's health. With Gallup working for Dewey, the DNC was worried about a surprise. Cantril found only a previously reported mid-July poll which showed that 84 percent of those planning to vote for Roosevelt felt his health would permit him to serve another term, while only 47 percent of those supporting Dewey felt FDR could do so. Cantril informed the DNC, "I am sure there will not be any other release of this kind before election."[12]

The campaign obviously needed a strong Roosevelt physical appearance. In October Roosevelt spoke at Ebbets Field during a drenching downpour and rode for four hours in the rain through fifty miles of crowd-packed New York streets. That evening he spoke in the Grand Ballroom of the Waldorf Astoria Hotel to the Foreign Policy Association. Six days later he repeated his performance in Philadelphia and then spoke again in Chicago. Through his actions, he appeared strong. He had been seen and had made news. He conspicuously exerted leadership. He spoke of close to sixty million jobs, new homes, hospitals, highways, airports, and cheap automobiles. He waylaid fears and he won.

Besides elections, polling groups such as the American Institute of Public Opinion at Princeton had continuously reported public response to national issues. The institute found that while Roosevelt's standing varied from time to time, a majority, usually an overwhelming majority, had supported the president's New Deal measures since 1935, including the Civilian Conservation Corps (CCC), social security, and wages-and-hours legislation, but not necessarily the National Recovery Administration (NRA) or the Agricultural Adjustment Administration (AAA). The institute's polls also showed that the public steadfastly refused to go along on the president's proposed changes in the Supreme Court.[13]

For a long time, Roosevelt appeared to have had some skepticism about public opinion polling on issues. Yet by 1940 FDR was very much interested in surveys testing one major issue—the possible U.S. intervention in the European war. During the spring of 1940, Anna Rosenberg of the War Manpower Commission began asking Hadley Cantril about his Office of Public Opinion Research surveys. She said that the president was intrigued by the question "Which of these two things do you think is more important for the United States to try to do, keep out of the war ourselves or help England win, even at the risk of getting into the war?"[14]

In meeting with the president, the pollster recounted that Roosevelt wanted data that might aid England. FDR innately understood how opinion changed and the importance of timing political actions. He asked for repeated questions to determine a statistical trend. Cantril later recalled that "nothing interested him more than trend charts" and that Roosevelt was right about trend changes concerning the war. In July 1940, when the people were asked whether the neutrality law should be changed to permit American ships to carry war supplies to England, 54 percent said "no"; by August, the "no" figure dropped to 47 percent.[15]

Not until after his November 1940 election did Roosevelt formulate a loan-and-lease arrangement for Great Britain. In an indirect reference to his public support, he said at a December 1940 press conference, "In the present world situation of course there is absolutely no doubt in the mind of a very overwhelming number of Americans that the best immediate defense of the United States is the success of Great Britain in defending itself. . . ." In March 1941 Congress overwhelmingly approved the measure.[16]

The administration asked Cantril for further analysis. During the Nazi invasion of the U.S.S.R. in the summer of 1941, Roosevelt was especially wary of Catholic reaction to any U.S. involvement with Bolshevism. Cantril found that Catholics were going along with the large majority of Americans who wanted Russia to defeat Germany. Cantril also analyzed why the president's May 27 speech seemed to have had so little effect. His analysis was two-fold: first, the speech was an unfocused declaration of a national emergency for delivering supplies to Britain; second, the speech failed to show how the national emergency would change the daily lives of the people. In this same report, Cantril contrasted this with data obtained after the escalation of the Battle of the Atlantic and the torpedoing of the American freighter *Robin Moore,* when the great majority of people favored some kind of more dramatic aid to Britain.[17]

Just before Pearl Harbor, Cantril began sending the president easy-to-read trend charts with marked margins nearly every week. He especially noted November 1941 data indicating that people thought Germany must be defeated at any cost. In reference to the growing Japanese menace, Cantril emphasized that 67 percent had answered "yes" to his September question, "Should the United States take steps now to keep Japan from becoming more powerful, even if this means risking war with Japan."[18]

Although the White House used other pollsters, Hadley Cantril became the president's major contact. Cantril was the only survey statistical adviser with direct and continual access to the president after 1941. In the fall of 1941 he began sending a series of special studies, which "the Office of Public Opinion Research hoped to get out during the next year." The financing of such studies was by "a foundation grant," he said. He explained that the survey results were based on methods comparable to the Gallop Poll and would have the same degree of reliability.[19]

Anna Rosenberg continued to be the go-between until 1942. After Pearl Harbor, she sent Roosevelt the results of a question asked before that fateful morning of December 7, "If the U.S. got in a war with Japan, do you think the country would win or lose?" The response had been that 92 percent thought the country would win. When asked if they thought the U.S. Navy was strong enough to defeat the Japanese navy, 80 percent responded "yes."[20]

After Pearl Harbor, Cantril began going directly to the White House himself, especially since the president had become even more interested in the Cantril pollings for political actions. Given the president's interest in a consistent set of survey findings and the need for independent funding, Cantril's Princeton neighbor Gerald B. Lambert, a financier, suggested he and Cantril set up their own nationwide survey mechanism that could launch studies at any time. Lambert offered to cover all expenses as his way to help the war effort and the president. The two men, who contributed ideas, reports, and financing, thus established the nonprofit Research Council, Inc. at the Office of Public Opinion Research, with the International Business Machines Corporation loaning all the tabulating equipment. There appears to have been no cost limit for this private polling outfit. The two men undertook research that the White House requested.[21]

Cantril's private survey work for the president was a well-kept secret. Cantril recalled that he and Lambert "made a point of being seen as little as possible in Government offices or agencies in order to minimize curiosity and preserve the informality of our relationships." From the beginning he told Anna Rosenberg, "I am trusting you and your friend not to let others in Washington know about them. The old problem of property rights—plus the fact that if certain Senators knew about this they would raise hell with Gallup and his faith in me would be shaken."[22]

Other White House aides also became quietly involved. Cantril recalled that he had two other presidential channels: David K. Niles and Grace Tully. Cantril later wrote that Niles "quickly saw the potential value of what we were trying to do and got everything to the President without change or editing." Roosevelt had told the two men to bring directly to his personal secretary anything they thought particularly important for him to see. Cantril recalled that it was through Grace Tully that he kept the president's trend charts up to date. Reports, especially those dealing with specific topics, went to the correct administrators and bureaus, and Samuel Rosenman received material for speeches.[23]

Cantril carefully revised and edited the reports down to two- or three-page, clearly written summaries. He recalled, "We always tried to remember that the President was one of the busiest men in the world and would completely lose interest if we became verbose or technical." He highlighted the crucial dates or conclusions with a red pencil in the margins and sometimes drew a face beside good or bad news. Whenever possible, Cantril provided a simple bar graph or chart indicating the major results and put the conclusions first with the details later.[24]

One question the president consistently watched was his public approval rating on how well he handled his job, especially concerning his policies to help Britain. After May 1941 the polls remained fairly constant, with the largest proportion of people being those who thought the president was about right and had not gone far enough. Cantril recalled, "This was precisely the situation he wanted to maintain during these critical months; hence his eagerness to learn the results of our periodical soundings."[25]

Cantril often followed up on various issues raised at press conferences.

Although only a few documents showed any White House requests for specific survey questions, there must have been pertinent conversations. For example, a reporter asked the president to comment on the so-called national complacency about the bad news in the Pacific; that same day, Cantril and his associates asked this morale question: "A Washington writer says that the people of the country are not alarmed enough about the war. Do you agree or disagree?" Cantril then sent Roosevelt the results, which showed 69 percent agreed and 21 percent disagreed.[26]

In fact, much of the polling was done in reaction to news coverage. Roosevelt might have thought news stories and editorial opinions were inaccurate, but such coverage did set the news agenda for public discussion. Throughout the war, many of the survey questions were based on the headline stories. As an example, Cantril wrote Grace Tully in August 1944, "In view of the New York *Times* dispatch today, reporting the attitude of Congress and the President on the peacetime draft, I thought the President might be interested in the latest poll of public opinion on the subject."[27]

Cantril also did a lot of polling concerning Roosevelt's wartime secrecy. He and Lambert believed good journalists often confused their own interest in getting a good story with the public's interest in learning about certain news, especially if it might endanger the lives of people in the armed services. Cantril thus conducted surveys designed to ascertain "whether or not people . . . consider the withholding of certain news as unjustified censorship or as sound news policy during wartime."[28]

For example, Cantril did opinion spot checks for the White House on withholding news coverage during the Nazi spy trial in June 1942. He tested public opinion on the secret military proceedings against the eight German saboteurs who had landed on the East Coast by posing three alternatives: should the trial be reported to the public; should the decision on whether or not to report the trial be left up to the person in charge of reporting news for the government; or, if the army says the trial should be kept secret for military reasons, should it be kept secret? Some 77 percent of Cantril's sample opted for keeping the trial secret if the army desired. The army desired to do so, despite complaints from the Office of War Information and the correspondents. As previously discussed, Roosevelt backed the army.[29]

Cantril also checked public reaction to the president's "secret," cross-country inspection trip in September 1942 to examine various aspects of the war effort. The "news lid" had included no advance public details about the trip. Only the three wire service representatives were allowed to accompany the president. Although the White House correspondents complained loudly about such unprecedented censorship, Cantril's public opinion surveys taken two days after Roosevelt returned found that some 78 percent of the public would have kept the trip secret. The public, still fearful of a Japanese invasion, agreed with FDR's decision. Cantril wrote that he and Lambert "immediately passed the comforting information on to the White House." The surveys only reinforced the administration's efforts. As the most vocal critics of the administration's secrecy, the nation's newspapers appeared to be alone.[30]

The focus of press criticism seemed to be not only the government's withholding information beyond the requirements of national security but also the administration's spoon-feeding selected information, such as the extent of the 1942 losses and the magnification of minor successes. The Office of War Information summarized the polling statistics in the "Report from the Nation," sent to the president. One survey repeated from February to late November 1942 showed a confirmation of Roosevelt's policies: 62 to 75 percent of the public agreed that the government gave the public as much information as it should about the war. Criticism of the war censorship was only markedly higher among those better educated. The public also indicated they did not want the enemy press and radio news stopped but merely labeled as "propaganda." Public opinion thus reinforced the administration's censorship policy. Only the nation's mass media—in particular, the print media—loudly complained.[31]

Cantril checked other secrecy areas and sent the information to FDR. Testing the public's reaction to governmental censorship of good military news, Cantril determined that a great majority of the American public, some 69 percent, did not sympathize with the war correspondents' demands for more immediate and detailed reports of the Allied defeat of the German offensive in December 1944. Cantril also found that the public supported the army's refusal to permit journalists on the warfront. Although Roosevelt overtly did nothing, Steve Early went to Paris in early 1945 in response to so many war correspondents' complaints.[32]

Roosevelt occasionally used Cantril's survey results for releasing dynamite news. One noteworthy case concerned public reaction to General Douglas MacArthur's retreat to Australia. Cantril knew from his surveys that half of the public would likely resent MacArthur's abandonment of the Philippines. Nazi propaganda also could be counted on to exploit such action as cowardice. He and Lambert suggested to the president that some kind of announcement be used to diffuse the controversy. Lambert then drafted a statement, deliberately phrased to involve all Americans in the president's decision to order MacArthur to leave and to make it seem the only reasonable choice under the circumstances.[33]

Just a few hours later, FDR initiated the topic at his press conference, "Then you have read the good news about General (Douglas) MacArthur." He then said, "I think you might as well quote it, or get Steve to give you a copy." In this particular case, Roosevelt followed Cantril's suggestion: "There will be, of course, immediately—we all know that—because we are accustomed to that sort of thing—there is going to be Axis propaganda that will appear this afternoon on their short-wave, and tomorrow morning, about how this is the abandonment of the Philippines. . . ." He continued, "And of course we know what they will say. On the other side of the picture, put it this way. . . ." The president then read verbatim Lambert's statement: "I know that every man and woman in the United States admires with me General MacArthur's determination to fight to the finish with his men in the Philippines. But I also know that every man and woman is in agreement that all important decisions must be made with a view toward the successful termination of the war. Knowing this, I am sure that every American, if faced individually with the question as to where General MacArthur could best serve his country, could come to only one answer." He then confided, "In other words, he will be more useful in Supreme Command of the whole Southwest Pacific than if he stayed in Bataan Peninsula, where of course the fighting is going on."[34]

The Cantril–White House partnership was evident again in September 1943 when Samuel I. Rosenman, Roosevelt's speech writer, requested that Cantril and Lambert learn more about the opposition to the president's proposed farm subsidy program. He said that the president was puzzled about so much opposition and wondered about the farmer's state of mind. Cantril subsequently found that the farmers lacked knowledge about the program and that only 13 percent of the farmers had a clear picture of the meaning of subsidies and over half of the farmers knew nothing about them at all. While the farmers agreed that some kind of government regulation was essential, they were unhappy about price controls, the lack of equipment, and the shortage of farm labor. The researchers advised clarification and repetition to assure understanding. They also warned that a "lengthy and detailed message to Congress cannot be counted on to enlighten the farmers, since it will not reach the masses."[35]

At his press conference on October 19, FDR spent much time defending the farm subsidy program. He said that "people get foggy thinking, and come out and say, 'No subsidies for anybody any more, beginning on the first of January.' Those same people, some of them professional farmers, they have been getting subsidies ever since 1933, and even before that." Despite Cantril's warning, the president's message to Congress on November 1 was an overwhelming 10,000 words in defense of food subsidies. The effort was not one of the president's more focused speeches, and overall it was not effective.[36]

This did not keep Roosevelt from thanking Cantril for his advice and polling efforts. After Sam Rosenman had urged the president to express his appreciation, "Cantril does the work and Lambert pays the bills," Roosevelt wrote Cantril in reference to the food subsidy report, "It is quite surprising and very instructive and I am sure will be helpful." He also told Lambert, "I would like to take this opportunity to thank you for making possible the work . . . by the Princeton Public Opinion Research Office in this connection and in connection with other subjects in the past. I think it has been a fine public service." Throughout the war, Grace Tully also continued thanking Cantril and Lambert for the president: "He hopes you will continue to send them along as they keep him in touch with what people are thinking."[37]

What the people were thinking outside the United States also became important to know. Cantril and his team even sampled, with much difficulty, the opinions of the French North Africans before the Allied invasion in the fall of 1942. Such interviewing had to be indirect and guarded in determining French resistance to an Anglo-American landing. A group of Americans under Cantril's absentee direction obtained 142 usable interviews, which indicated an American landing without British forces would not be met with resistance. The study led to the suggestion that the best-known American speak just after the landing. Indeed, it was Franklin D. Roosevelt who spoke on the radio in French to the French Algerian citizens, "Vive la France éternelle."[38]

It is difficult to detect just how much Roosevelt relied on the polls in any given action, but Cantril kept sending advice along with his reports. Cantril recalled, "As far as I am aware, Roosevelt never altered his goals because public opinion appeared against him or was uninformed. Rather he utilized such information to try to bring the public around more quickly or more effectively to the course of action he felt was best for the country." Steve Early read Cantril's reports and tried to emphasize their importance. He would separate the polls from the other intelligence summaries, and he wrote the president such memos as "These digests might provide some interesting reading on the way home," as Roosevelt traveled back and forth to Hyde Park or Warm Springs.[39]

The reports gave Early good information for news management. For instance, Cantril's September 14, 1941, report entitled "Comparison of Opinions of Those Who Do and Do Not Listen to the President's Radio Talks" was useful in preparing for the president's speeches. Using data on the president's May 27 and December 29 fireside speeches and the statistical variance between income groups, Cantril wrote, "There is a well-known tendency for people not to listen to or to read what they don't agree with or prefer not to know. . . ." He suggested, "If more efforts were made to publicize these speeches in advance, . . . the effect might be more noticeable." He also warned, "Press conference announcements concerning upcoming speeches do not show a difference." Such publicizing could backfire, as previously noted when both the Germans and the Japanese warlike actions vied for front-page headlines.[40]

It was of utmost importance to the White House to learn just what people were thinking. During the spring of 1944, American troops fighting on the Italian mainland met the German army's bitter resistance for seven months.

According to Cantril's sample, some 60 percent thought the fighting on the Italian front was going slower than anticipated. In April Cantril suggested that the public needed to be braced for a hard road ahead with occasional setbacks, especially that election year. Although there is no direct evidence of any presidential action here, Roosevelt told the White House correspondents after the Allies successfully moved into northern Italy that "that first day I was very much worried, because we didn't seem to be making much progress on that Italian push. . . . Things are distinctly better." On June 5, when Roosevelt went on radio to tell the American public about the capture of Rome, he appeared to have been influenced: "Victory still lies some distance ahead. . . . It will tough and it will be costly." The *New York Times* reported that "his speech was notable for its lack of heroics." While the president gave tribute to the United Nations, "he combined a solemn warning that much greater fighting lies ahead before the axis is defeated. . . ."[41]

Cantril's findings were one of many information sources Roosevelt and his advisers used to determine actions. The president used other pollsters too, such as George Gallup. In 1942 the president, while thanking Gallup for a confidential report concerning war opinions, also remarked that he was appalled by the percentage of the people who had no clear idea of what the war was about. FDR jokingly compared those people with the groups identified by a radio commentator some months earlier: "'There are three groups in this country who say they want to win the war (a) if, at the same time, Russia is defeated, (b) if, at the same time, Roosevelt is defeated, (c) if, at the same time, England is defeated.' "[42]

During the war, Roosevelt sought to discern public opinion for his reelections, his leadership, and his actions, especially during his last four years. Polling gave Roosevelt another statistical bit of confidence, another source of informational power. Public opinion surveys became but another secret informational weapon, as an accountability check on the president's performance, as check on the closure of the German spy trial or his 1942 inspection trip, or as a justification for such actions as lend-lease or General MacArthur's rescue. In the election process, public opinion polling became an important barometer of the electorate. Statistical polling could quantify the public's fears, hopes, and beliefs. It more and more replaced newspapers as a public opinion guage. It was more efficient than reports from scouts. Polling became one of the consummate forms of collecting information on the will of the citizen, the public's opinion, as another source of presidential power in yet another phase of the information age.

Notes

1. Leila A. Sussmann, *Dear FDR: A Study of Political Letter-Writing* (Totota, N. J.: Bedminister Press, 1963), especially pp. 66–70. John Franklin Carter, alias Jay Franklin, wrote the column "We the People" from 1936 through 1945 and sent reports to FDR from 1939 to 1945. See, for example, Carter to Grace Tully, December 26,

1941, President's Secretary's File (henceforth PSF), Franklin D. Roosevelt Library (henceforth FDRL). In October 1941 some $54,000 was allotted for confidential reports to be done by Carter. Harold P. Smith to Franklin D. Roosevelt, October 16, 1941, Official File (henceforth OF) 4514, FDRL. See also Report on Need for Coordination in Emergency Rescue Work, OF 4675, FDRL; Roosevelt to John Franklin Carter, September 18, 1943, OF 4514, FDRL. For the differences between the campaign results and the newspaper support, see Frank Luther Mott, "Newspapers in Presidential Campaigns," *Public Opinion Quarterly* 8 (Fall 1944): 348–67.

2. George Gallup and Saul Forbes Rae, *The Pulse of Democracy: The Public Opinion Poll and How It Works* (New York: Simon and Schuster, 1940), p. 35. See also Charles W. Roll, Jr., and Albert H. Cantril, *Polls: Their Use and Misuse in Politics* (New York: Basic Books, 1972), pp. 7–11; Frank Freidel, *The Ordeal*, Vol. 2 of *Franklin D. Roosevelt* (Boston: Little, Brown, 1954), p. 90.

3. "Topics of the Day: 'Digest' Poll Machinery Speeding Up," *Literary Digest*, August 29, 1936, p. 5; "Topics of the Day: Landon, 1,293,669; Roosevelt, 972,897," *Literary Digest*, October 31, 1936, p. 5; "Topics of the Day: What Went Wrong with the Polls?" *Literary Digest*, November 14, 1936, pp. 7–8. Gallup said that he had warned they would be wrong. See Gallup and Rae, *The Pulse of Democracy*, pp. 46, 71. *Fortune* was also close to the mark.

4. Gallup and Rae, *The Pulse of Democracy*, p. 47.

5. Frank Freidel, *The Triumph*, Vol. 3 of *Franklin D. Roosevelt* (Boston: Little, Brown, 1956), p. 360. For examples of Hurja's forecasting, see Emil Edward Hurja to FDR, July 15, 1932, Hurja to Howe, August 31, 1932, Hurja to Howe, October 25, 1932, and Hurja Memo, September 16, 1932, OF 300, FDRL.

Hurja, who the *New York Times* maintained was 97 percent accurate in 1932, mentioned that he was hired late that election year by Farley because of his ability to analyze political trends. In 1934 Hurja rejoined the DNC, according to the *New York Times*, March 9, 1937. DNC Chairman Edward J. Flynn was quoted as saying that Hurja had given Roosevelt only 376 electoral votes, an underestimation by some 40 percent for 1936. See *New York Times*, March 14, 1937.

Farley's method was to review the reports of the state chairmen, according to Harold F. Gosnell, *Champion Campaigner: Franklin D. Roosevelt* (New York: Macmillan, 1952), p. 166.

It is noteworthy that there is nothing on the use of polls in Alfred B. Rollins, Jr., *Roosevelt and Howe* (New York: Knopf, 1962), or in Charles Michelson, *The Ghost Talks* (G. P. Putnam's Sons, 1944).

6. For quote, see Archibald M. Crossley, "Methods Tested during 1940 Campaign," *Public Opinion Quarterly* 3 (March 1941): 85; see also Elmo Roper, "Checks to Increase Polling Accuracy," *Public Opinion Quarterly* 3 (March 1941): 87–89.

7. Hadley Cantril, "What the November 1942 Election Boils Down to," enclosure in Niles to Hopkins, December 16, 1942, Harry L. Hopkins Papers, FDRL; more on this in Robert E. Ficken, "The Democratic Party and Domestic Politics during World War II" (Ph.D. dissertation, University of Washington, 1973), p. 83. The specific quote used here is in Cantril and Lambert to Niles, December 21, 1942, Harry L. Hopkins Papers, FDRL.

Some eleven months after Pearl Harbor, Roosevelt's Bureau of Intelligence used polling data along with its usual clipping summaries to explain the lack of editorial support for the administration. Intelligence Report 49, November 13, 1942, PSF, FDRL.

8. Cantril to Dave [Niles], January 20, 1944, PSF, FDRL; Cantril to Niles, July 12, 1944, PSF, FDRL. See also Gosnell, *Champion Campaigner,* p. 212.

9. On findings, see Cantril to David K. Niles, January 20, 1944, PSF, FDRL. See also Hadley Cantril, *The Human Dimension: Experiences in Policy Research* (New Brunswick, N.J.: Rutgers University Press, 1967), pp. 96–97. For specific recommendations, see Cantril Memorandum, July 5, 1944, Harry L. Hopkins Papers, FDRL; "What People Feel Are the Main Problems Ahead for the Next Four Years and What They Think of the Candidates' Abilities to Handle These Problems," Confidential Report for David K. Niles, September 7, 1944, PSF, FDRL.

10. *Public Opinion Quarterly* 8 (Fall 1944): 332–39, 348.

11. Confidential Report for Samuel I. Rosenman, results from survey of March 16, 1944, attached to Rosenman's Memorandum to the President, March 20, 1944, re questions 4, 5, 6, PSF, FDRL. Also mentioned was that 69 percent of the public approved FDR's handling of the job as president. See Cantril to Grace Tully, July 26, 1944, PSF, FDRL.

12. William D. Hassett to Tully, enclosing a note from Elmo Roper, October 27, 1944, PSF, FDRL, as found in Ficken, "The Democratic Party and Domestic Politics," p. 254. This memo follows Cantril to Oscar Ewing, October 12, 1944, Democratic National Committee Papers, FDRL, and also *Public Opinion Quarterly* 8 (Fall 1944): 442.

13. Gallup and Rae, *The Pulse of Democracy,* p. 133.

14. Note in *F.D.R.: His Personal Letters, 1928–1945,* Vol. 2, Elliott Roosevelt, ed. (New York: Duell, Sloan and Pearce, 1950), p. 1158. Cantril's July 1940 results showed that 59 percent of the people thought the United States should keep out of war and that 37 percent thought the United States should risk war to help England. See references to the requests in Cantril, *The Human Dimension,* p. 35.

15. Cantril, *The Human Dimension,* pp. 43, 36. See also Robert Dallek, *Franklin D. Roosevelt and American Foreign Policy, 1932–1945* (New York: Oxford University Press, 1979), p. 253.

16. Franklin D. Roosevelt, *Complete Presidential Press Conferences of Franklin D. Roosevelt* (New York: Da Capo Press, 1972), Press Conference (henceforth PC) 702, December 17, 1940, Vol. 16: 350.

17. Cantril to Rosenberg, July 3, 1941, PSF, FDRL.

18. Hadley Cantril's notes, November 17, 1941, PSF, FDRL. As another example, see Cantril to Anna Rosenberg, September 13, 1941, PSF, FDRL. He gave the president geographical breakdowns indicating the highest support from the Rocky Mountain states (81 percent) and the lowest in the East and West Central areas (62 percent each). Cantril also noted the change in the trend by late August when the "yes" percentages had gone up some 15 percentage points from July.

19. Cantril Memo with the Special Studies, September 17, 1941, PSF, FDRL.

20. Rosenberg Memo to the President, December 11, 1941, OF 4075, FDRL.

21. Cantril, *The Human Dimension,* pp. 38–39. The bureau also referred to other polls. For example, the April 22, 1942, report mentioned the *Fortune* poll which showed a tendency among Americans to feel that their fellow citizens were somewhat complacent about the war.

22. Cantril, *The Human Dimension*, p. 40; Cantril to Rosenberg, n.d., 1941, PSF, FDRL. Cantril also acknowledged that "several times ambassadors from friendly powers flew up to Princeton to look at my master charts, since I did not want to let them have copies of their own." See Cantril, *The Human Dimension*, pp. 43–44.

23. Cantril, *The Human Dimension*, pp. 40–41.

24. Ibid., p. 41.

25. Ibid., pp. 40, 44; Cantril to Rosenberg, n.d., 1941, PSF, FDRL.

26. Roosevelt, *Complete Press Conferences*, PC 804, February 10, 1942, Vol. 19: 129. Hadley Cantril, ed., *Public Opinion 1935–1946* (Princeton, N.J.: Princeton University Press, 1951), p. 483.

27. Cantril to Tully, August 17, 1944, PSF, FDRL.

28. Cantril, *The Human Dimension*, pp. 65–66.

29. Ibid., p. 66.

30. Ibid.

31. "Report from the Nation," December 7, 1942, pp. 52–55, PSF, FDRL.

32. Cantril to Tully, December 27, 1944, OF 36, FDRL.

33. Cantril, *The Human Dimension*, p. 68. For further discussion, see D. Clayton James, *The Years of MacArthur, 1941–1945*, Vol. 2 (Boston: Houghton Mifflin, 1975), chapters 2 and 3.

34. Roosevelt, *Complete Press Conferences*, PC 812, March 17, 1942, Vol. 19: 208–9.

35. Cantril, *The Human Dimension*, pp. 69–71.

36. Roosevelt, *Complete Press Conferences*, PC 923, October 19, 1943, Vol. 22: 173. For an assessment of the speech, see William Hassett, *Off the Record with F.D.R., 1942–1945* (New Brunswick, N.J.: Rutgers University Press, 1958), p. 218.

37. SIR [Samuel I. Rosenman] Memorandum for Grace Tully, October 28, 1943, PSF, FDRL; Roosevelt to Dr. Hadley Cantril, October 28, 1943, PSF, FDRL; Roosevelt to Gerald B. Lambert, October 28, 1943, PSF, FDRL; Tully to Hadley Cantril, August 24, 1944, PSF, FDRL. See also Early's response, Early to Dr. Cantril, December 30, 1942, PSF, FDRL.

38. Hadley Cantril, "Evaluating the Probable Reactions to the Landing in North Africa in 1942: A Case Study," *Public Opinion Quarterly* 29 (Fall 1965): 400–410; Grace Tully, *F.D.R., My Boss* (New York: Charles Scribner's Sons, 1949), p. 264; James MacGregor Burns, *Roosevelt: The Soldier of Freedom* (New York: Harcourt, Brace, 1970), p. 292.

39. Cantril, *The Human Dimension*, pp. 41–42; see digest of December 6, 1943, OF 5015, FDRL, where Early sent FDR the references to editorials and columns from sixty-four newspapers of opinion about twenty radio commentators on December 2, 1943.

40. Hadley Cantril, "Comparisons of Opinions of Those Who Do and Do Not Listen to the President's Radio Talks," September 17, 1941, PSF, FDRL.

41. Burns, *Roosevelt: The Soldier of Freedom*, p. 559 and notes on p. 580; Roosevelt, *Complete Press Conferences*, PC 950, May 16, 1944, Vol. 23: 174; *New York Times*, June 6, 1944.

42. FDR to George H. Gallup, October 2, 1942, *F.D.R.: His Personal Letters, 1928–1945*, Vol. 2, p. 1349.

A communications apex for subsequent presidents. FDR speaking to a street crowd from his car, May 11, 1937. Courtesy of the Franklin D. Roosevelt Library.

12

The Legacy of Roosevelt's Press Relations

The constant free flow of communication among us—enabling the free interchange of ideas—forms the very bloodstream of our nation. It keeps the mind and the body of our democracy eternally vital, eternally young.
　　　—Franklin D. Roosevelt, radio address given at the *New York Herald-Tribune* Forum, October 24, 1940

In times of peace the people look to their representatives, but in war to the executive only.
　　　—Thomas Jefferson to Caesar A. Rodney, February 10, 1810

Free expression is a necessary concomitant to self-government, dependent on public information. The bulk of the electorate's knowledge comes from the mass media. The American press helps the citizens by being a watchdog of government. Yet, as Steve Early explained to correspondent Raymond Clapper before the 1933 inauguration, Franklin D. Roosevelt did not want the Washington correspondents to serve in a "watchdog capacity." Indeed, Roosevelt mangled the entire watchdog concept by artfully controlling access and the tremendous flow of presidential news during his twelve-year presidency. FDR might have defended the free flow of information, and indeed there was a tremendous flow of communications then, but he did not like media criticism of his programs or strong oppositional viewpoints. He wanted the White House correspondents to act as conveyor belts, stenographers, and accurate reporters of spot news from his perspective. Like other presidents who found it difficult to tolerate premature disclosure of information, Roosevelt carefully managed the release of government information on great pressing questions, whether on the judicial reform bill, the lend-lease act, or the war and the subsequent victories.

Many publishers were Roosevelt's domestic adversaries. They critically and closely watched the president from afar. Perhaps they attempted to be the unelected other government. As previously noted, Roosevelt was most concerned because newspapers were perhaps "the only book" people read daily. He had plenty of reasons for being anxious in that print-media age. Not only did the president lack endorsement from most American dailies for his reelections but he did not have editorial support for many of his New Deal programs or for his proposals for American aid to Britain and military readiness before Pearl Harbor. Despite record circulations, the same group of owners obtained more and more newspapers during the 1930s. The more antagonistic William R. Hearst's and Robert McCormick's holdings comprised over 50 percent of the country's Sunday circulation. In their attempt to save money during those depression years, editors throughout the country increasingly relied on the same homogenized news, the same features, and the same columnists. Roosevelt became even more concerned when publishers such as Hearst began purchasing radio stations.

Ironically, it was during World War II that another Roosevelt adversary, Henry Luce, owner of *Time, Life,* and *Fortune,* established a foundation to study the freedom of the press. Luce was concerned about government control of information and the American mass media. Under the leadership of University of Chicago President Robert Hutchins, the commission reported in 1947 that American press freedom had been fettered more by a lack of press responsibility and an increasingly large corporate structure that limited diverse voices than by governmental strictures.[1]

Years before the Hutchins Commission, Franklin D. Roosevelt also had complained about a lack of press responsibility, the press's corporate structure, multimedia ownership of radio, and bias. He often chided the correspondents and press organizations about their pro-management emphasis, their lack of labor news and viewpoints, and their editorial biases that spilled over into their news columns. After his landslide victory in 1936, he kidded the American Society of Newspaper Editors at their annual meeting about losing their original function as purveyors of public opinion. Indeed, that same year he pointedly remarked in a Gridiron speech that any fear about regimenting the American press was due not to government interference but rather to the press itself.

The president's overall excellent relations with the Washington correspondents and his finely developed newsgathering skills might have been a means to an end, a *raison d'être* for his news media actions. The question is then, would Franklin D. Roosevelt so carefully have charmed the working press into becoming his allies if the publishers and the editors had not been his adversaries? Roosevelt's semiweekly press conferences took time and preparation. There were weeks when he was overwhelmingly busy or ill, yet he still met with the press and reached out to the correspondents in between his speeches and trips. There were other times when the press meetings appeared contrived because he had so many pressures. Although there were many gaps during 1943 and 1944, FDR did not stop the conferences. They were too useful for disseminating information, defusing criticism, and handling simmering problems. For the most part, he truly enjoyed the camaraderie he had with the White House correspondents, perhaps more than any other president. From the teasing he initiated at the meetings, he obviously had a good time with his "beloved wolves" and his "club."

Roosevelt used different leadership methods and assumed greater responsibilities for governing, depending on whether there was a domestic crisis, as with the Great Depression, or an international crisis, as with World War II. During crises, the public expects leadership, action, and control. As Jefferson noted, in war "the people look to . . . the executive only." During such crucial events, the public expects the president to seize the moment and do something. Roosevelt most certainly did that.[2]

When the crisis was basically internal, as with the Great Depression, the president could tolerate diverse viewpoints and have an open, free exchange of ideas, even critical ones, not only from among the public but also from among his own advisers and administrators. The government, no matter how severe the economic crisis, did not appear in any danger of toppling. There was no need to impose press restraints. Rather, as a new president and as an experimenter, Franklin D. Roosevelt benefited from diverse viewpoints. The public could be and was let in on the details, the inside information. He needed to garner public support to formulate and implement his policies.

During the international crisis, there was a threat to the nation's survival. The stresses on the stability of the government were real: the surprise attack on Pearl Harbor, more surprise attacks, spies, shootings off the coast of California, and a possible invasion. These hostile, aggressive acts were communication enough to rally public support. News of the specifics of this world crisis was not necessary; an overall impression was enough. The public tacitly agreed that the president alone should speak, that Roosevelt could be the only American voice speaking to the world.

During the depths of war, information and even diverse viewpoints and arguments about administrative actions or proposals could become yet another weapon for the enemy. Details about damage, such as that incurred at Pearl Harbor, or about speculative war plans could help the enemy and hurt the country's morale. Given his World War I experience, Roosevelt no longer needed to be such an experimenter. He knew how to respond. Like Wilson, he became sensitive to criticism. Although more tolerant than Wilson, by necessity he publicly presented a united administrative effort and drew his information wagons in a circle.

Chapter 1 presented the classic conflict between confidentiality and openness—confidentiality, which must be preserved to some extent if the government is to operate, versus the people's right to know in order to make reasoned decisions in a democracy. The citizens have a right to obtain information relevant to those matters affecting their lives. At the same time, the president had to preserve the government. From 1933 to 1941, Franklin D. Roosevelt maintained an open government, one of the most open presidencies since Teddy Roosevelt's. When the president did operate with an air of secrecy, as he did with a budget message, his plan to pack the Supreme Court, and his decision to appoint Hugo Black to the Supreme Court, he did not do so to preserve the government. Rather, Roosevelt wanted to preempt public opposition. His reticence in these incidents was designed to give him flexibility and to forestall speculative news coverage. Such secrecy could backfire, as it did with the Supreme Court proposal and Hugo Black's appointment.

Yet by 1941 confidentiality became wartime covertness for protecting military and diplomatic plans. Despite Steve Early's reference to "the people's right to know," the public did not know or care to know all that was happening in the war zones or about American or enemy ship damage and battle casualties. Such information was thought to be so damaging that the American public and the journalists wanted to contain it. No one was more surprised than Steve Early at how complacent the correspondents were over legalized censorship. The military dictates for censorship became troublesome, despite few wartime convictions for sedition, compared with the almost 2,000 during World War I. In a democracy, the choice can be between coordination and clearance or conflict and confusion. As Elmer Davis once wrote, "One makes a better war effort, the other makes better headlines." Many times, as pointed out, censorship after 1942 became absolute and the question became "secrecy for whom?"[3]

The basis for a free press in a democracy may be the right to criticize government, yet citizens must have enough information upon which to base an opinion before criticizing. The lack of information during World War II did not stop either the public or the press from holding the president accountable, but the criticisms might have been more credible had there been more reliable information. Control of information is a source of tremendous political power. Roosevelt had that control and that power, especially in the military sphere. He knew that public knowledge about the government's war activities could be dangerous, whether it concerned the American lack of readiness, battle results, or even the president's inspection trips. During World War II, the American government's actions became mostly military, more authoritative, and more censored. Roosevelt followed the advice of his military advisers, especially after Pearl Harbor through 1942. He and the military thought that the enemy was mighty and everywhere and that American lives were in jeopardy.

At the same time, Roosevelt needed to keep in touch with the American public. He needed to educate the public as well as exert his leadership role. When Roosevelt released information to the press during the war, he understandably remained protective; he wanted flexibility to act quickly. During the war, unlike during the New Deal, he resented those news stories that pointed out divisiveness, and he tried to prevent speculative stories, even domestic ones. Roosevelt wanted to be able to get other officials' judgments on issues without the press's interference in the decision-making process. In a few instances, he ordered secret investigations to learn the journalists' news sources and to stop leaks. After the disastrous Pearl Harbor attack, Roosevelt used the FBI to investigate the press disclosures of the losses, which the Japanese already knew. In this latter case, Roosevelt believed that secrecy was necessary to preserve the national security for morale reasons. Yet, unlike Wilson's war years, the Roosevelt administration sent no journalists to prison over their views.

One function of the press is to provide enough information for the public to judge the president's leadership. If the electorate's vote was an affirmation of Roosevelt's efforts and the press coverage, then the public must have indeed been convinced through the information they had that Roosevelt would be the better choice for leadership. They continued to reelect him, despite the publishers' criticisms. The thirty-second president's actions were information enough. He had been able to convince Congress to pass most of his New Deal and wartime legislation. That he was able to make government more responsive to the human needs and wartime goals of the country might have been in part a measure of his success in managing the news.

There is also a second press function. The press presents not only an account of what is being said or done but also an account of what is being thought about what is being done. If Roosevelt's complaints were an indication, then FDR clearly did not believe the print media were performing this function well. He constantly complained about newspaper opinion pieces and their interpretations of his policies and programs, his motives, and his leadership. He contradicted those critical accounts of what was being thought about him and his administration, and he relied on other methods for learning what was being thought about what was being done.

In our populist conception of a democratic government, a supreme value has been placed on critical information to permit the people to decide issues and vote. The government in giving out information cannot be superior in the information process, nor can the press. There must be a balance. During the 1930s and 1940s, the publishers in their opinion function tried to be superior. The balance shifted in favor of the government because of the president's astute news management abilities for whatever kind of mass media that existed then. The electorate in most cases ignored those newspaper opinion pieces offering a critical analysis of Roosevelt's leadership and policies. FDR made news with the verbal and visual image of his actions, and he held the advantage despite the publishers' control of America's daily newspapers and many radio stations.

In the larger picture of presidential press relations, Franklin D. Roosevelt left a communications legacy for subsequent presidents. As a benchmark, Roosevelt showed the importance of a dynamic personality. His easygoing manner, his charm, and his optimistic nature were an integral part of his overall news management abilities. In fact, with these skills he might have created unreasonable expectations for less personable presidents.

FDR also demonstrated that the mass media can be a major political weapon for leadership. He needed the press as his principal vehicle to keep in touch with the people, to inform the public, to arouse the people to the dangers of the period, to reassure them, and to garner public support to coerce Congress to pass his programs. At the same time, those journalists of the 1930s and 1940s wanted as much fast-breaking news as possible. Newsgathering is a dependent process. What journalists learn about government is derived almost exclusively from the persons involved. FDR was the journalists' foremost high-level source. As such, he could give out the necessary information, he could define the issues, and he could set the news agenda.

The president also influenced the news through his institutionalized news conferences. By having such regularly held press conferences, he created an expected flow of White House news. The White House correspondents complained loudly if the meetings were omitted. His news management tactics are still part of the informational chess game. Roosevelt, like succeeding presidents, wore the armor of the nation's highest office, and the correspondents who covered him remained his subordinates. Although journalists could and did try to question him, Roosevelt would remark, "This is not an interrogation." Presidents following FDR could stifle the questioning with humor, an anecdote, or even a phrase of "There you go again," or they could refuse access. Just as Roosevelt did, they or their spokespeople can give the correspondents a front-page byline and a top-head dispatch as well as display their mastery of leadership through national exposure in a time-saving thirty minutes.

Although Roosevelt's press meetings were private background events, news conferences have been live, televised forums since 1961. Press conferences, though battered, bruised, and almost abandoned today, still provide an opportunity for public accountability and access to the president. Despite the fact that these news conferences have become a direct channel to the American public, few presidents since Roosevelt have enjoyed them. With broadcasts, there can be no off-the-record remarks or background statements. By being live, they might have become more formal, but they can still expose what is or is not on the president's mind and show possible error, misstatement, and ignorance.

Are press conferences worth the effort? Some presidents, not so knowledgeable and confident as FDR, have been so concerned about their public performance that they have been briefed as much as two days ahead of time. A president's cold sweat has become apparent under the glare of television lights. In general, press meetings have decreased from Roosevelt's average of five a month, the greatest number of press interactions that journalists have ever had with a president, to as few as three a year. Franklin D. Roosevelt might have indeed excelled, even with background meetings, to the point that no other president sees news conferences as worth the effort.

At times Roosevelt, like other presidents, might not have managed the correspondents' final product as much as he desired, yet the news conference forum still gave the nation's chief executive a chance to express viewpoints without immediate challenge. To focus the news on himself, FDR used a number of fundamental news management devices that other presidents have copied. Many times Roosevelt began his press conferences with an opening statement, an agenda-setting technique that presidents almost always use today. This tactic ensured this one bit of news would be reported, especially when the chief executive had documents mimeographed for the correspondents to have afterwards. That opening statement could divert attention from a subject the president did not wish to discuss further, even though the correspondents and the public might want an explanation. Roosevelt skillfully used this technique the very day of the embarrassing defeat of the judiciary reform measure and Justice Van Devanter's resignation. Roosevelt showed that the president is the most authoritative national news source. He has the first words. First words on a topic can and do make front-page and lead-broadcast-news stories.

Roosevelt showed that a president's casual social relations with journalists can lead to other background sessions, unofficial press conferences. His informal Sunday night suppers provided ample opportunity for off-the-record discussions. With only a small group of correspondents, FDR would discuss the policies in intricate detail. Succeeding presidents and high government officials have had such informal press relations at stag dinners, poker games, barbecues, and softball games.

FDR sought a two-way publicity system. It was not enough to give out the information. Roosevelt also wanted a follow-up organization to check his efforts. To determine press content, editorial comment, and national response, he used a Press Intelligence Bureau report, "Howe's Daily Bulletin." He also had both journalists and others send him written reports from various sections of the country on major issues, and he read his mail summaries. Other presidents have also carefully followed press content. Richard Nixon read daily summaries of some fifty newspapers and Ronald Reagan had news synopses, which also included the daily network news coverage and even editorial cartoons.

Roosevelt used embryonic public opinion surveys during his 1932 election campaign, and by 1940 he was seeking polls on what people were thinking about the war. The American print media, no longer reliable as a check on public opinion, lost out to more statistically accurate methods. Such poll results were newsworthy, too, and became the basis for news stories and regular columns. More recent presidents have paid so much attention to public opinion polls that they have hired full-time polling specialists as advisers.

The executive branch's press bureaucracy, in place long before FDR, is now an accepted part of the federal government. Information officers in every agency now speak for departments, write speeches, issue handouts, release press statements, and hold press conferences and briefings, much as was done during the New Deal years. This news bureaucracy exists not only in the executive branch but also in Congress and in state and local governments. The information policy is hierarchical and filters from the president downward, as it did in Roosevelt's era. During the New Deal when FDR was more open, the rest of the executive branch followed accordingly. When he closed off access during World War II, so did departments and agencies.

Roosevelt's Office of War Information and Office of Censorship, both gone by the end of 1945, begot other formalized information agencies, such as the United States Information Agency and the Voice of America. With the dismantling of the OWI and the OC, many of those seasoned workers transferred into the State Department and later into the CIA. Subsequent presidents have attempted even more formalized domestic information offices. From Richard Nixon's Office of Telecommunications Policy through Ronald Reagan's Office of Public Liaison, presidents have tried to improve the flow of information.

Roosevelt established the recognized position of a press secretary. Subsequent press secretaries have been compared to Steve Early, who had access to the president, an understanding of issues, a mastery of details, and an astute ability to get along with the press. The press secretary's position has grown so much that it is difficult to imagine it was Steve Early alone who met daily with the president, held daily briefings with the press, advised the president before his semiweekly press conferences, organized the entire executive branch's New Deal press system, and oversaw the release of all announcements and press statements. Today, hundreds of White House staffers devote their talents to exalting not only the president and his image but also the first lady.

FDR also showed the importance of technological artistry for whatever mass media existed. During the Roosevelt era, there were motion pictures, newsreels, still photographs, and radios. By the time of Eisenhower and Kennedy, there was also black-and-white television; by the time of Reagan and George Bush, there were color cable television and satellite feeds. Roosevelt reaffirmed the subsequent continual presidential search for the most direct method of sending information to the American public.

FDR, while now always excelling, had enough triumphs that he left an apex for presidential leadership of public opinion, and he reached a peak in presidential press relations. He was the transitional figure in the evolution of the relationship between the American presidency and the public during the twentieth century. Foremost a greater communicator, FDR knew when to speak and when not to. He knew how to use his charm and withdraw it. Succeeding presidents, regardless of political party, have compared their communication tactics and their leadership abilities to Franklin D. Roosevelt's.

There was and still is a danger of a possible media tyranny by an adroit president and his advisers over a mediocre press. As demonstrated in this study, Franklin D. Roosevelt did indeed "manage" the newsgathering process throughout those twelve years. What if these media skills were held by a less honorable, more selfish president? The most recent fears have included more executive cover-up policies, a lack of openness in government, and closed access to information. Madison's warning is noteworthy: "A popular government without popular information or the means of acquiring it, is but a prologue to a farce or a tragedy, or perhaps both."[4]

There was indeed popular information during the Roosevelt era. FDR's news management, although astounding, seems mild compared with several of the more recent presidents' efforts. There still is a likelihood that the right combination of personality, media talents, presidential actions, and power can create a tyranny over the mass media to the great detriment of a democratic people. The balance between access and governing is still a delicate balance between frankness and caution. Franklin D. Roosevelt's presidency brought an American victory over the Great Depression, the Germans, and the Japanese. Yet the question remains, was there also a legacy of a great victory over the control of governmental information in a democracy?

Notes

1. Commission on Freedom of the Press, *A Free and Responsible Press* (Chicago: University of Chicago Press, 1947), pp. 1–2.

2. Thomas Jefferson to Caesar A. Rodney, February 10, 1810, *The Writings of Thomas Jefferson*, Vol. 5 (Monticello, Va.: Thomas Jefferson Memorial Association, 1903), p. 510.

3. Elmer Davis, "War of Words," in *Dateline: Washington, the Story of National Affairs Journalism in the Life and Times of the National Press Club*, Cabell Phillips et al., eds. (Garden City, N.Y.: Doubleday, 1949), p. 223.

4. James Madison to W. T. Barry, August 4, 1822, *The Complete Madison*, Saul Padover, ed. (New York: Harper and Brothers, 1953), p. 337.

Appendix:
The White House Correspondents

It is difficult to discern an official list of White House correspondents, those journalists who specifically covered the president. The names of the White House correspondents given here were compiled from (1) the 1934 membership list found in the White House Correspondents' Folder, Stephen T. Early Papers, Franklin D. Roosevelt Library; (2) birthday greetings sent to FDR from the "Gang in the Press Room," January 30, 1934, President's Personal File, Franklin D. Roosevelt Library; (3) a list of correspondents accompanying FDR on his trip to Gettysburg and New York, May 28, 1934, President's Official File 36, Franklin D. Roosevelt Library; (4) a telegram to FDR from "We, the White House Faithfuls . . . ," November 4, 1936; (5) the 1941 membership list found in the White House Correspondents' Folder, Stephen T. Early Papers, Franklin D. Roosevelt Library; and (6) the list of correspondents who traveled with the president and were assigned specifically to the White House, as found in Grace Tully, *F.D.R., My Boss* (New York: Charles Scribner's Sons, 1949), pp. 290–91. The correspondents' affiliations are not given because so many of them changed during the twelve years.

Some of the names of those who covered both the White House and Capitol Hill were omitted from these lists. Leo Rosten, *The Washington Correspondents* (New York: Harcourt, Brace, 1937), pp. xvii–xx, mentions several correspondents who were not on these lists but who have been mentioned elsewhere, such as in the press conferences or in the Early or Roosevelt papers: Joseph W. Alsop, Jr., Delbert Clark, Kenneth G. Crawford, Robert W. Horton, William P. Kennedy, John L. Lambert, David Lawrence, Clinton L. Mosher, Louis Stark, Arthur T. Weir, and James Russell Wiggins.

The 1934 birthday greeting to the president, the roster of the May 1934 trip, the 1936 telegram, and Grace Tully's list may be the best sources for ascertaining which correspondents were considered insiders.

The White House Correspondents

	1934 Member- ship List	1934 Birthday Greetings	1934 May Trip List	1936 Telegram Names	1941 Member- ship List	Grace Tully List
Adams, Phelps H.	X					
Akers, M. T.	X					
Allen, James	X					
Allen, Robert S.	X				X	X
Anderson, Paul Y.	X	X				
Andrews, Bert						X
Armstrong, Robert B., Jr.	X					
Atchison, John C.	X					
Authier, George F.	X					
Auxier, Vance K.	X					
Baer, Frank L.	X					
Baker, Richard R., Jr.	X					
Bargeron, Carlisle	X					
Barkley, Frederick R.	X					
Baukhage, Hilmar Robert	X					
Bean, Rodney	X					
Beatty, J. Frank	X					
Belair, Felix, Jr.						X
Bell, Samuel W.	X					
Bell, Ulric	X					X
Benson, George	X					
Bingham, Barry	X					
Biondi, Leone F.	X					
Black, Ruby A.	X				X	
Blaisdell, Richard S.	X					
Bledsoe, S. B.	X					
Boettiger, John	X	X	X			
Bonwit, Julia A.	X					
Boyle, John	X					
Brandt, Raymond P.	X					X
Brayman, Harold	X	X				
Brookover, Lyle A.	X					
Brooks, Ned	X				X	
Brown, Ashmun N.	X				X	
Brown, Constantine A.	X					
Brown, Walter	X					
Browne, Merwin H.	X				X	
Bruckart, William	X					
Bruner, Felix F.	X					

The White House Correspondents (Continued)

	1934 Member-ship List	1934 Birthday Greetings	1934 May Trip List	1936 Telegram Names	1941 Member-ship List	Grace Tully List
Bryant, George B., Jr.	X					
Bryant, H. E. C., Jr.	X					
Buck, Robert M.	X					
Buel, Walker S.	X					
Bugbee, Emma	X					
Bullen, Percy S.	X					
Butler, James J.					X	
Byers, Clyde	X					
Cadou, Eugene	X					
Canham, Erwin D.	X	X	X			X
Cannon, James	X					
Carswell, Howard J.	X					
Catledge, W. Turner	X				X	
Chance, W. S., Jr.	X					
Chaplin, W. S.	X	X				
Cherry, Ralph L.	X					
Childs, Marquis W.					X	X
Chinn, James E.	X					
Clapper, Raymond					X	
Clark, Kenneth	X					
Codel, Martin	X					
Cole, William R.	X					
Collier, N. Rex	X					
Collins, M. F.	X					
Collins, Ralph A.	X					
Combs, George W.	X					
Conness, Leland S.	X					
Connor, Francis J.	X					
Cornell, Douglas B.	X					X
Cotten, Felix T.					X	
Cottrell, Jesse S.	X				X	
Cox, George H.	X					
Craig, Elizabeth May	X					
Crane, James B.	X					
Crawford, Arthur W.	X					
Cullinane, James J.	X					
Daly, John J.	X					
Davis, Watson	X					
Dayon, Katherine	X					

The White House Correspondents (Continued)

	1934 Member-ship List	1934 Birthday Greetings	1934 May Trip List	1936 Telegram Names	1941 Member-ship List	Grace Tully List
DeGreve, Arthur F.					X	
Denoyer, Pierre	X					
de Zappe, Rudolphe	X			X		
Doyle, James F.	X					
Dudley, Mayo	X					
Duffield, Eugene S.	X				X	
Dufour, Pierre	X					
Dure, Leon, Jr.	X					
Durno, George E.	X				X	X
Dutcher, Rodney	X					
Edmunds, Thomas F.	X	X		X		
Edwards, Willard						X
Eichler, Alfred E.	X					
Emery, Fred A.	X					
Engle, Parke F.	X					
Ervin, Morris D.	X				X	
Erwin, John D.	X	X				
Essary, J. Fred	X	X			X	
Ewing, Donald M.	X					
Finney, Ruth	X					
Fitzgerald, John C.	X					
Fitzpatrick, John J.	X					
Fleeson, Doris	X		X			X
Fleming, Dewey L.	X				X	
Flynn, Henry C.	X					
Flythe, William P., Jr.	X					
Flythe, William P., Sr.	X					
Folliard, Edward T.	X					
Foos, Irvin D.	X					
Foote, Mark	X				X	
Foss, Kendall	X					
Fox, Joseph A.	X					
Francis, Warren B.	X				X	
Frandsen, Julius, Jr.	X					
Frank, Pat	X					
Frey, Robert	X					
Friedheim, Eric	X					
Gableman, Edwin W.	X				X	
Garner, George A.	X					

The White House Correspondents (Continued)

	1934 Member-ship List	1934 Birthday Greetings	1934 May Trip List	1936 Telegram Names	1941 Member-ship List	Grace Tully List
Gauss, Harry B.	X					
Getty, Frank	X					
Gillilan, Strickland	X					
Godwin, Earl				X		
Goodwin, Mark L.	X					
Gorrell, H. T.	X					
Gridley, Charles O.	X				X	
Griffin, Bulkley S.	X				X	
Grimes, W. H.	X					
Grover, Preston					X	
Groves, Charles S.	X					
Grunewald, Hudson	X					
Gusack, Harry	X					
Hachten, Arthur	X				X	
Hadley, Edward	X					
Hall, Frank A.	X					
Hamilton, Charles A.	X					
Hard, William	X					
Harder, Bernie	X					
Harkness, Richard L.						X
Harris, Ned B.	X					
Harsch, Joseph C.	X					
Hart, Lee Poe	X					
Hawthorne, Roger	X					
Hayden, Jay G.	X				X	
Healey, Thomas F.	X	X				
Heap, Earl N.	X					
Heath, Edwin J.	X					
Heiss, A. E.	X					
Helgerson, Ray	X					
Henderson, Robert E.				X		
Henle, Raymond Z.	X	X				
Henning, Arthur S.	X				X	
Hennesey, Michael E.	X					
Henry, John C.						X
Herrick, Genevieve Forbes	X					
Herrick, John	X					
Higgins, E. Worth	X					
Hill, William	X					

The White House Correspondents (Continued)

	1934 Member- ship List	1934 Birthday Greetings	1934 May Trip List	1936 Telegram Names	1941 Member- ship List	Grace Tully List
Hodges, Paul	X	X				
Holmes, George R.	X					X
Horan, Harold J. T.			X			
Hornaday, James P.	X					
Hornaday, Mary	X				X	
Hurd, C. W. B.	X	X	X			
Hutchinson, William K.	X				X	
Hyde, Henry M.	X				X	
Irwin, Jesse	X					
Jamieson, William Edward	X					
Jefferson, Mary F.	X					
Jermane, W. W.	X					
Johnson, George Mack	X					
Jones, Coleman B.	X					
Kahn, Karl M.	X					
Kelley, Ralph J.	X					
Kelly, Eugene A.	X					
Kennedy, John A.	X					
Kent, Russell	X					
Keyser, Charles P.	X					
Kieldsen, James N.	X					
King, Tom W.	X					
Kinnear, Isabel	X					
Knorr, Ernest A.	X					
Koine, John F.	X					
Kreiselman, Lee	X		X			
Krock, Arthur					X	
Kury, Fred H.	X					
Lamm, Lynne M.	X					
Lander, William H.	X					
Lane, Harold S.	X					
Lane, Robert R.	X					
Leach, Paul R.	X				X	
Lehrbas, Lloyd	X					
Lerch, Oliver B.	X					
Lewis, Dorothea J.	X					
Lewis, Edward W.	X					
Lewis, Fulton, Jr.	X					
Lincoln, G. Gould	X				X	

The White House Correspondents (Continued)

	1934 Member-ship List	1934 Birthday Greetings	1934 May Trip List	1936 Telegram Names	1941 Member-ship List	Grace Tully List
Wilson, Duane	X					
Wilson, Lyle C.	X				X	X
Wilson, Richard					X	
Wilson, Richard L.	X					
Wimer, Arthur C.					X	
Wood, Lewis	X					
Wooton, Paul	X				X	
Wright, James L.	X				X	
Wrigley, Thomas	X					
Yates, Paul	X					
Young, John Russell	X					
Young, Marguerite	X					

Selected Bibliography

Unpublished Sources

Manuscripts

Biddle, Francis. Papers, Diaries, Franklin D. Roosevelt Library (FDRL), Hyde Park, N.Y.

Clapper, Raymond. Papers, Diaries, Censorship File, Reference File, Manuscripts Division, Library of Congress (LofC), Washington, D.C.

Davis, Elmer. Papers, Library of Congress (LofC), Washington, D.C.

Early, Stephen T. Papers (STEP), Franklin D. Roosevelt Library (FDRL), Hyde Park, N.Y.

Howe, Louis McHenry. Papers, Franklin D. Roosevelt Library (FDRL), Hyde Park, N.Y.

Krock, Arthur. Papers, Manuscripts, Speeches, Princeton University, Princeton, N.J.

McCormick, Anne O'Hare. Selected Documents, Franklin D. Roosevelt Library (FDRL), Hyde Park, N.Y.

Mellett, Lowell. Papers, Franklin D. Roosevelt Library (FDRL), Hyde Park, N.Y.

Roosevelt, Franklin D. Official File (OF), Franklin D. Roosevelt Library (FDRL), Hyde Park, N.Y.

———. President's Map Room Papers (MR), Franklin D. Roosevelt Library (FDRL), Hyde Park, N.Y.

———. President's Personal File (PPF), Franklin D. Roosevelt Library (FDRL), Hyde Park, N.Y.

———. President's Secretary's File (PSF), Franklin D. Roosevelt Library (FDRL), Hyde Park, N.Y.

Interviews and Personal Communication

Allen, Robert S. Interview at his office in the National Press Club in Washington, D.C., June 8, 1976.

Allen, Ruth Finney. Interview at her Washington, D.C., home, June 8, 1976.

Canham, Erwin D. Letter in answer to a series of questions, June 28, 1976.

Folliard, Edward. Interview at his Washington, D.C., home, June 3, 1976.

Lindley, Ernest K. Interview at the Cosmos Club in Washington, D.C., June 4, 1976.

Livezey, Emilie Tavel. Phone interview, August 18, 1985.

Strout, Richard L. Interview at the *Christian Science Monitor* office in Washington, D.C., June 2, 1976.

Theses

Bloomfield, Douglas MacArthur. "The Presidential Press Secretaries." Master's thesis, Ohio State University, 1963.

Moore, William McKinley. "F.D.R.'s Image: A Study in Pictorial Symbols." Ph.D. dissertation, University of Wisconsin, 1946.

Ragland, James F. "Franklin D. Roosevelt and Public Opinion, 1933–1940." Ph.D. dissertation, Stanford University, 1954.

Rinn, Fauneil J. "The Presidential Press Conference." Ph.D. dissertation, University of Chicago, 1960.

Schoenherr, Steven E. "Selling the New Deal: Stephen T. Early's Role as Press Secretary to Franklin D. Roosevelt." Ph.D. dissertation, University of Delaware, 1976.

Sharon, John H. "The Psychology of the Fireside Chat." Senior honors thesis, Princeton University, 1949.

Published Sources

Collected Works

Kimball, Warren F., ed. *Churchill and Roosevelt: The Complete Correspondence.* 3 vols. Princeton, N.J.: Princeton University Press, 1984.

Roosevelt, Franklin D. *Complete Presidential Press Conferences of Franklin D. Roosevelt.* 25 vols. New York: Da Capo Press, 1972.

———. *F.D.R.: His Personal Letters.* 3 vols. Edited by Elliott Roosevelt. New York: Duell, Sloan and Pearce, 1947–50.

———. *Franklin D. Roosevelt Reader: Selected Speeches, Messages, Press Conferences and Letters.* Edited by Basil Rauch. New York: Rinehart, 1957.

———. *The Public Papers and Addresses of Franklin D. Roosevelt.* 13 vols. Edited by Samuel I. Rosenman. New York: Random House, 1938–50.

Report

Conference on the Press under the Auspices of the School of Public and International Affairs, Princeton University, April 23–25, 1931. Princeton, N.J.: School of Public Affairs, 1932.

Books

Alsop, Joseph. *A Centenary Remembrance, FDR.* New York: Viking Press, 1982.

Alsop, Joseph, and Catledge, Turner. *The 168 Days.* Garden City, N.Y.: Doubleday, Doran, 1938.

Alsop, Joseph, and Kintner, Robert. *Men around the President*. Garden City, N.Y.: Doubleday, 1938.

Asbell, Bernard. *When F.D.R. Died*. New York: Holt, Rinehart and Winston, 1961.

Baughman, James L. *Henry R. Luce and the Rise of the American News Media*. Boston: Twayne Publishers, 1987.

Beasley, Maurine H. *Eleanor Roosevelt and the Media: A Public Quest for Self-Fulfillment*. Urbana: University of Illinois Press, 1987.

Bent, Silas. *Ballyhoo: The Voice of the Press*. New York: Boni and Liveright, 1927.

Biddle, Francis B. *The Fear of Freedom*. Garden City, N.Y.: Doubleday, 1951.

———. *In Brief Authority*. Garden City, N.Y.: Doubleday, 1962.

Black, Ruby. *Eleanor Roosevelt: A Biography*. New York: Duell, Sloan and Pearce, 1940.

Black, Theodore Milton. *Democratic Party Publicity in the 1940 Campaign*. New York: Plymouth, 1941.

Brinkley, David. *Washington Goes to War*. New York: Alfred A. Knopf, 1988.

Brucker, Herbert. *The Changing American Newspaper*. New York: Columbia University Press, 1937.

Burns, James MacGregor. *Roosevelt: The Lion and the Fox*. New York: Harcourt, Brace, 1956.

———. *Roosevelt: The Soldier of Freedom*. New York: Harcourt, Brace, 1970.

Byrnes, James F. *All in One Lifetime*. New York: Harper and Brothers, 1958.

Cantril, Hadley. *The Human Dimension: Experiences in Policy Research*. New Brunswick, N.J.: Rutgers University Press, 1967.

———, ed. *Public Opinion 1935–1946*. Princeton, N.J.: Princeton University Press, 1951.

Carlisle, Rodney P. *Hearst and the New Deal*. New York: Garland, 1979.

Cater, Douglas. *The Fourth Branch of Government*. New York: Vintage Books, 1965.

Childs, Marquis W. *I Write from Washington*. New York: Harper and Brothers, 1942.

Clark, Delbert. *Washington Dateline*. New York: Frederick A. Stokes, 1941.

Conkin, Paul K. *The New Deal*. 2d ed. Arlington Heights: Harlen Davidson, 1975.

Cornwell, Elmer E., Jr. *Presidential Leadership of Public Opinion*. Bloomington: Indiana University Press, 1965.

Creel, George. *Rebel at Large: Recollections of Fifty Crowded Years*. New York: G. P. Putnam's Sons, 1947.

Davis, Kenneth S. *FDR, the New Deal Years, 1933–1937: A History*. New York: Random House, 1986.

Donovan, Hedley. *Roosevelt to Reagan: A Reporter's Encounters with Nine Presidents*. New York: Harper and Row, 1985.

Emery, Edwin, and Emery, Michael. *The Press and America: An Interpretive History of the Mass Media*. 5th ed. Englewood Cliffs, N.J.: Prentice-Hall, 1984.

Erickson, Aaron J. *Get That Picture!* New York: National Library Press, 1938.

Essary, J. Fred. *Covering Washington*. Boston: Houghton Mifflin, 1927.

Farley, James A. *Behind the Ballots*. New York: Harcourt, Brace, 1938.

———. *Jim Farley's Story*. New York: McGraw-Hill, 1948.

Fielding, Raymond. *The American Newsreel, 1911–1967*. Norman: University of Oklahoma Press, 1972.

Freidel, Frank. *Franklin D. Roosevelt*. 4 vols. Boston: Little, Brown, 1952–73.

Gallapher, Hugh Gregory. *FDR's Splendid Deception*. New York: Dodd, Mead, 1985.

Goldberg, Richard T. *The Making of Franklin D. Roosevelt: Triumph over Disability*. Cambridge: Abt Books, 1981.

Gosnell, Harold F. *Champion Campaigner: Franklin D. Roosevelt*. New York: Macmillan, 1952.

Graham, Otis L., Jr., and Wander, Meghan Robinson, eds. *Franklin D. Roosevelt, His Life and Times: An Encyclopedic View*. Boston: G. K. Hall, 1985.

Greer, Thomas H. *What Roosevelt Thought: The Social and Political Ideas of Franklin D. Roosevelt*. East Lansing: Michigan State University Press, 1958.

Gunther, John. *Roosevelt in Retrospect*. New York: Harper and Brothers, 1950.

Harrity, Richard, and Martin, Ralph G. *The Human Side of F.D.R.* New York: Duell, Sloan and Pearce, 1960.

Hassett, William D. *Off the Record with F.D.R., 1942–1945*. New Brunswick, N.J.: Rutgers University Press, 1958.

Hurd, Charles. *When the New Deal Was Young and Gay*. New York: Harper, 1965.

Ickes, Harold L. *America's House of Lords*. New York: Harcourt, Brace, 1939.

———. *The Secret Diary of Harold L. Ickes*. 3 vols. New York: Simon and Schuster, 1953–54.

Irons, Peter. *Justice at War*. New York: Oxford University Press, 1983.

Kilpatrick, Carroll. *Roosevelt and Daniels: A Friendship in Politics*. Chapel Hill: University of North Carolina Press, 1952.

Kinnaird, Clark. *The Real F.D.R.* New York: Harper and Brothers, 1945.

Kirby, John B. *Black Americans in the Roosevelt Era: Liberalism and Race*. Knoxville: University of Tennessee Press, 1980.

Krock, Arthur. *Memoirs: Sixty Years on the Firing Line*. New York: Funk and Wagnalls, 1968.

Larrabee, Eric. *Commander-in-Chief: Franklin Delano Roosevelt, His Lieutenants and the War*. New York: Harper and Row, 1987.

Lash, Joseph P. *Dealers and Dreamers: A New Look at the New Deal*. New York: Doubleday, 1988.

Leuchtenburg, William E. *Franklin D. Roosevelt and the New Deal, 1932–1940*. New York: Harper and Brothers, 1963.

———. *In the Shadow of FDR: From Harry Truman to Ronald Reagan*. Ithaca, N.Y.: Cornell University Press, 1983.

Lindley, Ernest K. *Franklin D. Roosevelt: A Career in Progressive Democracy*. New York: Blue Ribbon Book Co., 1931.

———. *Half Way with Roosevelt*. New York: Viking, 1937.

———. *The Roosevelt Revolution: First Phase*. London: V. Gollancz, 1933.

Lippmann, Walter. *Interpretations, 1931–1932*. New York: Macmillan, 1932.

Louchheim, Katie, ed. *The Making of the New Deal: The Insiders Speak*. Cambridge: Harvard University Press, 1983.

Lowitt, Richard, and Beasley, Maurine. *One Third of the Nation: Lorena Hickok's Reports on the Great Depression*. Urbana: University of Illinois Press, 1983.

McCamy, James L. *Federal Publicity: Its Practice in Federal Administration*. Chicago: University of Chicago Press, 1939.

McIntire, Ross. *White House Physician*. New York: G. P. Putnam, 1946.

Marbut, F. B. *News from the Capital: The Story of Washington Reporting*. Carbondale: Southern Illinois University Press, 1971.

Melosi, Martin V. *The Shadow of Pearl Harbor: Political Controversy over the Surprise Attack, 1941–1946*. College Station: Texas A & M Press, 1977.

Meyersohn, Maxwell. *The Wit and Wisdom of Franklin D. Roosevelt*. Boston: Beacon Press, 1950.

Michael, George. *Handout*. New York: G. P. Putnam's Sons, 1935.

Miller, Nathan. *F.D.R.: An Intimate History*. Garden City, N.J.: Doubleday, 1983.

Moley, Raymond. *After Seven Years*. New York: Harper and Brothers, 1939.

Mott, Frank Luther. *American Journalism, a History: 1690–1960*. New York: Macmillan, 1962.

Newstadt, Richard E. *Presidential Power: The Politics of Leadership*. New York: John Wiley and Sons, 1960.

Nimmo, Dan D. *Newsgathering in Washington: A Study in Political Communication*. New York: Atherton, 1964.

Parrish, Michael. *Felix Frankfurter and His Times*. New York: Free Press, 1982.

Peel, Roy V., and Donnelly, Thomas C. *The 1932 Campaign: An Analysis*. New York: Farrar and Rinehart, 1935.

Perkins, Francis. *The Roosevelt I Knew*. New York: Viking Press, 1946.

Phillips, Cabell et al., eds. *Dateline: Washington, the Story of National Affairs Journalism in the Life and Times of the National Press Club*. Garden City, N.Y.: Doubleday, 1949.

Pollard, James E. *The Presidents and the Press*. New York: Macmillan, 1947.

Prange, Gordon W. *At Dawn We Slept: The Untold Story of Pearl Harbor*. New York: McGraw-Hill, 1981.

Richberg, Donald. *My Hero*. New York: G. P. Putnam's Sons, 1954.

Reilly, Michael F. *Reilly of the White House*. New York: Simon and Schuster, 1947.

Rivers, William L. *The Adversaries: Politics and the Press*. Boston: Beacon Press, 1970.

———. *The Opinionmakers: The Washington Press Corps*. Boston: Beacon Press, 1967.

———. *The Other Government: Power and the Washington Media*. New York: Universe Books, 1982.

Rollins, Alfred B., Jr. *Roosevelt and Howe*. New York: Knopf, 1962.

Rosen, Elliot A. *Hoover, Roosevelt and the Brains Trust: From Depression to New Deal*. New York: Columbia University Press, 1977.

Rosenbaum, Herbert D., and Berthelme, Elizabeth, eds. *Franklin D. Roosevelt: The Man, the Myth and the Era, 1882–1945*. Westport, Conn.: Greenwood Press, 1987.

Rosenman, Samuel I. *Working with Roosevelt*. New York: Harper and Brothers, 1952.

Rossiter, Clinton. *The American Presidency*. New York: Mentor Books, 1960.

Rosten, Leo C. *The Washington Correspondents*. New York: Harcourt, Brace, 1937.

Ryan, Halford R. *Franklin D. Roosevelt's Rhetorical Presidency*. Westport, Conn.: Greenwood Press, 1988.

Schlesinger, Arthur M., Jr. *The Age of Roosevelt*. 3 vols. Boston: Houghton Mifflin, 1957–60.

Seldes, George. *Lords of the Press*. New York: Julian Messner, 1938.

Seligman, Lester G., and Cornwell, Elmer E., Jr., eds. *The New Deal Mosaic: Proceedings of the National Emergency Council*. Eugene: University of Oregon Press, 1964.

Sheeham, Marion Turner, ed. *The World at Home: Selections from the Writings of Anne O'Hare McCormick*. New York: Knopf, 1956.

Sherwood, Robert E. *Roosevelt and Hopkins: An Intimate History*. New York: Harper and Brothers, 1948.

Smith, A. Merriman. *Thank you, Mr. President: A White House Notebook*. New York: Harper and Row, 1946.

Steele, Richard W. *Propaganda in an Open Society: The Roosevelt Administration and the Media, 1933–1941*. Westport, Conn.: Greenwood Press, 1985.

Stiles, Lela. *The Man behind Roosevelt*. Cleveland and New York: World Publishing, 1954.

Stokes, Thomas L. *Chip Off My Shoulder*. Princeton, N.J.: Princeton University Press, 1940.

Swain, Martha H. *Pat Harrison and the New Deal Years*. Jackson: University of Mississippi Press, 1978.

Swanberg, W. A. *Citizen Hearst*. New York: Charles Scribner's Sons, 1961.

Tebbel, John. *The Media in America*. New York: Mentor Books, 1974.

Tebbel, John, and Watts, Sarah Miles. *The Press and the Presidency: From George Washington to Ronald Reagan*. New York: Oxford University Press, 1985.

Trohan, Walter. *Political Animals: Memoirs of a Sentimental Cynic*. Garden City, N.Y.: Doubleday, 1975.

Tugwell, Rexford G. *The Brains Trust*. New York: Viking Books, 1968.

———. *In Search of Roosevelt*. Cambridge: Harvard University Press, 1972.

———. *Roosevelt's Revolution: The First Year, a Personal Perspective*. New York: Macmillan, 1977.

Tully, Grace. *F.D.R., My Boss*. New York: Charles Scribner's Sons, 1949.

Venkataramani, M. S. *The Sunny Side of FDR*. Athens: Ohio University Press, 1973.

Washburn, Patrick S. *A Question of Sedition: The Federal Government's Investigation of the Black Press during World War II*. New York: Oxford University Press, 1986.

Weiss, Nancy J. *Farewell to the Party of Lincoln: Black Politics in the Age of FDR*. Princeton, N.J.: Princeton University Press, 1983.

White, Graham J. *FDR and the Press*. Chicago: University of Chicago Press, 1979.

Winkler, Allan M. *The Politics of Propaganda: The Office of War Information, 1942–1945*. New Haven, Conn.: Yale University Press, 1978.

Wolfskill, George, and Hudson, John A. *All but the People: Franklin D. Roosevelt and His Critics, 1933–1939*. Toronto: Macmillan, 1969.

Articles

Bain, George W. "How Negro Editors Viewed the New Deal." *Journalism Quarterly* 44 (Autumn 1967): 552–54.

Becker, Samuel L. "Presidential Power: The Influence of Broadcasting." *Quarterly Journal of Speech* 47 (February 1961): 10–18.

Berchtold, William E. "Press Agents of the New Deal." *New Outlook,* July 26, 1934, pp. 23–30, 61.

Bleyer, Willard G. "Freedom of the Press and the New Deal." *Journalism Quarterly* 11 (March 1934): 22–35.

Boorstin, Daniel. "Selling the President to the People: The Direct Democracy of Public Relations." *Commentary* 20 (November 1955): 421–27.

Braden, Waldo W., and Brandenburg, Ernest. "Roosevelt's Fireside Chats." *Speech Monographs,* November 1955, 290–307.

Brandenburg, Ernest, and Braden, Waldo W. "F.D.R.'s Voice and Pronunciation." *Quarterly Journal of Speech* 27 (February 1952): 23–30.

Brandt, Raymond P. "The President's Press Conference." *Survey Graphic,* July 1939, pp. 446–50.

Brinkley, David. "An Age Less than Golden: Roosevelt vs. the Wartime Press." *Washington Journalism Review* 10 (June 1988): 39–44.

Brown, Ashmun. "The Roosevelt Myth." *American Mercury,* April 1936, pp. 390–94.

Burke, Robert E. "Election of 1940." In *History of American Presidential Elections, 1789–1968,* Vol. 4, edited by Arthur M. Schlesinger, Jr., and Fred L. Israel. New York: Chelsea House, 1971, pp. 2917–46.

———. "The Roosevelt Administration." *Current History* 59 (October 1960): 220–24.

Canham, Erwin. "Democracy's Fifth Wheel." *Literary Digest,* January 5, 1935, p. 6.

Casey, Ralph D. "Republican Propaganda in the 1936 Campaign." *Public Opinion Quarterly* 1 (April 1937): 27–45.

Clapper, Raymond. "Cuff-Links Gang." *Review of Reviews,* April 1935, pp. 47–50.

———. "Why Reporters Like Roosevelt." *Review of Reviews,* June 1934, pp. 14–17.

Clark, Delbert. "The President's Listening-in Machine." *New York Times Magazine,* September 1, 1935, pp. 3, 14.

———. "Steve Takes Care of It." *New York Times Magazine,* July 27, 1941, pp. 11, 22.

Cornwell, Elmer E., Jr. "Presidential News: The Expanding Public Image." *Journalism Quarterly* 36 (Summer 1959): 275–83.

———. "The Presidential Press Conference: A Study in Institutionalization." *Midwest Journal of Political Science* 4 (November 1960): 370–89.

Crawford, Kenneth. "Presidents and the Press." In *The Making of the New Deal: The Insiders Speak,* edited by Katie Louchheim. Cambridge: Harvard University Press, 1983.

Creel, George. "The Amateur Touch." *Collier's,* August 3, 1935, pp. 12–13, 34.

———. "Looking Ahead with Roosevelt." *Collier's,* September 7, 1935, pp. 7–8, 45–46.

———. "Roosevelt's Plans and Purposes." *Collier's,* December 26, 1937, pp. 7–9, 39, 49; January 27, 1945, pp. 11–13; February 3, 1945, pp. 16–17.

———. "What Roosevelt Intends to Do." *Collier's,* March 11, 1933, pp. 7–9, 34, 36.

Davenport, Walter. "The President and the Press." *Collier's,* January 27, 1945, pp. 11–13, 47, 49; February 3, 1945, pp. 16–17.

"Franklin D. Roosevelt." *Fortune,* December 1933, pp. 24–30.

Gosnell, Harold F. "How Accurate Were the Polls?" *Public Opinion Quarterly* 1 (January 1937): 100–108.

Hanson, Elisha. "Official Propaganda and the New Deal." *Annals of the American Academy of Political and Social Science* 179 (May 1935): 176–86.

Herrick, John. "With Reporters at the Summer White House." *Literary Digest,* August 12, 1933, pp. 5, 29.

Herring, E. Pendleton. "Official Publicity under the New Deal." *Annals of the American Academy of Political and Social Science* 179 (May 1935): 167–75.

Howe, Louis McHenry. "The President's Mail Bag." *American Magazine,* June 1934, pp. 22–23.

Hurd, Charles W. B. "President and the Press: A Unique Forum," *New York Times Magazine,* July 9, 1936, pp. 3, 14.

Kang, Joon-Mann. "Roosevelt and James L. Fly: The Politics of Broadcast Regulation, 1941–1944." *Journal of American Culture* 10 (Summer 1987): 23–33.

Kany, Howard L., and Bourne, William C. "Just One More, Please." In *Dateline: Washington, the Story of National Affairs Journalism in the Life and Times of the National Press Club,* edited by Cabell Phillips et al. Garden City, N.Y.: Doubleday, 1949, pp. 141–52.

Kelly, Eugene A. "Distorting the News." *American Mercury,* March 1935, pp. 307–18.

Krock, Arthur. "The Press and Government." *Annals of the American Academy of Political and Social Science* 180 (July 1935): 162–67.

Larson, Cedric. "How Much Federal Publicity Is There?" *Public Opinion Quarterly* 2 (October 1938): 636–44.

———. "OWI's Domestic News Bureau: An Account and an Appraisal," *Journalism Quarterly* 24 (March 1949): 3–14.

Lasswell, Harold D., ed. "Government." *Public Opinion Quarterly* 1 (April 1937): 97–101.

Lee, Alfred McClung. "Violations of Press Freedom in America." *Journalism Quarterly* 15 (March 1938): 19–27.

McCamy, James L. "Discussion: Measuring Federal Publicity." *Public Opinion Quarterly* 3 (July 1939): 473–75.

———. "Variety in the Growth of Federal Publicity." *Public Opinion Quarterly* 3 (April 1939): 285–92.

Mallon, Paul. "Roosevelt's Ear to the Ground." *New York Times Magazine,* January 14, 1934, pp. 1–2, 14.

Martel, James. "Washington Press Conference." *American Mercury,* February 1938, pp. 197–210.

Meiklejohn, Alexander. "Is the First Amendment an Absolute?" *Supreme Court Law Review* (1961): 245–66.

Mott, Frank Luther. "Newspapers in Presidential Campaigns." *Public Opinion Quarterly* 8 (Fall 1944): 348–67.

Nicholas, H. G. "Roosevelt and Public Opinion." *Fortnightly,* May 1943, pp. 303–8.

Pearson, Drew, and Allen, Robert. "How the President Works." *Harper's,* July 1936, pp. 1–14.

Pollard, James E. "The White House News Conference as a Channel of Communication." *Public Opinion Quarterly* 15 (Winter 1951): 663–78.

Pringle, Henry F. "Franklin D. Roosevelt." *The Nation*, April 27, 1932, pp. 487–89.

———. "Profiles: The President, I." *The New Yorker*, June 16, 1934, pp. 20–25.

———. "Profiles: The President, II." *The New Yorker*, June 23, 1934, pp. 20–24.

———. "Profiles: The President, III." *The New Yorker*, June 30, 1934, pp. 20–23.

Ragland, James F. "Merchandizers of the First Amendment: Freedom and Responsibility of the Press in the Age of Roosevelt, 1933–1940." *Georgia Review* 16 (Winter 1962): 366–91.

Ray, Royal H. "Economic Forces as Factors in Daily Newspaper Concentration." *Journalism Quarterly* 29 (Winter 1952): 31–42.

Rogers, Lindsay. "President Roosevelt's Press Conferences." *Political Quarterly* 9 (July–September 1938): 360–72.

Rosten, Leo C. "Political Leadership and the Press." In *The Future of Government in the United States*, edited by Leonard D. White. Chicago: University of Chicago Press, 1942, pp. 88–99.

Sharon, John H. "The Fireside Chat." *Franklin D. Roosevelt Collector* 2 (November 1949): 3–20.

Shaw, Albert. "One Year of President Roosevelt." *Review of Reviews*, March 1934, pp. 11–15.

Steele, Richard W. "The Great Debate: Roosevelt, the Media and the Coming of the War, 1940–1941." *Journal of American History* 71 (June 1984): 69–72.

———. "News of the 'Good War': World War II News Management. *Journalism Quarterly* 62 (Winter 1985): 707–16, 783.

———. "The Pulse of the People: Franklin D. Roosevelt and the Gauging of Public Opinion." *Journal of Contemporary History* 9 (October 1974): 195–216.

Sussman, Leila A. "F.D.R. and White House Mail." *Public Opinion Quarterly* 20 (Spring 1956): 5–16.

———. "The Personnel and Ideology of Public Relations." *Public Opinion Quarterly* 12 (Winter 1948): 697–708.

Timmons, Bascom N. "This Is How It Used to Be." In *Dateline: Washington, the Story of National Affairs Journalism in the Life and Times of the National Press Club*, edited by Cabell Phillips et al. Garden City, N.Y.: Doubleday, 1949, pp. 38–55.

Washburn, Patrick S. "FDR versus His Own Attorney General: The Struggle over Sedition, 1941–1942." *Journalism Quarterly* 62 (Winter 1985): 717–24.

———. "J. Edgar Hoover and the Black Press in World War II." *Journalism History* 13 (Spring 1986): 26–33.

Weaver, Paul. "New Journalism and Old: Thoughts after Watergate." *Public Interest* 35 (Spring 1974): 70–87.

Weinfeld, William. "The Growth of Daily Newspaper Chains in the United States: 1923, 1926–1935." *Journalism Quarterly* 13 (December 1936): 357–80.

Winfield, Betty Houchin. "FDR Wins and Loses Journalistic Friends in the Rising Age of News Interpretation." *Journalism Quarterly* 64 (Winter 1987): 698–706.

————. "F.D.R.'s Pictorial Image: Rules and Boundaries." *Journalism History* 5 (Winter 1978–79): 110–14, 136.

————. "Franklin D. Roosevelt's Efforts to Influence News during His First Term Press Conferences." *Presidential Studies Quarterly* 11 (Spring 1981): 189–200.

————. "New Deal Publicity: The Information Foundation for the Modern Presidency." *Journalism Quarterly* 61 (Spring 1984): 40–48, 218.

Newspaper

New York Times, 1932–45.

Index

Note on the Author

Betty Houchin Winfield was educated at the University of Arkansas and the University of Michigan, from which she took B.S. and M.A. degrees, and the University of Washington, from which she obtained her Ph.D. in communications history. She is a professor in the School of Journalism at the University of Missouri at Columbia. She has also taught at Washington State University and has been a visiting scholar at Columbia University, the University of Washington, and Texas Woman's University. She was co-author (with Lois B. DeFleur) of *The Edward R. Murrow Heritage: A Challenge for the Future* (1985) and is currently working on a book on the First Amendment and the presidency.